Social Life

Sara Miller McCune founded SAGE Publishing in 1965 to support the dissemination of usable knowledge and educate a global community. SAGE publishes more than 1000 journals and over 800 new books each year, spanning a wide range of subject areas. Our growing selection of library products includes archives, data, case studies and video. SAGE remains majority owned by our founder and after her lifetime will become owned by a charitable trust that secures the company's continued independence.

Los Angeles | London | New Delhi | Singapore | Washington DC | Melbourne

Social Life

Contemporary Social Theory

Matthias Benzer

Kate Reed

Los Angeles | London | New Delhi
Singapore | Washington DC | Melbourne

Los Angeles | London | New Delhi
Singapore | Washington DC | Melbourne

SAGE Publications Ltd
1 Oliver's Yard
55 City Road
London EC1Y 1SP

SAGE Publications Inc.
2455 Teller Road
Thousand Oaks, California 91320

SAGE Publications India Pvt Ltd
B 1/I 1 Mohan Cooperative Industrial Area
Mathura Road
New Delhi 110 044

SAGE Publications Asia-Pacific Pte Ltd
3 Church Street
#10-04 Samsung Hub
Singapore 049483

Editor: Natalie Aguilera
Assistant Editor: Eve Williams
Production editor: Katherine Haw
Copyeditor: Camille Bramall
Proofreader: Rebecca Storr
Indexer: Elizabeth Ball
Marketing manager: George Kimble
Cover design: Stephanie Guyaz
Typeset by: C&M Digitals (P) Ltd, Chennai, India

Library of Congress Control Number: 2018960846

British Library Cataloguing in Publication data

A catalogue record for this book is available from the British Library

ISBN 978-1-4739-0783-6
ISBN 978-1-4739-0784-3 (pbk)

Contents

About the Authors

Matthias Benzer is Lecturer in Sociology in the Department of Sociological Studies at the University of Sheffield. He previously worked as a researcher at the Centre for Analysis of Risk and Regulation at the London School of Economics and Political Science and as a Lecturer in Sociology in the Department of Sociology at the University of Manchester. He is the author of *The Sociology of Theodor Adorno* (2011, Cambridge University Press) as well as writings on critical theory (published in the *Journal of Classical Sociology* and *Philosophy & Social Criticism*) and poststructuralist social thought. Matthias is also currently conducting research on social and political questions regarding resource allocation in the United Kingdom National Health Service.

Kate Reed is Professor of Sociology in the Department of Sociological Studies at the University of Sheffield. She is currently Principal Investigator of the Economic and Social Research Council funded project 'End of or Start of Life'? Visual Technology and the Transformation of Traditional Post-Mortem. Her research interests are focused on the areas of reproductive genetics, gender, technology and health, and social theory. Kate is the author of *New Directions in Social Theory: Race, Gender and the Canon* (2006, Sage) and *Gender and Genetics: Sociology of the Prenatal* (2012, Routledge).

Introduction

In sociology, the idea that people live in society is widely accepted. At the same time, this idea is not always made explicit in sociological research. Social theory comprises attempts to conceptualise, analyse, understand, explain, and critically scrutinise social relations and conditions. The questions that this area of sociology has addressed in the twentieth and twenty-first centuries have included whether current social conditions must be considered as radically modern, postmodern, or not at all modern, where the lines of social inequality and discrimination are drawn, how relationships of power are shaping the social world, how social relations and social interaction are to be characterised, and where the potential for the transformation of society lies, to name a few. A range of social theorists, crucially, have, in their endeavours, explicitly raised and examined the problem of living in society. In other words, they have sought to investigate human life in social relations, contexts, and conditions. *Social Life* contains expositions, explorations, and discussions of such work in contemporary social thought. The focus of the book rests on eight socio-theoretical analyses of social life: writings by Anthony Giddens, Pierre Bourdieu, Bruno Latour, Donna Haraway, Zygmunt Bauman, Jean-François Lyotard, Michel Foucault, and Jean Baudrillard. The works of these sociologists have had a tremendous impact on the sociological research of the present day. The following chapters aim to highlight, detail, and discuss the contributions and challenges of the analyses of social life put forward by these eight thinkers to sociology's ongoing quest for conceptualising and interrogating the contemporary social world.

The chapters approach the socio-theoretical ideas under discussion from two angles. Each of the social theorists in focus has developed a set of concepts, statements, and arguments for analysing and critically scrutinising contemporary social relations and conditions. The first part of every chapter concentrates on decisive elements of those conceptions of, arguments about, and inquiries into, present-day society. At no point does this amount to a summary overview either of the respective body of thought in its entirety or even of large parts of it. Instead, the first parts of the chapters identify and spotlight key components of each thinker's conception and analysis of contemporary society and explore those in detail. At issue are elements that have made particularly sustained contributions or raised particularly far-reaching challenges to sociology's project of critically examining the social world of today. For instance, an elaborate account of Foucault's thinking about power is prioritised over a summary of his major interventions from the 1960s and 1970s *tout court*. In a similar fashion, a detailed exposition of Baudrillard's distinctions between the way in which life and death are treated in symbolic exchange relationships and the way in which they are treated in capitalist society is offered instead of an overview of his entire work on the symbolic, illusion, reality, simulation, and hyperreality.

Informed by their conceptions of social relations and conditions, each of these thinkers' interpretations, examinations, and critical interrogations of the social world has, in turn, in different ways informed their investigations of particular phenomena of that world. The second part of every chapter discusses the respective theorist's analyses of the ways in which the wider social contexts in focus in the first part shape, manifest themselves in, are expressed through, and receive influence from more specific phenomena. At the centre of attention here are chiefly phenomena – or phenomena that resemble phenomena – many people are likely to have experienced immediately, may frequently hear or read about, or are simply able to imagine independently of having been exposed to sociological research. For instance, Chapter 5 explores the problem of fear in liquid modernity as it is addressed in Bauman's work, whilst Chapter 1 discusses climate change as Giddens problematises it sociologically. The aim of the second part of each chapter is to elucidate ostensibly abstract theoretical ideas about prevalent social relations, contexts, and conditions by linking them to analyses of such phenomena.

Simultaneously, the second parts of each chapter thereby pursue a further objective. What these sections are concerned with more precisely are decisive components of the eight thinkers' analyses of how wider social conditions are interrelated with particular phenomena variously, but mostly quite explicitly, associated with the ways in which people live, with living, with the question of human life. The second part of Chapter 4, for instance, engages with Haraway's thinking on immunology, that of Chapter 6 with Lyotard's considerations of the 'questions: how to live, and why' (1997: vii), and Part 2 of Chapter 8 with Baudrillard's writings on the massive extinction of life during, the suicides central to, and the ramifications of, the attacks on New York City on September 11, 2001. The growing importance of the problem of life in critical investigations of social contexts, economic relations, and political conditions, which is indicated by the ever more frequent appearance of the prefix 'bio' in designations of socio-scientific fields of study (e.g. Birch and Tyfield 2012; Lemke 2011), is widely recognised. The following chapters suggest that the ways in which social relations and contexts shape, manifest themselves in, and are affected by, specific aspects and phenomena of human life and the lives of people constitute a sustained and encompassing concern of a much wider array of sociology, especially of social theory. The objective, in other words, is to highlight and discuss how the thinkers in focus in this book intertwine analyses of social conditions with analyses of phenomena characteristic of people's lives, of living, and of life – however variously understood – in today's society. Their *œuvres* have much to offer to sociological inquiries into contemporary social life understood in this very sense.

Thematically, the aim to explore socio-theoretical analyses of the problem of living in society is not especially restrictive. In itself, it would doubtless allow, arguably call for, an engagement with a broader range of works in social theory. A further objective of the present text, however, is to explore key components of such socio-theoretical analyses in detail. An orientation by this objective precludes an inclusive, let alone an exhaustive, account of current social theory's inquiries into life in the contemporary social world. The authors readily admit that the specific problems that have occupied them in their other research, the contributions of sociology that have guided their teaching, and their respective notions of sociology's most vital concerns and conceptions today are expressed in the thematic composition of the book's chapters.

The discussions in these chapters concentrate on specific primary texts. This is consistent with the book's overall aim to engage closely and in depth with decisive elements of the conceptions, investigations, and analyses in question, which has rendered the pursuit of overviews of wide arrays of sources inappropriate. The chapters endeavour to unpack and decipher particular, often convoluted, cryptic writings – and passages in the writings – of each theorist and trace their interconnections within each *œuvre*. They contain attempts to expose, explore in detail, and discuss concepts, configurations of concepts, and arguments that constitute particular inquiries and analyses of the theorists. The first parts of the chapters draw on sources that support the reconstruction and discussion of key components of the eight thinkers' conceptions and examinations of contemporary social conditions. The second parts turn to sources that support what may be described as theoretical case studies – explorations of the theorists' inquiries into interrelations between the wider conditions at issue in the first parts and more specific phenomena linked to the problem of living in today's social world.

Of those sources, many were not originally published in English. Most of the latter first appeared in French. The approach to the sources taken – that is to say, demanded by the objectives of the book's chapters – necessitated recourse to the original language versions of some of them. It is probably prudent to declare in this context that French is not the native tongue of either author. It became nevertheless apparent that some of the published English translations of central sources of this book are more accurate than others. For instance, the English version (Lyotard 1984b) of Lyotard's *La Condition Postmoderne* (1979) is very faithful to the original text, whereas the translation (Baudrillard 1993) of Baudrillard's *L'Échange Symbolique et la Mort* (1976) is problematic in places. In the following, several directly quoted translations of passages from various sources have been modified on the basis of the French texts. The sole objectives of doing so were the correction of translation errors in some instances and greater linguistic precision in all others. For the purpose of ensuring their defensibility, some modified translations were checked against German translations (notably Baudrillard 1982b and Lyotard 1994) of the French originals where those were readily available. Translations that have been modified are marked with the designation 'trsl. modified' within the relevant in-text references.

Numerous secondary works – monographs and articles, commentaries and critiques – dedicated to many of the eight thinkers are available. It has not been possible to survey even the majority of this body of literature. All sections of this book are mainly based on engagements with primary sources rather than on explorations of secondary texts. Nonetheless, each chapter provides not only references to those secondary works that have informed aspects of the analyses presented, but also references to secondary literature that offers readers richer insights into issues that cannot be elaborated here. Moreover, recommended further readings are listed at the end of each chapter. The following eight chapters explore each theorist's ideas in turn. The ninth chapter revisits some common concerns of the socio-theoretical investigations of social life explored throughout the preceding eight.

1

Anthony Giddens: Living with Radical Modernity

PART 1: RADICAL MODERNITY

In *The Consequences of Modernity* published in the early 1990s Giddens argued that, although not yet living in a postmodern world, we were nonetheless witnessing 'the emergence of ways of life and forms of social organisation' that were different to those facilitated by 'modern institutions' (CM 52). This indicated what he refers to as a radicalised version of modernity – a future-oriented reflexive and globalised form (RW). This version of modernity is for Giddens unsettling: 'Its most conspicuous features – the *dissolution of evolutionism*, the *disappearance of historical teleology*, the recognition of *thoroughgoing, constitutive reflexivity*, together with the *evaporating of the privileged position of the West* – move us into a new and disturbing universe of experience' (CM 52–3). One of the key problems of radical modernity – climate change – according to Giddens requires radical political solutions beyond traditional politics of the left and right (BLR, TW). This chapter seeks to explore the particular dilemmas and problems that radical modernity poses for human life as outlined in Giddens's socio-theoretical framework. Focusing specifically on the potential threat posed by climate change (PCC), the chapter also examines his proposed solutions with a view to their potential to inform concrete policy.

Radicalised Modernity

Modernity tends to refer in sociology texts to 'modes of social life or organisation that emerged in Europe from about the seventeenth century onwards and that subsequently became more or less worldwide in their influence' (CM 1). According to Giddens we now stand at the dawn of 'a new era' to which the social sciences must respond and which is taking us beyond modernity itself' (CM 1). Sociologists have attempted to describe and define this era through concepts such as postmodernism, post-Fordism, postcapitalism, and so on. Post-modernism is a slippery concept and, as Giddens himself points out, can mean any number of things: that the '"foundations" of epistemology are unreliable and that "history" is devoid of teleology and consequently no version of "progress" can plausibly be defended' (CM 46). It may also refer to the emergence of 'a new social and political agenda' including an 'increasing prominence of ecological concerns and perhaps of new social movements generally' (CM 46). While Giddens acknowledges that significant social changes have occurred in society in recent decades, rather than seeing these as evidence of us living in a society beyond modernity, he argues that they actually 'provide us with a fuller understanding of the reflexivity inherent in modernity itself' (CM 49). Giddens is not alone in his attempts to suggest we are living in a modern not postmodern, society. Other theorists such as Bourdieu and Habermas also – in different ways – have sought to develop socio-theoretical positions that are at odds with postmodernity (Callinicos 1999). What is specific to Giddens's approach, however, is his focus on radical modernity. He argues that 'we have not moved beyond modernity but are living precisely through a phase of its radicalisation' (CM 51).

In order to understand the times we live in Giddens argues 'it is not sufficient merely to invent new terms, like post-modernity and the rest. Instead, we have to look again at the nature of modernity itself' (CM 3). This for Giddens includes an analytical focus on the Janus-faced nature of modernity. Modernity he argues 'is a double-edged phenomenon' (CM 7). It has created vast opportunity for 'human beings to enjoy a secure and rewarding existence' but it also has a 'sombre side' (CM 7). It was only Weber according to Giddens out of the classical theorists who acknowledged this sombre side of modernity, as Marx thought class conflict would lead to a better society: 'Yet even he did not fully anticipate how extensive the darker side of modernity would turn out to be' (CM 7). Through developing his theory of radical modernity, therefore, Giddens seeks to include a focus on its dual-edged potential, as well as suggesting sociological strategies for managing its darker side.

The dynamism of modernity

Giddens begins his theory of modernity by outlining what he calls a 'discontinuist' interpretation of modern development. In particular he wants to focus on outlining the ways in which modern institutions are different from the traditional order (CM 3, RM). The big differences between traditional and modern institutions according to Giddens are their 'dynamism' and 'global scope' (CM 16). Giddens distinguishes three dominant and interconnected sources of dynamism that underpin modernity: the first is *the separation of time and space*. This is what Giddens refers to as the condition of time–space distanciation, a means of precise temporal and spatial zoning. Giddens argues that modernity 'tears space away from place fostering relations between "absent" others', and different locales are penetrated by and shaped in terms of social influences quite distant from them (CM 19).

The second source of dynamism for Giddens is the development of dis-embedding mechanisms. Giddens refers here to the "lifting out" of 'social activity from localised contexts, reorganising social relations across large time–space distances'(CM 53). Giddens gives the example of two types of disembedding mechanisms 'symbolic tokens' (e.g. money) and 'expert sys-tems' (e.g. medicine). Expert systems refer to 'systems of technical accomplishment or professional expertise that organise large areas of the material and social environments in which we live today' (CM 27). According to Giddens 'expert systems are disembedding mechanisms because, in com-mon with symbolic tokens, they remove social relations from the immediacies of context' (CM 28). Both types of disembedding mechanisms presume, but also foster, the separation of time from space (CM 28). Essential to these disembedding systems, according to Giddens, is trust and therefore trust is involved in an essential way with the institutions of modernity.

The final source of dynamism according to Giddens is '*The reflexive appropriation of knowledge*. The production of systematic knowledge about social life becomes central to system reproduction, rolling social life away from the fixed nature of tradition' (CM 53). He argues that the reflexivity of modern social life consists in the fact that 'social practices are constantly examined and reinformed in the light of incoming information about those very practices, thus constitutively altering their character' (CM 38). Giddens argues that sociology as an academic discipline occupies a key position in the reflexivity of modernity, because sociology offers a 'generalised type of reflec-tion upon modern social life' (CM 41). 'The discourse of sociology and the concepts, theories, and findings of the other social sciences' 'reflexively restruc-ture their subject matter, which itself has learned to think sociologically'. According to Giddens therefore '*modernity is itself deeply and intrinsically sociological*' (CM 43).

The institutional dimensions of modernity

Giddens identifies four institutional dimensions of modernity – capitalism, industrialism, surveillance, and military power. These dimensions according to Giddens are irreducible to one another, each consisting of a different set of causal processes and structures. However, they work together to provide a structure for understanding some of the key features, developments, and tensions in modern societies. *Capitalism* is the first dimension that he identifies. This 'is a system of commodity production, centred upon the relation between private ownership of capital and propertyless wage labour'. It is this relationship, according to Giddens, which forms 'the main axis of a class system' (CM 55). Industrialism is viewed separately from capitalism and, for Giddens, forms the second institutional dimension of modernity: 'The chief characteristic of *industrialism* is the use of inanimate sources of material power in the production of goods, coupled to the central role of machinery in the production process' (CM 55–6).

The nation state occupies a central place in capitalist societies according to Giddens, and the administration of the capitalist system and modern society in general is coordinated control over delimited territorial arenas. In this respect capitalism depends on '*surveillance* capacities well beyond those of traditional civilisations' (CM 57). For Giddens, therefore, *surveillance* capacity constitutes a third institutional dimension associated with the rise of modernity (CM 57–8). He states that 'surveillance refers to the supervision of the activities of subject populations in the political sphere' – although not confined to that sphere (CM 58). The final institutional dimension is *military power* (control of the means of violence in the industrialisation of war): successful monopoly of the means of violence within the state. This also refers to the industrialisation of war – total war and nuclear war (CM 58). According to Giddens, 'behind these institutional clusterings lie the three sources of dynamism of modernity' referred to earlier: '*time–space distanciation*, *disembedding*, and *reflexivity*' (italics my emphasis). These facilitate the conditions for change. 'They are involved in as well as conditioned by the institutional dimensions of modernity' (CM 63).

Globalisation, trust, and risk

Modernity for Giddens is dynamic, and also inherently globalising. Globalisation therefore occupies a central role within Giddens's theory of modernity. He defines globalisation as 'the intensification of worldwide social relations which link distant localities in such a way that local happenings are shaped by events occurring many miles away and vice versa' (CM 64). Globalisation is, according to Giddens, essentially 'action at a distance' (RM 96). Giddens regards the world capitalist economy as one of four dimensions of globalisation, the nation state is the second, the world military order is the third, and industrial development: 'the most obvious aspect of this is the expansion of the global division of labour', for example difference between more and less industrialised countries) is the fourth. The media – for Giddens that is 'mechanised technologies of communication' – 'have dramatically influenced all aspects of globalisation' (CM 77). According to Giddens the point is not that 'people are contingently aware of many events, from all over the world, of which previously they would have remained ignorant'. Rather 'it is that the global extension of the institutions of modernity would be impossible were it not for the pooling of knowledge which is represented by the "news"' (CM 77–8).

A key part of Giddens's theory of radical modernity is the relationship between modern institutions and abstract systems. According to him modern institutions are bound by '*the mechanisms of trust in abstract systems*, especially trust in expert systems' (CM 83). The future-oriented nature of modernity is largely structured by trust vested in abstract systems, in particular in the trustworthiness of established expertise (CM 83–4). According to Giddens 'the reliance placed by lay actors upon expert systems is not just a matter (as was often the case in the premodern world) of generating a sense of security about an independently given universe of events. It is a matter of the calculation of benefit and risk in circumstances where expert knowledge does not just provide that calculus but actually *creates* (or reproduces) the universe of events, as a result of the continual reflexive implementation of that very knowledge' (CM 84).

What this means in a globalised modernity according to Giddens is that no one can opt out of 'the abstract systems involved in modern institutions' (CM 84). There are no others (Kaspersen 2000). In modernity 'the dangers we face no longer derive primarily from the world of nature'. Rather, threats (such as ecological decay) 'are the outcome of socially organised knowledge, mediated by the impact of industrialism upon the material environment' (CM 110). They are part of what Giddens calls the new '*risk profile*' introduced by the advent of modernity. By a risk profile he means the particular 'portmanteau of threats or dangers characteristic of modern social life' (CM 110). According to Giddens, risk and danger (like everything else) have become secularised in modernity (CM 111). He focuses on the menacing nature of the globalisation of risk, the potential, for example, of nuclear war, ecological disaster, etc. However, he argues that because we are constantly bombarded with information about global risks on an everyday basis we tend to switch off: 'Listing the dangers we face has itself has a deadening effect. It becomes a litany which is only half listened to because it seems so familiar' (Bailey cited in Giddens, CM 128). Risk discourses in this sense are, according to Giddens, background noise. Furthermore, he also states that the more we know about modern risk, the more we recognise the limits of so-called 'expert' knowledge. This according to Giddens 'forms one of the "public relations" problems that has to be faced by those who seek to sustain lay trust in expert systems' (CM 130).

Riding the juggernaut of modernity

'Radical' or 'high' modernity is according to Giddens a 'runaway world', a 'juggernaut' veering out of control. No specific individuals or groups are responsible for this juggernaut or can be compelled to 'set things right' (CM 131). While sociologists have often criticised Giddens for making sweeping generalisations in his theory of radical modernity (Kaspersen 2000), he is keen to stress that he recognises the juggernaut of modernity is not all of a piece. It is made up of diverse and contradictory forces. However, despite the bleak picture Giddens paints, it is not – according to him – all hopeless. We should not/cannot 'give up in our attempts to steer the juggernaut' (CM 154). Giddens puts forward his notion of utopian realism, a critical theory without 'guaran-tees'. This theory he argues must be *'sociologically sensitive'* and *'geopolitically, tactical'*, in order to *'create models of the good society'*. His focus here is on linking what he calls 'emancipatory politics' with *'life politics, or the politics of self-actualisation'* (CM 156). Emancipatory politics for Giddens refer to 'radical engagements concerned with the liberation from inequality or servi-tude'. Social movements, he argues, provide instruction to potential future transformations (e.g. labour movements, ecological movements) (CM 160–1). One of the biggest challenges we face in a radical modern world is environ-mental decay. 'Since the most consequential ecological issues are so obviously global, forms of intervention to minimise environmental risks' will, as Giddens argues, need to be on a global scale (CM 170). He states that an 'overall system of planetary care might be created, which would have as its aim the preserva-tion of the ecological well-being of the world as a whole' (CM 170). Giddens ends his analysis by stressing the urgency of the need for change on a global scale with respect to environmental decay, lest we end up as a 'republic of insects and grass' (CM 173).

Radical politics

According to Giddens, the problems prevalent within radical modernity – such as ecological decay – require radical political solutions. In *Beyond Left and Right* (Giddens 1994b) and *The Third Way* (Giddens 1998) Giddens seeks to develop what he calls a radical politics of the centre, a widespread philosophy and approach for the left. He restates many points articulated in CM, that the world of the late twentieth century has not turned out as the founders of socialism anticipated. They felt that the more we collectively know 'about social and material reality', the more we will become masters of our own des-tiny (BLR 3). As Giddens outlines in his work on radical modernity, the world we live in today is not one subject to tight human mastery. Almost to the con-trary, it is one of dislocation and uncertainty, a juggernaut veering out of control, a 'runaway world' (BLR 3, CM).

Risk again forms a central position in Giddens's work on radical politics; in this context he focuses in particular on what he calls *'manufactured uncer-tainty'* (BLR 4). Giddens argues that 'manufactured risk is a result *of* human intervention into the conditions of social life and into nature' (BLR 4). Manufactured uncertainty for Giddens is the outcome of 'the long-term matu-ration of modern institutions'. However, it has also rapidly increased as a result of 'a series of developments that have transformed society (and nature) over no more than the past four or five decades' (BLR 4). There are four main contexts in which we confront high-consequence risks coming from the exten-sion of manufactured uncertainty. Each of these corresponds to an institutional dimension of modernity as outlined in CM. These are: the impact of modern social development on the world ecosystem, the develop-ment of poverty on a large scale, and the widespread existence of weapons of mass destruction, together with other situations in which collective violence looms as a possibility. The fourth and final source of global crisis concerns the large-scale representation of democratic rights, including the inability of vast numbers of people to develop even a small part of their human potential (BLR).

Beyond socialism and conservatism

Giddens argues that if we are to effectively address these problems posed by radical modernity we need to develop a radical political position beyond the political left or right. According to Giddens socialism and conservatism have disintegrated, and neoliberalism is paradoxical (BLR 10). Giddens poses the question: 'If the oppositional force of socialism has been blunted, must a capitalistic system reign unchallenged?' (BLR 11) He argues not. There would be several dire consequences should capitalist markets go unchecked including 'the dominance of a growth ethic, universal commodification and economic polarization' (BLR 11). A critique of these potential trends remains for Giddens essential. However, he argues that in a radical modern society it cannot be derived from a cybernetic model of socialism. Although this 'cybernetic model implicit in socialism as a whole, and developed in its most advanced way in Soviet communism was quite effective as a means of 'generating economic development in conditions of simple modernization' (BLR 66), the reflexivity inherent within a radicalised modernity, coupled with globalisation, 'introduces quite different social and economic circumstances' requiring radical political solutions (BLR 66).

According to Giddens, neoliberals have 'appropriated the future-oriented radicalism that was once the hallmark of the bolder forms of socialist thinking' (BLR 73). In contemporary society the 'conservative has become radical and the radical conservative' (BLR 73). Giddens argues that the 'main emphasis of socialist conservatism' is the turn towards the 'protection of the now embattled welfare state' (BLR 73). The critique of capitalism that Giddens develops is still focused on economic oppression and poverty but 'from a different perspective from those characteristic of socialist thought' (BLR 12). He focuses on radicalism but seeks to unhook its connection to either the political left or right: 'radicalism reverts to its original meaning as daring: it means being prepared to contemplate bold solutions to social and political problems' (BLR 49). Viewed in this way radicalism is not merely 'valued for its own sake but instead is tempered by that awareness of the importance of continuity on which philosophic conservatism exists' (BLR 50). 'Radical political programmes today', Giddens argues, 'must be based on a conjunction of life politics and generative politics' (BLR 246). He refers back to his institutional analysis of capitalism, surveillance, industrialism, and the means of violence (CM). He argues that: 'along each of these dimensions' the question that radical politics must pose is: 'what alternative sociopolitical forms could potentially exist?' (BLR 101).

Utopian realism and the third way

A framework of radical politics should, according to Giddens, be informed by utopian realism, a critical theory 'with no guarantees' (CM 154), an approach that he introduces in his earlier work on radical modernity (CM). This should relate in particular, Giddens argues, to the four overarching dimensions of modernity: combating poverty; redressing the degradation of the environment; contesting arbitrary power; and reducing the role of force and violence in social life. These, according to Giddens, 'are the orienting contexts of utopian realism' (BLR 246). Giddens attempts to outline the philosophy behind his radical politics in BLR. However, he develops more concrete proposals for how this might work in practice in *The Third Way*, focusing in particular on the role of the state. Giddens argues that while 'neoliberals want to shrink the state; the social democrats, historically, have been keen to expand it'. The third-way approach argues that it is necessary to reconstruct, the state, to go beyond those on the right 'who say government is the enemy' and those on the left 'who say government is the answer' (TW 70).

Third-way politics for Giddens advocates a new *mixed economy* (TW 99). The new mixed economy looks for a 'synergy between public and private sectors, ultilizing the dynamism of markets but with the public interest in mind' (TW 99–100). It requires a reform of the welfare state, which, although not easy to achieve, 'can be sketched out quite readily' (TW 116). A radically reformed welfare state, according to Giddens, would involve social investment in a positive welfare society' (TW 127). 'Expenditure on welfare, understood as positive welfare', would according to Giddens 'be generated and distributed not wholly through the state, but by the state working in combination with other agencies including business' (TW 127–128). Furthermore, any future welfare society according to Giddens 'is not just the nation, but stretches above and below it. Control of environmental pollution, for example, can never be a matter for a national government alone, but it is certainly directly relevant to welfare' (TW 128).

Managing the dual-edged nature of modernity

In his work on radical politics Giddens seeks again to re-emphasise the Janus-faced nature of radical modernity. He argues that unpredictability, manufactured uncertainty, and fragmentation are only one side of a globalising order. 'On the reverse side are the shared values that come from a situation of global interdependence, organized via the cosmopolitan acceptance of difference' (BLR 253). In a world where there are no others, Giddens argues that we all share common interests and face common risks (BLR 253). Giddens uses this opportunity to reinforce his arguments that we are still living in a modern world – albeit a radical one. Far from seeing the disappearance of 'universal values' (as those favouring a postmodern approach would suggest), Giddens argues: 'this is perhaps the first time in humanity's history when such values have real purchase' (BLR 253).

Giddens uses the example of ecological politics to think through ways of dealing with manufactured uncertainty. Ecological politics for Giddens is a politics of loss (of both nature and tradition). It is also for him 'a politics of recovery' (BLR 227). According to Giddens, 'we can't return to nature or to tradition' (BLR 227). However, both individually and collectively we can seek to 'remoralize our lives in the context of a positive acceptance of manufactured uncertainty' (BLR 227). 'Put in this way, it isn't difficult to see why the ecological crisis is so basic to the forms of political renewal' that Giddens discusses in his work on radical politics (BLR 227: TW). The ecological crisis 'is a material expression of the limits of modernity, repairing the damaged environment can no more be understood as an end in itself than can the redress of poverty' (BLR 227). According to Giddens, modernisation that is ecologically sensitive is not about 'more and more modernity'. Rather, it 'is conscious of the problems and limitations of modernizing processes'. It is alive to the need to re-establish continuity and develop social cohesion in a world of erratic transformation, where the intrinsically unpredictable energies of scientific and technological innovation play such an important role' (TW 67–8). Giddens attempts to offer insight into some of the problems created by modernity, as well as developing effective strategies to deal with them. The following section extends this analytical focus to his substantive sociological work on climate change. Examining his work on climate change in more depth allows for an assessment both of his core socio-theoretical concepts as outlined in CM, and his attempts to develop more concrete policy solutions (BLR, TW).

PART 2: CLIMATE CHANGE

Climate change has for some years been at the centre of a global political agenda. As numerous scholars have argued, a continued increase in the world's temperature has the potential to 'transform human and animal life as it has been known' (Urry 2009: 87). However, while climate change is at the centre of public debates about global politics (Klein 2015), according to Urry (2009) there continues to remain a limited number of good 'sociological analyses' that focus on exploring the various ways in which we can move 'societies into a different path-dependent pattern' (Urry 2009: 89). Giddens attempts to offer a sociological analysis of climate change in *The Politics of Climate Change*, which he sees as 'a prolonged inquiry into a single question'. Why do most people, most of the time, act as though a threat of such magnitude can be ignored?' (PCC 1). As will be explored in the following section, Giddens's work on climate change elaborates on certain key concepts from his earlier work on radical modernity and politics, such as the concept of risk. Giddens also seeks to offer a detailed analysis of existing climate change policies, as well as outlining his own suggestions for moving societies into new path-dependent routes.

Climate Change and Giddens's Paradox

Giddens begins his work on climate change by outlining what he calls 'Giddens's paradox', a theme that takes central place throughout the text: 'since the dangers posed by global warming aren't tangible, immediate or visible in the course of day-to-day life, many will sit on their hands and do nothing of a concrete nature about them' (PCC 2). He argues that 'Giddens's paradox affects almost every aspect of current reactions to climate change' (PCC 2). It is the reason according to him why, for most citizens, climate change is an issue that is often at the back of people's minds. Giddens's paradox effectively refers to the disjuncture between knowledge and behaviour. He uses a range of examples to illustrate what he means by this. For example, even though we know smoking is bad for us, we find it hard to face the impact that smoking may have on us in the future and modify our behaviours in the present (PCC 3). For him Giddens's paradox explains perhaps why politicians have only just woken up to the scale and urgency of the problem of climate change on a global scale, introducing a range of ambitious climate change policies.

Giddens begins his analysis by offering a summary of where debates on global climate change currently are. The first phase of global initiatives have focused on bringing climate change to the political agenda; the next focus, according to Giddens, 'must involve embedding it in our institutions and in the everyday concerns of citizens, and here, for reasons just mentioned, there is a great deal of work to do' (PCC 3). Although international organisations such as the UN, are, according to Giddens, committed to getting global reductions in greenhouse gas emissions, there is little in the way of concrete results so far (PCC 3–4). Climate change as an expression of radical modernity is 'like a "juggernaut" careering at full pace to the edge of the cliff' (Urry 2009: 89). It is difficult to see how in this context we might gain control of the juggernaut. It is not simply, according to Giddens, a question of the survival of the planet – as advocates of the green movement may argue – but rather it is about preserving a planet fit for human life and habitation. In order to gain control of this runaway juggernaut of climate change it is necessary, Giddens argues, to introduce a long-term perspective into politics, domestically and internationally, a perspective that goes beyond a politics of the left or right.

Climate change, beyond left and right

Giddens rehearses many of the arguments in his work on climate change that are articulated in both BLR and TW. Perspectives on climate change, as Giddens points out, reflect a variety of political viewpoints. Underlying these perspectives, however, remain the old left and right political divisions. 'Those who want to respond to climate change through widespread social reform mostly tend towards the political left; most of the authors who doubt that climate change is caused by human agency, on the other hand, are on the right' (PCC 49). However, it is vital in order to develop effective climate change policy according to Giddens, that we go beyond the traditional politics of the left and right (PCC 49). Giddens argues that the majority of scientists and politicians have woken up to the urgency of climate change. However, there are some who remain 'sceptics' – those who dispute the claims being made about the scale of climate change. These unfortunately, as Giddens argues, receive a good deal of attention in the media (PCC 3). Sceptics often argue that climate change is not really proven, or that there 'is nothing new about the increasing temperatures observed today', and that 'the world climate has always been in flux' (PCC 23). Other authors, writing on risk more generally, have argued that we live in an 'age of scares', climate change is just one of these (PCC 24).

Drawing on the arguments he develops in BLR and TW, Giddens argues that we need to develop a radical politics beyond traditional political divisions if we are to effectively deal with climate change. Climate change for Giddens 'is not a left–right issue'. The green movement for Giddens cannot be seen as the new socialism, 'the new red'. He argues that we need to build a long-term 'cross-party framework' (PCC 7). While appreciating that critiques of centre politics are well-worn, Giddens argues that it could be a major advantage to develop this approach in the field of environmentalism. Giddens is keen to stress that equating the political centre with an absence of radicalism only applies in the case of traditional left–right issues. He argues that 'it is entirely possible to have a "radicalism of the centre" – indeed, in terms of climate change and energy policy it is an essential concept' (PCC 114). We need to go 'beyond the rhetoric of immediate party politics' (PCC 114). For Giddens there has to be an agreement reached across different parties as the issue is too important for political point scoring. We should according to Giddens 'perhaps speak of a *concordat* rather than a consensus, because there should be a clear statement of principles that are publicly endorsed' (PCC 116).

Risk and uncertainty

The concept of risk is central to Giddens's work on both radical modernity and politics (CM, BLR, and TW). Manufactured risk and uncertainty are also central themes running throughout his work on climate change. While manufactured risk penetrates other areas of life, for example, marriage and the family (RW 27), most environmental risks such as global warming fall into the category of manufactured risk (RW 26). Giddens elaborates on his earlier conceptualisation of risk by focusing specifically on the dual nature of the concept in his work on climate change. According to Giddens 'taking risks adds edge to our lives, but, much more importantly, is intrinsic to a whole diversity of fruitful and constructive tasks' (PCC 56). It is a central part of capitalism. 'Capitalism is actually unthinkable and unworkable without it' (RW 25). According to Giddens, when it comes to tackling climate change, we need to harness the positive side of risk. We have no hope of responding effectively 'unless we are prepared to take bold decisions. It is the biggest example ever of he who hesitates is lost' (PCC 57).

Giddens seeks to pose the question: 'Where do we stand at the moment in terms of the risk posed by global warming?' (PCC 8). He begins by outlining various changes that have taken place over the past 150 years or so. For example, the levels of greenhouse gases in the atmosphere have progressively increased with the expansion of industrial production. Recent studies show the temperature of oceans rising. 'Mountain glaciers are retreating in both hemispheres and snow cover is less, on average, than it once was' (PCC 14). Giddens makes the same kinds of connections between manufactured risk and global environmental decay here that he does elsewhere (CM, BLR, TW). However, in his work on climate change he draws more directly on policy-related evidence in order to illustrate the scale of the problem. For example, he argues that the Intergovernmental Panel on Climate Change of the UN (IPCC) in 2007 stated that 'warming of the climate system is unequivocal' (PCC 15–16). They warn of the potential for the twenty-first century to be dominated by 'resource based wars', with the potential for coastal cities to become flooded. This according to the IPCC would provoke both destitution and migration on a mass scale (PCC 18).

Climate change and risk prevention

Giddens does explore some of the ways in which we might 'harness' some of the threats posed by global risk and uncertainty in his work on radical modernity and politics. For example, through the perspective of utopian realism, or via his radical politics or third-way approach (CM, BLR, TW). However, in his work on climate change he also offers a more detailed analysis of existing concrete risk prevention strategies used in this context. He examines some of the key concepts coming out of the green movement – for example, the 'precautionary principle' (PP), 'sustainability', and the principle that 'the polluter pays' (PCC 55). Giddens traces the concept of the PP back to the early 1980s, when it was used in Germany in the context of the ecological debates. 'At its simplest, it proposes that action on environmental issues (and, by inference, other forms of risk) should be taken even though there is insecure scientific evidence about them' (RW 32). 'In several European countries, programmes were initiated to counter acid rain'; however, as Giddens argues, in the UK a 'lack of conclusive evidence was used to justify inactivity about this and other pollution problems too' (RW 32).

Giddens explores the ways in which the PP has been used well beyond the green movement. It was built into the 1992 Rio Declaration[1] and into various programmes of the European Commission (PCC 55). The core meaning of PP is 'better safe than sorry' (PCC 55); however, Giddens also argues that PP 'isn't always helpful or even applicable as a means of coping with problems of risk and responsibility' (RW 32). Here he returns to his focus on the dual concept of risk. Giddens argues that the main problem with PP is that it 'concentrates only on one side of risk, the possibility of harm' (PCC 57). As Giddens argues, the notion of staying close to nature or of limiting innovation rather than embracing it isn't always appropriate. 'The reason is that the balance of benefits and dangers from scientific and technological advance and other forms of social change too' are difficult to assess (RW 32). He also states that precaution over some risks can create others, so PP can often be self-contradictory (PCC). Giddens advocates that we operate through a different type of PP, what he calls percentage principle. We have to assess risks and opportunities in relation to benefits obtained (PCC). According to Giddens, however, risks that 'shade over' into uncertainties, like those involved in global warming, mean that 'there will be an element of guesswork, perhaps large element, in whatever we do (or do not do)' (PCC 58).

Giddens provides an analysis of other climate change strategies including a focus on 'sustainable development', which he argues helped bring together two discrepant communities ('greens' and 'pro-market authors') but is none-theless 'more of a slogan than an analytical concept'. Another strategy 'polluter pays' focuses on making those who cause pollution pay through taxes. Giddens states that this is hard to pin down and has practical limits. However, polluter pays is still a 'guiding thread in bringing climate change into the sphere of orthodox politics' (PCC 67). In assessing the different ways of deal-ing with 'risks' posed by climate change, however, Giddens advocates that we should discard PP and the concept of sustainable development, replacing these with more sophisticated modes of risk analysis.

The role of technology and the state

Central to Giddens's analysis of climate change is technology. 'Technological innovation', Giddens argues, 'has to be a core part of any successful climate change strategy and the same is true of energy policy' (PCC 131). As argued in both BLR and TW, the state must play a key role in combating problems posed by radical modernity such as environmental decay. In his work on climate change Giddens argues that the state and government must have a significant role in making technological innovation possible 'since a regulatory framework, including incentives and other tax mechanisms, will be involved' (PCC 131). The literature on low-carbon technologies is, according to Giddens, 'a minefield of claims and counter-claims' (PCC 132). However, he returns again to his focus on the dual concept of risk, and argues that: 'Risks and problems there are plenty. Yet, as I have stressed throughout this book, it is the balance of risks we have to consider and there are no risk-free options' (PCC 132). Overall Giddens argues that there are 'no guaranteed technological solutions', hence 'radically increasing energy efficiency has to be high on the agenda' (PCC 139). Whatever happens over the next 20 years or so a diversification of energy sources will be required 'to reduce emissions and break dependence on oil, gas and coal' (PCC 140). Regardless of what technologies are backed by states, new areas of uncertainty will undoubtedly be created in the process (PCC 145).

Giddens returns to the concept of utopian realism, first outlined in *The Consequences of Modernity*. Rather than examining this concept in future-oriented philosophical terms (as he does in CM) however, he attempts to offer practical examples of what a utopian realist society could look like in his work on climate change (PCC 160). He gives examples of so-called 'utopian' societies. For example, he discusses Malmo in Sweden, a location where whole communities are built around eco-friendly policies (e.g. homes, parking, and waste). He uses the notion of utopian realism not only to explore more environmentally friendly ways of living but also travelling. He focuses in particular on cars and the need to reduce CO_2 emissions. Whilst acknowledging the potential for the growth of new modes of transport powered by renewable sources he also states that we do not know 'how quickly, new forms of propulsion for vehicles, such as electricity from renewable sources, or hydrogen, can come into use on a large scale' (PCC 161). He does also explore alternative forms of social organisation and states there may be a movement against globalisation and a return to localism driven by more effective planning strategies. This could, according to Giddens, enable us to envisage a future where we do not rely so heavily on cars (PCC 161). Whatever happens from now on Giddens states that 'climate change is going to affect our lives and we will have to adapt to its consequences' (PCC 162).

Adapting biological and social life

In order to preserve human life in the future we must, Giddens argues, adapt to climate change. Adaption, is a concept, according to Giddens, that is 'borrowed from evolutionary biology, the term 'adaptation' has come into widespread use in the climate change literature' (PCC 163). For Giddens this is not just about 'reacting to the consequences of climate change once it has occurred'. 'Adaptation as far as possible has to be anticipatory and preventative' (PCC 163). Giddens elaborates on this concept focusing on what he calls *proactive adaptation* (PA). 'PA is about diagnosing and responding to *vulnerabilities*'. Vulnerability for Giddens is all about risk: 'the risk of suffering damage to a valued activity, way of life or resource' (PCC 164). Vulnerability for Giddens stands in contrast to *resilience*. 'Resilience can be defined as *adaptive capacity*, the capacity not only to cope in the face of external changes or shocks, but, wherever possible, to respond actively and positively to them' (PCC 164). Ultimately, it is the richer countries, he argues, that must shoulder most of the responsibility for adaptation, as far 'as the developing world is concerned, just as they have to in limiting the progress of global warming' (PCC 165).

The majority of greenhouse gas emissions are produced by only a limited number of countries. According to Giddens, 'what the majority of states do pales in significance compared to the activities of the large polluters' (PC 220). Innovation at all levels has to be a key aspect of the world's attempts to contain climate change (PCC 227). Giddens argues that three things are of particular importance in dealing with climate change: states – working individually, bilaterally, or in larger groupings. According to Giddens, 'a great deal of power in world society still remains in the hands of states, and no other organizations approach them in terms of legitimacy' (PCC 227). Businesses – both big and small – must also play a role. We also need to witness the emergence of a diverse and dynamic global civil society mediated by electronic means of communication and by the ease of modern transportation. He also stresses the importance of a strong form of global governance and the need to rehabilitate the United Nations, which currently seems to have lost its way. State leaders may come to realise that it is the lack of effective global governance that is a prime reason why the dangers associated with climate change have become so acute (PCC 228). Giddens rearticulates his earlier radical political or third-way position (BLR, TW), stating that we need to go beyond a politics of either the left or right, and instead focus on developing a 'cross-party concordat' (PCC 115). This would provide 'a firm anchor for climate change as a continuing preoccupation of the "policy stream"' (PCC 115).

Giddens concludes his work on climate change by stating that, for better or worse, modern industry has unleashed a sheer volume of *power* into the world vastly beyond anything witnessed before (PCC 229). He moves from policy analysis back to social theory, reflecting again on the work of classical social theorists. He states that the enlightenment thinkers saw such capabilities as essentially benign – and as Marx argued – problems created by humans could be resolved by humans. However, others (most notably Weber) saw the powers created by industrial development as destructive or threatening the control of their creators (PCC 229). According to Giddens, this debate continues today:

> Doomsday is no longer a religious concept, a day of spiritual reckoning, but a possibility imminent in our society and economy. If unchecked, climate change alone could produce enormous human suffering. So also could the drying up of the energy resources upon which so many of our capacities are built. (PCC 230)

According to Giddens, there can be no 'going back'. 'The very expansion of human power that created such deep problems' in the first place through the process of industrial development 'is the only means of resolving them, with science and technology at the forefront' (BLR 230).

CONCLUSION

Giddens's substantive work on climate change does incorporate elements of his work on both radical modernity and politics. In *The Consequences of Modernity* he identifies climate change as one of the most pressing problems posed by radical modernity. In *Beyond Left and Right* and *The Third Way* he begins to map out a strategy to deal with environmental decay. This is something that he then elaborates on more fully in his work on climate change (PCC). A number of scholars, however, have argued that Giddens loses sight of his socio-theoretical moorings in his work on *The Third Way* (see Giddens 2000 and also Callinicos 2001) and in *The Politics of Climate Change*, both of which are aimed at a popular rather than an academic audience, and as a result his work lost credibility. For example, Giddens's theory of globalisation as outlined in *The Consequences of Modernity* afforded him the position of a respected figure in the field of globalisation. However, according to James and Steger (2014), the term Giddens's paradox (2014: 421) that he developed in PCC seemed to show a lack of integrity. The notion of Giddens's paradox to describe the core problem of climate change – the discrepancy between what people know and how they act – is not only an act of vanity on his part perhaps, but also may indicate a shift from serious socio-theoretical analysis in Giddens's work.

Throughout BLR, TW, and PCC Giddens articulated and developed his radical political position. However, it is perhaps the concept of risk that is used most consistently across all the texts explored in this chapter. Giddens continues to reinforce the message that 'our age is not more dangerous – not more risky – than those of earlier generations, but that the balance of risks and dangers has shifted' (RW 34). Giddens reinforces the message that 'we live in a world where hazards created by ourselves are as, or more threatening than those that come from outside. Some of these hazards are genuinely catastrophic', such as climate change. Others affect us as individuals much more directly, for instance, those involved in diet, medicine, or even marriage (RW 34). However, what he seeks to demonstrate is that there is 'no question of merely taking a negative attitude towards risk. Risk always needs to be disciplined, but active risk-taking is a core element of a dynamic economy and innovative society' (RW 35). Risk and opportunity, as Giddens argues, belong together; the greatest opportunities often arise from the biggest risks (PCC 230). Despite any differences identified in all the work analysed in this chapter, the message Giddens ends on in each text is not dissimilar: a mix of doomsday philosophising and of hope for the future, which he pitches through the conceptual lens of the centre ground: 'A new Dark Ages, a new age of enlightenment, or perhaps a confusing mixture of the two – which will it be? Probably the third possibility is the most likely. In that case, we all have to hope that the balance will be tilted towards the enlightenment side of the equation' (PCC 232).

Abbreviations

BLR: *Beyond Left and Right: The Future of Radical Politics* (1994b)

CM: *The Consequences of Modernity* (1990)

PCC: *The Politics of Climate Change* (2011)

RM: *Reflexive Modernization* (1994a)

RW: *Runaway World* (1999)

TW: *The Third Way: The Renewal of Social Democracy* (1998)

Selected Further Reading

The following two readings provide a good and comprehensive introduction and overview of Giddens's sociological project:

Bryant, C. G. A. and Jary, D. (eds) (2001) *The Contemporary Giddens: Social Theory in a Globalizing Age*. Basingstoke: Palgrave.

Kaspersen, L. B. (2000) *Anthony Giddens: An Introduction to a Social Theorist*. Oxford: Blackwell Publishers.

Callinicos, A. (2001) *Against the Third Way*. Cambridge: Polity Press provides a thought-provoking critique of the third-way perspective.

Note

1   United Nations, General Assembly, Rio Declaration on Environment and Development, Rio de Janeiro, 3–14 June 1992, www.un.org/documents/ga/conf151/aconf15126-1annex1.htm (accessed May 2017).

2

Pierre Bourdieu: Capital and Forms of Social Suffering

PART 1: FORMS OF CAPITAL

Bourdieu views capital as accumulated labour, 'a force inscribed in objective or subjective structures', 'the principle underlying the immanent regularities of the social world' (FC 46). According to Bourdieu, 'it is what makes the games of society – not least, the economic game – something other than simple games of chance' (FC 46). Capital for Bourdieu exists in different forms – economic, cultural, and social – which, when legitimated, are converted into symbolic capital and power. Bourdieu argues that the social position of individuals, groups, or institutions is determined by the *volume* and *composition* of capital they hold (Wacquant 2008: 268), and that the distribution of cultural and economic capital is the main source of class differentiation in society (D). Capital therefore frames his understanding of social inequality in contemporary society and, as articulated in Part 2 of this chapter, is also embedded in his work on suffering.

Habitus, Capital, and Field

The concepts of field, capital, and habitus are often perceived to be the organising concepts of Bourdieu's work (Wacquant 1989). Together these are used to formulate his socio-theoretical approach, a 'synthesis of objectivism and subjectivism, social physics and social phenomenology' (Wacquant 2008: 266). Bourdieu uses these concepts together, and it is impossible to make sense of capital without recognising its relationship to the other two. We begin our analysis, therefore, by situating his concept of capital in relation to habitus and field.

Habitus is 'the durably installed generative principle of regulated improvisations' (OTP 78). It acts as a 'system of durable and transposable *dispositions* through which individuals perceive, judge, and act in the world' (Wacquant 2008: 267). Through the habitus 'unconscious schemata' are acquired via ongoing exposure to a particular set of social conditions and through the internalisation of 'external constraints and possibilities' (Wacquant 2008: 267). It is habitus that forms a 'mediating link between individual's 'subjective worlds and the cultural world into which they are born and which they share with others' (Jenkins 1992: 75). According to Wacquant it 'is at once *structured*, by the patterned social forces that produced it, and *structuring*: it gives form and coherence to the various activities of an individual across the separate spheres of life' (Wacquant 2008: 268).

According to Wacquant (2008) 'the system of dispositions' (habitus) people acquire depends, however, on their particular endowment in *capital* (258). For Bourdieu, 'capital is accumulated labor (in its materialized form or its "incorporated", embodied form) which, when appropriated on a private, i.e., exclusive, basis by agents or groups of agents, enables them to appropriate social energy in the form of reified or living labor' (FC 46). Capital 'takes time to accumulate' and can be reproduced in 'identical or expanded form', although, according to Bourdieu, it has a tendency to persist in its existing state (FC 46). At any given point in time the structure and distribution of different types of capital represent the inherent structure of the social world, that is, a 'set of constraints inscribed in the very reality of that world, which govern its functioning in a durable way' (FC 46). In order to understand and account for the structure and functioning of the social world, Bourdieu argues for the need to acknowledge capital in all its forms and 'not solely in the one form recognized by economic theory' (FC 46). Bourdieu identifies three fundamental forms of capital:

> *economic capital*, which is immediately and directly convertible into money and may be institutionalized in the form of property rights; as *cultural capital*, which is convertible, on certain conditions, into economic capital and may be institutionalized in the form of educational qualifications; and … *social capital*, made up of social obligations ('connections'), which is convertible, in certain conditions, into economic capital and may be institutionalized in the form of a title of nobility. (FC 47)

Alongside economic, cultural, and social capital Bourdieu also uses the term symbolic capital, which is taken according to Skeggs 'to refer to the form the different types of capital take once they are perceived and recognized as legitimate. Legitimation is the key mechanism in the conversion to power. Capital has to be legitimated before it can have symbolic power' (Skeggs 1997: 8).

In contemporary societies, however, 'people do not face an undifferenti-ated social space' (Waquant 2008: 268). According to Wacquant (2008) 'the various spheres of life, art, science, religion, to the economy, the law, politics and so on tend to form distinct microcosms endowed with their own rules, regularities and forms of authority – what Bourdieu calls fields' (Wacquant, 2008: 208). Bourdieu defines fields as 'a network, or a configuration, of objec-tive relations between positions objectively defined' (Bourdieu in Wacquant 1989: 39). It 'is a social arena within which struggles or manoeuvres take place over specific resources or stakes and access to them' (Jenkins 1992: 84). 'It is a structured space of positions, a *forcefield* that imposes its specific determina-tions upon all those who enter it' (Waquant 2008: 268). It is also an arena of struggle through which agents and institutions seek to preserve or overturn the existing distribution of capital (Wacquant 2008: 268).

Bourdieu employs this particular conceptual 'arsenal', as Wacquant refers to it, in order to explore the ways in which 'social and mental' structures are reproduced or transformed in society (Wacquant 2008: 267). Bourdieu argues that these concepts are closely linked and operate most effectively when used together.[1] As will become apparent in Part 2, it is not possible or desirable to completely isolate these concepts from one another. However, for Bourdieu it is capital – most notably economic and cultural capital – that underpins the major social divisions in contemporary social life. There is significant merit, therefore, in offering a detailed analysis of the different types of capital, which he outlines in some detail in his essay 'The forms of capital' (1986), and which is both informed by and illuminated through his substantive work on school-ing and taste (Bourdieu and Passeron 1977).

Cultural Capital

Bourdieu argues that cultural capital requires familiarity 'with the dominant culture in society', and particularly 'the ability to understand and use educated language' (Sullivan 2001: 893). Cultural capital for Bourdieu can exist in three different forms:

> in the *embodied* state, i.e., in the form of long-lasting dispositions of the mind and body; in the *objectified* state, in the form of cultural goods (pictures, books, dictionaries, instruments, machines etc.), which are the trace or realization of theories or critiques of these theories, problemat-ics etc.; and in the *institutionalized* state, a form of objectification which must be set apart because, as will be seen in the case of educational qualifications, it confers entirely original properties on the cultural capital which it is presumed to guarantee. (FC 47)

The notion of cultural capital was developed by Bourdieu originally through his own empirical research in education (Bourdieu and Passeron 1977). Cultural capital is the theoretical hypothesis that made it possible for him to explain the unequal academic achievements of children from different social classes (FC 47). In developing the concept of cultural capital Bourdieu breaks from what he argues is common-sense theory, which views academic success as related to natural aptitude. Bourdieu's approach also departs from an economic approach, which links educational success to finance (i.e. having the means to privately educate your children) and from a human capital approach, which views investments in education (e.g. in training programmes) as a means to achieve a more productive workforce.

For Bourdieu, existing approaches to educational attainment fail to account for the complex intersection of economic/cultural investment in educational attainment. They disregard 'the best hidden and socially most determinant educational investment, namely the domestic transmission of cultural capital' (FC 48). They ignore the importance of cultural capital previously invested by the family, neglecting 'the contribution which the education system makes to the reproduction of the social structure by sanctioning the hereditary transmission of cultural capital' (FC 48). In making these claims, Bourdieu has often been criticised for not being precise enough about exactly which of the resources associated with the higher class home constitute cultural capital, and how these resources are converted into educational credentials (Sullivan 2002). However, by acknowledging the interpenetration of family, cultural capital, and educational attainment in this way, Bourdieu offered a significant challenge to economic theories of capital and existing sociological work on education.

Transferring embodied cultural capital

One of the key properties of cultural capital according to Bourdieu is that 'it is linked to the body and presupposes embodiment' (FC 48). 'The accumulation of cultural capital in the embodied state' *Bildung* presumes 'a process of embodiment' (FC 48). Bourdieu argues that embodied capital is external wealth converted into an integral part of the person, into a habitus. This form of capital cannot be transmitted immediately ('unlike money' or 'property rights') 'by gift or by bequest, purchase, or exchange'. It may however be acquired unconsciously (FC 48). By focusing on the embodied nature of cultural capital, Bourdieu uniquely draws together notions of biological and cultural inheritance, the former an innate property, the latter acquired through primary socialisation. Embodied cultural capital for Bourdieu 'cannot be accumulated beyond the appropriating capacities of an individual agent' (FC 49). It decays with the biological capacity (and memory etc.) of its owner. This, for Bourdieu, is because embodied capital is linked in various ways to biological personhood 'in its singularity' and is subject to a hereditary transmission (FC 49). According to Bourdieu through the notion of embodied capital one is able to combine the prestige of innate property with the merits of acquisition, biological inheritance with socialisation. He argues that the social conditions in which such capital is transferred and acquired are therefore subtler than those of economic, capital making it function as symbolic capital (FC 49).

'The structure of the field, i.e., the unequal distribution of capital, is the source of the specific effects of capital' (FC 49). However, for Bourdieu, it is through the logic of transmission that cultural capital acquires its symbolic power (FC 49). The ability to obtain objectified cultural capital depends on the familial embodiment of cultural capital. The ability to accumulate all forms of cultural capital (embodied, objectified, and institutionalised) arises from the outset only with the children of families endowed with strong cultural capital (FC 49). Bourdieu argues that this hidden (domestic) transmission of cultural capital plays a significant role in the reproduction of different forms of capital (and subsequently an agent's position within social space). According to Bourdieu, the hereditary transmission of cultural capital 'therefore receives proportionately greater weight in the system of reproduction strategies, as the direct, visible forms of transmission tend to be more strongly censored and controlled' (FC 49). This transmission occurs through the socialisation of children within the family and therefore takes time to accumulate. For Bourdieu, 'the link between economic and cultural capital is established through the mediation of time needed for acquisition' (FC 49) of capital.

Objectified and institutional forms of capital

According to Bourdieu, 'cultural capital in the objectified state has a number of properties that are defined only in the relationship with cultural capital in its embodied form' (FC 50). 'The cultural capital objectified in material objects and media, such as writings, paintings, monuments, instruments, etc., is transmissible in its materiality' (FC 50). Bourdieu uses the example of a collection of paintings to illustrate his argument. Cultural capital can be transmitted through changes in the legal ownership of paintings along with economic capital. However, there is also the possession of the means of 'consuming a painting or using a machine', which are embodied capital, and as such is subject to the same laws of transmission (FC 50). According to Bourdieu, cultural capital in its objectified state presents itself as autonomous. It is the product of historical action and has its own laws that transcend individual desires. However, he also argues that it exists as 'symbolically and materially active, effective capital only insofar as it is appropriated by agents and implemented and invested as a weapon and a stake in the struggles which go on in the fields of cultural production' (FC 50).

This is something that Bourdieu elaborates in his work on taste (D). Here he argues that 'to appreciate' certain objective forms of capital such as 'a painting, a poem, or a symphony' presumes the 'mastery of the specialized symbolic code' (Wacquant 2008: 270). Mastery of this type of cultural capital 'can be acquired by osmosis in one's milieu of origin or by explicit teaching' (Wacquant 2008: 270). According to Wacquant (2008) when it comes through family and inheritance (as with children of cultured upper class families), this capacity is experienced as an innate inclination (Wacquant 2008: 270). He also states that the field of social classes involves the 'struggles in which the agents wield strengths and obtain profits proportionate to their mastery of this objectified capital, and therefore to the extent of their embodied capital' (FC 50).

According to Bourdieu, the objectification of cultural capital in the form of academic qualifications is one way of neutralising some of the limits of embodied capital (i.e. the fact that it decays along with its bearer) (FC 50). 'It institutes cultural capital by collective magic' (FC 51). Bourdieu argues that academic qualifications confer 'institutional recognition on the cultural capital possessed by any given agent', and in doing so 'also makes it possible to compare qualification holders and even to exchange them (by substituting one for another in succession)' (FC 51). Bourdieu also argues that this 'makes it possible to establish conversion rates between cultural capital and economic capital by guaranteeing the monetary value of a given academic capital' (FC 51). For Bourdieu, the material and symbolic profits guaranteed by academic qualifications also depend on their rarity. When qualifications become less rare they are more difficult to convert (e.g. as is the case with the expansion of higher education). In this case the investments made (in time and effort) to acquire academic qualifications may turn out to be less lucrative than was anticipated (FC 51).

Social Capital

While Bourdieu focuses in detail on cultural capital and its relationship to economic capital, he does not neglect the importance of social capital. Social capital refers to group association or membership: 'social capital is the aggregate of the actual or potential resources which are linked to possession of a durable network of more or less institutionalized relationships of mutual acquaintance and recognition – or in other words, to membership in a group' (FC 51). According to Bourdieu, this group then provides its individual members with the support of the collectively owned capital. 'These relationships may exist only in the practical state, in material and/or symbolic exchanges which help to maintain them. They may also be socially instituted and guaranteed by the application of a common name' (FC 51). According to Bourdieu, the amount of social capital possessed by an individual will therefore depend on 'the size of the network of connections he can effectively mobilize' (FC 51). It is also contingent on the volume of the capital (economic, cultural, and symbolic) that an individual possesses in their own right (FC 51). According to Bourdieu, 'the existence of a network of connections is not a natural or even a social given' (FC 52). The reproduction of social capital requires a continual effort of sociability, and 'a continuous series of exchanges in which recognition is endlessly affirmed and reaffirmed' (FC 52). Those who are richly endowed with social capital, particularly inherited social capital (e.g. as symbolised through possessing an elite family name), are more likely to be able to 'transform all circumstantial relationships into lasting connections' (FC 52).

Economic Capital and Capital Conversions

According to Sullivan (2002) sociologists have often critiqued Bourdieu for placing too much weight in his theory of capital to 'symbolic relations at the expense of material ones' (Sullivan 2002: 146; Willis 1983). This is perhaps unfair, as Bourdieu makes clear that both cultural and social capital can be derived from economic capital (FC 53). He argues that it can be assumed that 'economic capital is at the root of all the other types of capital', and that these disguised forms of capital 'conceal (not least from their possessors) the fact that economic capital is at their root' (FC 54). He argues that 'the convertibility of the different types of capital is the basis of the strategies aimed at ensuring the reproduction of capital (and the position occupied in social space) by means of the conversions least costly in terms of conversion work and of the losses inherent in the conversion itself (in a given state of the social power relations)' (FC 54). As Bourdieu argues, the conversion rate between different forms of 'capital, set by such institutional mechanisms as the school system, the labour market, and inheritance laws, turns out to be one of the central stakes of social struggles, as each class or class fraction seeks to impose the hierarchy of capital most favourable to its own endowment' (Wacquant 2008: 271).

Through his theory of capital, therefore, Bourdieu demonstrates that people are distributed in 'social space according to: the global *volume* of capital they possess; the *composition* of their capital', and the relative weight of the various forms of capital (Skeggs 1997: 8; Wacquant 2008). In his empirical work on taste and education Bourdieu emphasises the ways in which different forms of capital work together to underpin class difference in contemporary society. The following section extends this analytical focus to his broader sociological and political work on social suffering. Examining his ethnographical work on the experience of suffering in everyday life allows for an assessment of the extent to which Bourdieu's work on capital can further inform sociological analyses of how positions of disadvantage are reproduced, reinforced, and experienced in contemporary society.

PART 2: SOCIAL SUFFERING

Suffering has been described as a social experience that opposes rationality and 'exhausts the limits of practical reason' (Morgan and Wilkinson 2001: 204). Sociologists increasingly focus on conceptualising experiences of suffering in contemporary social life, particularly in the area of health and illness (Frank 2001; Kleinman et al. 1997). Bourdieu's work on social suffering belongs to a body of literature that seeks to speak to 'the experience of people living under the impact of extreme social hardships and events of political atrocity' (Wilkinson 2005: 4). *La Misère du Monde*, translated as *Weight of the World* (WOTW), is a co-authored ethnographical account of people's experiences of social suffering.[2] The book prioritises themes simultaneously central to sociology and encountered – personally or in mediated form – by large numbers of people in their daily lives, such as: poor housing and unemployment, social and symbolic forms of exclusion, intergenerational and interethnic conflict, and urban dystopia. In what follows we seek to examine Bourdieu's application of the concept of capital in this work on suffering, focusing in particular on his methodology, analysis of family and education, and social and physical space.

Researching Social Suffering in Everyday Life

In *Weight of the World* Bourdieu states: 'I am loath to engage too insistently here in reflections on theory or method' (WOTW 607). Despite this claim, however, discussions on reflexive sociology are prevalent throughout his ethnographic approach to suffering (Wacquant 1989).[3] Furthermore, it is through this discussion on the relationship between the researcher and the 'object' of research that we see elements of his theory of capital. In *Weight of the World* Bourdieu and co-authors attempt to juxtapose a sociological analysis with the individual points of view of their respondents through the direct inclusion of interview transcripts in the main text. As Bourdieu argues, it is necessary to analyse and understand respondents' points of view but without 'setting up the objectivizing distance that reduces the individual to a specimen in a display case' (WOTW 2). Bourdieu argues for the importance of juxtaposing of different points of view (the space for points of view) in research in order to 'bring out everything that results when different or antagonistic visions of the world confront each other' (WOTW 3).[4] Bourdieu argues that 'using material poverty as the sole measure of all suffering keeps us from *seeing* and understanding a whole side of the suffering characteristic of a social order' (WOTW 4). By adopting an approach that allows space for different points of view Bourdieu seeks to capture all forms of suffering including *positional suffering*, which is often taken as the point of reference for criticism ('you really don't have anything to complain about'), as for consolation ('you could be worse off you know') (WOTW 4). Through taking this approach – as will become clearer in a moment – Bourdieu is able to capture the subtle differences in the operation of various forms of capital that inform everyday experiences of suffering.

Capital and the research relationship

Bourdieu also stresses the methodological importance of acknowledging that the research relationship is first and foremost a social relationship. As such it often reflects and reproduces inequalities and hierarchies of the wider social structure. Bourdieu introduces his theory of capital directly into this discussion in this text on the research relationship. Bourdieu argues that the asymmetry in the research relationship is reinforced by 'social symmetry every time the investigator occupies a higher place in the social hierarchy of different types of capital, cultural capital in particular' (WOTW 609). He states that 'the *market for linguistic and symbolic goods* established every time an interview take place varies in structure according to the objective relationship between the investigator and the investigated or, what comes down to the same thing, the relationship between all the different kinds of capital, especially linguistic capital, with which each of them is endowed' (WOTW 609). In emphasising the operation of capital in the research situation, Bourdieu illustrates one of the ways in which the research relationship is an implicitly social one. However, he argues that sociologists have often failed to recognise this. They neglect to 'objectivize themselves' and therefore do not 'realize that what their apparently scientific discourse talks about is not the object but their relation to the object' (Bourdieu in Wacquant 1989: 33).

In order to acknowledge this relationship effectively Bourdieu argues that sociologists need to take a reflexive approach to research. However, this requires the development of an approach that goes beyond the particular type of reflexivity favoured by some American anthropologists (Clifford and Marcus 1986). According to Bourdieu, such authors spend too much time reflecting on themselves rather than their research object, opening the door potentially to a thinly veiled nihilistic relativism (Bourdieu in Wacquant 1989: 35). Bourdieu argues that the sociologist must go beyond this and objectivise her or his position in cultural production (Bourdieu in Wacquant 1989 HA). In his work on suffering, therefore, he advocates the need to adopt a particular type of reflexivity in research: 'a *reflex reflexivity* based on a craft, on a sociological "feel" or "eye", allows one to perceive and monitor *on the spot*, as the interview is actually taking place, the effects of the social structure within which it is occurring' (WOTW 608).[5] It is through the adoption of this sociological 'eye' or 'feel' that Bourdieu is able to explore the plurality of experience of social suffering in everyday life without losing sight of the effects of the wider social structure on the research relationship itself.

Social and Physical Sites of Capital

As already articulated above, Bourdieu has a multifaceted notion of social space. In contrast to Marx, he sees 'social space in modern societies not as focused around one organizing principle (relations to the means of economic production) but as a space with multiple (if interrelated) fields of competition where different forms of capital are at stake' (Couldry 2005: 356). For Bourdieu, individual action is the key site where social structure can be reproduced: social structure is not a determining force in itself. Bourdieu refers specifically to 'actions of individuals that are based on the dispositions those individuals have acquired and whose acquisition is itself structurally determined by the objective conditions in which that individual has lived his or her life (the individual's position in social space, including both inherited capital and actual resources, economic, cultural, and symbolic)' (Couldry 2005: 356). The relationship between physical (geographical) space and an agent's position in social space is present in Bourdieu's discussion of social capital in 'The forms of capital' (FC). However, the intersection of social and physical space, and more specifically the role of capital in this context, is extended in his work on suffering.[6]

According to Bourdieu, as bodies (and biological individuals) human beings are situated in a site and they occupy a place: 'The site (*le lieu*) can be defined absolutely as the point in *physical space* where an agent or a thing is situated, "takes place", exists: that is to say, either as a *localization* or, from a relational viewpoint, as a *position*, a rank in an order' (WOTW 123). 'People are constituted in, and in relationship to, a *social space* (or better yet, to needs fields)' (WOTW 124). According to Bourdieu, there is no space in a hierarchical society that is not also hierarchical and that does not articulate these unequal relationships 'in a form that is more or less distorted and, above all, disguised by the *naturalization effect* produced by the long-term inscription of social realities in the natural world' (WOTW 124). He argues that social space converts into physical space,

> but the translation is always more or less *blurred*: the power over space that comes from possessing various kinds of capital takes the form in appropriated physical space of a certain relation between the spatial structure of the distribution of agents and the spatial structure of the distribution of goods and services, private or public. (WOTW 124)

According to Bourdieu, 'the structures of social space' are inscribed 'in physical space' and cannot be changed 'except by a *work of transplantation*, a moving of things and an uprooting or deporting of people, which itself presupposes extremely difficult and costly social transformations' (WOTW 124). For Bourdieu, 'the value of different regions of reified social space' (i.e. physically realised or objectified) 'is defined in this relation between the distribution of agents and the distribution of goods in social space' (WOTW 125). The result of this is that the rarest goods and the people that own them are concentrated in particular places.

This focus on social and physical space is prevalent throughout *Weight of the World*. It is illuminated early on by Bourdieu's interview with two young boys living in a French housing project:[7] one boy – Ali – is French Algerian, the other – François – is ethnically white. Bourdieu uses interview transcripts to examine the shared position of the boys in social and geographical space. He states: 'How could readers of their interview fail to see that in fact they share every trait except ethnic origin' (WOTW 62). Whilst emphasising the similarities between the two boys, he also illustrates the differences, which relate to race, ethnicity, and access to capital:

Ali is merely a sort of François taken to the limit: the ethnic stig-
mata inscribed in a permanent way on his skin or his facial
features, as well as in his name, intensifies, or rather radicalizes the
handicap linked to the lack of certificates or qualifications, itself
linked to the lack of cultural and more specifically linguistic capital.
(WOTW 62)

In his analysis of ethnic and racial inequality (here and elsewhere) Bourdieu
emphasises the importance of socio-economic position, or at least seeks to
use the same analytical framework to study these different but intersecting
forms of inequality. However, as Lane argues, racial discrimination is the
outcome of a 'complex of tastes, aversions, prejudices and ideas', it has 'its
own autonomous logic' and requires its 'own specific tools of analysis' (Lane
2006: 153). It is the product of a complex and contradictory set of processes
that include but are not exclusive to social and economic deprivation
(McRobbie 2002). Such complexity, however, does not appear to be fully
reflected in Bourdieu's discussion of capital and ethnicity in his work on
social suffering.

Capital and physical space

In *Weight of the World* Bourdieu focuses much of his analysis of social and
physical space on Paris,[8] which he states is: 'the site of capital, that is, the site
in physical space where the positive poles of all the fields are concentrated
along with most of the agents occupying these dominant positions' (WOTW
125). This, according to Bourdieu, means 'that the capital cannot be ade-
quately analyzed except in relation to the provinces ("and provincialness"),
which is nothing other than being deprived (in entirely relative terms) of the
capital and capital' (WOTW 125). He elaborates further here on the relationship between capital and physical and social space. He argues that: 'the
ability to dominate space, notably by appropriating (materially or symbolically) the rare goods (public or private) distributed there, depends on the
capital possessed' (WOTW 127). Capital makes it possible to keep 'undesirable' people together in a far away location. It also keeps desirable people
and goods close, 'minimizing the necessary expense (notably in time)' in
appropriating them. Bourdieu argues that 'those who are deprived of capital
are either physically or symbolically held at a distance from goods' that have
the highest social value: 'they are forced to stick with the most undesirable
and the least rare persons or goods'. The lack of capital according to
Bourdieu 'chains one to a place' (WOTW 127).

Embodied capital, time, and space

Alongside capital, habitus and field are never far away from Bourdieu's analysis of social and physical space. Bourdieu argues here that: 'If the habitat

shapes the habitus, the habitus also shapes the habitat' (WOTW 128). The importance of time and acquisition were already illustrated above with reference to the hidden domestic transmission of capital and related to both biological and cultural notions of inheritance. In *Weight of the World*, embodied capital, time, and acquisition are connected again through his examination of social and physical space. Bourdieu refers here to the properties acquired through prolonged occupation of a site and sustained association with its legitimate occupants. He emphasises the importance of the relationship between location and social capital:

> This is the case, obviously, with the social capital of relations, connections or ties (and most particularly with the privileged ties of childhood or adolescent friendships) or with all the subtlest aspects of cultural and linguistic capital, such as body mannerisms and pronunciation (accents) etc. all the many attributes that make the place of birth (and to a lesser degree, place of residence) so important. (WOTW 128)

Bourdieu focuses his analysis on Paris in order to illustrate the subtle operationalisation of different forms of capital in physical space. He argues that: 'One has the Paris that goes with one's economic capital, and also with one's cultural and social capital (visiting the Pompidou Museum is not enough to appropriate the Museum of Modern Art)' (WOTW 128). Furthermore, it is not only a case of economic and cultural capital. According to Bourdieu, 'certain spaces, and in particular the most closed and most "select", require not only economic and cultural capital but social capital as well' (WOW 128–9). This is acquired through what he calls 'the *club effect*' that derives from people in 'chic' neighbourhoods coming together on a regular basis, and sharing the fact that what they have in common is the fact that they are not common (WOTW 129).

Bourdieu's focus on France is extended by other authors of *Weight of the World* to include an analysis and comparison with different geographical areas. For example, in writing about social dystopia in the American ghetto, Wacquant draws comparisons with rising urban inequality in France[9] (WOTW 130–9). Much of the analysis in the text focuses on the use of interview transcripts to illuminate the ways in which the differentiation of social space is reproduced in physical space. However, Bourdieu also includes a discussion of policy in his analysis. He argues that the differentiation of physical space can also be reinforced 'at a national level concerning housing policies, or at a local level, with regard to the construction and allocation of subsidized housing or choices for public services'. Such policies lead to for example, policies 'the *construction of homogenous groups on a spatial basis*' for example as observed in run-down housing estates (WOTW 129). By drawing on different modes of analysis Bourdieu is able to elucidate the different ways in which experiences of social inequality and suffering are reinforced through physical space.

Cultural Capital, Inheritance, and Education

As articulated above, Bourdieu often focuses in his work on cultural capital and the interaction between family background and schooling (Bourdieu and Passeron 1977). Cultural capital for Bourdieu is 'inculcated in the higher class home, and enables higher-class student to gain higher educational credentials than lower-class students' (Sullivan 2002: 145–146). In his work on suffering, Bourdieu returns to his focus on the transmission of cultural capital, education, and family. Inheritance, in particular, takes a more central role in his work on suffering. Bourdieu uses it not only to illustrate class difference, but also to demonstrate the relativity of suffering.

Capital and inheritance

Bourdieu begins his discussion with an argument on paternal inheritance. He states, first, that in order to continue and embody the paternal line it is frequently necessary to go beyond the achievements of one's father (WOTW 507).[10] Second, Bourdieu argues that 'for all social categories (though to differing degrees), the transmission of inheritance depends on the judgements' of the 'schooling system'. The schooling system for Bourdieu is brutal. It is competitive and it 'is responsible for many failures and disappointments'. In the past, it was the family that set up the parameters of inheritance, making it appear preordained (WOTW 507). In contemporary society, according to Bourdieu, 'this work also falls to schools', whose judgements and sanctions may confirm but also contradict or counter those of the family (WOTW 507). It is unsurprising, therefore, that the school is so often at the core of social suffering. Bourdieu argues that this is certainly the case with the interviewees in his study, 'who have been disappointed either in their own plans or in their plans for their children or by the ways the job market has reneged on the promises and guarantees made by the educational system' (WOTW 507).

It is worth noting at this point that Bourdieu's discussion on inheritance is focused on the father–son relationship, excluding a discussion on inheritance through the maternal line. In reflecting on issues of gender in Bourdieu's extensive *œuvre*, Skeggs (2004) argues that he sees the family 'as a fiction and a social artefact', in the same way that feminists do.[11] He perceives it to be a 'well-founded illusion because it is produced and re-produced with the guarantee of the state and operates as a central site of normalisation and naturalisation' (Skeggs 2004: 21). According to Skeggs, however, this does not stop him from 'normalising his own conception of the family 'by defining it as *the* universal norm, in a similar way to how he defines working-class women as closer to nature' (Skeggs 2004: 21–2). For Bourdieu 'the family functions as a field in which normalcy or the ability to constitute oneself as the universal is the capital': yet he fails to examine the ways in which 'normalcy works *differently* through gender as a form of capital' (Skeggs 2004: 22). This is certainly reflected in his discussion on inheritance in *Weight of the World*, which fails to problematise the gendered nature of inherited capital.

The family and education

For Bourdieu, the family itself is a necessary 'matrix of the contradictions and double binds that arise from the disjunction between the dispositions of the inheritor and the destiny contained within the inheritance itself' (WOTW 507–8). Inheritance is transmitted unconsciously in and by the *father's* 'whole way of being, and also overtly by educational acts aimed at perpetuating the line' (WOTW 508). However, Bourdieu is clear in his work here that successful inheritance means embodying but also going beyond the parent. The gap between parents' expectations and what the child can actually achieve is a major source of suffering (WOTW 508). Focusing more specifically on cultural capital, Bourdieu argues that if (family) connection constitutes a necessary condition for the smooth transmission of the inheritance (particularly concerning cultural capital), it is nevertheless not an adequate condition for achieving succession. 'For the holders of cultural capital above all (but also for everyone else, though to a lesser degree), succession is subject to the verdicts of school and is therefore passed on by academic success' (WOTW 509).

The transmission of cultural capital features again in Bourdieu's work in this text on schooling and secondary education more directly. Bourdieu argues that the meritocratic school system cannot deal effectively with a diversity of student intellectual strategies and as a result education often 'inflicts wounds that are likely to reactivate basic traumas' (WOTW 509). The negative judgements given by schools affect an individual's self-image, reinforced by the parents in ways 'that no doubt vary in their force and form, magnifying suffering and confronting the child or teenager with the alternatives of either conforming or quitting the game through denial, compensation, or regression' (WOTW 509). He gives the example of the manual labourer father whose 'entire existence is carried in a dual injunction' (WOTW 510). The father wants his children to succeed and be upwardly mobile on the one hand, whilst maintaining identification with himself (be like me):

> He cannot want his son to identify with his own position and its dispositions, and yet all his behavior works continuously to produce that identification, in particular the body language that contributes so powerfully to fashioning the whole manner of being, that is, the habitus. (WOTW 510)

As a result, the son/daughter is 'guilty of betrayal if he succeeds, he is guilty of disappointing if he fails' (WOTW 510). Bourdieu uses these contradictions imposed by the family to illustrate positional forms of suffering: 'The family is at the root of the most universal part of social suffering, including the paradoxical form of suffering based in privilege' (WOTW 511).

Capital, education, and schooling

Bourdieu also focuses specifically on the democratisation of the education system. According to Bourdieu, the secondary school system was until the end of the 1950s characterised by great stability based on the early and brutal elimination of students from disadvantaged families (WOTW 421). One of the biggest changes is, he argues, the democratisation of the school system – the entry into academic enterprise of social categories previously excluded (e.g. shopkeepers, artisans, farmers) (WOTW 422).[12] According to Bourdieu, it is clear that the children of the most culturally and economically disadvantaged families cannot gain access to the higher levels of the school system without significantly modifying the economic and symbolic value of educational qualifications (WOTW 423).

However, 'official diversification (into tracks or streams) and unofficial diversification (into subtly hierarchized schools or classes', ... 'also help recreate a particularly well-hidden principle of differentiation' (WOTW 424). Bourdieu argues that the 'elite students who have received a well-defined sense of place, good role models, and encouragement from their families' are in position to apply their cultural capital in top streams in good schools (WOTW 424). In contrast, students who come from 'disadvantaged families, especially children of immigrants, often left to fend for themselves, from primary school on, 'are obliged to rely either on the dictates of school or on chance to find their way in an increasingly complex universe' (WOTW 424). This, according to Bourdieu, helps to explain 'their either untimely or inappropriate use of already extremely meagre cultural capital' (WOTW 424). Bourdieu concludes his examination of education by arguing that:

> The educational system excludes as it always has, but now it does so continuously and at every level of the curriculum ... and it keeps hold of those when it excludes, just relegating them to educational tracks that have lost more or less of whatever value they once had. (WOTW 425)

The arguments Bourdieu makes about cultural capital, family, and education in *Weight of the World* are very similar to those he makes elsewhere (FC; Bourdieu and Passeron 1977). In *Weight of the World*, however, his discussion is tied explicitly to a focus on education as a source of social suffering. His position is also updated to reflect changes in education brought about by the expansion and devaluing of educational qualifications. This is easily illustrated in the UK context by the proliferation of secondary school and degree level courses such as 'music management'. Such courses appear to have little academic content and also do not provide the students taking them with specific professional qualifications. They tend, however, to be taken by those attempting to make the most of what Bourdieu calls their meagre cultural capital.

Sociological debates surrounding *Weight of the World* have often been focused on issues relating to methodology or politics. While some sociologists argue that *Weight of the World* is best read as a political tract not a socio-logical analysis (Jenkins 1992), others suggest that Bourdieu's socio-theoretical framework cannot cope with the sheer breadth and weight of topics and data presented in the text (Martuccelli 1999). However, through the analysis of capital in his work on suffering in the second part of this chapter, we have sought to show that this is not necessarily the case. Rather, through focusing on the plurality of respondents' voices Bourdieu is able to illuminate more clearly the ways in which positions of disadvantage are not only experienced, but also reinforced or reproduced in contemporary society. In *Weight of the World* Bourdieu deftly applies what he calls the sociological 'eye' or 'feel' in order to illuminate the subtle ways in which capital and suffering operate in everyday social life (WOTW 608).

CONCLUSION

There is a consistency in Bourdieu's use of capital across all of his work explored in this chapter. One of the key threads present throughout his work perhaps is the connection he makes between forms of capital, time, and acqui-sition. This is illuminated through the hidden domestic transmission of cultural capital in his work on the family and education, and through the transmission of social capital in his discussion on social and physical space. Furthermore, the embodied nature of capital appears to underpin much of his work – from his focus on the inheritance of cultural capital to the biological occupation of particular social and physical spaces. With the rapid expansion of the biomedical sciences over recent decades, the notion of embodied capital has become increasingly important in contemporary socio-theoretical discus-sions on inequality. As Webster argues, for example, the growth of genetic testing in recent decades has the potential to create new forms of (economic) inequality based on one's *genetic* capital (Webster 2007: 91). However, as his work on the family shows, embodied capital for Bourdieu is not something that is just acquired only through biological notions of inheritance, but also through primary socialisation. In developing this concept, therefore, he has offered something particularly unique to the sociological study of inequality, paving the way perhaps for the recent advancement of 'carnal sociology', which focuses specifically on the embodied and embedded nature of inequality and social action (Wacquant 2015).[13]

Whilst methodological reflexivity permeates his entire *œuvre*, capital is particularly embedded in Bourdieu's methodological approach to suffering. He seeks through his methodological strategy to illuminate a full spectrum of experiences of suffering in contemporary social life, not just those associated with profound economic hardship. However, economic capital still appears to form the bedrock of much of his analysis in his work on suffering. This per-haps mitigates some of those earlier critiques levelled at Bourdieu which suggest that he focuses too much on other forms of capital to the detriment of an analysis of material conditions (Willis 1983). However, it also means that some forms of inequality (gender, and race and ethnicity) may still appear underrepresented in his work, or that, at the very least, their analysis is often reduced to issues of economic inequality (Lane 2006; Skeggs 2004). That said, it is worth remembering here, perhaps, that capital is only one of several key concepts used by Bourdieu to illuminate social suffering. Only when it is used alongside other key concepts, such as habitus and field, can sociologists hope to expose different aspects of inequality across a range of areas of contemporary social life (Wacquant 1989).

Abbreviations

D: *Distinction* (1984)

FC: 'The forms of capital' (1997)

HA: *Homo Academicus* (1988)

OTP: *Outline of a Theory of Practice* (1977)

WOTW: *The Weight of the World* (1999)

Selected Further Reading

Wacquant, L. (2008) 'Pierre Bourdieu', in R. Stones (ed.) *Key Sociological Thinkers*. Basingstoke: Palgrave, pp. 261–77 provides a comprehensive introduction to Bourdieu's sociology. It includes a useful discussion of the concepts of habitus, capital, and field.

Jenkins, R. (1992) *Pierre Bourdieu*. London: Routledge offers a detailed and critical analysis of Bourdieu's overall sociological framework.

The edited monograph Adkins, L. and Skeggs, B. (eds) (2005) *Feminism After Bourdieu*. Hoboken, NJ: John Wiley & Sons contains varied and detailed discussions on gender and capital, and the impact of Bourdieu's work on feminism.

Notes

1 Together these concepts help Bourdieu to 'sociologize' the notion of doxa, a term originally developed by phenomenologist Husserl. These concepts emphasise the close fit between subjective worlds and objective structures. 'Each relatively autonomous universe develops its own doxa as a set of shared opinions and unquestioned beliefs' that 'bind people together' (Wacquant 2008: 270).

2 Bourdieu is the lead author for WOTW. The text is nearly 700 pages long and includes chapters by 20 different authors. It is impossible to explore all of these chapters in detail. We have drawn on a range of chapters by Bourdieu to illuminate his use of capital. However, where appropriate we also refer to chapters by other authors.

3   Sociological reflexivity is not the central focus of this chapter. For further discussion, see Bourdieu and Wacquant (1992).
4   See 'Space of points of view' (WOTW 1–5).
5   See 'Understanding' (WOTW 607–26).
6   See also Bourdieu (1995).
7   See Bourdieu's chapter 'The order of things' (WOTW 60–77).
8   See Bourdieu's chapter 'Site effects' (WOTW 123–9).
9   See also the chapter by Lois Wacquant 'Inside the zone' (WOTW 140–67) and the chapter by Phillippe Bourgois 'Homeless in El Barrio' (WOTW 168–79).
10 See chapter on 'The contradictions of inheritance' (WOTW 507–13).
11 There is a significant body of feminist literature on Bourdieu. See Skeggs (2004).
12 See chapters 'Outcasts on the inside' (WOTW 421–6) and 'They were the days' (WOTW 427–40).
13 For a discussion on the development of carnal sociology, please see Waquant (2015).

3

Bruno Latour: Rethinking Modern Social Life

PART 1: BEYOND MODERN SOCIAL CONDITIONS

In *We Have Never Been Modern* Latour offers an alternative approach to the theorisation of modernity. Latour is not suggesting – as radical modernists or postmodernists do – that we are simply living in a radical or postmodern society. Rather he seeks to problematise the very idea that we have ever been modern (WHNBM). Latour also seeks to offer an alternative socio-theoretical view to the concept of the social in *Reassembling the Social*. Rather than seeking to use the word to develop social explanations, he focuses instead on networks and associations, including those involving both humans and non-humans (RAS). This chapter seeks to explore his analytical approach to these two key concepts, also examining their manifestation in *An Inquiry into the Modes of Existence* – his comparative anthropology. With the threat of ecological decay looming on a global scale, Latour seeks in AIME to revisit many of the questions he poses in his earlier works, such as: if we were never modern then what were we and what are we to become (AIME 11)?

Were We Ever Modern?

Socio-theoretical explanations of the development of society tend to rest on the premise that we have been through or are currently still living in a period of modernity. For Latour these dominant accounts of modernity fall short. He is not aiming here to offer an alternative socio-theoretical vision of modernity itself as theorists such as Giddens have done in their work on radical or high modernity. Nor is he attempting to suggest – as postmodernists such as Lyotard do – that there has been a radical rupture with modernity. Both Giddens and Lyotard in different ways assume that modernity has existed in some form and at some point in time. For these theorists and many others the society we currently occupy is either a radicalised version of modernity or a new type of society beyond modernity. Latour is arguing for something quite distinct. He seeks to problematise the existence of modernity. He begins by highlighting the plurality and contradictions often inherent in definitions of modernity:

> Modernity comes in many versions … yet all its definitions point, in one way or another, to the passage of time. The adjective 'modern' designates a new regime, an acceleration, a rupture, a revolution in time. When the word 'modern', 'modernization', or 'modernity' appears, we are defining, by contrast, an archaic and stable past. (WHNBM 10)

Latour also argues that the word 'modernity' refers to two distinct sets of practices that have nonetheless become blurred:

> The first set of practices, by 'translation', creates mixtures between entirely new types of beings, hybrids of nature and culture. The second, by 'purification' creates two entirely distinct ontological zones: that of human beings on the one hand; that of nonhumans on the other. Without the first set, the practices of purification would be fruitless or pointless. Without the second, the work of translation would be slowed down, limited, or even ruled out. (WHNBM 10–11)

According to Latour the first set of practices corresponds to what he calls 'networks' and the second to what he names as the modern critical stance (WHNBM 11). Latour argues that, providing we treat the two practices of translation and purification as distinct, then we can consider ourselves as 'truly modern' (WHNBM 11). However for Latour: 'as soon as we direct our attention simultaneously to the work of purification and the work of hybridization, we immediately stop being wholly modern, and our future begins to change' (WHNBM 11). It is at this point that Latour questions whether we have, in fact, ever been modern. This is because we become aware, on reflection that the two sets of practices have already been at work historically, and therefore our past also begins to change (WHNBM 11). Finally, Latour argues 'if we have never been modern – at least in the way criticism tells the story – the tourtuous relations that we have maintained with the other nature-cultures would also be transformed' (WHNBM 11).

The problem for Latour, which he returns back to again and again, is the relationship between humans and non-humans, and the ways in which modernity or being modern denies the simultaneous emergence of non-humans. According to Latour 'modernity is often defined in terms of humanism' (WHNBM 13). However, he also argues that this definition 'overlooks the simultaneous birth of "nonhumanity" – things, or objects, or beasts – and the equally strange beginning of a crossed-out God, relegated to the sidelines' (WHNBM 13). Modernity develops from the combined creation of these three entities (the birth of man, non-humanity, and God relegated to the sidelines). This combined creation is simultaneously masked and the three entities are treated separately (WHNBM 13). At the same time that these are being separated however 'underneath, hybrids continue to multiply as an effect of this separate treatment' (WHNBM 13). According to Latour, 'the common text that defines this understanding and this separation is called a constitution' (WHNBM 14).

The modern Constitution

Latour refers to what he calls the *modern Constitution*, which he spells with a capital 'C' to distinguish it from the notion of a political constitution. He uses it to define humans and non-humans, their attributes, relationships, abilities, and groupings (WHNBM 15). Latour begins by drawing on a seventeenth-century debate in philosophy between Hobbes (political philosophy) and Boyle (natural philosophy, physics, and chemistry) that arose over Boyle's air-pump experiments.[1] In his *Leviathan*[2] Hobbes simultaneously redraws the boundaries between different fields of physics, theology, psychology, law, biblical exegesis, and political science. Boyle on the other hand concurrently redesigns scientific rhetoric, theology, scientific politics, and the hermeneutics of facts. According to Latour:

> Together, they describe how God must rule, how the new King of England must legislate, how the spirits or the angels should act, what the properties of matter are, how nature is to be interrogated, what the boundaries of scientific or political discussion must be. . . (WHNBM 29–30)

Latour presents the arrangement that came out of the debate as 'being laid down in a "modern Constitution" that separates the powers of politics and science' (de Vries 2016: 124). He argues that this composition stayed in place 'for centuries because the internal, intellectual structure of this Constitution shields it from criticism and change' (de Vries 2016: 124). What Latour refers to here, however, is not a political constitution (such as we might think about in relation to the American political system, for example) and the separate powers of government. Rather the Constitution that Latour has in mind focuses on separating the powers of 'nature' (the domain of the natural sciences) on the one hand, and 'society' (values, human interaction, politics, and culture) on the other (de Vries 2016: 125).

At the heart of the modern Constitution, according to Latour, lies a paradox: when 'we consider hybrids we are dealing only with mixtures of nature and culture' (WHNBM 30). However, when we reflect on the work of purification, then nature and culture are separated (WHNBM 30). This is precisely what Latour is aiming to understand. The key point of the modern Constitution, according to Latour, is that 'it renders the work of mediation that assembles hybrids invisible, unthinkable, unrepresentable' (WHNBM: 34). The point that Latour is trying to make – and one that distinguishes his work from dominant socio-theoretical accounts of modernity – is that the modern Constitution allows for the creation of hybrids whilst simultaneously pretending that these hybrids don't exist. Latour argues that moderns are not actually unaware of what they do. Rather, he is saying that 'what they do – innovate on a large scale in the production of hybrids – is possible only because they steadfastly hold to the absolute dichotomy between the order of Nature and that of Society, a dichotomy which is itself possible only because they never consider the work of purification and that of mediation together' (WHNBM 40).

Modernity as illusion

In making the case that we were never modern however, Latour does not suggest that modernity is an illusion. Modernity according to Latour 'is a force added to others that for a long time it had the power to represent, to accelerate, or to summarize – a power that it no longer entirely holds' (WHNBM 40). For Latour, 'the modern Constitution exists and indeed acts in history', 'but it no longer defines what has happened to us' (WHNBM 40). Modernity is about the development of humanism, it is also about the development of progress and mastery of humans over nature. However, according to Latour, what the moderns have actually succeeded in doing is creating more and more hybrids. According to Latour, moderns think that they have been successful because 'they have carefully separated Nature and Society (and bracketed God), whereas they have succeeded only because they have mixed together much greater masses of humans and nonhumans, without bracketing anything and without ruling out any combination!' (WHNBM 41). By making this case Latour seeks to offer a unique and original socio-theoretical alternative to existing theories of modernity.

Latour moves away from a focus on social relations in his work. He argues that the modern Constitution facilitates the creation of collectives rather than societies made up of only social relations (WHNBM 43). Despite making this case Latour is clear, however, that the position he seeks to advance is not one that could be described as postmodern: Postmodernism does not offer solution. 'It lives under the modern Constitution, but it no longer believes in the guarantees the Constitution offers. It senses that something has gone awry in the modern critique, but it is not able to do anything but prolong that critique, though without believing in its foundations' (WHNBM: 46).

According to Latour, if we focus closely on the production of hybrids and the simultaneous 'work of elimination of these same hybrids', we then realise that 'we have never been modern in the sense of the Constitution'. According to Latour, postmodernism is unfeasible therefore as postmodernists claim to come after a time that hasn't even begun (WHNBM 46–7).

Entering a non-modern world

If we have never been modern or postmodern, then what kind of world are we living in or entering into? Latour concludes this work by tackling possibly the most difficult question: 'the question of the nonmodern world that we are entering', he argues, 'without ever having really left it' (WHNBM 130). As we enter this non-modern world that we have never actually left, Latour wants to know what attributes of the 'moderns' we might want to hold on to. 'The moderns' greatness' for him stems from a range of things including: their 'proliferation of hybrids, their lengthening of a certain type of network', their 'daring', 'research', and 'their innovativeness', as well as their 'youthful excesses', 'the creation of stabilized objects independent of society' and 'the freedom of a society liberated from objects'. All of these features, according to Latour, 'we want to keep' (WHNBM 133).

In seeking to develop a way forward Latour outlines what he thinks is worthy of retention: *'to retain the production of a nature and of a society that allow changes in size through the creation of an external truth and a subject of law, but without neglecting the co-production of sciences and societies'* (WHNBM 134). According to Latour this would involve using premodern categories to conceptualise the hybrids, whilst holding on to the moderns' final outcome of purification 'that is, an external Nature distinct from subjects' (WHNBM 134). In moving forward, Latour also wants to retain some aspects of postmodernism because, according to Latour, postmodernists have 'sensed the crisis of the moderns and attempted to overcome it'. He stresses that: 'take away from the postmoderns their illusions about the moderns, and their vices become virtues – nonmodern virtues!' (WHNBM 134). What Latour seeks to do in this work is simply reestablish symmetry between science and technology and human beings. According to Latour, nature and society are not two opposites, 'but one and the same production of successive states of societies–natures, of collectives' (WHNBM 139).

In WHNBM Latour aims to highlight the ways in which science studies have sought to reevaluate the division of labour between science and politics (WHNBM 144). Latour argues that we often ascribe ourselves disciplinary labels as sociologists, historians, scientists, philosophers, or anthropologists. But to such disciplinary labels 'we always add a qualifier: of science and technology', 'science studies', or 'science technology and society' (WHNBM: 3).

Rather than science studies appearing as an adjunct to social theory, however, Latour shows the value of placing it at the centre of socio-theoretical frameworks. Latour seeks to demonstrate throughout the text that there is something missing from existing social explanations and that is non-human entities or 'quasi-objects' as Latour calls them. Quasi-objects link the two poles between nature and society (WHNBM 55). They are agents (not operators) that bring people together in particular relations as well as drawing people into relations with other non-human entities (WHNBM: 51–55). This inclusion of non-human entities in his analysis and the movement beyond focusing solely on human social relations is primarily what distinguishes Latour's socio-theoretical framework from many others. Overall Latour suggests that 'modernism was not an illusion, but an active performing. If we could draft a new Constitution, we would, similarly, profoundly alter the course of quasi-objects' (WHNBM 144–5).

Reconfiguring the Social

In WHNBM Latour offers a way of conceptualising the development of society that is quite distinct from most other socio-theoretical approaches. He also offers an alternative approach to conceptualising the social. The 'social' is one of the defining concepts of social theory and sociology more generally. In *Reassembling the Social* (RAS) he seeks to rethink the meaning of the concept. According to Latour, 'when social scientists add the adjective "social" to some phenomenon, they designate a stabilized state of affairs, a bundle of ties that, later, may be mobilized to account for some other phenomenon' (RAS 1). For Latour, there is nothing problematic about using the concept in this way 'as long as it designates what is *already* assembled together, without making any superfluous assumption about the *nature* of what is assembled' (RAS 1, italics in original). Latour states that problems arise when 'social' begins to refer to a type of material, as if the adjective were roughly comparable to other terms like 'wooden' or 'steely' (RAS 1). For Latour it is at this point that the word's meaning breaks down as it now refers to two very different things: 'first, a movement during a process of assembling; and second, a specific type of ingredient that is supposed to differ from other materials' (RAS 1).

In RAS, Latour aims to 'show why the social cannot be construed as a kind of material or domain'. He also wants to dispute the project of providing a 'social explanation' of some other 'state of affairs' (RAS 1). He seeks, rather, to use the term to trace connections, which he believes was the original purpose of the term. Once this has been achieved, then the social sciences, according to Latour, can resume their traditional goal but with tools better suited to the task (RAS 1–2). Latour wants to: 'scrutinise more thoroughly the exact content of what is "assembled" under the umbrella of a society' (RAS 2). For Latour this appears to be the only way to remain faithful to the original aims of sociology, this 'science of the living together' (RAS 2). In *Reassembling the Social* he argues that we need to define the discipline of sociology. Latour takes us back to the original Latin or Greek definition 'socio-logy', which means the 'science of the social'. According to Latour there are problems with this definition, as scientific and technical enterprises 'bear little relation with what the founders of the social sciences had in mind when they invented their disciplines' (RAS 2). Science, according to Latour, was all about progress during the modernising period. However, as science has expanded it has been brought into much more of a co-extensiveness with society. This has resulted in changes to the actual meaning of science and society. For Latour 'neither science nor society has remained stable enough to deliver the promises of a strong "socio-logy"' (RS 2). He argues that it is time to 'modify what is meant by "social"' (RAS 2). He wants to 'devise an alternative definition for "sociology" while still retaining this useful label' and in doing so remaining true to its 'traditional calling' (RAS 2–3). This offers quite a significant departure from most existing socio-theoretical approaches.

What is society?

Sociology has sought to establish the existence of a specific sort of phenomenon ('society', 'social order', 'social practice', 'social dimension', or 'social structure'). According to Latour, in order to establish this sphere it has been important to distinguish it from others (such as law, science, politics etc.). Once the domain of 'society' had been defined the aim of sociology has been to 'shed some light on specifically social phenomena – the social could then explain the social' (RAS 3). This version of social theory has, according to Latour,

> become the default position of our mental software that takes into consideration of the following: there exists a social 'context' in which non-social activities take place; it is a specific domain of reality; it can be used as a specific type of causality to account for the residual aspects that other domains (psychology, law, economics etc.) cannot completely deal with. (RAS 3–4)

In this sense, according to Latour, 'the social sciences have disseminated their definition of society as effectively as utility companies deliver electricity and telephone services' (RAS 4). There is, according to Latour, an alternative approach to understanding the social. This second approach however does not claim there is anything specific about the social order, social context, or social dimension of any sort (RAS 4). For Latour 'the second position takes as the major puzzle to be solved what the first takes as its solution, namely the existence of specific social ties revealing the hidden presence of some specific social forces' (RAS 5). Latour argues that 'it is possible to remain close to the original intuitions of the social sciences by redefining sociology not as the 'science of the social', but as the *tracing of associations*' (RAS 5). According to Latour, here the 'social does not designate a thing among other things, like a black sheep among other white sheep, but *a type of connection* between things that are not themselves social' (RAS 5). This is important and is what really distances his approach from many other socio-theoretical frameworks. Latour argues that this may seem to 'dilute' sociology to a means for representing all aggregates 'from chemical bonds to legal ties'. However, he argues that this is precisely the point that this alternative division of social theory would like to make. This is because 'all those heterogeneous elements *might be* assembled anew in some given state of affairs' (RAS 5).

By widening his approach of the social to include non-humans (objects and animals etc.) Latour also seeks to problematise our understanding of 'collectivity' (of the notion of 'we'). According to Latour we no longer know what 'we' means as we are 'bound by ties that don't look like regular social ties' (RAS 6). Latour states that the overall project of what we are supposed to do as a collective is thrown into doubt and the notion of belonging enters a crisis. Another notion of social therefore has to be developed (RAS 7). A new version of 'the social' must be '*much wider* than what is usually called by that name, yet *strictly limited* to the tracing of new associations and to the designing of their assemblages' (RAS 7). Latour therefore seeks to 'define the social not as a special domain, a specific realm, or a particular sort of thing, but only as a very peculiar movement of re-association and reassembling' (RAS 7).

The social cannot be a safe and unproblematic category. According to Latour 'having rendered many useful services in an earlier period, what is called "social explanation" has become a counter-productive way to *interrupt* the movement of associations instead of resuming it' (RAS 8). In the traditional explanation the social is perceived 'to be made essentially of social ties' (RAS 8). However, the alternative explanation recognises that 'associations are made of ties which are themselves non-social' (RAS 8). Sociologists have traditionally 'imagined that sociology is limited to a specific domain', whereas, according to Latour (and the alternative explanation), 'sociologists should travel wherever new heterogeneous associations are made' (RAS 8).

Actor network theory (ANT)

The first approach he calls 'sociology of the social', the second approach, and the one he seeks to advance, he calls 'sociology of associations' (RAS 9). The name for the latter approach is 'actor-network-theory'. According to Latour, this is 'a name that is so awkward, so confusing, so meaningless that it deserves to be kept' (RAS 9). Latour has written extensively on ANT, in his work on Pasteur (Latour 1988) for example and elsewhere.[3] According to Latour the task of a social scientist is no longer to 'impose some order', nor is it to 'limit the range of acceptable entities' or 'teach actors what they are', or to 'add some reflexivity to their blind practice'. Rather '"you have to follow the actors themselves" (RAS 11–12). 'ANT. . . is a technique for detecting how connections between heterogeneous, human and non-human, entities make up a state of affairs that we used to call "social"' (de Vries 2016: 88).

It is the inclusion of non-human actants and agents in his analysis that really differentiates this approach to theorising the social from many other socio-theoretical approaches. 'Actants can be concrete or abstract'. According to Latour 'a good ANT account is a narrative or a description or a proposition where (de Vries 90) all the actors *do something* and don't just sit there' (RAS 128). Latour uses the term actant in order to permit 'agency for *anything* non-human' (de Vries 88). This does not just relate to science; for example, some people insist that they are being moved by divinities, spirits, and voices (RAS 236). Latour draws on a range of concepts to advance his ANT. In particular he uses terms such as intermediary and mediator. 'An *intermediary* is what transports meaning or force without transformation; *mediators* on the other hand, 'transform, translate, distort, and modify the meaning or the elements they are supposed to carry' (RAS 39; see also de Vries 90). An actor network refers to an assembly of actants who are 'networked' and defined by another actant through the translations they are involved in (de Vries 2016: 92). According to de Vries ANT 'introduces new terminology – such as "oligopticon"[4] – 'to account for the common experience of the annoying fact of society. That is, that individual actions and relations take place within a society (or economy and culture) 'that is perceived as a realm that guides and constrains individual actions' (de Vries 2016: 98).

Latour makes it clear that ANT 'is not an alternative theory *in* sociology' (i.e. it is not a theory competing with for example, Giddens's theory of structuration, de Vries 88). ANT rather 'is an alternative *to* the "sociology of the social", an alternative social science, a technique for redescribing the social world by tracing the associations of humans and nonhumans that make up a "collective"' (de Vries 2016: 88). The incorporation of non-human objects and entities into his analysis is a theme running throughout Latour's work – as we have already seen in WHNBM. Latour has often been criticised for the ways in which the same properties appear to be ascribed to both humans and non-humans in his work. According to Winner (1993) this fails to account for the intentionality that distinguishes humans from many other animals or objects. As will be explored in Part 2 however, Latour continues to extend his focus on non-human and human actants and agents, networks and associations in his comparative anthropology.

PART 2: DIFFERENT MODES OF LIVING

The current global ecological crisis is a reoccurring theme in Latour's more recent work. In *An Inquiry into the Modes of Existence* (AIME) for example, published 20 years after WHNBM he argues that we must choose between 'modernising' and 'ecologising'. Ecological problems force us, according to Latour, to reanalyse the values of the so-called moderns, to pose a series of questions: 'If we have never been modern, then what has happened to us? What are we to inherit? Who have we been? Who are we going to become? With whom must we be connected? Where do we find ourselves situated from now on?' (AIME 11). Latour refers to AIME as a comparative anthropology of the moderns.[5] As we explore in this section, Latour seeks to show us that there is not one outside world, but rather a plurality of worlds that relate directly to the key institutions that frame our lives (Muecke 2012). According to Latour the Earth is a plural collective. With the current threat of global ecological crisis, the key question we must face now is: how can this plural world we currently live in work as a collective to achieve common goals (de Vries 2016)?

Ecological Politics and Gaia

The questions that Latour poses to the moderns in AIME are set within the context of the ecological crisis. He states that: 'the scope of the ecological crises obliges us to reconsider a whole set of reactions, or rather conditioned reflexes, that rob us of all our flexibility to react to what is coming' (AIME 7). Since he wrote WHNBM ecological problems have been a serious concern for Latour. In *Politics of Nature* he reconfigured 'political ecology' and the role of science in democracy (de Vries 2016: 194). In AIME he seeks to develop his work on this further:

> For more than twenty years, scientific and technological controversies have proliferated in number and scope, eventually reaching the climate itself. Since geologists are beginning to use the term "ANTHROPOCENE" to designate the era of Earth's history that follows the Holocene, this will be a convenient term to use from here on to sum up the meaning of an era that extends from the scientific and industrial revolutions to the present day. (AIME 9)

Latour argues for a shift in the nature of the relationship between humans and the Earth throughout his work. This focus, however, becomes more pressing given the current ecological crisis. According to Latour, in light of the 'planetary negotiation that is already under way' we need to reflect on all the 'values that the notion of modernization had at once revealed and compromised' (AIME 17, de Vries 148). Latour argues that we are now called to appear before Gaia, 'the odd, doubly composite figure made up of science and mythology used by certain specialists to designate the Earth that surrounds us' (AIME 9). Gaia is a truly global entity that 'threatens us even as we threaten it' (AIME 9).

The name Gaia comes from Greek mythology – the primordial Greek goddess, the personification of the Earth. According to de Vries (2016) the novelist William Golding suggested Gaia to British Scientist James Lovelock as a potential 'name for his hypothesis that living organisms regulate the terrestrial atmosphere' – 'the balance between the levels of oxygen and carbon dioxide that makes life on Earth possible' (de Vries 2016: 195). Latour argues that if we (humans) through the expansion of transport, the development of industry, and large-scale livestock breeding 'continue to emit too much carbon dioxide, the subtle balance between oxygen and carbon dioxide will be disturbed. Gaia, "the living Earth", will be endangered', with devastating effects (de Vries 2016: 195). However, according to Latour 'there is only one Earth, but Gaia is not One' (Latour, cited in de Vries 2016: 195).

In order to effectively tackle climate change, we need to work collectively. Latour argues that we must choose between modernising and ecologising. This is a point he has been articulating since the publication of *Politics of Nature* (PON) in 2004. In PON Latour outlines the values of the politics that he thinks will be required. In contrast AIME 'suggests a platform for the diplomatic exchanges that will be necessary, if war, violence, and ecological catastrophe are to be avoided'. The purpose of AIME is to 'offer the moderns a clearer view of themselves' and other peoples (de Vries 2016: 199). In this text, however, Latour seeks to present 'a positive, rather than merely a negative, version of those who "have never been modern" (AIME xxvi; see also de Vries 199).

Latour focuses here on what he sees as 'the work of redescription', which he feels 'may allow us to give more space to *other values* that are very commonly encountered but that did not necessarily find a comfortable slot for themselves within the framework offered by modernity' (AIME 11). He gives the examples here of politics or religion, or law. According to Latour these are values that:

> the defences of Science in all its majesty had trampled along its way but which can now be deployed more readily. If it is a question of ecologizing and no longer of modernizing, it may become possible to bring a larger number of values into cohabitation within a somewhat richer ecosystem. (AIME 11)

According to Latour the intensity of the world's ecological problems is undeniable, and like others Latour argues that new ways of thinking about the world are needed. We need a deeper common sense than the modern Constitution offers. 'Once we have a clearer idea of our values', we may move forwards 'to explore our plural world' (de Vries 2016: 200–201). It is overall a positive message that Latour seeks to reinforce in his comparative anthropology: 'what risk do we run ...? The world is young, the sciences are recent, history has barely begun, and as for ecology, it is barely in its infancy: Why should we have finished exploring the institutions of public life?' (PON 227–8; de Vries 2016: 201).

A Plurality of Types of 'Beings'

Latour extends many of the themes from WHNBM and RAS in AIME, in particular the move beyond a focus on social relations to include other types of 'being' and other forms of life. At the end of part one of the text, according to Latour, 'we shall know how to speak appropriately about a plurality of types of beings by relying on the guiding thread of experience, on empiricism as William James defined it: nothing but experience, yes, but *nothing less than experience*' (AIME xxv). Rather than drawing on ethnographic detail to articulate his argument as Latour does in other work however,[6] in AIME the argument is set up by introducing a fictitious female anthropologist. The anthropologist proceeds by questioning the puzzles left by the moderns as they have tried 'to account for values in a wide variety of domains – science, technology, religion, politics, law, fiction, their emotions, morality, and the economy' (de Vries 2016: 152).

Latour encourages the fictitious anthropologist that he creates to distinguish between *being-as-being* and *being-as-other* (de Vries 158). Being-as-being 'seeks its support in a **SUBSTANCE** that will ensure its continuity'. In contrast, beings-as-other 'depend not on a substance on which they can rely but on a SUBSISTENCE that they have to seek out at their own risk' (AIME 162; see also de Vries 159). Introducing the notion of being-as-other allows us to explore 'how many *other forms of alterities* a being is capable of traversing in order to continue to exist' (AIME 163). By distinguishing being-as-being and being-as-other, according to de Vries Latour appears to give '(individual) *existence* pride of place over *substance* (essence)' (de Vries 163). Latour continues to focus on ontology as he seeks to move '*pluralism* from the level of language, culture, and society to the level of ontology' (reality) (de Vries 2016: 163).

From actor networks to modes of existence

According to Latour, ANT focused on redescribing 'each of the central institutions of contemporary societies by following the heterogeneous network of associations that make them up'. Through this process 'it has been shown that the grand narrative of modernization does not do justice to the very institutions developed by the Moderns'. A comparative anthropology, according to Latour, needs to have common ground (which actor networks provide) 'but also requires an instrument to make the differences among collectives emerge anew'.[7] He argues that in conjunction with research on networks another line of inquiry into modes of existence must be pursued in order to capture the 'various ways in which those associations were binding entities together'. According to Latour, 'such an inquiry into modes of existence (AIME) feeds on the research on networks, but tries to qualify the mode in which those networks expand' (all quotes taken from http://www.bruno-latour.fr.node/328).[8]

According to Norton, to speak of modes of existence 'is to inquire both into the existence of things (and, thus, to do ontology) and into all the relations into which things enter, as well as the behaviors and values they exhibit, in order to exist' (Norton 2013: 2). Modes of existence frame Latour's conceptualisation and understanding of contemporary life. There are crossovers between the different modes of existence and a tendency for each to want to be dominant (Muecke 2012). However, the 'principle of irreduction' that is at the heart of Latour's philosophy and the starting point of ANT – 'nothing is, by itself, either reducible or irreducible to anything else' (POF 158) – prevents this from occurring (Muecke 2012).

Latour returns again to ANT – the world 'is made up by actor networks, by actants relating, translating, and defining each other' (de Vries 156). Latour identifies a number of concepts – stages through which modes of existence pass. For Latour, each mode of existence has its own hiatus, trajectory, felicity/infelicity conditions, beings to institute, and alteration. According to Latour, however, each translation is an abstract, whereby a small discontinuity, a *hiatus*, needs to be practically overcome. The right *conditions of felicity* must be present in order for an actor network to function well. Furthermore, something is allowed to pass along the *trajectory* of associations that are established (de Vries 2016: 163).

A mode of existence is identified therefore by specifying the characteristics (see also de Vries 48–9) listed below:

- *Hiatus*, a disruptive condition that needs to be overcome. According to Latour 'every instance of continuity is achieved through a discontinuity, a HIATUS' (AIME 100).

- *Trajectory*, the continuity it allows through the results of these transformations.

- 'every leap across a discontinuity represents a risk taken that may succeed or fail; there are thus FELICITY and INFELICITY CONDITIONS proper to each mode' (AIME 100).

- The *beings* that are instituted and passed through and the alteration of beings-as-other it allows (i.e. the way these are transformed).

As Latour argues, 'the result of this passage, of this more or less successful leap, is a flow, a network, a movement, a wake left behind that will make it possible to define a particular form of existence, and consequently particular

BEINGS' (AIME 100). In the book 15 modes of existence are identified by Latour, which is the number that he claims is necessary to get an image of modern life 'as a whole with a satisfactory *resolution*' (AIME 479–80; see also de Vries 181).

The modes of existence

The 15 modes of existence are as follows: reproduction [REP], metamorphosis [MET], habit [HAB], technology [TECH], fiction [FIC], reference [REF], politics [POL], law [LAW], religion [REL], attachment [ATT], organisation [ORG], morality [MOR], network [NET], preposition [PRE], and [DC] for double click. The characteristics for each mode are summarized in what Latour calls a 'pivot table' (AIME 488–9). According to de Vries for 'each mode, the table specifies by what *hiatus* and *trajectory* it is distinguished; what its *conditions of felicity* and infelicity are; what beings are instituted; and, finally, to what alteration being-as-other is subjected' (de Vries 2016: 181).

In part one of the text, Latour examines the first few modes of existence to be encountered in the inquiry: network [NET], preposition [PRE], reference [REF], and reproduction [REP]. In addition he introduces double click [DC], 'which is an allusion to the digital mouse' (AIME 93). [DC] is not 'a proper mode of existence', but rather an adversary who pushes the notion that information can be shifted from one context to another without any need for translation' (Norton 2013: 2). [NET] and [PRE] are modes that appear to lead the way to other modes. While the [NET] mode identifies a collection of associations, [PRE] modes identify the differences between networks. Joined with [DC] these modes make up the final of five groups of modes, each group containing three modes. [TEC], [FIC], and [REF] 'provide alternative descriptions of science, technology, and fiction. [POL], [LAW] and [REL] offer descriptions of politics, law, and religion as modes of existence' (de Vries 2016: 184). There is no time or space to cover each of these modes in detail; here we will just look at a few.

The three modes of existence of the first group, [REP], [MET], and [HAB], 'are the ones that have been at most elaborated by other collectives and most ignored by our own' (AIME 288). According to de Vries by introducing them Latour has widened the area for discussions between the moderns and other peoples. For example, [MET] focuses on how to take into account experience that 'under the modern Constitution may be viewed as psychogenetic'. Its hiatuses might be described as emotional shocks and crises (de Vries 2016: 185). In common sense terms, when a person experiences an emotional shock (bereavement, relationship breakdown), their life continues but often in a radically different form. However, when Latour discusses [MET] he is not just referring to human beings but also to non-humans, spirits, and divinities. Through introducing [MET] Latour helps to break down distinctions between us (moderns) and them (others). According to Latour: 'the modernist believes that the others believe in beings external to themselves, whereas he "knows perfectly well" that these are only internal representations projected onto a world that is in itself devoid of meaning' (AIME 187; see also de Vries 185).

Given that Latour identifies [POL], [LAW], and [REL] as distinct modes of existence, why does he not do this for economics? Latour does not present this as a separate mode of existence. Latour explicitly distinguishes his work from existing critiques of capitalism. What is required in its place, according to Latour, is 'an alternative account that neither endorses nor deplores capitalism', but rather deconstructs the modern concept of the economy (Norton 2013: 4–5; AIME 385). One of the reasons for not identifying the economy as a separate mode of existence runs parallel to the reasons he set out in *Reassembling the Social* 'to abandon the concept of "Society". Like "Society", "the economy" mixes up process – a specific way of assembling collectives – and the outcome of these processes' (de Vries 2016: 188). This is where ANT is useful: it provides us with 'the language to account for the economy as process, rather than as something already given as hard economic facts determined by the laws of the market (de Vries 2016 189; Norton 2013).

CONCLUSION

According to Norton (2013) AIME draws together much of Latour's previous work to present 'a comprehensive relational metaphysics, an "ont-ecology" with the power to constructively and creatively confront the many challenges to which modern thought has led us' (Norton 2013: 5). AIME is not an easy text to navigate. It is philosophically complex and confusing at times. Furthermore, although ecological concerns – and the implications that these have for contemporary forms of life – provide the background for the book's aims and argument, the substantive concerns posed by climate change are often buried by the book's philosophical focus. There is, however, consistency across all the works examined here. We certainly see many of the themes that are present in both WHNBM and RAS in AIME. AIME was published 20 years after WHNBM, and, as articulated in Part 2 of this chapter, can be seen as a direct attempt to address many of the questions he raised in his earlier text. There is however one important distinction: while WHNBM has a some-what negative message overall, Latour seeks in AIME to offer a positive version of those who 'have never been modern'. He seeks in AIME to ask whether we can defend the values that we keep close to us – the values 'that the notion of modernization had at once revealed and compromised' in the 'planetary negotiation that is already underway over the future of [these] values' (AIME 17; see also de Vries 201)? In order to do this Latour argues that we need a new philosophical vocabulary. He presents AIME as a 'provisional report' on these issues (AIME xix, 476; see also de Vries 157). But he leaves us with more questions than answers. What have we learnt from our explorations into modes of existence? Can the inquiry lead to diplomatic arrangements with other peoples (AIME 477–80)?

According to de Vries (2016) Latour in his earlier work emphasises the 'heterogeneity of what makes up our world', 'suggesting that in order' to get a realistic picture 'of the world we must rid ourselves of the 'established distinctions' emerging from 'the primarily epistemological concerns of Western philosophy' (e.g. distinctions between 'nature' and 'society', humans and non-humans) (de Vries 2016: 153). Ontology rather than epistemology is still central to the argument Latour makes in AIME and he continues to show that practices are made out of heterogeneous components. Latour also suggests that ANT is still the most appropriate tool to describe them. As de Vries (2016) notes, however, while most of Latour's earlier work focuses on describing how actor networks are created, his focus in AIME is on what has passed in the actor networks that make up science, politics, law, religion: 'so under the word "network" we must be careful not to confuse what circulates *once everything is in place* with the *setups* involving the heterogeneous set of elements that allow circulation to occur' (AIME 32). Throughout his work Latour does provide us with the tools to problematise our existing understandings of 'modern' and 'social' life, moving beyond a socio-theoretical focus on human social relations. This is perhaps where his strongest contribution to social theory lies.

Abbreviations

AIME: *An Inquiry into the Modes of Existence* (2013)

POF: *The Pasteurization of France* (1988)

PON: *Politics of Nature* (2004)

RAS: *Reassembling the Social: An Introduction to Actor-Network-Theory* (2005)

WHNBM: *We Have Never Been Modern* (1993)

Selected Further Readings

The following text provides a detailed and critical overview of Latour's œuvre: de Vries, G. (2016) *Bruno Latour*. Cambridge: Polity.

Michaels, M. (2016) *Actor Network Theory: Trials, Trails and Translations*. London: Sage offers a comprehensive account of ANT.

Lynch, P. and Rivers, N. (eds) (2015) *Thinking with Bruno Latour in Rhetoric and Composition*. Carbondale, IL: Southern Illinois University Press, an edited collection, explores the use and relevance of Latour's work across disciplines, focusing in particular on writing and rhetoric.

Notes

1 Boyle played a significant role in the development of scientific methodology. His air-pump experiment relates to the association he made between the pressure and volume of gas within a closed system.

2 Hobbes's *Leviathan* was first published in 1651. It relates to the structure of society and legitimate government, it is regarded as one of the first and also most influential examples of social contract theory.

3 ANT is frequently associated with Michael Callon, Bruno Latour, and John Law. See Michaels (2016) for an overview of ANT and its relationship to sociology.

4 'Oligopticon' for Latour refers to a site for the manufacture of social structures (e.g. legal system) (RAS).

5 AIME is a large text accompanied by a bilingual website and readers are encouraged to contribute to the website, to 'extend the work … with new documents, new sources, new testimonies, and most, important, to modify the questions by correcting or modulating the project in relation to the results obtained' (AIME xx).

6 See, for example, Latour and Woolgar (1986).

7 See www.bruno-latour.fr/node/328 the companion website to AIME.

8 See www.bruno-latour.fr/node/328

4

Donna Haraway: New Modes of Sociality

PART 1: CYBORGS AND PARTIAL PERSPECTIVES

One of the distinguishing features of Donna Haraway's social theory is the emphasis she places on the role of non-human actants and agents, namely animals and technology. When social theorists talk about the social, what they often really mean, Haraway argues, is the study of social relations and history. Haraway develops the concept of the cyborg in order to displace the social from its 'exclusive location in human doings' (Gane and Haraway 2006: 142). She states that she is 'serious about the temporalities, scales, materialities, relationalities between people and our constitutive partners, which always include other people and other critters, animal and not, in doing worlds' (Gane and Haraway 2006: 143). What she makes clear in the development of her concept of the cyborg is that one cannot attempt to theorise contemporary social conditions without understanding the relationship between humans and other, non-human forms. She uses the deconstruction of the boundaries between humans and non-humans to develop her analysis of contemporary social life as well as to sketch out her specific blueprint for social change. The following outline of Haraway's concept of the cyborg frames her socio-theoretical vision and, as we will explore, underpins the development of her epistemological focus on what she calls 'partial perspectives'.

Cyborg Theorising

The cyborg is the metaphor through which Haraway carefully illustrates the contemporary human condition. Her clearest and most enduring statement of the concept comes in 'A cyborg manifesto' originally published in 1985. Haraway states that many of the entities appearing in her work have been birthed through the reproductive apparatuses of war, and that this is particularly true of 'A cyborg manifesto' (Haraway 2004a: 3). She writes that: 'For me, the "Cyborg Manifesto" was a nearly sober socialist-feminist statement written for the *Socialist Review* to try to think through how to do critique, remember war and its offspring, keep ecofeminism and technoscience joined in the flesh, and generally honor possibilities that escape unkind origins' (Haraway 2004a: 3). In an interview with Nicholas Gane, Haraway (Gane and Haraway 2006) argues that the manifesto is a feminist theoretical statement, a coming to terms with the social conditions of our times and a treatise that outlines how to move forward. The central question of the manifesto, which is a direct play on Lenin's 1902 tract, is: 'What is to be done' (Gane and Haraway 2006: 136)?

The 'cyborg is a cybernetic organism, a hybrid of machine and organism, a creature of social reality as well as of fiction (CM 149)'. In developing the concept, Haraway continually blurs the boundaries between reality and fiction: 'Social reality is lived social relations, our most important political construction, a world-changing fiction' (CM 149). The cyborg is also Janus-faced: it is both a source of inequality and a potential facilitator of social change. According to Haraway the cyborg era is a fairly recent one. It is, however, impossible to pinpoint when exactly it came into being. It could date from the late nineteenth century, or from the 1930s, or from the Second World War, or even after that. She is keen to point out that how it is dated depends on how one chooses to foreground the concept (Gane and Haraway 2006: 146). Implicit within this focus is Haraway's position on the development of society and her approach to modernity and post-modernity. She argues that there can be no logical development of society that can be charted from the period of the Enlightenment through to modernity and post-modernity. For Haraway, there are no beginnings and endings: we have only ever been in the middle of things (PM 77). At the start of the manifesto Haraway states that in the late twentieth century 'we are all chimeras, theorized and fabricated hybrids of machine and organism; in short we are cyborgs. The cyborg is our ontology; it gives us our politics' (CM 150). Haraway argues that her Cyborg Manifesto should be read as 'an argument for *pleasure* in the confusion of boundaries and for *responsibility* in their construction' (CM 150). This focus on boundary transgressions and the possibility and potential inherent in their deconstruction form the central tenet of Haraway's social theory.

Deconstructing Western universalism

In her development of the concept of cyborg Haraway moves away from theoretical claims about universality and objectivity. For Haraway, the cyborg is completely committed to partiality. She uses the cyborg to deconstruct the existing binaries of Western thought. She focuses her analysis on the dualisms that have been used to denigrate women and keep them confined to the domestic sphere (e.g. public/private, nature/culture).[1] The cyborg for Haraway collapses and transforms these dichotomies. She argues that the 'cyborg is a creature in a post-gender world' (CM 150). It is oppositional and utopian. However, it 'is not innocent' but deeply rooted within the 'monster' of global capitalism. Haraway locates the development of the cyborg in Cold War rhetoric, in financial investment in military technology,[2] and in cybernetics.[3] During this era, technological development and research became directly inter-linked with business interests and financial investment (Gane and Haraway 2006: 139). The cyborg for Haraway therefore is 'a military project, a late capitalist project in deep collaboration with new forms of imperial war' (Gane and Haraway 2006: 139). Haraway, however, wants to utilise the subversive potential of the cyborg. She argues that, while the cyborg is deeply embedded in global capitalism, it also opens up radical possibility (Gane and Haraway 2006: 139). As she states:

> The main trouble with cyborgs, of course, is that they are the illegiti-mate offspring of militarism and patriarchal capitalism, not to mention state socialism. But illegitimate offspring are often exceedingly unfaith-ful to their origins.[4] Their fathers, after all, are inessential. (CM 151)

Haraway signals three crucial boundary breakdowns central to her conceptu-alisation of the cyborg (although she tends to concentrate on the first two). These are: the boundary between human and animal, the boundary between animal–human (organism) and machine, and the boundary between the physi-cal and non-physical world (CM 151–2). The cyborg is about transgressed boundaries, and Haraway continually focuses on the dual potential of these transgressions. She argues that from one perspective a cyborg world with its rapid technological advancement could signal the further militarised control of populations across the globe. However, viewed from another perspective, a cyborg world might indicate new and more egalitarian social arrangements that celebrate new kinships between animals, humans, and machines, and that accept a partial rather than an objective view of the world (CM 154). This almost dialectical tension lies at the heart of her socio-theoretical vision. The boundary transgression that is so central to the conceptualisation of the cyborg could lead to the development of progressive politics but could also lead to the creation of further oppression for minority groups. She articulates this argu-ment through socialist feminism. She argues 'that most American socialists and feminists see deepened dualisms of mind and body, animal and machine, ideal-ism and materialism in the social practices, symbolic formulations, and physical artefacts associated with "high technology"' (CM 154). However, rather than seeing technology simply as a form of domination, Haraway argues that it offers potential ways to resist oppression. She seeks to use the cyborg myth to imagine other alternative more egalitarian versions of society. She argues for 'a politics rooted in claims about fundamental changes in the nature of class, race and gender in an emerging system of world order analogous in its novelty and scope to that created by industrial capitalism' (CM 161).

Communication, technology, biology

Central to Haraway's conceptualisation of the cyborg is the relationship between language, technology, and biology. While communication and language have formed a central focus of much existing social theory, her inclusion of biology and technology distinguishes Haraway's socio-theoretical approach from many others. She argues that information and communication technology along with biotechnologies are the crucial tools for recrafting bodies in the current era (CM 164). These technologies are transforming social relationships and the social conditions in which people live. In particular, for Haraway these are the tools that have the potential to fundamentally transform the position of women in society. She argues that 'these tools embody and enforce new social relations for women worldwide' (CM 164).

Haraway contends that:

> communications sciences and modern biologies are constructed by a common move – *the translation of the world into a problem of coding*, a search for a common language in which all resistance to instrumental control disappears and all heterogeneity can be submitted to disassembly, reassembly, investment, and exchange. (CM 164)

She continually states that humans are living in what can be termed as 'disassembling times' where their entire way of being is constantly deconstructed and reassembled in new ways through advances in science and technology. 'In communications sciences, the translation of the world into a problem in coding can be illustrated by looking at cybernetic (feedback-controlled) systems theories applied to telephone technology, computer design, weapons deployment, or data base construction and maintenance' (CM 164). In this context solutions to problems are based on 'determining the rates, directions, and probabilities of flow of a quantity called information' (CM 164). In modern biology, she uses examples from molecular genetics, ecology and sociobiology, evolutionary theory, and immunobiology to illustrate the problem of coding. She states that organisms have been translated into problems of genetic coding and read-out (e.g. DNA printing). Haraway argues that organisms no longer exist as objects of knowledge, but have become information-processing devices (CM 164). Haraway uses these examples to argue that it is science and technology that are fundamentally responsible for transforming contemporary social conditions. In making this case, Haraway is also quick to point out that it is largely economics that forms a central domain of these transformations (CM 165).

Production and reproduction

While Haraway's conceptualisation of the cyborg is focused on the relationship between humans, animals, and machines, processes of economic production still form the centre of her theorisation of contemporary social conditions. For Haraway, production is caught up with technology, biology, and processes of reproduction. While feminists have long criticised malestream social theory for its inability to acknowledge the relationship between production and reproduction, Haraway adds a further dimension to this through her exploration of technology. She argues that 'microelectronics mediates the translations of labor into robotics and word processing, sex into genetic engineering and reproductive technologies, and mind into artificial intelligence and decision procedures' (CM 165). According to Haraway 'Communications sciences and biology are constructions of natural–technical 'objects of knowledge in which the difference between machine and organism is thoroughly blurred; mind, body, and tool are on very intimate terms' (CM 165). She argues that the new biotechnologies go beyond human reproduction, redefining and revolutionising industry such as agriculture. For Haraway, science and technology provide fresh sources of power, requiring new sources of analysis and political action.

Haraway consistently argues against technological determinism – her position on this is perhaps best articulated in relation to her focus on production and reproduction. For example, she states that it is often argued that new technologies have caused the development of the homework economy. However, Haraway is quick to point out that the homework economy[5] is made possible (not caused) by new technologies. She relates the development of robotics, for example, to putting men out of work in developed countries and exacerbating failure to generate male jobs in developing contexts (CM 168). At the same time, there has been a feminisation of work. In the context of sex and reproduction, Haraway argues that 'new technologies affect the social relations of both sexuality and of reproduction, and not always in the same ways' (CM 168–9). The intimate ties of sexuality and instrumentality, of private satisfaction on one hand and utility on the other reinforce male and female gender roles. Haraway refers to these as sociobiological stories that 'depend on a high-tech view of the body as a biotic component or cybernetic communications system' (CM 169). A central part of this, Haraway argues, is the medicalisation of pregnancy and childbirth – whereby women's bodies become permeable, subject to both 'visualisation' and 'intervention'. Haraway argues that: 'sex, sexuality, and reproduction are central actors in high-tech myth systems structuring our imaginations of personal and social possibility' (CM 169).

The cyborg and social change

In detailing the development of technology one thing that is crucial to Haraway and perhaps demarcates her position from other feminist perspectives of the time is that she acknowledges the potential for change inherent in human

couplings with other actants and agents. She wants to move away from a somewhat nostalgic position articulated by socialist feminists that less technologically
driven times were less oppressive for women. Some virulent forms of oppression
have been lost through advances in technological development. She argues that:

> ambivalence towards the disrupted unities mediated by high-tech cul-
> ture requires not sorting consciousness into categories of 'clear sighted
> critique grounding a solid political epistemology' versus 'manipulated
> false consciousness', but subtle understanding of emerging pleasures,
> experiences, and powers with serious potential for changing the rules
> of the game. (CM 172–3)

This is centrally important to Haraway's approach to social change.

Haraway uses the concept of the cyborg to describe contemporary social
conditions. She also uses it, however, to outline her blueprint for social change
through the metaphor of science fiction. She argues that 'certain dualisms have
been persistent in Western traditions', such as self/other, mind/body, culture/
nature, male/female, and so on (CM 177). She states that these dualisms have
been central to the oppression of 'women, people of colour, nature, workers,
animals, in short, domination of all constituted as others, whose task is to mirror
the self' (CM 177). With reference to the relationship between self and other
Haraway argues that in existing Western thought the 'self' is perceived as the
autonomous powerful 'God' like figure, while the 'other' is multiple with no clear
boundaries or power (CM 177). For Haraway, high-tech culture challenges these
dualisms in novel and interesting ways. The relationship between human and
machine is unclear, as is the relationship between self and other, mind and body.
Whether people refer to themselves in formal discourse (e.g. in terms of humans'
biology) or in daily practice (e.g. home/work), Haraway argues that people find
themselves to be 'cyborgs, hybrids, mosaics, chimeras' (CM 177). For Haraway,
there is no 'ontological separation in our formal knowledge of machine and
organism, of technical and organic' (CM 177–8). Overall, Haraway tries to make
two key points through the development of her cyborg perspective: first, that 'the
production of universal, totalizing social theory is a major mistake that misses
most of reality'. Second, she articulates the need for humans to take 'responsibility for the social relations of science and technology'. This is not about
demonising technology. Rather, it means 'embracing the skilful task of reconstructing the boundaries of daily life, in partial connection with others'. The
cyborg, she concludes, can help humans find 'a way out of the maze of dualisms'
in which they have 'explained' their 'bodies and ... tools' to themselves (CM 181).

Partial Perspectives

If the concept of the cyborg represents Haraway's ontological framework, then
the partial perspectives must be viewed as her epistemology. Cyborgs themselves are based on partiality, and cyborg visuality offers only a partial

perspective. In order to study and understand the cyborg world, sociologists need to develop an approach that reflects this partiality, somewhere between scientific objectivity on the one hand and postmodern relativism on the other. Haraway argues that in these disassembling times 'some of us have tried to stay sane' by 'holding out' for 'a feminist version of objectivity' (SK 578). The problem according to Haraway is the dilemma of attempting to maintain 'an account of radical historical contingency for all knowledge claims and knowing subjects', whilst at the same time cultivating 'a no-nonsense commitment to faithful accounts of a "real" world' (SK 579). According to Clough and Schneider what she is trying to articulate here is that as well as revealing the 'historical and ideological specificity of scientific practices' and 'deconstructing their absolute authority', feminists should also seek to offer a 'better account of the world' (SK 579; see also Clough and Schneider 2001: 342). She states that such an account comes with the acknowledgement of the 'irreducible difference and radical multiplicity of local knowledges' (SK 579; see also Clough and Schneider: 342).

Haraway accepts a version of scientific realism; however, this version of realism is expressed 'in partial visions or partial perspectives'. She wants to move away from postmodern relativist accounts. In particular, she wants to move away from what she calls the 'god trick – that is, seeing everything, everywhere, from nowhere' (Clough and Schneider 342). According to Haraway, partial views are not a universalising vision, a view from above. She argues that feminists do not need 'a doctrine of objectivity that promises transcendence'. However, for Haraway there needs to be a global network of connections that include the possibility 'partially to translate knowledges among very different–and power–differentiated–communities' (SK 580). She states that: 'We need the power of modern critical theories of how meanings and bodies get made, not in order to deny meanings and bodies, but in order to build meanings and bodies that have a chance for life' (SK 580).

Feminist objectivity

In developing what she calls the partial perspective, Haraway attempts to develop an approach between radical constructivism and feminist empiricism. She does acknowledge that 'it is, of course, hard to climb when you are holding on to both ends of a pole, simultaneously or alternatively' (SK 580). In this essay, she uses vision as a metaphor. Among many feminists 'vision' has been viewed as a source of oppression for women. She seeks to reclaim vision, however, arguing that it 'can be good for avoiding binary oppositions' (SK 581). Haraway argues for the 'embodied nature of all vision' (SK 581). She argues that feminist objectivity 'means quite simply *situated knowledges*' (SK 581). For Haraway, it is only the partial perspective that can promise objective vision. In short, the argument that she is seeking to articulate in this essay is 'an argument for situated and embodied knowledges'. She argues against 'unlocatable, and so irresponsible, knowledge claims' (SK 583). As with the development of the concept of the cyborg, Haraway attempts to create a path between universal generalisation on the one hand and postmodern relativism on the other. Clough and Schneider (2001: 342) argue that this is an epistemologically demanding perspective, as one must attempt to see from the perspective of those on the margins without romanticising or appropriating the vision of those who are less powerful (SK 583–4). Along with many other feminists, Haraway wants to argue for 'a doctrine and practice of objectivity that privileges contestation, deconstruction, passionate construction, webbed connections, and hope for transformation of systems of knowledge and ways of seeing' (SK 584–5). She clearly wants to take a stance against relativism at the same time, though. In sum, Haraway argues for a politics and epistemology of location. Through this perspective, 'partiality and not universality is the condition of being heard to make rational knowledge claims' (SK 589). Haraway situated knowledges require that the object of knowledge be pictured as an actor and agent, not as a screen or a ground or a resource, never finally as slave to the master that closes off the dialectic in his unique agency and his authorship of "objective" knowledge' (SK 592). Indeed this notion of agency underpins her broader socio-theoretical vision. Haraway argues that agency has the potential to transform the entire project of social theory; by acknowledging the agency of objects of knowledge we can avoid making false claims to objectivity and universality (SK 592–3).

The production of bodies

One of the key facets of Haraway's conceptualisation of the cyborg is her focus on the boundary transgressions between humans and animals and humans and machines. In her manifesto, she also makes reference to the boundaries between the physical and non-physical. However, a thorough articulation and analysis of this particular binary remain elusive in the context of the manifesto. It is discussed in the context of her epistemological work on partial perspectives (SK 595–6). In her discussion and development of the partial perspectives, Haraway returns to her focus on biology and, more specifically, the production of bodies. She draws on the work of Katie King (1987), a feminist literary theorist, who examines the ways in which poems are produced as objects of knowledge. Haraway applies this approach to understanding the 'production and reproduction-of bodies and other objects of value in scientific knowledge projects' (SK 595). First, Haraway asks whether bodies can be generated and produced in the same way that Romantic late eighteenth-century poems were. It is here that Haraway develops another key concept, the notion of *material-semiotic* actor. The concept of material-semiotic is Haraway's attempt to translate the third dualism outlined in 'A cyborg manifesto', the relationship between the physical and non-physical (Gane and Haraway 2006: 147). The concept of material-semiotic actor is used by Haraway to 'portray the object of knowledge as an active, meaning – generating part of apparatus of bodily production, without *ever* implying the immediate presence of such objects' (SK 595). Haraway argues that 'like "poems", which are sites of literary production where language too is an actor independent of intentions and authors, bodies as objects of knowledge are material-semiotic generative nodes' (SK 595). Bodily boundaries materialise in social interaction (SK 595). Haraway argues that 'boundaries are drawn by mapping practices; "objects" do not pre-exist as such (SK 595). In short, Haraway seeks to examine the ways in which bodies are produced through different types of discourse and practice. Haraway argues that 'various contending biological bodies emerge at the intersection of biological research and writing, medical and other business practices, and technology such as visualization technologies' (SK 596). She states that feminist embodiment, partiality, objectivity, and situated knowledges 'turn on conversations and codes at this potent node in fields of possible bodies and meanings' (SK 596). Bodies emerge as creations of both fact and fiction in Haraway's work on the cyborg and partial perspectives. As will be explored in Part 2 of this chapter, Haraway's work on immunology provides fertile ground for a more detailed examination of her discursive analysis of the body, as well as enabling in-depth reflections on her wider socio-theoretical vision.

PART 2: IMMUNE SYSTEM DISCOURSE

Whether we are talking about war, migration, or the proliferation of diseases such as AIDS, the immune system or immunity from contagion forms 'the symbolic and material linchpin around which our social systems rotate' (Esposito 2011: 2). This has led a number of scholars across the humanities and social sciences to study the immune system in scientific and public discourse, as well as its role in clinical practice. For example, feminist epistemologies have increasingly been applied to scientific discourse in order to 'assess competing claims of immune function within a feminist context' (Weasel 2001: 27). The immune system has figured frequently throughout Haraway's work. As she states: the immune system is a 'potent and polymorphous object of belief, knowledge, and practice' (BPB 200). It is the perfect example of the 'networked consciousness of the cyborg age', and a good example of what Haraway means when she denies there is such a thing 'as the abstract' (Kunzru 1996: 4). A critical reflection on her use of cyborg and partial perspective in her work on the immune system can shed light on Haraway's approach to biopolitics along with her conceptualisation of the relationship between self and other.

Cyborg Theory and Immune System Discourse

In 'The biopolitics of postmodern bodies' (BPB) Haraway explores the often competing popular and technical languages that construct biomedical, biotechnical bodies and selves in scientific culture in the 1980s. She takes the immune system as the focus of the essay and observes that 'immune system discourse is about constraint and possibility for engaging in a world full of "difference", replete with non-self' (BPB 211). According to Murray (2007) Haraway does not deny the clinical importance or significance of the immune system. She views it as an 'iconic mythic object' in which there is a close inter-connection of 'myth, laboratory and clinic' (BPB 201; see also Murray 2007: 159). The immune system

> is an elaborate icon for principal systems of symbolic and material "difference" in late capitalism. Pre-eminently a twentieth century object, the immune system is a map drawn to guide recognition and misrecognition of self and other in the dialectics of Western biopoli-tics. That is, the immune system is a plan for meaningful action to construct and maintain the boundaries for what may count as self and other. (BPB 200)

According to Haraway 'the immune system is imaged as a battlefield' and 'the self' as a 'stronghold' (Murray 2007: 159). It provides a picture of relation-ships and 'a guide for action in the face of questions about the boundaries of the self and about mortality' (BPB 210–11).

Haraway returns to several of the key themes present in the development of the cyborg and partial perspectives. In particular, she argues that bodies are not born but made. She argues that discourses of immunology are particularly powerful mediators of the experiences of illness and death in contemporary society. In the essay Haraway reintroduces readers to the notion of the material-semiotic actor, which she begins to develop in her work on partial perspectives. She argues that bodies 'are not ideological constructions' and are 'always radi-cally historically specific' (BPB 204). For Haraway, 'bodies have a different kind of specificity and effectivity', and 'invite a different kind of engagement and intervention' (BPB 204–5). She repeats the argument that she outlined earlier:

> 'Material-semiotic actor' is intended to highlight the object of knowl-edge as an active part of the apparatus of bodily production, without *ever* implying the immediate presence of such objects or, what is the same thing, their final or unique determination of what can count as objective knowledge of a biomedical body at a particular historical juncture. (BPB 205)

Haraway argues again that 'bodies as objects of knowledge are material-semiotic generative nodes. Their boundaries materialise in social interaction' (BPB 205). However, in her work on immunology she focuses more specifically on the ways in which biological bodies surface 'at the intersection of biological research, writing, and publishing' (BPB 205). She extends her analysis to examine the ways in which bodies are also made through 'medical and other business practices', and through 'cultural productions of all kinds, including available metaphors and narratives' (BPB 205). Furthermore, Haraway explic-itly examines the ways in which they are made through technology; for example, visualisation techniques that bring to life 'killer T cells and intimate photographs of the developing fetus' (BPB 205).

The cyborg, communication, and immunology

The cyborg is central to the focus of her argument in this essay. She extends her conceptualisation of the cyborg in a section in this essay entitled 'Cyborgs for earthly survival' (BPB 209). In the 'bio politics of postmodern bodies', Haraway elaborates on the notion of the cyborg as text, machine, body, and metaphor. This is again theorised through her focus on communications. She begins to unpack in more detail here the ways in which the cyborg 'not only blurs the boundaries between human beings, animals, and machines, but also that between between body and language' (Munnik 1997: 112). According to Haraway, modern technology textualises reality. In making this argument, she returns again to the issue of coding that appears in 'A cyborg manifesto' (CM 164). She argues that it is possible to see how technology textualises the body in biological discourses of the body. These discourses increasingly 'tends to conceive of the body primarily as expressing or bearing the genetically coded information of DNA molecules' (Munnik 1997: 112). Immunology is used by Haraway to illustrate this textualisation of the body (BPB 199–233). The entire discourse of immunology is permeated by notions of coding and decoding. For example, a virus in this discourse is a 'clever invader that sets out to produce an entirely new text that eventually is recognised as "foreign"' (Munnik 1997: 113; BPB 221). Immunology is about the immune system 'defending the body against invaders from the outside, which must therefore be able to establish the difference between friend and foe, health and sickness' (Munnik 1997: 113). Immunologists recognise this 'as a process involving original texts, textual corruptions, and the ability to recognize alien texts as such' (Munnik 1997: 113). Haraway sees the immune system above all as an object in contemporary scientific narratives that is used to create and maintain the boundaries between self and other – a war narrative (BPB 200). However, this is problematic for cyborgs who are themselves hybrids and who therefore do not need to defend their original selves from the other: 'their sickness stories have no need to be war narratives' (Munnik 1997: 113).

The central focus on communication in this essay is illustrated by an example from a study by Winograd and Flores on understanding *computers and cognition*, which is about the operation of computer systems in artificial intelligence. A key idea in this study is 'communication *breakdown*, which Haraway then adopts, in her essay in immunology as a metaphor for illness' (Munnik 1997: 113). Winograd and Flores show that breakdowns play a vital role in human understanding. They should not be viewed as a negative situation that should be avoided. Rather, they should be viewed as 'a situation of non-obviousness, in which some aspect of the network of tools that we are engaged in using is brought forth to visibility' (Winograd and Flores 1986 cited in BPB 211). A breakdown exposes the node of relations essential for us 'to accomplish our task'. . . 'to anticipate the form of breakdowns and provide a space of possibilities for action when they occur' (Winograd and Flores 1986 in BPB 211). Haraway draws 'a connection here between the political (war) narrative and the prevailing immunological narrative' (Munnik 1997: 114). She demonstrates how Winograd and Flores's interpretation highlights a radically different type of narrative than the existing one:

> This is not a Stars Wars[6] or Strategic Computing Initiative relation to vulnerability, but neither does it deny therapeutic action. It insists on locating therapeutic, reconstructive action (and also theoretic understanding) in terms of situated purposes, not fantasies of the utterly defended self in a body as automated, militarised factory, a kind of ultimate self as Robotic Battle Manager meeting the enemy (not self) as it invades in the form of bits of foreign information threatening to take over the master control codes. (BPB 211)

She returns again to the arguments made in her work on the cyborg and partial perspectives that in these completely denaturalised systems another opportunity for political action is uncovered. She argues that it is up to cyborgs to develop truthful narratives such as that of Winograd and Flores. 'The construction or "writing" of such a denaturalized narratives is one form of political action needed to disarm the state' (Munnik 1997: 114; BPB 209–11).

The cyborg and biopolitics

The argument Haraway articulates in this essay on the immune system should be read as her specific take on biopolitics. This is something that is implicit in the development of the concept of the cyborg in the manifesto, and in her introduction to the term material-semiotic in her work on partial perspectives. However, Haraway uses her work on the immune system to illustrate this position more fully. In particular, in this essay Haraway emphasises 'the dual potential that biopolitics holds for destruction or affirmation' (Esposito 2011: 145–7). Like Foucault, Haraway 'takes the centrality of the body as a specific object of biopower', however she does so from a 'material-semiotic' perspective through which she deconstructs the unitary character of the body (Esposito 2011: 146). In contrast to Foucault, Haraway approaches the body from the perspective of its deconstruction and multiplication, prompted by the rapid increase in the 'new bionic, electronic, and information technologies' (Esposito 2011: 146). This, according to Esposito (2011: 146), should be viewed as a 'real paradigm shift in interpretation': 'If in the 1930s the discursive regime on the body attained its ultimate ideological solidity in the concept of "race", and around the 1970s it was reconceived by Foucault in terms of "population" today it must be looked at from the standpoint of its technical transformation' (Esposito 2011: 146). Haraway does not lose sight of 'the actual relations of power into which the management of the living being is inscribed and which tends to change continuously' (Esposito 2011: 146). However, Haraway goes beyond this by arguing that the 'connection between politics and life is radically redefined by the unstoppable proliferation of technology' (Esposito 2011: 146). In conversation with Gane, Haraway herself expands on this, stating that 'Foucault's formulation of biopower remains necessary but it needs to be enterprised up' in light of this cyborg world in which we live. She argues that Foucault's 'sense of the biopolitics of populations has not gone away, but it has been reworked' and 'mutated', and in short 'technologized' (Gane and Haraway 2006: 148). As with the argument first articulated in the manifesto, therefore, the dual-edged potential of the cyborg is reinforced in her biopolitics essay. The cyborg articulated here thus continues to be poised as a potential source for radical change as well as a source for the continued and enhanced unequal structuring of social relations.

Producing Nature, Producing Knowledge

The immune system also plays a key role in Haraway's essay 'Promises of monsters' (PM 63–124). The immune system is used in this context to further revisit and illustrate various elements of her work on cyborg theory and partial perspectives. It also extends her focus on the relationship between self and other and illuminates her position on modernity and postmodernity. Haraway argues that one of the key aims of this essay is to reclaim vision from the ways it has been used in the past to oppress minority groups – she wants to remake vision for activists and advocates engaged in political action (PM). This is very similar to her original development of the partial perspective in 'Situated knowledges' (SK) where she states that she wants to reclaim vision for feminist theory. In promises of monsters, Haraway wants to use vision to see the world from the perspectives of socialist feminists and anti-racist environmentalism, and science for the people (PM).

The main focus of the essay is what she terms artifactualism. She refers again to the central tenet of her work on the production of bodies in both 'Situated knowledges' (SK 595) and 'The biopolitics of postmodern bodies' (BPB 205), arguing that organisms are not born but made (PM 67). She focuses her analysis this time on the production of nature. She argues that many think that the postmodern world is *denatured*. However, Haraway holds that the world has not been denatured as such; rather the contemporary world is merely a particular production of nature. In global capitalism, 'the whole world is remade in the image of commodity production' (PM 66). She returns again to her initial argument in 'A cyborg manifesto' on the importance of relationships between humans and other actants and agents. She argues that nature is made through a co-construction between humans and non-humans (PM 66). In promises of monsters, Haraway develops a path somewhere between materialism, constructivism, and postmodernism. She is keen to distinguish her approach from postmodernism. She argues that postmodernists tend to view the entire world as 'denatured and reproduced in images or replicated in copies' (PM 66). Haraway departs from this and argues that 'organisms emerge from a discursive process' (PM 67). In the essay she advances the same themes outlined elsewhere in this chapter, that 'biology is a

discourse, not the living world itself' (PM 67). She again stresses the importance of other actants and agents in this context. Humans, she argues, 'are not
the only actors in the construction of the entities of any scientific discourse'
'machines' and 'other partners' are 'active constructors of natural scientific
objects' (PM 67).

The production of bodies

The term 'material-semiotic actor' again plays a central role in promises of
monsters. She uses it to 'highlight the object of knowledge as an active part of
the apparatus of bodily production' (PM 67). As argued earlier, for Haraway
'"objects" like bodies do not pre-exist as such' (PM 67); the same argument is
applied in this context to nature. It cannot 'pre-exist as such, but neither is its
existence ideological' (PM 68). Haraway argues that 'nature is a common
place and a powerful discursive construction' (PM 68). She again rehearses the
same arguments about politics and the potential for change. She argues in this
essay that 'perhaps our hopes for accountability for techno-biopolitics in the
belly of the monster turn on revisioning the world as coding trickster with
whom we must learn to converse' (PM 68).

In 'Promises of monsters', Haraway develops what she calls the four-
square cyborg in order to 'play havoc with some of the finest technology of
structuralist and poststructuralist analysis' (Haraway 2004a: 4). This square
consists of four categories: real space (Earth), outer space (the extra-terrestrial),
virtual space (science fiction), and inner space (the biomedical body (PM 78)).
This last category, 'the biomedical body', will form the central focus of this
analysis and in particular her work on the immune system. Haraway argues
that the immune system is a construct of an elaborate 'apparatus of bodily production' (PM 68). But, she argues that 'neither the immune system nor any other
of biology's world-changing bodies – like a virus or an ecosystem – is ghostly
fantasy' (PM 68). She focuses here on the artefactual production of nature.

By doing so she makes another important theoretical statement that again
further develops her work on the partial perspective. She emphasises the corporeality of theory, asserting that overwhelmingly theory is embodied (PM
68). She seeks to place the lived body at the centre of social theory not apart
from it. She also states that lives are built just as technologies are. Because of
this she argues that 'we had best become good craftspeople with the other
worldly actants in the story' (PM 68). She restates her argument that this is
not about the rationalist progress of science in potential league with progressive politics (PM 77). However, she is also quick to point out that this is not
about the social construction of science and nature that situates agency on the
side of humanity. She makes reference to Bruno Latour in this essay to elaborate her position on the development of society and argues that the modern
will not be superseded by or infiltrated by the postmodern (PM 77). She agrees
with Latour in maintaining that 'belief in something called the modern' has
always been 'a mistake'. Haraway makes a very important point here: there is

an 'absence of beginnings, enlightenments, and endings' (PM 77). She states that: 'the world has always been in the middle of things, in unruly and practical conversation, full of action and structured by a startling array of actants and of networking and unequal collectives' (PM 77).

Haraway returns to the connections she makes between language and biology in immune systems discourse. In this essay, however, she grounds her argument in a range of examples, from print media to medical texts through to examples from the entertainment industry. Thus, Haraway illustrates and extends her earlier argument that the immune system is used as a battle ground metaphor, referring to science sections of newspapers and magazines. She gives the example of the *National Geographic*, which openly punned on the notion of Star Wars in its use of the phrase 'Cell Wars' (Jaret in PM 101). Medical texts on the immune system also abound with militarised metaphors. However, what is interesting about immune system discourse is that it works both ways. As Haraway says, it is not just the 'imagers of the immune system' discourse that learn from military cultures, 'military cultures draw symbolically on immune system discourse'. She draws on a range of examples to support and illustrate her arguments here; for instance, the Disney World thrill ride called 'Body Wars'. She argues that 'immune system discourse is about the unequally distributed chances of life and death' (PM 102). She states, however, that this is not just about death' but also life; for example, '*living* with AIDS' (PM 103).

Theorising the self and other

In 'Promises of monsters' Haraway also emphasises the ubiquitous nature of the immune system. She states that with about 10^{12} cells, the immune system 'has two orders of magnitude more cells than the nervous system' (PM 103). The immune system is regenerated throughout life from the pluripotent stem cells. The immune system starts with embryonic life and is there right through the lifecourse. It is dispersed across the body in various tissues and organs, and 'a large fraction of its cells are in the blood and lymph circulatory systems and in body fluids and spaces' (PM 103). Haraway stresses that the immune system is a very dispersed system with a flexible communication system, she argues that: 'The immune system is everywhere and nowhere. Its specificities are indefinite if not infinite, and they arise randomly; yet these extraordinary variations are the critical means of maintaining bodily coherence' (PM 104). Haraway uses the immune system here to further elaborate on her conceptualisation of the relationship between the self and other. Haraway argues that the immune system is a highly dispersed system yet despite such dispersal it is responsible for holding the body together. She uses the immune system here as a metaphor for self and other, alluding perhaps to a more fluid or liquid sense of self (Murray 2007: 162). However, Haraway uses this conceptualisation to position her approach against traditionally postmodern approaches. According to Murray, in postmodern theories the self is portrayed as 'more fragmented in terms of symbolic consistency and narrative texture, and is characterized by ambiguities, ambivalence, discontinuity, dread, flux, multiplicity – and turmoil. The 'self' may be recognised as a composite of contending discourses, practices, representations, images and fantasies' (Murray 2007: 162 referring to Elliot 2001). However, despite these ambiguities and contradictions, for Haraway there is something that holds the self together. In illustrating this point through the immune system, Haraway again avoids the relativism of postmodern conceptualisations of the self, thus again delineating her specific socio-theoretical contribution.

CONCLUSION

In the conclusion to her essay 'Promises of monsters' Haraway states that:

> The whole argument of 'The Promises of Monsters' has been that to 'press enter' is not a fatal error, but an inescapable possibility for changing maps of the world, for building new collectives out of what is not quite a plethora of human and unhuman actors. (PM 110)

This is perhaps the principal argument underlying all of the essays examined in this chapter. For Haraway a theory of society does not rest on an examination of the relationship between individual and society. Rather it includes meaningful relationships between humans and other organisms and technology. Furthermore, to engage with other non-human actants and agents does not necessarily lead to greater inequality but can open up new possibilities for social change.

There are of course those who have questioned whether the cyborg, which is made up of both fact and fiction, really does have the political potency that she ascribes to it (Munnik 1997: 115). However, this critique is perhaps a little unfair. What Haraway tries to show through the development of the concept of the cyborg is that one can imagine a better and fairer world. Such a world for Haraway has the potential to be realised one day through the expansion of new biological, technical, and social relationships. This is the central premise upon which the concept of the cyborg is based and through which the epistemology of the partial perspectives is built. It is also the position that is illuminated by Haraway's work on the immune system: first, through an elaboration of her position on biopolitics; and second, by illustrating her theory of the relationship between the self and other. While the manifestation of the concept of the cyborg and partial perspectives in her work on the immune system is reasonably clear, there is perhaps a lack of analytical clarity between the actual concepts themselves. This, coupled with Haraway's rather abstruse essay style, often makes it difficult to analyse the manifestation of each individual concept in Haraway's work effectively. However, to make this criticism is perhaps to miss the point, as for Haraway boundaries both real and imagined must be transgressed in order for meaningful and egalitarian ones to be reconstructed. This after all is perhaps the most powerful contribution that Haraway makes to contemporary social theory.

Abbreviations

BPB: 'The biopolitics of postmodern bodies' (1993)

CM: 'A cyborg manifesto' (1991)

PM: 'Promises of monsters' (2004b)

SK: 'Situated knowledges' (1988)

Selected Further Readings

The following two readings offer short but comprehensive introductions to Haraway's works:

Reed, K. (2006) *New Directions in Social Theory: Race, Gender and the Canon.* London: Sage, pp. 132-6.

Clough, P. T. and Schneider, J. (2001) 'Donna J. Haraway', in A. Elliot and B. S. Turner (eds) *Profiles in Contemporary Social Theory.* London: Sage, pp. 338-48.

For a more detailed and critical account of her cyborg theory, see:

Munnik, R. (1997) 'Donna Haraway: Cyborgs for earthly survival', in H. Achterhuis (ed.) *American Philosophy of Technology.* Bloomington and Indianapolis, IN: University of Indiana Press, pp. 95-118.

Notes

1 For a feminist discussion on binary thought and women's oppression, see Oakley (1979).
2 The Cold War era is commonly defined as the period commencing at the end of World War Two and ending with the collapse of communism (1946–1991). For a discussion on the relationship between Cold War politics, technological investment, and the military, see Mackenzie (1993).
3 Cybernetics is a transdisciplinary field that focuses on the study of regulatory systems and their structures. The systems that come under study are diverse including: biological, cognitive, mechanical, and social.
4 Some authors have suggested that Haraway is often too quick to dispense with the notion of origin and history. Kirby (1997), for example, argues that origin cannot be separated from the question of identity itself.
5 The discussion of homework presumes a particular set of relations of production. According to Leach (1998) a homeworker is someone 'who receives work for which she is paid by the piece from the supplier, the latter being responsible for the disposal of the finished product. In industrialized societies there is also a tendency to use a category of "home-based work"'. This refers to work such as childminding, small business ventures, etc. (Leach 1998: 97). Haraway (in CM) uses the term to explore the exploitation of female labour in developing nations as well as the feminised nature of work in industrial contexts.
6 Stars Wars refers to the Strategic Defence Initiative (SDI) developed during Ronald Reagan's US presidency. This was a proposed missile defence system intended to protect the US from nuclear attack.

5

Zygmunt Bauman: Liquid Social Life

PART 1: LIQUID SOCIETY

Zygmunt Bauman's conception of contemporary social reality turns on his distinction between 'solids' and 'fluids' such as 'liquids' (LM 1–2). A solid, he clarifies, generally maintains its 'shape': its 'spatial dimensions' are definite; 'time' has limited relevance for it. A liquid is always about 'to change' 'shape': it takes up a 'space' only momentarily; for a liquid, 'the flow of time' is essential. 'Fluids' are also more mobile, and thus commonly considered 'lighter', than 'solids'. Bauman argues that the current stage of 'modernity' can be captured by the 'metaphors' of '"fluidity" or "liquidity"' and that this 'phase' is, in many respects, new (LM 2).

> The kind of modernity which was the target, but also the cognitive frame, of classical critical theory strikes the analyst in retrospect as quite different from the one which frames the lives of present-day generations. It appears 'heavy' (as against the contemporary 'light' modernity); better still, 'solid' (as distinct from 'fluid', 'liquid', or 'liquefied'); condensed (as against diffuse or 'capillary'); finally, systemic (as distinct from network-like). (LM 25)

Bauman draws this distinction in numerous ways, in respect of multiple domains of modern society. Whilst an exhaustive survey is beyond this chapter's scope, reconstructing his distinction in view of individualisation and modernisation as well as in view of the changing relationships between time and space and between capital and labour is indispensable for an exposition of his conception of contemporary social conditions.

Individualisation

One of the domains in relation to which Bauman develops his distinction of liquid from solid modern society is 'individualization' (LM 31). Prior to the onset of modernity *tout court*, he argues, people were '"born into" their identities' (LM 32). Among the principal 'frames' that defined the scope of what humans could choose to do in their lives were 'hereditary estates' (LM 6). Estates were ascribed to people (LM 6, 32), 'inherited' (LM 33) rather than '"joined"' (LM 32). The 'frames of estates' were rigid (LM 32, see also 6). People could hardly 'contest' their position (LM 33, see also 6). Modernity, by contrast, is inseparable from individualisation. In fact, Bauman insists that the two are 'the same social condition' (LM 32). Individualisation, he explains, involves making 'human "identity" … a "task" and charging the actors with the responsibility for performing that task …' (LM 31). Throughout the modern era, people have had to attend to 'the self-constitution of individual life' and to the establishment and maintenance of relationships 'with other self-constituting individuals' (LM 49; see also Davis 2016: 78, 94).

Bauman distinguishes specifically early modern conditions, though. Whilst 'the estate-order' was declining (LM 33, see also 6, 32), new 'frames', especially the modern *classes*, were forming (LM 7). They came to define the 'life projects and life strategies' people could conceivably engage in. The class frames were the 'ready-made niches' of the young modern era (LM 7; see also Blackshaw 2008: 120–1). Yet now the individual herself or himself had 'to find the appropriate niche' (LM 7) and work on 'conforming to the emerging class-bound social types and models of conduct' by 'imitating' (LM 32), obeying 'rules' (LM 7), and keeping to 'the norm' (LM 32). Moreover, individuals had constantly to reaffirm their class 'membership' (LM 32). Crucially, though, class frames, too, were rigid (LM 7). 'Class', but also, for example, 'gender hung heavily over the individual range of choices', like '"facts of nature"'. People's ability 'to escape' the confines of their class was severely limited (LM 33). This illustrates Bauman's more encompassing view that whilst 'modernity' has been a project of liquefying 'deficient', often already unstable 'solids', its objective initially was to forge better, more durable ones (LM 2–3). Installed in place of its 'defunct … predecessor', the 'industrial order' as a whole was built for the eons (LM 143–4). 'New solids were to be … constructed'; and who- and whatever had been 'set afloat' when the previous context was undone was 'to be … "re-embedded"', notably workers (LM 142–3; see also Poder 2008: 100–1).

In today's 'fluid and light' phase of the modern era, people must continue to partake 'in the individualizing game' (LM 34; see also Blackshaw 2008: 120–1). They also still draw 'on society for the building materials and design blueprints' of life (LM 7). But the present is characterised by a whole range of 'patterns and configurations' with conflicting 'commandments' and pliable constitutions. The 'patterns' are not '"self-evident"' anymore, leaving the end point of each individual's efforts of self-constitution 'underdetermined' (LM 7). In fact, individuals themselves are increasingly responsible for configuring 'patterns of dependency and interaction', which, in turn, are as difficult to hold 'in shape' as any fluid (LM 8; see also Poder 2008: 101). The frames 'postulated and pursued' today resemble '"musical chairs"' with their propensity to switch 'positions' or disappear abruptly. Individuals must repeatedly reorient themselves and are always in transit, with no hope of arriving at a 'final destination' (LM 33–4).

In solid modernity, Bauman continues to draw his distinction along very similar lines, some people made laws, planned routines, and determined 'ends', whilst others – 'other-directed men and women',[1] namely – carried out those activities in pursuit of these goals. The former included 'authorities' such as 'leaders' and 'teachers' (LM 63). Everyone else could concentrate on 'learning and following the rules set down for them' (LM 59). By contrast, liquid modernity, which knows, instead of a 'Supreme Office', only competitions 'for supremacy' among multiple 'offices', has no – and certainly not only one – answer to 'the question of objectives' (LM 60). Rather than gauging 'means' in view of a 'given end', people are likely to spend the majority of their time 'agonizing about the choice of goals' (LM 61). And it is the task of each 'individual' alone to discover 'what she or he is capable of', to enhance these skills as much as possible, and to choose the goals most consistent with these abilities (LM 62). The present conditions allow for multiple 'law-proffering authorities', which undermine one another (LM 63–4). The era of 'great leaders' giving people directions, instructions, and orders is over. Nowadays, a great number of 'individuals' offer various 'advice' on and 'examples' for living one's life. Every person must examine this range of suggestions and choose themselves which 'example to imitate', and the 'responsibility for the consequences of investing ... trust in this example rather than another' is theirs alone (LM 30; see also Campain 2008: 201; Davis 2016: 54–5, 78, 100–2; Poder 2008: 101, 104). Bauman differentiates sharply 'between leaders', who must 'be followed', and the 'counsellors' so frequently encountered today, who 'need to be hired and can be fired' (LM 64).

Modernisation

Bauman develops his distinction between the two modernities further in view of what he terms '*modernization*'. Perpetual modernisation, a desire for '"clearing the site"' for 'a "new and improved" design', constitutes a distinctive characteristic of the whole of modernity (LM 28). From the outset, Bauman writes with reference to Peter Gay, a mode of procedure according to a medical model was envisaged: 'diagnose the ailment, ... design the therapy course, apply it, and make the ill healthy again – or even healthier ... than ... before' (LL 130–1). The people of modernity have never been able to terminate these endeavours, because for modern society '[f]ulfilment is always in the future' (LM 28).

However, crucially, 'early' modernity still harboured 'the belief' that the transformations of history might – be it in a day, be it in a thousand years – reach a conclusion in the form of a 'good society' in which 'needs' are met, 'order' is immaculate, and 'all contingency' and 'ambivalence' of humans' activities have been eliminated (LM 29, see also 143; Poder 2008: 101). In the eyes of the key 'characters' of that phase's 'story' – a privileged few, Bauman points out, rather than the whole population (LL 133–4) – overcoming 'the world as found' and installing another meant striving for the '*perfect* world' which would warrant no additional changes (LL 132–3). Moreover, they imagined that a better management of 'the world' could help realise 'greater happiness' for 'all humans' and understood the quest for it as 'a *collective task*', a joint project of conceptualising and constructing 'a better world' (LL 132).

Twenty-first century society, Bauman holds, is unquestionably 'modern' in that it still pursues constant '*modernization*' with an 'unquenchable thirst for creative destruction' (LM 28; see also Poder 2008: 100). The 'motif' resounding in the chants of 'ministers' everywhere is 'modernize, modernize, change or perish'. The 'characters' central to the narratives of the modernities of the year 2000 and of the year 1800, respectively, share an inability to 'stand still' and a dissatisfaction 'with what is' (LL 131). Yet although the desire for change of both types of characters has been fuelled by the vital sustenance that the assurance of the transformability of 'what is' lends to 'the hope of satisfaction' (LL 131–2), contemporary 'modernity' can be told apart from 'early' modernity by the 'swift decline' of any 'illusion' that consummate conditions might ever be achieved (LM 29; see also Poder 2008: 101). When the 'heroes' of today's 'story' – and these are now 'all' the 'players' – do not downright 'resent the thought of ever stopping', they keep their minds off any ultimate goals, conscious of their being in the dark about the moves that their modernisation endeavours would require beyond the immediate next 'step' now engaging them completely (LL 133–4). In their eyes, 'change is an end in itself' (LL 133). No longer looking to a link between 'happiness' and a 'state of the world', they are convinced that the escape from misery hinges on each person's work on her- or himself, thus conceiving it as an entirely '*private task*' (LL 132). Nowadays, the chores of modernisation tend to be 'left to individuals' management and individually administered resources' (LM 29).

Time and Space

Bauman's aforementioned introduction to solids and liquids with reference to time and space already indicates that these dimensions are important for his investigations. Indeed, the key quality of modernity, 'from which all other characteristics follow', he surmises, '… is the changing relationship between space and time' (LM 8). This transformation leads Bauman to affirm and further specify his distinction between the two modernities.

Technological component

In 'pre-modern' epochs, Bauman argues, time and space were 'locked in a … one-to-one correspondence' (LM 8–9). Questions about the distance between two locations could be answered with reference to the length of time it took 'human or animal muscles' to travel it: '"Far" and "long", just like "near" and "soon", used to mean nearly the same: just how much or how little effort it would take for a human being to span a certain distance – be it by walking, by ploughing, or harvesting' (LM 110). In the specific sense that no king could traverse a distance in any less time than anyone else, inequality was minimal (LM 112).

The onset of modernity coincided with the dissociation of time and space (LM 8, 112). Of central importance were inventions of transport technologies that enabled people to travel given 'distances' in ever 'less time' (LM 111, see also 9). 'Time was different from space because, unlike space, it could be … manipulated' by human-made means (LM 111). Those disposing of better means of transport could travel the same distance more quickly, and thus seize a larger 'territory', than everyone else (LM 112).

The technological contraction of the time of movement for the purpose of seizing ever wider spaces, the fortification of these spaces, and populating them with things became characteristic modern endeavours (LM 112–14, see also 9). Bauman mentions the growing size of factories, numbers of employees, and volume of machines, as well as imperial expansion (LM 113–14). 'Wealth and might' were augmented by enlarging 'the place they occup[ied]', 'protected by protecting that place' (LM 115), and, crucially, 'tied to their place', that is, 'immovable' (LM 114). Controlling such spaces, in turn, hinged on 'neutralizing' time's 'inner dynamism': on carving time up into segments of equal length and establishing 'monotonous and unalterable sequences' – in factory work, for instance – so that nothing would happen sooner than planned (LM 115). These time–space configurations were decisive for solid or '*heavy* modernity' (LM 113).

Modernity's current phase is distinct from its heavy stage not because it has steered the development of the time–space relationship in a new direction, but because it has radicalised its already ongoing development. Tendentially (LM 119), Bauman emphasises, in this 'software' or 'light modernity' (LM 118), 'space may be traversed, literally, in "no time"' (LM 117). At the speed of 'electronic signals', far away localities can now be 'acted upon'. Crucially, if, to argue with Georg Simmel, the value of anything hinges on what must be sacrificed to obtain it, then, continues Bauman, where 'no time needs to be … "sacrificed" … to reach … places, places are stripped of value in the Simmelian sense' (LM 117). Plus, insofar as not an instant is required for getting anywhere, no location 'has "special value"'. In these conditions, it is difficult to justify investment in gaining 'access to', and in the 'management' and 'cultivation' of, any place (LM 118).

Power component

Whilst Bauman thus clearly understands the modern condition as decisively shaped by technological developments and the changing time–space configuration, he closely associates these with transformations in social power relationships characteristic of modernity's unfolding.[2] Foucault's analysis of panoptic spaces conceived in the 1700s and 1800s, such as factories, schools, and prisons (1991: 195–228), serves Bauman as a cardinal reference point. In the panopticon, every inmate was immobilised, trapped in a cellular space (LM 9–10). First, inmates were aware that they could be watched all the time but unsure whether their supervisors were occupying their posts at any particular time (LM 9–11, see also 26). Second, 'the flow of [their] time' was strictly 'routiniz[ed]'. The supervisors were mobile to an extent that supported 'their domination' in the former respect, but 'routinization', among other duties, required them to remain present in the spaces of confinement. Hence, crucially, panoptic space was one of 'mutual engagement and confrontation between the two sides of the power relationship' (LM 10; see also Davis 2016: 100–1, 105n7; Poder 2008: 101).

The recent successes in humans' endeavours to increase 'the speed of movement', argues Bauman, are having a deep impact on contemporary power relations. Now that devices such as mobile phones allow a 'command' to travel from anywhere to anywhere in no time, no part of the exercise of power requires those exercising it to stay put in any specific location. The 'power-holders' are able to remove themselves from proximity to those on whom power is exercised, which brings the panoptical arrangement to an end: 'The end of Panopticon augurs *the end of the era of mutual engagement*: between the supervisors and the supervised, capital and labour, leaders and their followers, armies at war' (LM 10–11; see also Campain 2008: 202–3).

Capital and Labour

The social relationship arguably most important to Bauman's analyses of modernity's solid and liquid phases is that between capital and labour. He describes the former phase as simultaneously that of 'heavy capitalism' and that of the '*dependency*' of 'capital and labour' on one another, which 'tied them' permanently to each other (LM 145; see also Poder 2008: 101).

'Heavy capitalism was obsessed with bulk and size' (LM 58): with gigantic factories populated with masses of workers and huge machines (LM 144) behind insurmountable walls (LM 58). Henry Ford, Bauman remarks citing Daniel Cohen, gave his workers a 100% raise specifically in order to bind them to his factory (LM 58, 144). 'Routinized time', too, as already mentioned, 'tied labour to the ground' (LM 116; see also Davis 2016: 100–1). And 'labour' bound to the workplaces, together with the gargantuan and heavy sites and tools of production, kept 'capital' immobile (LM 116). Emphasising labour's '*embodied*' quality, Bauman points out that to 'mov[e] around' and 'hire … labour' employers needed to move and hire 'labourers', and 'to control the work process' they needed 'to control the workers'. This 'brought capital and labour face to face' (LM 120–1; see also Davis 2016: 101n6). The relationship between the two was characterised by daily struggles and occasional intense clashes that took the form of direct confrontations (LM 116, CL 14, 19). Yet since neither could do without the other and both were aware that they required 'solutions' agreeable to both, clashes and 'bargaining' could reinforce their 'unity' (LM 146–7). Moreover, both needing the exchange of labour for wages, both had to be maintained in a condition 'fit for that transaction', and both 'had "vested interests" in keeping the other side in the right shape' (LM 145). A key element of their 'settlement' (LF 164), 'the state' contributed to keeping 'capitalists' able 'to buy labour' (LM 145) and to stimulating the 'expansion of the capitalist economy' as well as to 'rehabilitating labour' (LF 163) and to ensuring that the jobless were prepared for being 'called back into active service' (LM 145, see also CL 7–8). Generally, workers of that era had a degree of certainty: an 'apprentice' starting to work for Ford, for example, could look forward to a lifetime of 'employment' in an enterprise whose life expectancy was even longer (LM 146).

Liquid modernity, by contrast, is witnessing the emergence 'of light … capitalism' (LM 149). Whereas the ability to work still cannot be fulfilled without 'the presence of capital' (LM 121), capital's 'reproduction and growth' are now 'largely independent from the duration of any particular local engagement with labour'. Their bonds are 'loosening' (LM 149; see also Campain 2008: 202–3; Davis 2016: 66–7; Poder 2008: 106).

In the current 'software era', which is contemporaneous with the '"disembodiment"' of the 'labour' fuelling 'capital', capital need no longer manage cumbersome control and training apparatuses. Hence, it is not 'tied' down and 'into direct engagement' with the workers anymore. Today's 'capitalists' are keen to jettison unnecessary weight, especially the 'onerous' duty of managing countless employees (LM 121–2; see also Campain 2008: 202–3; Poder 2008: 101). Unburdened from 'bulky machinery and massive factory crews, capital travels light' – 'briefcase', notebook, mobile (LM 150, see also 58). It is able to reach virtually any place, need not remain anywhere longer than is satisfactory, and can always swiftly move on (LM 58, 121–2; see also Campain 2008: 202–3; Davis 2016: 101n6, 105). A firm 'engagement' would only hamper 'movement' and 'competitiveness', leaving opportunities potentially to improve 'productivity' unused (LM 150–1).[3] Capital's ability to move rapidly from one locality to another allows it to issue the 'threat of' – for any locality devastating – 'capital disinvestment'. Politics on the ground responds by 'deregulation', and the people's capacity and will 'to put up an organized resistance' is corroding (LM 150, see also LF 159; Campain 2008: 202–3). Bauman adds that 'profits' no longer flow from things but from 'ideas', which 'are produced only once'. Rendering them 'profitable' does not hinge on a large workforce 'replicating the prototype', but on a large crowd of 'consumers'. When capital arranges its journeys, it is therefore ever less concerned about whether a locality provides a workforce, whose '"holding power" ... on capital' is, as a result, atrophying (LM 151). Today's employee, finally, experiences 'uncertainty', a world of 'work on short-term contracts, rolling contracts or no contracts' under the sign of '"Flexibility"' in which people will change employment increasingly frequently (LM 147; see also Campain 2008: 202–3; Poder 2008: 106).

Politics and Individualisation

Bauman's analysis of the relationship between capital and labour constitutes one component of his multifaceted investigation of the political dimension of contemporary social conditions. Bauman also highlights the present obstacles to the transformation of liquid society for the better. Whilst a complete account of this part of his work cannot be given here, an argument in connection with 'individualization' (LM 34) may illustrate the kinds of dilemmas he attempts to tackle.

It is doubtful, emphasises Bauman, that people can spare themselves 'frustration' by their own individual means (LM 34). Nonetheless, individuals today concentrate 'on their own performances' rather than on the social conditions in which the 'contradictions' of their lives are generated (LM 38). Indeed, the frustrated are advised to blame themselves and their personal shortcomings (LM 34). As a consequence, Bauman argues citing Ulrich Beck (1992: 137), people come to live '"... *biographical solution[s] to systemic contradictions"*': the latter are 'socially produced', but the obligation to deal with them is 'individualized' (LM 34; see also Davis 2016: 133–6). Yet '"biographic solutions to systemic contradictions"' do not exist (LM 38).

The liquid age, Bauman insists, is sustaining a chasm 'between the right of self-assertion' and the power over the social conditions that determine whether 'self-assertion' is 'feasible' (LM 38, see also 39). The 'individual' does not presently control 'the resources' that proper 'self-determination' would require (LM 40). No individual is free to determine 'the range of choices and the agenda of choice-making' (LM 51; see also Davis 2016: 51, 75–8, 136–7; Poder 2008: 103). Bauman concedes that individual capacities amalgamated 'into a collective stand and action' might provide 'a remedy' (LM 35; see also Campain 2008: 203). However, the message disseminated everywhere is that the individual 'is the master of his or her own fate' (LM 39, see also 64; Davis 2016: 133–6). The primary lesson of observing others today is that everybody is exposed to 'risks ... to be ... fought alone'. People have become 'sceptical' of appeals to the '"common good"' or the '"good society"', asking only that everybody be allowed to pursue their own path. 'Sharing intimacies', 'worries', 'anxieties', Bauman argues drawing on Richard Sennett, is now virtually the only mode of forming 'communities', which are correspondingly transient (LM 36–7; see also Campain 2008: 203–4; Davis 2016: 135–7). Today, he adds, 'communities' also often form with reference to 'celebrities', those 'liquid modern characters' whose celebrity Daniel Boorstin ascribed to their '"… well-knownness"' (LL 49–50). Yet a celebrity's 'notoriety' rarely lasts; celebrity-centred 'imaginary communities' require 'no commitment' and are fragile, always prone to disband (LL 50). The 'colonization of the public sphere by the private', continues Bauman, has in fact become the foremost barrier to liberation (LM 51, see also 37, 39). Personal problems 'will not congeal' and form 'a "common cause"', so 'individual grievances' do not easily coalesce 'into shared interests', let alone 'joint action' (LM 35; see also Davis 2016: 67, 135–6). In this situation, replenishing 'public space' with substance becomes a key emancipatory 'task' (LM 39, see also 41). What needs addressing is the problem of turning 'private problems into public issues' and of 'recollectivizing the privatized utopias' in order to transform them into 'visions of the "good society"' (LM 51; see also Campain 2008: 203; Davis 2016: 132–5, 138).

PART 2: LIQUID LIVING

Whilst the problem of life in contemporary social conditions can be heard to reverberate throughout Bauman's examinations of liquid modernity, he also raises this problem explicitly. What goes by 'the name of "modernity"', he says, is 'our bizarre way of life' (LL 130). '"Liquid life"', he specifies, 'is a kind of life that tends to be lived in a liquid modern society… Liquid life, just like liquid modern society, cannot keep its shape … for long' (LL 1). Like his depiction of liquid society, Bauman's portrayal of the liquid life seeks to capture a wide range of its properties. His problematisation of individuality and of life's modernisation, the concept of the consuming life, and his analysis of contemporary fears contain some of his decisive considerations.

Individual Life

Bauman's emphasis on individualisation renders it unsurprising that he identifies the problem of individuality as a key characteristic of the liquid life. Bauman understands individuality as a typically modern problem. When the 'capacity' of 'the community' to 'regulat[e] the lives of its members … matter-of-factly' according to standards or norms was waning, the 'shaping' of people's conduct was coming to light as something to be chosen (LL 20). The 'normative powers' of modern society did not take control over the sphere of 'interpersonal relations'; such ties could henceforth be established and severed 'freely'. A person's 'individuality is asserted and daily renegotiated' in that 'face-to-face' sphere. More specifically, the very idea of being 'an "individual"' is inextricable from that of taking 'responsibility' for one's 'interaction'. This 'responsibility' can only be thought if it is assumed that people 'have the right to choose' how to 'proceed'. In fact, in contemporary society, such 'free choice' is also a 'duty' (LL 21). This right and duty notwithstanding, for many people 'practising … free choice' is, of course, often out of 'reach' (LL 22).

For Bauman, 'individuality' is truly a problem. It contains 'an *insoluble* contradiction': both the 'cradle' and the 'destination' required by individuality is 'society' (LL 18). That one 'be an individual', namely distinct, is, he emphasises, a central 'demand' of contemporary 'society' on all people indiscriminately: 'individuality is a "universal must"'. In turn, so as to demonstrate their 'individuality' persuasively, people cannot but utilise 'tokens' that are 'shared' and 'commonly recognizable' (LL 16; see also Davis 2016: 142–3). As might be expected, in trying to construct their individuality, people 'listen' out for signals emitted by their innermost 'feelings', the supposed quintessence of '"uniqueness"' (LL 17). However, purchasing assistance for decoding these signals, they all too often end up with 'recipes for individuality … peddled wholesale' (LL 18).

According to Bauman, '[c]onsumerism' has certainly become a vital strategy for responding to the social demand on everyone to build, maintain, and renew 'their individuality'. Pointing to the advertising slogan '"Be yourself – choose Pepsi"', he argues that people's effort to stand out constitutes 'the main engine' of the 'production' of commodities *en masse* and of their 'consumption' by the masses (LL 23–4). Everybody seeks to form 'the friable stuff of life' into an 'identity' – a word one cannot dissociate from a vague notion of 'consistency' (LM 82). Yet insofar as nobody's identity is now fixed, 'it is the ability to "shop around" in the supermarket of identities' that supports the realisation of notions of identity (LM 83). The inhabitants of this 'liquid modern world' tour its shopping centres for 'publicly legible identity badges' (LL 34; see also Davis 2016: 56–7, 63–4, 73). Here people appear 'free' to assemble and disassemble 'identities' as they wish. In actual fact – as another brazenly frank advert, this time for a 'brand of hair conditioner': '"All unique; all individual; all choose X"', reveals – they must buy 'mass-produced' goods bought by thousands of others for building their particular identities, whilst the 'life' they want for themselves is more often than not a life they have seen on one of the many 'screens' surrounding them (LM 83–4, see also LL 86–7; Davis 2016: 73, 76–80, 86; Poder 2008: 102). This is evidently a tricky situation.

Modernising Life

Indeed, people's longing to be different can support the 'mass consumer market' only in 'a consumer economy' in which articles quickly become outdated. A contemporary strategy for rendering oneself distinct consists of divesting oneself of goods 'relegated from premiership league' and acquiring the latest faster than others (LL 24). However, the situation thus remains tricky with regard to consistency. Today, the objects out of which identity is constructed are made not to last, 'standards' are highly 'flexible', and 'identities' are inevitably 'unstable', so that the individual ends up perpetually having to readapt rapidly to 'the changing patterns of the world "out there"' (LM 85–6).

In this respect, individual identity is a site of the modernisation of life. From Bauman's aforementioned contention that modernisation is increasingly focused on the individual rather than on social conditions it may be inferred that identity constitutes a key site of modernisation. 'Life in a liquid modern society', he argues, '… must modernize' (LL 3). In the fluid present, one's 'assets' and 'abilities' quickly become 'liabilities' and 'disabilities' (LL 1). People live in dread of becoming laden with what has become outmoded and of not keeping step 'with fast-moving events'. Accordingly, 'getting rid of things' is now a vital activity (LL 2). '"Creative destruction" is the fashion in which liquid life proceeds'. For a life, to modernise means precisely to continue to rid oneself 'daily of attributes … past their sell-by dates' and to undo one's present 'identities' (LL 3). People are enabled and obliged to deactivate their 'past', to strive for fresh starts, to go through an entire 'series of families, careers, identities' (CL 100–1). Bauman reads the growing prominence of 'cosmetic surgery' as an expression of the current appeal of '"serial births"'. Scores of people have come to use such interventions regularly as tools for periodically reconstructing their 'visible self'. Each of the consecutive surgical procedures allows the individual to respond to today's 'fast-changing standards' and successively replace 'an image that has outlived its utility or charm' with 'a new public image' and, if possible, 'a new identity' (CL 101). Personal 'identity' is 'living through' a number of chapters steered by the need to obliterate one's 'history' instead of the will to design a 'future'. It means endeavouring 'to embrace' whatever is deemed necessary 'today' accompanied by the knowledge that all of this may well be considered problematic 'tomorrow'. Individual identity is always tied to its own respective 'present'. As its only stable – yet possibly even solidifying – kernel remains 'homo eligens', a human being continuously choosing without ever having definitively chosen (LL 33).

It is indispensable to add, however, that for Bauman this activity of constructing and repeatedly refreshing an individual identity manifests economic inequality: hinging on consumption in the above sense, this activity is clearly very expensive, open exclusively to those with substantial means (LL 25). A sizeable 'remainder' of the population is shut off from the 'costly extras' required for preparing trendy 'identity cocktails'; given 'no choice', they must accept 'identity concoctions' – however bland – 'as they come' (LL 35; see also Davis 2016: 87–9, 92–6; Poder 2008: 102, 110).

Life in the Market

As the foregoing considerations already strongly indicate, Bauman understands liquid modernity as the phase of 'the society of consumers' (CL 68, see also LL 80, LM 73). The 'consumer society' values people mainly according to 'capacities and conduct' relevant to 'consumption' (LL 82, see also LM 76). It compels them to choose 'a consumerist lifestyle and life strategy' (CL 53). Formerly, in the 'society of producers and soldiers', people were 'trained' to adapt to their assigned station, bear 'drudgery' and 'routine', and agree 'to working for the work's sake'. That society sought to render people 'fit' to operate on 'the factory floor and the battlefield' (CL 54). In the consumer society, by contrast, everybody is supposed to approach 'consumption as a vocation'

(CL 55). From an early age, people are meant to develop a fitness for operating in shopping centres (CL 54).

Shopping and non-satisfaction

'The code in which our "life policy" is scripted', Bauman asserts, 'is derived from the pragmatics of shopping' (LM 73–4, see also LL 83). 'Shopping' – that is, 'scanning' what is on offer, inspecting the items, considering prices in relation to one's funds or 'credit limit', and selecting – takes place everywhere today, not just in 'shops'. It is what people do for 'food, shoes, cars', of course, but also 'for new and improved examples and recipes for life'. They '"shop" for the skills' required for winning a livelihood, for instance, or 'for ways to earn the love of the beloved' and for cheap ways of splitting up with them, as much as for the best sound systems (LM 73–4, see also LL 87–8; Blackshaw 2008: 119–20; Davis 2016: 73, 76–8; Poder 2008: 104). This extension of 'consumer patterns', Bauman surmises, is probably due to the pervasive '"marketization" of life processes' characteristic of contemporary society (LL 88).[4]

Contemporary 'consumerism', however, is not primarily a matter of meeting 'needs', which were once considered scarcely malleable (LM 74–5). Even 'desire', which lends itself more easily to being inflated but is expensive for sellers of commodities to cultivate in people, is making way for the still more flexible '"wish"' as the 'stimulant' of consumption (LM 75–6). 'Life' in a producer society, argues Bauman, was 'regulated' by norms (LM 76). People needed a certain minimum to be able to work and could not easily want what lay beyond a socially permitted maximum. The key issue was '*conformity*'. 'Life organized around consumption' is not 'normatively' modulated but 'guided by seduction', continually expanding 'desires', and fickle 'wishes' (LM 76). What matters chiefly now is '*adequacy*': being able 'to develop new desires' that match ever novel 'allurements' (LM 77).

The 'case' of the society of consumers is underpinned by 'the promise to satisfy human desires' like no formation before it (LL 80). Indeed, whereas in the producer society people still considered it decent to postpone gratification, the period between 'wanting' and 'getting' has contracted (LL 83, see also CL 85–6, 98, LM 155–60). In the former formation, emphasis rested on the principle of forgoing instant 'rewards' for the sake of 'future benefits' and 'individual rewards for the benefit of the "whole"', for example, the 'nation' (CL 69). Liquid modernity's consumer society, by contrast, posits the '*obligation ... to choose*' – though presenting it 'as *freedom* of choice' – and 'to seek pleasure and happiness' (CL 74–5; see also Davis 2016: 74). However, if people were ever convinced that their 'desires' have been wholly met, the prospect of 'satisfaction' would cease to lure them to the shops (LL 80), 'consumer demand' might deteriorate, and 'the consumer-targeted economy' might stop turning (LL 81; see also Poder 2008: 105). The latter is driven by a '"buy it, enjoy it, chuck it out" cycle' (CL 98). It thrives on the enduring '*non*-satisfaction of desires' (LL 80, see also 92). To a 'society' which states that its principal 'purpose' is 'customer *satisfaction*', Bauman argues from an only slightly different angle, any permanently '*satisfied* consumer' poses a threat. So 'the ethical guideline of the consuming life' must instruct 'to avoid *staying satisfied*' (CL 98).

Bauman mentions several ways in which 'non-satisfaction' is sustained (LL 80). What is acquired might certainly simply fail to create the 'fulfilment' it promised (LM 72). But even if gratification ensues, it will, owing to the inexhaustible amount of further 'seductive ... offer[s]', be short-lived (LM 72, see also 73). In particular, holds Bauman, goods that are essential and up-to-date one day are rivalled by novel products the next and become inessential, out-of-date, or worse, and ready to be discarded (LL 85–9, see also CL 102–3). Articles heavily promoted today can even be maligned in the harshest terms tomorrow (CL 96–7, 99–100, LL 80). Finally, gratification itself will produce 'new needs/desires/wants' (LL 80). Reports that some skincare products have caused skin problems and thus boosted 'consumer demand' for the next versions of such articles provide an illustration (LL 81, see also LM 74). Of course, if people are to consume to help stimulate the economy, they must have money or credit (CL 78–9). In fact, in the society of consumers, '"living on credit"' is meant to become 'second nature' (CL 79; see also Blackshaw 2008: 125).

Ultimately, Bauman holds, the inhabitants of the consumer society approach their entire 'social setting' and all the 'actions' it arouses under the direction of the '"consumerist syndrome"'. The term 'syndrome' designates here a bundle of *inter alia* 'attitudes', 'cognitive dispositions', and 'value judgements' (LL 83; see also Blackshaw 2008: 117–18; Poder 2008: 106). 'The consumerist cultural syndrome' involves the valuation of 'transience' and 'novelty' over 'duration' (CL 85, see also LL 83). Belongings are desired and deemed useful only for a short while; they are sought to be got rid of soon after they are acquired (CL 85–6, LL 83–4). People try to avoid keeping things for too long, happily 'consigning' them 'to waste' (CL 86, LL 84). 'Fully fledged consumers' are relaxed, even positive, about the objects' 'short lifespan', perceiving their flaws at the same time as heralds of 'new joys' (CL 86, LL 84).

Consumers as commodities

A proper understanding of life in the consumer society, Bauman accentuates though, hinges on recognising not only that individuals are consumers, but also that many 'inhabit' markets as '*commodities*' (CL 6, see also 57, 62), notably, of course, labour markets (CL 10). As mentioned, Bauman, drawing on Jürgen Habermas, argues that until recently 'the capitalist state' – responding to the requirement that 'capital' be able and keen to purchase 'the commodity' 'labour', and that the latter remain capable of catching the attention and securing the 'approval' of 'potential buyers' – was vital in 'encouraging capitalists to spend their money on labour' as well as in 'making labour attractive to capitalist buyers' (CL 7). Yet whereas states still support 'capital' in many ways, 'the recommoditization of *labour*' is undergoing 'deregulation and privatization' (CL 8–9, see also 62). Education and healthcare, for example, are increasingly provided by private suppliers, and individuals themselves are responsibilised for rendering 'labour sellable', for instance by obtaining skills (CL 9, see also 57–9). Simultaneously, people are ever busier '*marketing*', '*promot[ing]*' themselves as '*commodities*' (CL 6). To 'become a subject', Bauman asserts, one must become 'a commodity', and to maintain one's 'subjectness', one must constantly revive 'the capacities expected and required of a sellable commodity' (CL 12).

Now, Bauman describes this '*transformation of consumers into commodities*' as the consumer society's primary characteristic (CL 12). This is not to say, however, that it outweighs the constitution of humans as consumers in characterising that society. Rather, the two are inseparable. For it is, in turn, precisely by consuming that people render themselves distinct 'from the mass of indistinguishable objects' and able to draw the attention of buyers (CL 12, see also 79). From Bauman's perspective, 'consumption' constitutes 'an investment' in articles that can influence one's '"social value" and self-esteem', an investment in one's '"saleability"' (CL 56–7). In fact,

[t]he crucial, perhaps the decisive purpose of consumption in the society of consumers ... is not the satisfaction of needs, desires and wants, but ... *raising the status of consumers to that of sellable commodities...*

It is by their potency to increase the consumer's market price that the attractiveness of consumer goods – the current or potential objects of consumers' desire triggering consumer action – tends to be evaluated. (CL 57)

Bauman specifies humanity's 'passage' into the consumer society as the 'colonization of life by the commodity market'; market 'laws' have become the 'precepts' of 'life' (CL 61–2). Humans turn to the market for the means they have to deploy 'in making themselves "fit for being consumed" – and so market-worthy'. Consumers consume consumer articles to accomplish a mission '"outsourced"' to private, 'individual' 'consumers', namely the consumers' own '"commoditization"' (CL 62). Competing with everyone else, they are supposed to strive for their 'optimal selling price', better 'ratings', or a superior ranking in some 'league table' (CL 62–3).

Living with Fear

Bauman considers the liquid life problematic not only due to individualisation and modernisation or due to the consumerist syndrome and commodification, but also, perhaps above all, because life in contemporary conditions involves suffering. He has already been shown to accentuate the non-satisfaction that characterises people's lives today. Yet Bauman is particularly concerned with the fears that pester people, describing the contemporary epoch as one 'of fears' (LF 2; see also Davis 2016: 51). Some beset specific groups, others everyone in the world (LF 20), and combating 'fears' has become 'a lifelong task' (LF 8). The 'dangers' fuelling them are now thought to accompany 'human life' constantly (LF 8). Fears can emanate from a range of objects and daily surroundings, from nature as well as fellow humans – both 'threatening' to wreck 'our bodies' and 'homes' (LF 4). Moreover, Bauman points to a fear-inducing sphere of simultaneously 'natural and human' calamities, of market debacles, of firms dissolving 'together with dozens of services … and thousands of jobs', of plane crashes etc. (LF 5). Contemporary 'fears', diagnoses Bauman, stir a 'feeling of impotence': people have virtually no notion of where their fears come from, do not know how to protect themselves against them, let alone 'preven[t]' or 'figh[t]' the 'dangers', and are unable even to envisage the necessary 'tools' and 'skills' (LF 20). '"Fear"' stands here for 'our *uncertainty*', not knowing what exactly 'the threat' is and what one should do about it (LF 2).

Existential tremors

Bauman's discussion of what he calls existential tremors contains key components of his multifaceted analysis of 'liquid modern fears' (LF 21). The variety of today's dangers notwithstanding, people's 'insecurity', Bauman holds, centres on the 'fear' of 'humans' doing harm (LF 131). Most people harbour the notion that other people are 'a source of existential insecurity'. This is unsurprising in contemporary society, especially, as people are compelled 'to pursue their own interests' and hence unlikely to count on much 'disinterested compassion and solidarity' from others (LF 132). Among the 'horrifying … fears' of today are those 'of being left behind', 'of *exclusion*' (LF 18). The British television shows *Big Brother* and *The Weakest Link* (LF 22–8), Bauman claims, are 'moral tales' for the inhabitants of the 'liquid modern world' (LF 28). They convey the 'truths' that individuals are threatened with social expulsion, but 'that blows hit at random', that causal connections between people's actions and what happens to them are extremely faint at best, and that hardly anything, if anything at all, can be done to 'stave off' the 'fate' of 'eviction' (LF 28, see also 18–19, 47; Blackshaw 2008: 129).[5] Such 'tales', Bauman states, instil 'fears' that come to 'penetrate and saturate the whole of life', to suffuse 'body and mind' (LF 28–9).

Individuals, elaborates Bauman, are indeed living in the 'presence of … [e]xistential tremors' (LF 133). He describes as 'shaky' the supposed underpinnings of 'life prospects', people's employment and employers, 'partners' and friendship 'networks', and social status and 'self-confidence'. '"Progress"' has come to mean 'the threat of relentless … change', whereby a moment's 'inattention' can lead to definitive 'exclusion' (LL 68, see also LF 3–4, 19–20, 139, 148; Blackshaw 2008: 128–9; Poder 2008: 105). However, crucially, the focus of contemporary 'fears' is shifting to 'areas of life' which, whilst reassuringly 'within sight and reach', are 'largely *irrelevant* to the genuine source of anxiety' (LF 133, see also 4).

Bauman places this shift of focus within a wider historical context:

> The long crusade against socially begotten and gestated terrors culmi-
> nated in collective, state-endorsed insurance against individually
> suffered misfortune (like unemployment, invalidity, disease or old
> age), and in collectively guaranteed provision, similarly countersigned
> by the state, of the amenities essential to individual self-formation and
> self-assertion, which was the substance, or at least the guiding objec-
> tive, of the social (misnamed as 'welfare') state. (LF 157)

Yet this 'social state' is pulling back. Few in contemporary politics reiterate
the 'promise', made in 1933 by US president Roosevelt, of an age in which
nothing but fear would need to be feared. People are once more pestered by
'fear of social degradation', ultimately 'of poverty and social exclusion' (LF
157, see also 1; Davis 2016: 92–3). Owing to the cutbacks in the social
state's collective efforts to insure individuals against 'misfortune', 'security'
is increasingly at the mercy of 'market' caprices and 'global forces' (LF 134).
People are having to try to solve 'socially produced' problems individually
through 'solitary actions', deploying their own private means, which cannot
but fall short. The 'messages' released by 'political power' create perspectives
of still further 'privatization of troubles' and thus still greater 'uncertainty',
rather than of 'collectively assured existential security'. They motivate people
to funnel their attention on their *safety* (LF 136, emphasis added; see also
Davis 2016: 67–9, 92–4). For Bauman, the latter term chiefly points to
'material, bodily ... aspects of security' (LF 138); by 'safety', he means 'shelter from ... threats to one's own person and its extensions' (LF 134), for
example, 'homes and their contents' (LF 138, see also 3, 158; Poder 2008:
105–6). Indeed, since individuals can neither decelerate the aforementioned
inexorable 'change' nor tell and determine where it is going, they concentrate
instead on what they 'can, or believe [they] can, ... influence'. They endeavour to spot '"the five symptoms of depression"', avoid 'cigarette smoke' and
direct sunlight, build a protective arsenal of CCTV, 'SUVs', and 'martial arts'
skills etc. (LL 68–9, see also LF 143; Davis 2016: 68, 161–5).[6] People aspire
to obtaining the means necessary to gain 'control' in this *safety* sphere, leaving other fear-emitting spheres – which could not be controlled through
individual efforts anyway – 'unattended' (LF 138–9). The actions upon those
life 'areas' onto which the focus of 'fears' is shifting are insufficient for deac-
tivating the 'genuine sources' of fears and allaying 'the original anxiety' (LF
133–4, see also 139).

Bauman specifies the curtailment of the function of the state in this context. Assessing globalisation, Richard Rorty notes: '"... the economic situation
of the citizens of nation states has passed beyond the control of the laws of
that state ..."'; '"... a global overclass ..."' now takes the key '"economic decisions ..."' independently '"of the legislatures ... of any given country ..."'
(cited in LF 146). Bauman includes 'extraterritorial capital', whose relationship

with labour was discussed above, together with 'its neoliberal acolytes' in that class (LF 147). He affirms:

> ... society is no longer adequately protected by the state; it is now exposed to the rapacity of forces the state does not control and no longer hopes or intends to recapture and subdue – not singly, not even in combination with several other similarly hapless states. (LF 147; see also Davis 2016: 51, 65–7)[7]

Much of the state's power is dissolving 'into global space', whilst much of the state's 'political acumen and dexterity' is being transferred to each person's '"life politics"'. The thus ever slimmer state is largely confined to operating as 'a *personal safety state*'. The latter's 'political formula' revolves increasingly around pledges 'to defend' individuals against 'the threat of a paedophile let loose, a serial killer, an obtrusive beggar, mugger, stalker, prowler, poisoner of water and food, terrorist ...'; it revolves ever less around the promise, made by the '*social state*' of the relatively recent past, to protect people from 'social degradation' (LF 148, see also 4, 158; Davis 2016: 51, 67–8).

Fear of death

Like in several *œuvres* engaging this book, in Bauman's writings the problem of life in contemporary society raises that of death. Bauman's sociological considerations of death predating *Liquid Modernity* are quite well known (see e.g. Tierney 1997: 56–62). The analysis of the fear of death in his later work retraces in an intriguing way the contours of the liquid social condition and the liquid life led within it.

The 'fear of death', asserts Bauman, is both humans' and animals' '"original fear"'. However, only the human being experiences also a '"secondary fear"' fuelled by the constant consciousness of the certainty of death, the 'knowledge' that eventually, inevitably, he or she will die (LF 30, see also 50). Death, an '*irreversible*' termination that issues into an unending 'absence', concretises the graspable 'meanings' of the notions of 'finality' and 'eternity' (LF 42, see also 29–30). The 'cultures' of humankind, in turn, constitute contrivances for rendering '*life with the awareness of mortality liveable*' (LF 31; see also Tierney 1997: 56–7).

Among several 'strategies' (LF 49, see also 31–9), Bauman lists the '*banalization*' of death (LF 39). The passing of somebody 'near and dear', with whom one had an '"I-Thou"' connection, who cannot be wholly 'replaced', creates a sense of the '*finality* and *irrevocability*' that all deaths revolve around (LF 43). In fact, argues Bauman, any severance of 'an interhuman bond', which involves losing 'a partner', the 'disappearance' of something special, bears 'a stamp of "finality"', allowing for an indirect 'death experience' (LF 44–5). In liquid modernity, crucially, interhuman ties are temporary and easily split (LF 44).[8] Thus, 'life' becomes 'a daily rehearsal of death ... performed by proxy', and indirect 'death experience' becomes a recurrent event. The radical other-ness distinguishing 'death experience' turns into a 'familiar' part of the everyday (LF 44). Upon every 'separation' follows the establishment of new 'bonds' (LF 45). The repeated '"metaphorical rehearsal" of death' *qua* '"irre-versible" end' is supposed to ensure that such terminations end up appearing 'revocable' to people (LF 49, see also 6). Incidentally, the above-mentioned TV 'tales' of eviction present comparable regular 'public rehearsals of death' with the purpose of 'banalizing the sight of dying' so as to render people immune to the fear of the end (LF 29). Yet ultimately, this deep-seated 'fear' will, in some 'form', remain a part of 'human life'[9] (LF 52). 'Threats', Bauman argues referring to Freud, come from different 'directions', but the 'destination' in each case is physical 'pain and suffering', that is, 'dress rehearsals' of death; and each of those 'sources' provides 'infinite supplies of fear' (LF 52–3).

CONCLUSION

For many years, Bauman's inquiries into contemporary social conditions revolved around the differences between solid and liquid modernity, which manifest themselves in a whole range of domains of society. Inextricable from those inquiries is the question of life in twenty-first-century society. Bauman formulates it as, *inter alia*, the questions of the liquid life, the con-suming life, and living with fear. Not least, it appears, because of the suffering and anxiety that continue to shape it, the human life of the present is a focal point of Bauman's work. In turn, these writings suggest that the liquid life cannot be understood separately from liquid social conditions – and thus that questions about human life today cannot but also be addressed to sociology.

Abbreviations

CL: *Consuming Life* (2007)

LF: *Liquid Fear* (2006)

LL: *Liquid Life* (2005)

LM: *Liquid Modernity* (2000)

Selected Further Reading

The following texts – a monograph and an edited volume – contain critical engagements with Bauman's work on liquid modernity, liquid life, and consumerism:

Davis, M. (2016) *Freedom and Consumerism: A Critique of Zygmunt Bauman's Sociology.* London: Routledge.

Jacobsen, M. H. and Poder, P. (eds) (2008) *The Sociology of Zygmunt Bauman: Challenges and Critique.* Aldershot: Ashgate.

For an engaging discussion of several themes raised in this chapter, see also Bauman, Z. (2003) *Liquid Love: On the Frailty of Human Bonds.* Cambridge: Polity Press.

Notes

1   Bauman does not unpack the term 'other-directed' in this context. He probably has in mind the difference between 'inner-directed' and 'other-directed' persons famously examined by David Riesman in *The Lonely Crowd* (1953).
2   For a discussion of Bauman's views on power, see for instance Campain (2008).
3   The ideal 'business organization' of the 'exterritorial elite', Bauman remarks with reference to Nigel Thrift, is now not 'solid' but 'fluid', so that it can always be quickly 'dismantled and reassembled' (LM 154).
4   According to Blackshaw, Bauman 'holds up a mirror to a culture whose stamp is the *market-mediated mode of life* …' (Blackshaw 2008: 117).
5   For a more detailed, critical discussion of Bauman's reading of the two TV programmes, see Davis (2016: 96–100, see also 69–70, 94, 168).
6   Bauman also comments on the 'commercial' aspects (LF 143–4, see also 7–8, LL 69–70).
7   Briefly, for Bauman 'globalization' has hitherto been completely '*negative*': a 'globalization' primarily 'of trade and capital' and of 'crime and terrorism, all now disdaining territorial sovereignty and respecting no state boundary' (LF 96), without a simultaneous 'globalization … of political and juridical institutions able to control them' (LF 135). See Davis (2016: 51, 65–71) for a discussion.
8   On this well-known argument of Bauman's, see above all his *Liquid Love* (2003; see also Davis 2016: 69–70, 163–5; Poder 2008: 106).
9   And it will, Bauman warns, continue to lend itself to being economically and politically 'manipulated and capitalized on' (LF 52).

6

Jean-François Lyotard: Living in Postmodernity

PART 1: SOCIETY AND THE GAMES OF LANGUAGE

The dimension of Jean-François Lyotard's *œuvre* that has had the deepest impact on sociology is doubtless his examination of postmodernity. In *The Postmodern Condition* from 1979, Lyotard notes that the term '*postmodern*' is used in sociology to capture present-day 'culture'. His famous book employs the term specifically to characterise 'the condition of knowledge', namely 'in the most highly developed societies' (PC xxiii; see also Malpas 2003: 15, 17; Williams 1998: 26). According to the 'working hypothesis' of *The Postmodern Condition*, 'the status of knowledge' is changing at a time when 'cultures' are arriving in the so-called 'postmodern', and 'societies' in the so-called 'postindustrial', era (PC 3; see also Malpas 2003: 18). Lyotard indicates in this context several reasons why *A Report on Knowledge* – the subtitle of that book – might have relevance for those seeking insight into contemporary social conditions (PC 3–6; Malpas 2003: 16–20). Importantly for the following discussion, Lyotard proposes that '[s]cientific knowledge is a kind of discourse' (PC 3), whilst a particular conception of language is indispensable to his conception of society.

Language Games

Outlining the 'Method' of his study, Lyotard refers to Ludwig Wittgenstein's investigations of 'language'. These concentrate 'on the effects of different modes of discourse' (PC 9–10; see Wittgenstein 1953: esp. § 23; see also

Malpas 2003: 20–2; Williams 1998: 27). Lyotard mentions the 'denotative' type of 'utterance' or 'statement' – his example being '"The university is sick …"' – as one illustration of what he has in mind. An utterance of this type has a 'sender' emitting it, an 'addressee … receiv[ing] it', and a 'referent'. It also has a series of effects. For instance, it puts 'the sender in the position of "knower"' and the recipient in that 'of having to give or refuse … assent' (PC 9). It is possible similarly to identify other 'kinds of utterances', including the 'declaration', the 'question', the 'promise', and many more, each with its own 'effects' (PC 9–10, see also 16, 20–1).

Crucially, Lyotard proposes to conceive of an 'utterance' or statement 'as a "move" in a game' (PC 10; see also Malpas 2003: 21–3; Williams 1998: 30). He adopts the concept of 'language-games' from Wittgenstein (1953: § 23). According to Lyotard, Wittgenstein seeks to articulate that every 'categor[y] of utterance' must be determinable by 'rules' that pinpoint its respective 'properties' as well as possible 'uses'. These 'rules', Lyotard makes explicit, 'define' a 'game'; the slightest change to a single 'rule' changes the whole 'game'; and any '"move" or utterance' contravening those 'rules' is not part of that 'game' (PC 10; see also Malpas 2003: 21–3; Williams 1998: 27–30, 35).

Language Games and Social Relations

Lyotard's approach draws vital inspiration from philosophy, but it is also strongly shaped by sociology (see also PC 16–17). This is unsurprising. One cannot, he holds, 'know' the present 'state of knowledge' whilst remaining ignorant about 'the society within which it is situated' (PC 13). In turn, before one can deal with 'knowledge' within current social conditions specifically, it is necessary to decide on a 'methodological representation' of these conditions (PC 11), on the way in which 'society' is interrogated and can respond (PC 13).

What Lyotard proposes for his own overall methodology are, precisely, 'language games' (PC 15). In his remarks on these games, he formulates as a clear 'principle' for his inquiries 'that the observable social bond is composed of language "moves"' (PC 10–11; see also Malpas 2003: 23). In slightly different terms, 'language games … combine to form the social bond' (PC 25). In his remarks on the latter, Lyotard stops short of asserting – albeit also of ruling out – that 'social relations' consist entirely of 'language games' (PC 15). He does, though, insist that such 'games' constitute 'the minimum relation' without which there can be no 'society' at all, and that in the present conditions 'language' is acquiring 'a new importance' (PC 15–16).

Lyotard – unlike Jean Baudrillard (1983) in his view – emphatically rejects the diagnosis of the current 'dissolution of the social bond and the disintegration of social aggregates [orig. *collectivités* (Lyotard 1979: 31)] into a mass of individual atoms …' (PC 15). For every 'self', so Lyotard argues, '… is always located at a post through which … messages pass'. In this sense, everyone is enmeshed 'in a fabric of relations …'. As also already indicated, 'the messages' crisscrossing that self put it in the position 'of sender, addressee, or referent'

(PC 15; see also Malpas 2003: 23, 29). Lyotard emphasises that every self has some 'powe[r] over' those 'messages'; it is possible for the self to shift 'in relation to these language game effects', in relation to the position in which one has been put (PC 15).

Lyotard's remarks on language games reveal that his approach is based on a further tenet, namely, 'to speak is to fight, in the sense of playing' (PC 10; see also Williams 1998: 30). To repeat, as 'messages' travel across somebody – that is, during every '"move"' that somehow concerns her or him – this person is 'displaced'; she or he is changed in one way or another with regard to the ability to send, receive, and be a 'referent' of, further messages. Such '"moves"', Lyotard states, underscoring this 'agonistic' quality of language games, will 'provoke "countermoves"'. The issue for the players in this moment is by which type of 'countermove' one can reshape 'the balance of power' once more (PC 16). Consistently with his ascription of a major role in the social world to language games, Lyotard's 'idea of an agonistics of language' (PC 10; see also Williams 1998: 30) finds its complement in his description of 'society' as 'the sum total [orig. *l'ensemble* (Lyotard 1979: 46)] of partners in the general agonistics' (PC 25, see also 10).

Lyotard has observed that in modernity 'language games' tend to take 'the form of institutions ...' (PF 25). A 'battle' such as a debate among 'friends' has 'rules' permitting maximum 'flexibility of utterance': the participants throw whatever they have – 'questions, requests, assertions' etc. – at each other. By contrast, every 'institution' needs 'constraints'. Within institutions, some 'things' must 'not be said', whilst others 'should be said', and in specific ways – for example, 'orders' in military or 'denotation' in educational institutions. However, Lyotard seeks to avoid a '"reifying" view of what is institutionalized' (PC 17). Reifying translates Lyotard's '"chosiste"' (1979: 35) here. In sociology, the term '*chosisme*', literally thingism, is sometimes (e.g. Adorno 2000: 77, 81, 106, 175n26) used to refer to Émile Durkheim's 'rule' of sociology '*to consider social facts as things*' (Durkheim 1982: 60). For Lyotard, any institutional restrictions 'on potential language "moves"' emerge themselves from 'language strategies'; far from final, they are 'provisional' and changeable (PC 17).

System and Division

Lyotard has also inspected other 'representational models for society' (PC 11), which, whilst he has not adopted them, play a role in his thinking. One of them is 'society' *qua* 'functional whole' (PC 11). This 'model' is illustrated by the sociology of Talcott Parsons (1970), for instance, for whom 'society' constitutes 'a self-regulating system' (PC 11). That said, and although Lyotard brands it 'technocratic' and 'cynical', German systems theory seems to be a more persistent reference point in his work, as will become clearer. Briefly, from this theoretical perspective society is a 'system' that aims primarily for 'performativity', that is, for the best overall 'output' to 'input' ratio. Alterations to 'rules', 'innovations', and 'dysfunctions', including 'political revolutions', all amount merely to 'an internal readjustment', leading to an improvement of 'the system's "viability."' (PC 11). What Lyotard finds in several bodies of thought, including Parsonian social theory and Niklas Luhmann's systems theory, is the notion of 'society' as 'a unified totality' (PC 12).

Contrary to these, Marxist thought offers another model, namely, society 'is divided in two' (PC 11). Here, as is well known, 'the principle' is that 'of class struggle' (PC 11, 12). Importantly for Lyotard's investigations, the 'decision' to conceptualise the social world in terms of the first model or the second determines how one can conceptualise the 'role' or 'function' of 'knowledge' within that world (PC 13).[1] Lyotard himself, though, as may be expected, advances his inquiry primarily in terms of language games instead.

The Language Game of Science

As mentioned, Lyotard examines scientific knowledge as a discourse. From his perspective, 'science' consists of 'statements'. These are understood as '"moves" made by ... players' according to 'rules' (PC 26). Sketching the language 'game' of 'scientific ... research', Lyotard specifies that what is subject to 'regulat[ion]' is what makes a 'statement' acceptable 'as "scientific."' For instance, a 'sender' is meant to state 'the truth about the referent', that is, to be capable of both proving what is being said and rebutting all 'statements' to the contrary. Simultaneously, an 'addressee' is supposed to be able 'to give (or refuse)' their agreement with the assertion 'validly', thus also being 'a potential sender' (PC 23).

'Scientific knowledge', Lyotard points out, demands the separation of the 'language game' of 'denotation' from 'all others', which are to be 'excluded'. In this respect, the sole 'criterion' for an utterance's 'acceptability' is its 'truth-value' (PC 25; see also Connor 1989: 29). Every 'statement' must remain 'verifiable' by 'argumentation and proof'. An 'accepted' statement is, of course, always disputable. Yet every 'new statement ... contradict[ing]' an already accepted utterance about 'the same referent' is itself only acceptable if it fulfils those conditions, that is, 'refutes' that utterance by dint of 'arguments and proofs' (PC 26).

Discursive Species

It must be emphasised that for Lyotard '[k]nowledge [*savoir*]' is more than just 'learning [*connaissance*]', and learning more than just 'science' (PC 18, see also 7). 'Learning' comprises only 'statements ... denot[ing] ... objects', which one can say to be 'true or false' (PC 18). A '"learned"' person is defined as someone capable of 'a true statement about a referent' (PC 25). 'Science' is even more specific, including only 'denotative statements' whose 'objects' one can 'access ... in explicit conditions of observation' and which one can identify as part or not part of a 'language' that 'experts' accept as 'relevant' (PC 18). A 'scientist' is someone capable of 'verifiable or falsifiable statements about referents accessible to the experts' (PC 25).

'Knowledge', however, instead of simply being equated with 'denotative statements', is associated with a 'competence'. Moreover, it amounts to a wide-ranging 'competence', rather than to one concerning a single type of utterance. It enables a person to produce '"good" denotative', 'prescriptive', 'evaluative', and other kinds of statements; it enables '"good" performances' regarding various 'objects of discourse', regarding those 'to be … decided on' or 'evaluated', but also those to be 'transformed' (PC 18). A '"good"' statement or 'performance' is one that meets certain 'criteria', for example, 'truth' or 'efficiency' (PC 19).

Lyotard draws a thorough distinction between, for instance, 'science' and 'narrative knowledge' (PC 25), which, he claims, have been in perpetual 'conflict' (PC 7, see also xxiii). This well-known distinction cannot be revisited here (see PC 19–23, 25–7; Connor 1989: 28–30; Malpas 2003: 20–1, 24–5; Williams 1998: 30). It is important to bear in mind, though, that, for Lyotard, the 'existence' of 'nonscientific (narrative) knowledge' is just as 'necessary' as that of scientific knowledge. Each consists of 'statements' *qua* '"moves" … by … players within … rules'. But the very 'rules' of scientific differ from those of narrative knowledge. The '"moves"' considered '"good"' in the latter are of a different kind to moves deemed '"good"' in the former. One can neither 'judge' the former's 'validity' in terms of the latter nor the latter's in terms of the former (PC 26, see also xxiii; Williams 1998: 30). One can only 'gaze in wonderment at the diversity of discursive species …' (PC 26; see also Connor 1989: 34).

Dispersal and Heteromorphy

An important attribute of 'science', explains Lyotard, is that it must provide 'legitimation' for 'the rules' that regulate the scientific 'game' (PC xxiii, see also 18, 27–31; Connor 1989: 28–30). In the Western world, 'legitimacy' is itself 'a referent' for 'inquiry' (PC 23). Consistently with earlier considerations, Lyotard argues that what applies to the language game applies to social relations: 'the institutions governing the social bond … must be legitimated as well' (PC xxiv). Through 'legitimation' as Lyotard understands it 'a legislator' is given the authority to proclaim 'a law' – a law which demands that certain 'citizens' act in a particular way. In his work, though, 'legitimation' simultaneously means that someone is given the authority to state a 'rule' concerning utterances – 'to prescribe' specific 'conditions' of the sort already mentioned, for instance 'experimental verification', which 'a statement must fulfill' so that it is considered 'scientific' (PC 8; see also Williams 1998: 31).

Lyotard designates a 'science' as *modern* if it gives itself legitimacy in terms of 'a metadiscourse' that draws on a 'grand narrative' (PC xxiii; see also Malpas 2003: 24–5; Williams 1998: 27). He proceeds to detail 'a narrative of emancipation' and 'a speculative narrative' (PC 37), a 'more political' and a 'more philosophical' variant, which have been especially prominent in modernity (PC 31; see e.g. Connor 1989: 30–1; Malpas 2003: 24–7; Williams 1998: 32–3). What is more important for this discussion, though, is his diagnosis that in today's 'postindustrial society' and 'postmodern culture' both variants of the 'grand narrative' (PC 37) are met with 'incredulity' (PC xxiv; see also Connor 1989: 8–9, 31; Malpas 2003: 16, 24, 27–8; Williams 1998: 27–8, 32–5, 83). Notably, examining the difficulties accompanying certain 'legitimation' efforts leads to a recognition that scientific 'discourse' is 'a language game with its own rules', but without any 'special calling' to regulate any other 'game', such as the practical or aesthetic games. 'The game of science is ... put on a par with ... others'. Here, too, Lyotard simultaneously keeps a close eye on the social world. In further course, as 'language games' disperse, the 'social subject itself seems to dissolve'. Lyotard reiterates the 'linguistic' quality of the 'social bond'. Yet, crucially, this bond constitutes a weave in which 'an indeterminate number ... of language games', each following its own distinct 'rules', cross (PC 40; see also Connor 1989: 9, 31–2, 34; Malpas 2003: 29; Williams 1998: 5, 27–35, 62, 69–70, 79–83, 103–5).

These considerations are decisive for Lyotard's characterisation of postmodernity. He is unconvinced, namely, that one can define rules shared by 'all ... language games'. He doubts that a consensus – even 'a revisable consensus' – might comprise all the rules 'regulating' all the 'statements circulating in the social collectivity', that 'all speakers' reach a consensus on a set of 'rules ... valid for all language games' (PC 65, trsl. modified; see also Connor 1989: 34; Williams 1998: 27–8, 32–5, 83). Societies, writes Lyotard, comprise 'vast clouds of language material' (PC 64, see also xxiv). But their 'pragmatics' consist of an imbrication of 'networks of ... classes' of statements – 'denotative' ones, 'prescriptive' ones, 'evaluative' ones etc. – of different forms. For Lyotard, it is vital to recognise 'that language games are heteromorphous' and 'subject to heterogeneous ... rules' (PC 65, see also WIP 72–3; Connor 1989: 32, 34, 37–8; Malpas 2003: 21–2, 30; Williams 1998: 5, 27–35, 62, 69–70, 79–83, 103–5). A major issue in his discussion of postmodernity is how these conditions are and should be responded to, respectively.

The System's Decision Makers

Lyotard is critical of the response of today's 'decision makers' (PC xxiv). 'The ruling class', he points out, is, now and for the time being, that of the 'decision makers'. It has come to consist of 'corporate leaders, high-level administrators ... heads of the major professional ... organizations', and others, in place of 'the traditional political class' (PC 14). Crucially, the 'decision makers' are trying to administer the 'clouds of sociality' described above in accordance with 'a logic ... of maximum performance'. This logic 'implies that their elements are commensurable' (PC xxiv). A 'terror' is exercised to ensure that 'language games' take the same form (PC 66). The decision makers' endeavour is 'to manage' the social world in 'input/output matrices'. Ultimately, 'all … games' are meant to answer to the standard of 'efficiency', which is to say, of 'optimizing the system's performance' (PC xxiv; see also Connor 1989: 32–3; Malpas 2003: 28, 30; Palumbo-Liu 2000: 202, 213n6; Williams 1998: 126–7).

The resonances with Lyotard's already mentioned reading of Luhmann's theory of society as a system are clear. An important point of Luhmann's, Lyotard adds, is that this 'system' needs to arrange for people's different 'aspirations' (PC 61) – or *expectations* (Lyotard 1979: 99, orig. English) – to be adjusted to the system's 'ends' (PC 61, see also 64). 'Administrative procedures', Luhmann is said to argue, can 'make individuals "want" what the system needs' for its own performativity (PC 62). Lyotard finds similar conceptions in the sociological works of David Riesman (1953) and Herbert Marcuse (2002), for example. What he appears to have in mind is the former's conception of the other-directed character and the latter's critique of the creation of false needs.

Inventions

Lyotard further develops his own perspective on the contemporary social world with reference to scientific research. According to Lyotard, striving for 'proof' is a pursuit of something 'unintelligible', striving for 'an argument' a quest 'for a "paradox"' and the creation of 'new rules' of the 'reasoning' game (PC 54; see also Connor 1989: 33–4). Each 'new statement', 'observation', or 'theory' unfailingly raises 'the question of legitimacy'. What is conspicuous about 'postmodern scientific knowledge', Lyotard maintains, is that it contains 'the discourse on the rules that validate it' within itself (PC 54). What is important is that this 'science … suggests a model of legitimation' which is not that of the best 'performance', but rather that of 'difference' in the sense of 'paralogy' (PC 60; see also Malpas 2003: 31).

Lyotard reiterates two points in this context: scientific 'pragmatics' involves chiefly 'denotative' statements, and discussing these requires 'rules' – in other words, 'metaprescriptive' statements of the sort that determine 'moves' acceptable within 'language games' (PC 65). He concedes that debates about those rules enter a 'state' of 'consensus' (PC 65, see also 63; Williams 1998: 30). Crucially, though, consensus is not the 'end' of such debates; 'paralogy' is (PC 65–6). 'Paralogy' is understood as one – decisive – type of 'move … in the pragmatics of knowledge'. Eventually, namely, a player will appear who disrupts 'the order of "reason"'. Lyotard assumes 'a power that destabilizes the capacity for explanation'. This power is behind each 'proposal of new rules of the scientific language game …' (PC 61, trsl. modified, see also 63; Connor 1989: 33–4, 40–2; Malpas 2003: 31). In scientific 'pragmatics', Lyotard explains, a 'statement' is to be held on to as soon as it, on the one hand, contains something that diverges from the 'known' and, on the other, can be argued and proven. This 'differential or imaginative or paralogical activity' makes the 'metaprescriptives', the prevalent scientific '"presuppositions"',

come to the fore and demands that the partners 'accept different ones' (PC
64–5; see also Connor 1989: 33–4; Malpas 2003: 30–3). This 'will generate
ideas', generate 'new statements' (PC 65, see also 64) – 'dissension' gives rise
to 'invention', says Lyotard (PC xxv; see also Connor 1989: 34, 39) – and that
constitutes the sole 'legitimation' capable of rendering such a demand permis-
sible (PC 65, see also 64).

On the basis of his insights, Lyotard comes to espouse a mode of thinking about the social world that is characterised by a clear set of components:
the acknowledgement that 'language games' have different forms and the
diagnosis of the diversity of these games' rules, as outlined earlier; and the
twofold 'principle that any consensus on the rules defining a game … *must*
be local', that is, reached only by the particular game's current 'players', as
well as temporary, that is, open to dissolution (PC 66; see also Connor 1989:
32, 34, 37–8; Malpas 2003: 30, 32; Williams 1998: 5, 27–35, 62, 69–70,
79–83, 103–5). Lyotard notes that such thinking is in tune with current
developments in 'social interaction': in various 'domains', including, for
instance, the 'international' sphere, politics, the world of work, or the 'family', 'permanent institutions' are being replaced by 'the temporary contract'
(PC 66). Simultaneously, it jars with the thinking of the decision makers of
the system.

PART 2: LIVING IN THE SYSTEM

The Postmodern Condition does not thematise life in postmodernity elaborately or very explicitly. Of note, though, '*knowledge*' as the wide-ranging
'competence' as which Lyotard has been shown to frame it in that book
comprises, *inter alia*, '"knowing how to live …" … [… *savoir-vivre* …]' (PC
18). A later, much less famous book of Lyotard's on postmodernity, a collection of 'notes' (PF vii) from the late 1980s and early 1990s entitled
Postmodern Fables (PF)[2] (originally *Moralités Postmodernes* (1993)), does
pose key 'questions' about the problem at the centre of that knowledge
domain: 'how to live, and why?' (PF vii). In the present conditions, a vital
question for those engaged in critical thinking and writing, *Postmodern
Fables* seems to suggest, is how to live without solely or chiefly serving the
system's improvement. The 'moral [orig. *moralité* (1993: 11)]' at the end of
a 'fable', Lyotard points out, 'draws' from it a local and temporary 'bit of
wisdom' (PF vii; see also Palumbo-Liu 2000: 204–5). Several of Lyotard's
considerations have been inspired by his encounters in his own life as a
thinker and writer as well as by his reception of works of art. There are, of
course, differences between 'fables' and 'science' (PC 27, see also xxiii). But
'scientific knowledge' is not all there is to 'knowledge [orig. *savoir* (1979:
18)]' (PC 7, see also 18; Palumbo-Liu 2000: 205). 'The answers' to the questions posed, Lyotard admits, 'are deferred' (PF vii). What he doubts is that
'we know' what appears to be known today, namely 'that life is going every

which way'. Instead, this is what people 'represent ... to' themselves. One can currently observe '[e]very which way of life' being 'flaunted' and 'enjoyed' – but, specifies Lyotard, they are flaunted and enjoyed 'for the love of [orig. *en amateur de* (1993: 11)] variety' (PF vii). The system itself, as will become clearer, promotes variety, yet inside a range delimited by rules. Lyotard's considerations point to what might be recalcitrant against the pressures of the system.

The System and Exploitation

If one turns to the 13th piece in *Postmodern Fables*, 'The intimacy of terror' from 1993,[3] for further clues about what Lyotard means by the system, one appears at first sight to be offered little: 'the system', he writes, '... is quite simply called the system' (PF 199). In fact, here and throughout the book Lyotard goes on to accentuate – albeit partly in terms familiar from *The Postmodern Condition* – properties of this system that the earlier, more widely known study does not illuminate particularly strongly.

Lyotard's notion of the system is not identical with a reiteration of Marx's theory of capitalist society. However, his references in more than one of the pieces in *Postmodern Fables* to Marx's conception of labour power, for instance, do reveal important aspects of the orientation of the system Lyotard has in mind. In 'Interesting?', Lyotard presents a dialogue between a woman, SHE, and a man, HE. The latter squarely equates 'what we are calling the system' with 'capitalism' (PF 63). It may revolve chiefly around 'seizing upon what one doesn't have, and making it "(sur)render."', HE suggests (PF 63). As Lyotard puts it in 'Unbeknownst', the 12th piece, and in more widely familiar terminology, Marx argues that 'the capitalist organization of being together' entails 'the exploitation of labor power' (PF 191). According to Marx's critique of capitalism, as is well known, the capitalist pays the worker a daily wage equal to the value of what is required for replenishing labour power for another day. The worker provides the capitalist with labour power for a day (Marx 1990: 270–93). The upshot of 'the capitalist organization' of social life as Marx understands it, writes Lyotard, is a 'sacrifice of pure creative power' (PF 191). For Marx holds that the capitalist's 'usage' of the labour power purchased yields 'more value than it consumes' (PF 64). That is to say, labour power 'consum[es] *less* energy (less value) than it produces as it goes into ... productive action ... , as it goes to work ...' (PF 191). In Marx's critical analysis, '[c]apital', Lyotard reasserts, 'deprive[s] the proletariat of the use of [labor] force', which is all the proletariat owns, with the purpose of acquiring 'the fruits of its strange power: creating more value than it consumes' (PF 72). This, adds Lyotard, constitutes '[a]n eminent case of "good productivity" ...' (PF 72) – in other words, greater output than input as a clear instance of good performativity, the principle of which has been said to guide the system as such.

The System's Openness

And yet, for Lyotard class struggle no longer poses as great a threat to the system as one might have once thought, and the political potential of social critique, too, needs to be carefully reconsidered. Lyotard clarifies this, in part at least, in his reflections in the fifth piece of *Postmodern Fables*. Here, he addresses the transformations that have shaped 'the historical situation' generally and the kind of critical endeavour he himself has been participating in specifically (PF 68). Lyotard begins by looking back on his time at *Socialisme ou barbarie* (*Socialism or Barbarism*), which he retrospectively describes as a 'sort of "Institute" of critical theory and practice' (PF 67, see also PC 13, 89n46; Palumbo-Liu 2000: 206). During the 1950s and 1960s, Lyotard recalls, he and his fellow members were working on a 'critical analysis of "late capitalism"', but also 'of supposedly "communist" society' (PF 71). The 'strategy' they were following was one of 'offense' (PF 69). They were engaged in 'situation analysis'. This involved examining 'events' perceived as crucial to 'the historical context at that time' for the purpose of attempting to grasp 'the contemporary world and its development'. Simultaneously, however, these inquiries were inextricable from 'a practical project' (PF 67). The aim that he and his colleagues were pursuing, Lyotard accentuates, was to find out through which 'intervention' they could 'help those subject to exploitation and alienation emancipate themselves' (PF 68). In this context, '[e]mancipation' meant nothing less than 'an alternative to reality' *tout court* (PF 69).

The 'interventions' put forward nowadays, argues Lyotard, are, by contrast, confined to the word: to 'petitions', 'texts', 'conferences', 'books', etc. Moreover, today's 'strategy' revolves around 'defense':

> We must constantly reaffirm the rights of minorities, women, children, gays, the South, the Third World, the poor, the rights of citizenship, the right to culture and education, the rights of animals and the environment, and I'll skip over the rest.

Importantly here, the 'rules' of what it is to be 'an intellectual' in the present day allow for and promote such activities (PF 68–9; see also Palumbo-Liu 2000: 202–3). 'Emancipation' understood in a particular way, Lyotard explains, has become something 'the system' itself tries to achieve, namely within certain of its discrete – for instance, the familial, sexual, racial, or educational – 'sectors' (PF 69).

Lyotard recognises that 'the system' encounters 'resistance' and 'obstacles' in this regard. Yet he maintains that they lead it to foster 'new enterprises' and 'become … more open' (PF 69). Its operations nowadays include '*venture programs*' (PF 70, orig. English, see PF 3n1), which, more exploratory in their orientation, will increase its 'complexity and make room for more "flexible" institutions' (PF 70). Incidentally, this development seems to come as no surprise to Lyotard. Conducting his reflections in the autumn of 1990 (PF 74),

he reads the end of twentieth-century Central and Eastern European communism as the most recent demonstration of the tendency of any 'system' that
is 'more "open"' to be 'more performative' and of the proneness of any system
that 'closes in on itself' either to fall victim to 'competitors' or to die of 'entropy'
(PF 80). What appears to him to determine a system's success in its contest with
others – a 'competition' to be inspected more closely in a moment – is that
'openness', that is, 'the "free play"' it protects in its 'mode of functioning' (PF
80). It is emancipation in this sense that is at issue here. To come back to the
situation of the intellectual, it is assumed, Lyotard reiterates, that such 'emancipation' has become the responsibility 'of the system itself'. The latter
appears to have considerable appetite for 'critiques'. Indeed, what critics
critically identify is 'every failure of the system with regard to emancipation'.
Thus, encouraging criticism helps the system meet its responsibility of emancipation (PF 70). Even 'before speaking or acting', and no matter what their
'intervention' is, his fellow thinkers and writers of today, suggests Lyotard,
are as aware as he is 'that it will be taken into account by the system as a
possible contribution to its perfection' (PF 204, see also PC 13; Palumbo-Liu
2000: 202–3, 213n7).

Lyotard draws further insight into the contemporary situation of political critique from two visits to the German Democratic Republic shortly
before and shortly after the fall of the Berlin Wall. He reports that during his
travels he encountered 'East German intellectuals ... concerned about ...
elaborating a position' that might make it possible to criticise not only the
'totalitarianism' of Central and Eastern Europe but also 'Western liberalism'
(PF 71). In the month of the reunification of Germany less than a year after
that momentous night in November 1989, Lyotard notes the difficulty of
envisaging how the sort of 'radical critique' that his 'East German colleagues'
called for might be accomplished. Cornelius Castoriadis and Claude Lefort,
founders of the *Socialisme ou barbarie* group with which Lyotard was once
associated, have demonstrated that 'criticism' needs 'an open social and mental space'. Yet today it is precisely 'the system' itself that, requiring such an
open space, 'alone ... guarantees' it (PF 74).

Intertwined with these considerations are Lyotard's own thinly disguised
doubts about certain strands of the politics of the left today. What Marxism
was once concerned with, he argues, was a diversity of 'working classes' – in
other words, of 'communities of laborers' enchained in 'capitalist relations'.
The objective of Marxism was the transformation of these classes into one
'proletariat', namely into one 'collective subject' that would be 'emanci-
pated', 'conscious and autonomous'. As such, this subject was meant to be
'capable of emancipating all of humanity' (PF 72). However, in place of what
was once an 'international workers' movement', Lyotard now identifies 'local
institutions'. The purpose of each of these is not the transformation of different groups of workers into one collective subject, but 'defending the
interests of this or that category of laborers'. 'Class struggles' of this sort do
'put up a resistance to the development of the system', Lyotard concedes

(PF 73). Yet this resistance is again to be understood in the sense of the afore-mentioned 'obstacles', which the system requires so as 'to improve its performance' in the manner already indicated (PF 73, see also PC 13).

The System of Competition

These observations notwithstanding, the system's permissiveness should not be overestimated. *The Postmodern Condition*, as mentioned, emphasises the importance to the system of commensurability. 'The intimacy of terror' in *Postmodern Fables* underscores the importance of 'competition' as a further key property of the system (PF 199, though see also PC 48). Competition, Lyotard claims here, is the system's only 'means'. The system cannot allow 'peace'. Not only does it accept 'multiculturalism', but the system also 'arouses disparities', even 'solicits divergences' (PF 199; see also Connor 1989: 40–1; Goux and Wood 1998: 3–4). And yet his argument does not deviate dramatically from his earlier point in *The Postmodern Condition*. For the system, Lyotard specifies, does so only to the extent that there is 'consensus' – in other words 'agreement' about 'the rules of disagreement'. They state which 'elements' and 'operations' are 'permitted'; complete 'freedom of strategy' reigns inside these boundaries (PF 199–200; see also Goux and Wood 1998: 3–4; Palumbo-Liu 2000: 200–2, 206).

Correspondingly, the system uses competition for a twofold purpose. On the one hand, through a 'competition' in which all 'operations' remain inside a range defined by a given set of rules, the system 'guarantees security'. Its 'constitution' is not open 'to radical upheaval' (PF 199–200). On the other hand, through competition the system ensures 'development'. From competition emerge 'winning strategies', which it can then 'integrat[e]'. Thus, the 'constitution of the system' can always undergo 'revision' (PF 199–200, see also PC 15; Palumbo-Liu 2000: 201–2).

Lyotard, as already indicated above, and to add this only briefly, deploys the concept of competition also to characterise a different level of the contemporary condition. The 'authority' of the current arrangement of 'the world', he argues, is supported by the widespread acceptance of a 'fact'. Humans, it is said, have been experimenting with various 'communitarian organizations' for thousands of years. A 'competition' is thought to have been in operation for just as long – here, namely, as the engine of a 'natural selection ... of the best performing' form of organisation as such (PF 201). The past hundred years or so specifically have witnessed the endeavours of different 'regimes' to enforce 'fascism, nazism, communism' as 'modes of community organization' (PF 70). Yet the latter were 'eliminated from the competition' (PF 70), whereas 'capitalist democracy', going by the 'name of system', is understood to have come out on top (PF 201). In Lyotard's use of the term, 'the system' means 'a triumphant liberal, imperialist capitalism' (Goux and Wood 1998: 4; see also PF 199). Capitalist democracy's 'superiority' is not disputed anymore (PF 201).

The System's Rules

In Lyotard's experience, the pressure on critics to restrain their moves can, in fact, be considerable. He maintains that this 'world in which we live' contains much still to 'be said[,] ... done, and ... proposed' (PF 203). He has even compiled a list – incomplete to boot, by his own admission – of issues requiring discussion and resolution. Several of its items – 'the status of immigrants and refugees', for instance, or 'the protection of minority cultures', or 'help for the sick and the old', or 'the right of women over their own bodies' (PF 202) – remain just as pressing two decades into the twenty-first century. Many who, like him, are engaged in thinking and writing, Lyotard continues, collaborate with one or another 'association' striving to help in solving 'difficulties' of that kind, contribute to 'debates', and even enter into 'combats' (PF 203). Crucially, though, issues such as those he has identified are to be tackled within 'the rules of the game, in consensus with the system' (PF 202).

That is to say, any 'attention' paid to 'thought and writing' today is attached to certain prerequisites (PF 204). Lyotard reads a 1980 piece by the historian Pierre Nora, which appears to have left a deep impression on him, as both a complaint about the works of certain French intellectuals and an assertion of certain of those prerequisites (PF 204–6, WIP 71). The objection, Lyotard recalls, was that different 'groups' – or rather 'sect[s]' – of intellectuals were engaged in 'a war of words', but without any effort 'to make themselves understood by each other or ... the public' (PF 205). What was being precluded 'in French criticism and philosophy', so the diagnosis went, was 'debate' (PF 204). The corresponding proposition, reports Lyotard – without naming Nora, but doubtless referring to him – in his essay from 1982 'Answering the question: What is postmodernism?', was to 'impos[e] on the intellectuals a common way of speaking' (WIP 71). This would enable the regeneration of 'the conditions for a fruitful exchange' (WIP 71). It was a request 'for some communicational consensus ... and a general code of exchanges ...' (WIP 73, see also PF 215). The current 'anarchy' was supposed to be turned into 'order', the intellectuals' 'domestic squabbles' domesticated under a Roman Peace (PF 205). Much, notes Lyotard, has indeed been done with the aim of enforcing 'dialogue and argument' among those 'aggressive and confused scriveners' (PF 205). In his view, Nora's proposition contains one of a host of recent demands that 'experimentation, in the arts and elsewhere', be terminated (WIP 71, see also 73). The 'color of the times', Lyotard observes, is 'slackening' accordingly (WIP 71).

The Marketplace of Singularities

Lyotard provides yet another perspective on the system's particular tolerance of variety in the first piece of *Postmodern Fables*. There, he tells of Marie, a Frenchwoman who has travelled to Japan to give a lecture and a seminar (PF 3–4, 10, 13). Marie relates her encounters and begins to reflect on her situation more widely. She has observed that, whereas Immanuel Kant encouraged people to 'think for yourself',[4] nowadays doing so is considered 'not *politically correct*'. All 'streams ... must converge', and the myriad 'colloquia, interviews, seminars' are merely to assure everyone that all are 'saying the same thing'. What is on all 'lips', highlights Marie, is 'alterity, multiculturalism' (PF 6, *politically correct* orig. English, see PF 3n1; see also Palumbo-Liu 2000: 207). 'If you are a woman, and Irish, and still presentable, and some kind of professor in Brazil, and a lesbian, and writing non-academic books, then ... [c]ultural capital is interested in you' (PF 6). Marie holds – her contention being quite similar to Bauman's aforementioned problematisation of individuality – that this constitutes a demand on everyone equally. Everyone should 'express' their respective 'singularity' (PF 7).

What appears decisive, namely, is that 'cultural capitalism has found ... the marketplace of singularities' (PF 7; see also Connor 1989: 40–1; Palumbo-Liu 2000: 200–2, 205–7). Marie describes herself as a 'little stream' of '*cultural capital*' (PF 3, *cultural capital* orig. English, see PF 3n1, see also PF 4). She is someone 'they buy culture from' (PF 3). Simultaneously, Marie describes herself as a 'cultural labor force they can exploit' (PF 3), and who – like the exploited labourer in Marx's critique of political economy (e.g. Marx 1990: 270–80) but also, for instance, in Adorno's more recent sociology (e.g. Adorno 2008: 96–9) – has signed a 'contract' to this effect (PF 3). She is, she says, a 'wage earner' as much as a 'craftsperson' (PF 3). With a vague echo of Horkheimer and Adorno's (2002: 94–136) famous concept, Marie notes that 'the culture industry' of the late nineteenth century, which was centred on the production and sale of standardised artefacts, left 'no future' for 'minorities' and 'singularities'. Yet customers have become dissatisfied with 'snacking always on the same images, the same ideas at the cultural fast-food outlets' (PF 11; see also Palumbo-Liu 2000: 200–2, 207). Marie's own challenge is to come up with ever novel 'product[s]': 'to invent, read, imagine' (PF 3, see also 9, 12). The crux nowadays is that 'new energy is always available' as well as 'manageable'; 'multiculturalism' has de facto become 'profitable' (PF 10–11; see also Connor 1989: 40–1).

According to Marie, 'all the streams' are to enter – all 'singularities to enrich' – 'the museum' (PF 7). The achievements of the past, from the Lascaux caves to the Maginot Line to the writings of Agatha Christie, have already been 'stored'. The task today is to do the same with all things 'contemporary', the 'great works', of course, but also 'the ways of living' of the present, 'the means of preparing fish', current 'slangs', and so forth (PF 8). Marie knows that her lecture, too, will be heard with the question if her work is 'worth preserving' in mind (PF 9). Again, what is under consideration here is '[c]ultural capital'; what she is witnessing, Marie is convinced, is 'the capitalization of all cultures in the cultural bank' (PF 8). Marie insists on her identification of 'cultural institutions' with 'banks' proper in that the former are 'laboratories' rather than mere 'repositories': their 'managers' have to 'put' the items stored in these institutions 'to work', for instance, to exhibit, examine, or restore them (PF 9–10), much like banks are expected not merely to hold on to, but to do something with, the capital entrusted to them.

The Question of Resistance

Yet Lyotard also offers perspectives on recalcitrance against such conditions. This recalcitrance can be noticed particularly, though by no means exclusively, in the sphere of art. In response to the question of what postmodernism is, Lyotard calls 'postmodern ... that which ... puts forward the unpresentable' (WIP 81; see also Connor 1989: 212; Malpas 2003: 49–50). Drawing on Kant's work, he sketches the situation where 'the imagination fails to present an object which might ... come to match a concept'. He illustrates this situation by noting that people harbour an 'Idea of the world ...' as 'totality of what is' yet no one can 'show an example of it' (WIP 78; see also Malpas 2003: 46–7; Williams 1998: 21–3, 88). Lyotard locates 'the postmodern' inside 'the modern'. The objective of 'modern painting', for instance, is '[t]o make visible that there is something which can be conceived' but not 'seen' or 'made visible' (WIP 78–9; see also Malpas 2003: 45–50).

'The postmodern' can nonetheless be distinguished. Lyotard specifies it as 'that which ... puts forward the unpresentable *in presentation itself* ...'. Vital to the postmodern, in other words, is the quest 'for new presentations' so as to create 'a stronger sense of the unpresentable' (WIP 81, emphasis added; see also Connor 1989: 212; Malpas 2003: 47–50; Williams 1998: 23, 108–13). The 'postmodern artist or writer', says Lyotard, '... are working without rules ...'. The product of their work, like that of a philosopher's work, is 'not in principle governed by ... rules' that have already been set. Nor can one 'judg[e] ...' such works 'by applying' to them 'categories' that are already known. Rather, the piece of art or writing is still in the process of 'looking for' the 'rules' that might respectively govern it (WIP 81; see also Malpas 2003: 45–50; Williams 1998: 22–3, 109–13). Lyotard identifies a similar process in the realm of 'knowledge', where '"progress"' can mean either 'a new move' in a language game and merely inside 'the established rules' or an 'invention of new rules', which entails 'a change to a new game' (PC 43, see also 53). This demarcation of the truly postmodern is vital for the question of recalcitrance.

In 'The intimacy of terror', Lyotard proceeds to question whether certain works of philosophy, literature, art, and music – Edmund Husserl's phenomenology, Franz Kafka's *The Castle*, Pablo Picasso's *Young Ladies of Avignon*, or Pierre Boulez's *Répons*, to name a few – can ever be a subject matter for 'debate' (PF 206). These 'works', he notes, are not products of 'the system'. What is decisive is that they bear a 'solitude', a 'retreat', and an 'excess beyond all possible discourse'. A certain 'measurelessness' distinguishes them (PF 206–7). As 'cultural objects' such works are relatively 'accessible to the community', yet they cannot be reduced to the existing 'usages or mentalities' of that community (PF 207). Echoing *The Postmodern Condition*'s thematisation of science, Lyotard adds that the emergence of science's 'inventions' is just as 'wondrous' – namely inexplicable through, and frequently 'resisted by', their contemporaneous 'state of knowledge' (PF 207). Marie, to return to her fable briefly, is aware that the lecture she is about to give to her audience in Japan will not be understood. She is also aware that what would be demanded of her is clarity, and clarity would mean contextualisation of what she is saying in relation to already existing and known works (PF 6).

Here, though, Lyotard's focus remains on art. In a famous note by Charles Baudelaire,[5] Lyotard makes out '[p]oetic hysteria' as it 'confesses' to '… cultivat[ing] its retreat with joy and terror' (PF 209). Art, literature, but also thinking, Lyotard explains, 'hysterically cultivate' a relationship with an 'inhuman stranger' that resides inside the person. Indeed, it is necessary to 'trace' that relationship in 'colors, sounds' or 'words' (PF 214). Those engaged in 'writing, painting, or composing' will work with '[w]ords, sounds, colors', which are, emphasises Lyotard, always 'already organized by the rhetorics' that have been 'inherited', and which will have a certain 'eloquence' (PF 215). In the tracing of that relationship with the inner stranger, in turn, words, sounds, and colours are to be brought 'back to *their* silence' (PF 214). 'Poetic hysteria', asserts Lyotard referring to Baudelaire again, promptly terminates 'the circuit of repetitions' (PF 209, see also 215). Thus emerge instances of genuine recalcitrance against the demand for commensurability and also against the demand for mere variety within a range delimited by given rules.

This issue also surfaces from the above-mentioned dialogue on 'the interesting' between the unnamed woman and the unnamed man, which Lyotard presents in the fourth of the *Postmodern Fables* (PF 49). Towards the end of the exchange, the question what 'the interesting' might be for an 'artist', a 'scholar', or an 'engineer' is raised (PF 60). Referring, as does *The Postmodern Condition* on several occasions, to Wittgenstein, SHE describes a situation in which a person in receipt of 'some tennis balls and … rules about how to play with them' encounters another person who is also playing with tennis balls. Instead of playing tennis, however, the latter handles them in a manner the former fails to comprehend (PF 62). She claims that 'data', the 'given', from 'physical effects' to 'cosmic phenomena' to 'the color of a landscape' and so forth, are similarly encountered as though they were 'signs', but 'in an unknown language' (PF 61). Finally, SHE points to 'something or someone' within herself 'who is … speaking', but in a 'language' different to hers (PF 62).

In what seems like a direct response to the question Lyotard poses in the *Fables'* 'Preface' – to its first part, 'how to live … ?', anyway (PF vii) – SHE urges that the person encountering another who handles tennis balls in an incomprehensible fashion nonetheless absolutely not 'stop playing with' the latter (PF 62). Nor, SHE holds, can the 'clandestine host' within her 'be ignored'. Rather, her advice for each situation is: first, to posit 'a hypothesis about that other language' and about its rules; and, second, to experiment with – indeed 'to invent' – 'responses' in accordance with those 'supposed rules' and with the other's 'enigmatic messages' (PF 62). Again, great artworks serve as illustrations. Paul Cézanne, SHE argues, has 'com[e] to "speak" Mount Sainte-Victoire in little chromatic strokes' (PF 62–3). What the 'interesting' is, in her view and, so she appears to claim, from the viewpoint of artists, scholars, and engineers, 'is to try to speak the language of another that you don't understand' (PF 61, see also 63). The moves Lyotard sketches here against different backdrops show recalcitrance against being related to the already familiar; they do not remain within the limits set by already established rules. As such, they show resistance to the more stubborn pressures of the system.

CONCLUSION

In a system with an appetite for critical interventions because they can help make it better, the political potential of social critique is in question. This would certainly sharpen the conundrum of how to live without only or mainly operating for the system's improvement, especially from the critic's perspective. Yet the system's 'decision makers' consecrating 'our lives' to 'the growth of power' also treat language games with a view to their commensurability (PC xxiv; see also Connor 1989: 32–3). Indeed, the system thrives on competition, encouraging variety within a range delimited by rules. Occasionally, the pressures on those engaged in thinking and writing to conduct moves in a manner that is debatable because it is relatable to what is already there is considerable. Finally, in these conditions even singularities have come to circulate in the marketplace. What Lyotard calls 'innovation' will contain little by way of clues for resisting these conditions: innovation 'is under the command of the system, or at least used by it to improve its efficiency'. 'Paralogy', distinct from innovation (though the 'one' de facto often turns 'into the other') (PC 61), constitutes a more promising point of reference; but it is not the only one.[6] In his remarks on Baudelaire, Lyotard locates the poet among 'the first … to confront the stupidity of the system' (PF 208). Specifically, Baudelaire confronted 'the stupid world' of nineteenth-century capitalism (PF 209). Lyotard picks up on the concept – from Marx's (1990: 138–63) analysis of that world, of course – of 'money' as 'the general equivalent for all commodities' (PF 209). Consistent with Marx's concept of labour power, Lyotard's notion of commodities includes not only 'goods' but also 'bodies … and souls' (PF 209). Unfolding 'under the poet's horrified eyes', says Lyotard, was the 'world of total exchangeability under the rule of money'. Today's 'system', he continues, is, in at least one important respect, but an advanced stage in the development of that world. It is 'the extension … of the same routine of exchange' into the – for Lyotard decisive – dimension of 'language'. In 'interlocution, interactiveness, … and debate', he insists, 'words are exchanged for words as use value is exchanged for use value' (PF 209, see also 12; Williams 1998: 126–7). In their solitude and measurelessness, not contained within existing rules, the works of art mentioned above show recalcitrance against such conditions.

Abbreviations

PC: *The Postmodern Condition* (1984b)

PF: *Postmodern Fables* (1997)

WIP: 'Answering the question: What is postmodernism?' (1984a)

Selected Further Reading

An inclusive discussion of Lyotard's work, including his conception of postmodernity, is provided by Williams, J. (1998) *Lyotard: Towards a Postmodern Philosophy*. Cambridge: Polity Press.

Malpas, S. (2003) *Jean-François Lyotard*. London: Routledge also provides further discussion of themes raised in the chapter above.

For an edited volume containing engagement with Lyotard in relation to education, see Dhillon, P. and Standish, P. (eds) (2000) *Lyotard: Just Education*. London: Routledge.

Notes

1 See in this context Lyotard's (PC 12) remarks on Max Horkheimer's (1972) seminal distinction between traditional and critical theory.
2 For a critical discussion of the fable in Lyotard, see Palumbo-Liu (2000: 204–13).
3 An alternative translation is available as 'Terror on the run' (Lyotard 1998). The latter was consulted, but this discussion refers to 'The intimacy of terror'. Readers aiming for an in-depth engagement with the piece and unable to access the French original are advised to consult both translations.
4 Marie is probably referring to Kant's (1991) 'An answer to the question: "What is enlightenment?"' from 1784, the title of which may also have inspired that of Lyotard's aforementioned early 1980s essay 'Answering the question: What is postmodernism?' (WIP).
5 '"I cultivated my hysteria with joy and terror. Now, I've always got this vertigo, and today January 23, 1862, I felt before me *the breeze of imbecility flapping its wing*"' (Baudelaire in PF 208; see also Baudelaire 1950: 205).
6 For a critical discussion, which, however, predates most of *Postmodern Fables*, see Connor (1989: 40–3). See also remarks by Malpas (2003: 30–3) and Williams (1998: 23, 111–12).

7
Michel Foucault: Power over Life

PART 1: POWER

Around the turn of the nineteenth century, remarks Michel Foucault, it was becoming customary 'for kings to lose their heads' (PP 20). George III of the United Kingdom, however, had not been 'decapitated' by the guillotine, but by the insanity that had 'seized hold of the king's head' (PP 21). In 1800, Pinel described to French readers how their neighbours' mad monarch had been treated (PP 19–20). In what Foucault, drawing on Pinel, calls a 'ceremony' of 'dethronement' (PP 20–1), the king was stripped of '"all trappings of royalty"' and told plainly that he was not '"sovereign"' anymore (Pinel in PP 20). Locked in '"a room ... covered with matting"' (PP 20), he could no longer issue commands to anyone and was 'reduce[d] ... to his body' (PP 21). When he furiously smeared a doctor who was visiting him with faeces (Pinel in PP 20, see also PP 22–5), the 'insurrectional gesture' (PP 25) was met by the 'restrained ... force' of a quiet servant (PP 23), who calmly undressed the lunatic, cleaned him up (PP 25), and had to ensure his docility (PP 22, see also 20). Foucault observes in this 'scene' a manifestation of a decisive development in the formation of contemporary social conditions: the recession of one form of power, the power of 'sovereignty' (PP 22), and 'the emergence and definitive installation' of another form, 'disciplinary power' (PP 41, see also 26–7). Foucault places the question of power at the centre of the study of social conditions. Every society's 'social body', he argues, is fundamentally shaped by power relationships (SD 24).

Sovereign Power

The relationship between a sovereign and a subject, says Foucault, corresponded with the power mechanisms of 'feudal-type societies' (SD 35).

Of medieval origin, the theory of sovereignty is principally concerned with the workings of power in the 'feudal monarchy'. It also helped legitimise the 'great monarchical administrations' (SD 34). Sovereign power remained operative as late as 'post-feudal, pre-industrial government' (PP 27) and still operates in certain guises in spheres of contemporary society (e.g. PP 79, SD 36–40). Yet Foucault mentions sovereign power chiefly in order to distinguish from it those forms of power that truly characterise the social conditions of the present.

The theory of sovereignty, argues Foucault, centres on 'the monarch and the monarchy' (SD 34). The medieval monarchic institutions of power were established upon multiple intertwined, conflict-ridden power relations, such as those of suzerainty and vassalage, promising to establish order within them. Crucially, the monarchy's power mechanisms developed the form – which actually masked some of their operations – of an overarching juridical edifice of right and law (HS1 86–8; see also Sheridan 1990: 182). This edifice was constructed around the king and to justify and serve 'royal power' (SD 25, see also BP 7–8). It needed to be shown 'that the monarch was indeed the living body of sovereignty, and that his power, even when absolute, was perfectly in keeping with a basic right' (SD 26). In this modality, power could be said to be held or possessed by someone – a king, for example (PP 21–2, DP 192).

The power of sovereignty operated on a bounded territory and its produce (SD 36, STP 11). The conquest of new and defence of conquered land were major concerns (STP 64, see also 65, 91–2). Yet whilst the notion of 'sovereignty over an unpopulated territory' was by no means deemed outlandish (STP 11), sovereign power was de facto 'exercised ... on a territory ... and ... the subjects ... inhabit[ing] it' (STP 96, see also 11). More precisely, it involved a relationship between the sovereign's will and the wills of subjects, whereby the sovereign issued laws and regulations that mediated his will and dictated what subjects, who were supposed to obey, had to do (STP 65, 70, see also 98; Sheridan 1990: 141).

Sovereign power, Foucault specifies further, constituted a relationship of power that connected the sovereign and subjects through 'deduction' and 'expenditure' (PP 42). The expenditures of the sovereign included, for instance, gifts to subjects or services, notably protection (PP 42, see also BP 66). However, expenditure was generally smaller than deduction (PP 42) and is, Foucault seems to think, less important for describing sovereign power. For sovereign power functioned primarily as a 'subtraction mechanism'. It 'was ... a right of seizure'. What distinguished the sovereignty relation in the main was the sovereign's seizing a share of the wealth, products, time, and services of the subjects through levies (HS1 136, see also 89, PP 42, 46, SD 35–6; Lemke 2011: 35; Sheridan 1990: 191–2).

Although the theory of sovereignty revolves around the king, Foucault notes that in 'feudal-type societies' the sovereignty relation characterised the exercise of power 'from the highest to the lowest levels' (SD 35). That said, the various sovereignty relationships, for example, between suzerain and feoffee, lord and serf, or priest and laity, formed no 'unitary hierarchical table with subordinate and superordinate elements'; these relations were not classificatory; there was 'no common measure' (PP 43, cf. 52). The 'elements' of sovereignty relations, Foucault emphasises, were non-equivalent: a sovereignty relation could operate between 'a suzerain ... and a family, a community, or the inhabitants of ... a region', that is, 'human multiplicities'; yet 'sovereignty may also bear on something other than ... human multiplicities', 'on land, a road, an instrument of production', and their 'users' (PP 44). What is decisive in this context for tracing the trajectory of Foucault's analyses of power is his contention that in sovereignty relations 'the subject-element' was usually not 'an individual body' (PP 44, see also 46n, 55). Sovereignty relations operated on 'multiplicities' such as 'families' or 'users' (PP 44). Alternatively, they operated on 'fragments ... of somatic singularity': it was specifically as 'son of X' or as 'bourgeois of this town', for instance, that someone might be 'sovereign' or 'subject' in sovereignty relationships, and one could 'be both subject and sovereign in different aspects' (PP 44).

By contrast, 'individualization' could be witnessed 'towards the top'. At the peak of the sovereign power configuration, Foucault argues, albeit with qualifications, 'the king in his individuality, with his king's body', could be located (PP 45, see also DP 192–3; Sheridan 1990: 155–6). This 'single, individual point' had the role of arbitrator between the various sovereignty relations: what was required was 'something like a sovereign who, in his own body, is the point on which all these multiple, different, and irreconcilable relationships converge' (PP 45, see also 82).[1]

Power Relationships

The monarchy, Foucault diagnoses in 1976, is haunting contemporary analyses of power: right, law, will, state, and sovereignty remain major concerns. However, increasingly prevalent new processes of power (HS1 88–9) demand that power be reconceptualised (HS1 102, see also SD 34; Sheridan 1990: 182–3). Foucault famously proposes to sidestep questions of sovereignty and obedience (SD 27) in favour of exploring 'a multiple and mobile field of force relations' (HS1 102, see also 97; Sheridan 1990: 139, 183, 186, 218).

Force relations

At the core of Foucault's opposition to extant conceptualisations of power is his disagreement with the idea of power as a right which, like a commodity, can be owned, contractually surrendered, and appropriated by some but not others (SD 13–14, 29, HS1 94; Sheridan 1990: 139, 184–5, 218). Power, he contends, is force in operation between points; it 'functions' (SD 29); 'it exists only in action' (SD 14); it is the reciprocal '"... exercise of an unbalanced force"' (Davidson 2006: xv, citing PP 14; see also Sheridan 1990: 139, 184, 218). Power is a *relationship* of unequal force between points (HS1 93–5, SD 15; Davidson 2006: xvi; Sheridan 1990: 139, 184, 218). This means that all power also involves the exercise of 'resistance'. Power relations cannot exist without 'points of resistance' that 'play the role of adversary, target, support, or handle' (HS1 95–6; see also Davidson 2006: xxiin9; Sheridan 1990: 139, 184–5).

Force relations, Foucault instructs, must be analysed in their 'multiplicity' (HS1 92; Davidson 2006: xv–xvi; see also Sheridan 1990: 139, 183, 186, 218). In fact, given the indelibility of resistance, power must be seen as a range of incessant 'struggles and confrontations' (Davidson 2006: xv; HS1 92; Sheridan 1990: 183). Indeed, Foucault doubts that one headspring feeds all revolting and rebelling in society, insisting instead on the 'plurality of resistances' (HS1 96; see also Sheridan 1990: 139–40, 184–5).

Relations of force, Foucault points out, can draw 'support' from each other, coming together as a 'chain' (HS1 92) or as 'local systems of subjugation' (SD 34), whereas mutual discrepancies may keep them apart (HS1 92). Similarly, the 'focuses of resistance are spread over time and space at varying densities', sometimes 'mobilizing' people and generating social 'cleavages' (HS1 96; see also Sheridan 1990: 139–40, 185). Finally, force relationships may be 'coded' or consolidated (HS1 93) in keeping with 'the logic' (HS1 97) or 'more general lines' of wider 'strategies' (Davidson 2006: xv; see also Sheridan 1990: 184–6). The 'design' or 'crystallization' of such 'strategies' can be found in the 'state apparatus', for instance, or in different 'social hegemonies'. From this perspective, neither states nor instances of social 'domination' of some over others are pre-given, but are among the ultimate 'forms power takes' (HS1 92–3, see also 96–7; Sheridan 1990: 218–19). From the same vantage point Foucault argues that revolutions can occur thanks to 'the strategic codification of ... points of resistance' (HS1 96; see also Sheridan 1990: 139–40, 185).

Investigating power

Foucault therefore suggests to examine first of all the most minuscule workings of power (SD 30) and to investigate it 'in its most regional' domains (SD 27). It can then be established how the 'procedures' playing out in these domains are 'used', 'invested', and 'annexed' by ever more encompassing 'mechanisms' and, finally, by 'forms of overall domination' (SD 30–1, see also HS1 94); how local 'tactics' begin to link up with each other and together draw the contours of larger apparatuses (HS1 95; see also Sheridan 1990: 184–6). The 'school apparatus' of a society, for instance, is best understood in respect of extensive 'strategies' traversing, utilising, and interlinking much smaller 'mechanisms' and 'local tactics of domination', which in turn interlink tiny relations of subjugation such as those between children and grownups, offspring and parents, or families and administrations (SD 45–6).

In his analyses, Foucault seeks to avoid all attempts to reduce power. Notably, he challenges the Marxist view that the economy constitutes power's 'historical raison d'être' and that power's purpose is basically to maintain the existing 'relations of production' and 'class domination' (SD 13–14, see also HS1 94; Sheridan 1990: 219). Power relationships are certainly closely intertwined with economic – but also other, for instance sexual – relationships, yet they are 'effects' as well as 'conditions' of 'divisions, inequalities', or 'differentiations' in other relations (HS1 94, see also SD 14; Sheridan 1990: 184, 219).

Foucault, as is well known, highlights the inseparability of power and knowledge. The exercise and mechanisms of power depend on, and are strengthened by, the operation of discourses of truth (SD 24, 33–4, HS1 101; Sheridan 1990: 131, 138, 165, 169–70, 186, 220). For instance, power can work on sexuality thanks to 'techniques' for knowing and 'procedures' of speaking and writing about sexuality (HS1 98, see also 97; Sheridan 1990: 165–6, 169–70, 185).[2] Conversely, power fashions the devices for knowledge production, for example, techniques of observation, documentation, and inquiry (SD 33). In fact, power generates 'statements', 'negations', 'discourses', and 'theories' themselves (PP 13, also cited in Davidson 2006: xviii; see also HS1 101; Sheridan 1990: 131, 138, 165–6, 169–70, 185–6, 220). Moreover, it 'institutionalizes', 'professionalizes', and 'rewards' the pursuit of 'truth' (SD 25). And as far as sexuality is concerned, it was only insofar as 'power had established it as a possible object' that it could become a field of inquiry (HS1 98, see also 97; Sheridan 1990: 165–6, 169–70, 185).

This point about sexuality illustrates a more far-reaching argument. What power works upon, Foucault insists, does not precede its operations but is produced by it (see e.g. Davidson 2003: xix–xx). The individual, in particular, is by no means a basic entity which subsequently comes under the purview of power or is crushed by it. Instead, it is 'power' that 'allows bodies, gestures, discourses, and desires to be identified and constituted as something individual … The individual is … a power-effect' (SD 29–30, see also 28; Sheridan 1990: 140, 152, 154–6, 165). Thus, analyses of power should not seek a foothold in components that pre-exist power relations, but proceed from an 'actual or effective relationship of domination' and investigate how it 'determines the elements to which it is applied' (SD 45). The problem of disciplinary power already strongly reverberates here.

Disciplinary Power

Much of Foucault's work on power is dedicated to disciplinary power. Utterly 'incompatible with relations of sovereignty' (SD 35), discipline became a major modality of power in Western societies in the 1600s and 1700s (DP 137, SD 35). 'It was', says Foucault, 'one of the basic tools for the establishment of industrial capitalism and the corresponding type of society' (SD 36).[3] It is, he holds, among the most widespread forms of the exercise of power today (PP 40, 79).

Discipline's target

Sovereign power was exercised on legal subjects in a territory and their produce. Disciplinary power grabs hold of bodies rather than products (PP 40, 46, AN 193, DP 136; Sheridan 1990: 138–9, 148–9, 192, 217, 219). Whereas 'vassalage', for example, '... bore less on the operations of the body than on the products of labour' (DP 137), discipline, Foucault emphasises, is a 'modality by which ... power ... reaches the level of bodies' (PP 40; see also Lagrange 2006: 361–2). More precisely, disciplinary power acts on the individual body (STP 12, PP 40, 46; Lemke 2011: 36; Sheridan 1990: 192, 217, 219).

Disciplinary power works chiefly upon 'bodies and what they do' (SD 35). Indeed, whereas the sovereign seized but a part of the subjects' work and time (PP 46, HS1 136), discipline aims for a comprehensive 'hold' on the individual's actions, including words, and habits (PP 40, 46, see also DP 138): on the individual's 'time in its totality' (PP 46).

In this context, the body is not approached as an indivisible 'unity', though. Disciplinary power disassembles it, reconfigures it, and operates on its components: movements, gestures, behaviours, attitudes etc. (DP 137–8; see also Lagrange 2006: 361–2; Sheridan: 1990: 149, 217). The body is treated 'at the level of the mechanism' (DP 137). Power's grab for the body coincided with the conception of 'Man-the-Machine' (DP 136; see also Lemke 2011: 36; Sheridan 1990: 148–9, 192–3).

What disciplinary power ultimately targets are the body's forces: its aptitudes, capabilities, skills, and energies. This procedure has two aspects. Discipline enhances the body's forces – for instance, training certain of its capacities – in order to make the body more useful. At the same time, it weakens the body's forces – restraining certain of its energies – and makes it more docile (AN 193–4, DP 137–8; Lemke 2011: 36; Sheridan 1990: 139, 148–52, 192, 219). '[D]isciplinary coercion establishes in the body the constricting link between an increased aptitude and an increased domination' (DP 138).

Disciplinary operations

Where disciplinary power is exercised, the body – its habits, parts, and potential – is seen as deeply mouldable (DP 135–6). Nonetheless, for Foucault 'power need not be violent' (Davidson 2003: xx; see also Sheridan 1990: 139). One crucial mechanism of disciplinary power is 'constant surveillance' (SD 36): individuals are permanently under supervision (PP 47; Lemke 2011: 36; Sheridan 1990: 152–3). Surveillance is tied to the production of written records of people's every word and deed (PP 48–9). The 'police discipline' emerging in the 1700s illustrates this (PP 50). The police received the task of always and everywhere observing – without becoming visible itself – everything that was happening, done, and said down to the details and of documenting them in 'reports and registers' (DP 213–14, see also PP 50–1).

Foucault outlines a whole set of broad operations of power on the body, each of which is supported by several disciplinary 'techniques' (DP 139, 141). The 'distribution of individuals in space' (DP 141; see also Sheridan 1990: 150), for instance, involves the technique, among others, of defining *functional sites* (DP 143). In the late 1700s, factories were divided into spaces for discrete operations of the production process and the corresponding sections of the workforce. These spaces were then respectively partitioned into identical individual workplaces. This facilitated the observation of each worker and their comparison in view of their activities and ability, whilst 'each variable' of the workforce, such as 'promptness' or 'skill', could be 'assessed ... and related to the individual who was its particular agent' (DP 145).

Controlling activity in time is supported – again by way of example – by an 'instrumental coding of the body' or '*body-object articulation*' technique. Discipline prescribes exactly how a series of body parts and a series of parts of an object are to connect through several 'simple gestures', before arranging these connections in a temporal sequence (DP 152–3; see also Sheridan 1990: 151). The role of 'disciplinary power', then, is not 'deduction', appropriating a product, but 'synthesis', constructing 'a body-weapon, body-tool, body-machine complex' (DP 153).

Foucault also underscores discipline's training function. One of the means of disciplinary training is 'normalizing judgement' (DP 170; see also Sheridan 1990: 148–55). Operant, for instance, in schools or workshops, this tactic involves micro-punishments such as 'minor deprivations' or 'petty humiliations'. These are dished out for activities and behaviours such as 'negligence' or 'impoliteness', which, whilst not necessarily breaking any laws, fail to 'measure up to' rules determined by prescriptive 'regulations' or 'observable ... regularit[ies]' (DP 178–9; see also Sheridan 1990: 153–4). 'To punish', crucially, 'is to exercise': behaviour which falls short entails obligatory repetitive training in good behaviour so that behaviour is corrected according to the rule (DP 179–80). Simultaneously, correct behaviour is rewarded to make those whose behaviour departs desire conformity. Behaviours are thereby precisely distributed between various opposing poles of 'good and evil', every person receives a 'punitive balance-sheet', and 'individuals' are finely 'differentiat[ed]' (DP 180–1; see also Sheridan 1990: 154).

In addition to correcting, micro-punishment also prevents. The disciplinary workshop, an area of close 'supervision', penalises 'anything that might involve distraction', such as loud singing or sharing lewd stories during work (PP 51). This is to create 'continuous punitive pressure' on 'potential behavior', generate aversion to offending, and thus enable discipline to 'intervene' in advance of 'the actual manifestation of the behavior', before bodies can do or say what they are not supposed to do or say (PP 51–2).

It is important to underline that for Foucault the individual on which disciplinary power operates in various ways is not given in advance. Rather, disciplinary power deals with 'multiplicities' and turns them into individuals. 'The individual is ... a particular way of dividing up the multiplicity for a discipline' (STP 12; see also Lemke 2011: 37–8). By attaching the 'subject-function' to the 'somatic singularity' – to the body's actions, words, movements, and forces – through surveillance, documentation, and other procedures, disciplinary power creates the individual (PP 55–6, see also 49–50; Sheridan 1990: 140, 152, 154–6, 165). It is discipline which, by dint of operations, techniques, and training methods such as those illustrated above, manufactures bodies into individuality with its specific properties (DP 167, 170, 192, see also 194, 217). Thus, in contradistinction to sovereign power, 'the disciplinary system entails ... individualization at the base' (PP 55, see also DP 192–3; Sheridan 1990: 154–6).

Security and Government

Foucault distinguishes discipline from a further major type of power, 'the apparatus (*dispositif*) of security' (STP 6). Security is younger than disciplinary power, having emerged roughly in the mid-1700s, and differs from it (e.g. STP 55–6, 64, 66; Lemke 2011: 37, 47). Foucault asks if security, too, increasingly characterises the operations of power in contemporary society (STP 10–11; Senellart 2009: 378).[4]

Security and population

The development of security apparatuses, Foucault argues, is connected to the appearance of a particular 'idea' and 'reality' of 'population' (STP 11, see also 67; Lemke 2011: 37; Senellart 2009: 379). Here it is 'the population' that constitutes the 'pertinent level' of power operations (STP 66, see also 42). To this population, in turn, is attributed a certain '"naturalness"' (STP 70; see also Lemke 2011: 45).

Its 'naturalness' emerges, firstly, as the regularity of numerous population phenomena, for instance, as the constant ratios of various illnesses' casualties each year (STP 74). Moreover, the population is seen as naturally affected by a range of 'variables', especially the 'means of subsistence', but also climate, material environment, conventions, and many others (STP 70–1, see also 345, 366). These 'factors' are not 'all natural'; they can potentially be modified to an extent (STP 366; see also Lemke 2011: 46–7). Thirdly, it is held that each 'individual acts out of desire', which cannot be changed. 'Desire' is the sole driving force of the actions of the population (STP 72). And the 'play' of people's desires will ensure advantageous outcomes for the population as a whole (STP 73). Notably, the 'game of the interest of competing private individuals who each seek maximum advantage for themselves' will yield 'the most favorable economic situation' for the population (STP 346).

The onset of this political concern with the population, argues Foucault, constituted 'the entry of a "nature" into the field of techniques of power'. Securitising power does not, however, involve a sovereign's imposition of laws from on high demanding 'obedience' against nature, but the application of 'reflected procedures of government within this nature, with the help of it, and with regard to it' (STP 75). Indeed, given the population's dependence on so many 'variables', it is hard to transform it directly 'by decree' (STP 71; see also Lemke 2011: 47). 'If one says to a population "do this," ... there is quite simply no guarantee that it can do it' (STP 71). Instead, one envisages influencing a population indirectly by acting upon the various 'remote factors' that are known to affect it (STP 71–2). Eighteenth-century town planning projects illustrate security's orientation towards organising spaces so as to steer the interactions of their natural elements, for example rivers, and artificial elements that function like natural ones, for example clusters of houses, with the nature of the population within them (STP 21–3).

Rather than centring on legal 'prohibition' or disciplinary 'prescription', security, Foucault continues, chiefly 'works on the basis of' and 'within reality'. Through conducting 'analyses' and configuring 'arrangements', it seeks to make reality's elements 'work in relation to each other'. Its operations thus remain within 'the interplay of reality with itself' (STP 47–8, see also 344; Lemke 2011: 47). Whereas disciplinary power aims to control every detail, 'security ... "lets things happen ..."' to some extent (STP 45). It ensures that 'reality' proceeds along its proper path correspondingly with its own 'laws, principles, and mechanisms' (STP 48). Security 'relies' on 'natural processes' for achieving particular results in the population (STP 45). The potential of desire suggests that government ought to 'stimulat[e] and encourag[e]' (STP 73; see also Lemke 2011: 47) 'desire' and allow it to 'play' freely so it can generate 'the general interest of the population' (STP 73). Notably, if the 'private interest[s]' of 'competing' individuals are permitted to function of their own accord, the actions of each individual will help ensure the 'good of all' (STP 346).

Government and liberalism

His considerations of population and security lead Foucault to a more persistent discussion of government (STP 76, 88; Lemke 2011: 44–5; Senellart 2009: 379). The appearance of 'the problem of population', especially through statistical demonstrations of its 'regularities' and 'effects', facilitated the development of an explicit 'art of government' (STP 103–4; see also Lemke 2011: 45–6). The purpose of such government is to enhance the population's situation, its wealth, health, longevity etc. (STP 105).

The sphere in which politics thus intervenes is conceptualised as processes and mechanisms with a certain 'naturalness' – 'the naturalness of society' (STP 349; see also Lemke 2011: 45–7). The population, specifically, 'has its own laws of transformation' and is 'characterized by the law of the mechanics of interests' (STP 351–2). This naturalness entails that government does not operate primarily through prohibitions and orders, but maintains 'respect' for those 'natural processes': to govern means to be mindful of them, to 'work with them', 'to arouse', 'facilitate', and *laisser faire* to safeguard the functioning of 'the necessary and natural regulations' (STP 352–3; see also Lemke 2011: 46–7). Government deploys means that are intrinsic to the population itself (STP 105), from '"campaigns"' to alter its views and habits (STP 366) to 'techniques' whose operations people may not even notice, focusing particularly on their interests (STP 105). Moreover, those 'natural phenomena' are considered scientifically knowable, and 'scientific knowledge' of them is deemed a prerequisite of 'good government' (STP 350; see also Lemke 2011: 46–7). Successful, 'rationally reflected' government depends on 'observations and knowledge' of the population (STP 106). Government thus understood does not, then, centre on a sovereign's rule through the imposition of laws on subjects (STP 115–16), but constitutes rather a 'management' – involving 'apparatuses of security' (STP 107–8) – of 'the mass of the population' (STP 110; see also Senellart 2009: 379).

In this context, Foucault unpacks his well-known concept of '"governmentality"' (STP 108; Senellart 2009: 379–80). He uses this 'ugly word' (STP 115) to designate *inter alia* the trajectory towards the primacy of government over sovereign and disciplinary power as well as precisely the combination of 'institutions, procedures', and 'analyses' that enables the workings of this 'power' on the population that involves 'apparatuses of security' and 'political economy as its major form of knowledge' (STP 108; see also Senellart 2009: 388). Ours, insists Foucault in 1978, is 'the era of a governmentality discovered in the eighteenth century' (STP 109).[5]

This problem of government, finally, is also at the centre of liberalism.[6] Foucault explores liberalism 'as a principle and method of the rationalization of the exercise of government' (BP 318, see also 321; Lemke 2011: 45). The exact 'question of liberalism' is that of 'frugal government' (BP 29, see also 321).[7] Of major importance here is the notion that the market operates according to 'natural mechanisms', and that if these mechanisms are left to operate, they will allow the 'true price', which 'fluctuates' around a product's 'value', to form. Market mechanisms and their revelation of the 'natural price' make it possible to distinguish 'correct' from 'erroneous' government action:

> ... inasmuch as it enables production, need, supply, demand, value, and price, etcetera, to be linked together through exchange, the market constitutes ... a site of verification-falsification for governmental practice. (BP 31–2; see also Lemke 2011: 46–7; Senellart 2009: 383–4)

Moreover, 'frugal government' is subject to 'internal' limits (BP 37). A particularly persistent mode of defining these limits (BP 43) was developed by 'English radicalism' (BP 40). Government is set 'desirable' as well as factual restrictions based on examinations of its aims, its objects, and which governmental practices would be 'useful' (BP 40; see also Lemke 2011: 46). In the Western world after 1800, Foucault emphasises, 'individual and collective utility ... will be the major criteria for working out the limits of the powers of public authorities ...' (BP 43–4; see also Senellart 2009: 384). What underpins 'exchange' and 'utility' in turn is 'interest' (BP 44). Ultimately, it is 'interests' that 'constitute politics'; the power of government may be exercised exclusively where 'interests' render something 'of interest' to people (BP 45).

PART 2: POWER OVER LIFE

Whilst Foucault concedes that several of the juridical monarchy's 'forms' still exist, he maintains that the 'new mechanisms of power' are more – and ever more – influential today. Crucially, the new 'mechanisms are', certainly 'in part, those that, beginning in the eighteenth century, took charge of men's existence, men as living bodies' (HS1 89; see also Lemke 2011: 33–6; Sheridan 1990: 182–3, 191–3). In fact, 'existence' in this passage is meant to translate the original's 'la vie' (Foucault 1976: 117). In the work of Foucault, who argues that 'in any society ... mu[lt]iple relations of power traverse, characterize, and constitute the social body' (SD 24; see also Sheridan 1990: 139), the problem of life in contemporary social conditions is that of life and power. Once again, he distinguishes the area of his investigations from the context of sovereignty.

Right of Death

Sovereign power, Foucault has been shown to argue, was generally understood in terms of right. Importantly here, the 'classical theory of sovereignty' ascribed to the sovereign 'a right of life and death' (SD 240; see also Sheridan 1990: 191). That is to say, neither subjects' lives nor their deaths were 'natural or immediate phenomena ... outside the field of power', but could themselves 'become rights only as a result of the will of the sovereign'. Yet the sovereign's 'right of life and death', Foucault emphasises, was actually mainly a 'right to kill'. The sovereign could not make people live as he could make them die (SD 240). His 'right ... formulated as the "power of life and death" was in reality the right to *take* life or *let* live'. Foucault therefore suspects that this right must be linked to the aforementioned mechanism of 'deduction' in the sovereign power relationship. Sovereign power was the 'right' to subtract slices of people's wealth, parts of their time, 'and ultimately life itself' (HS1 136, see also 89, SD 240–1; Lemke 2011: 35–6, 38–9; Sheridan 1990: 191–2).

Albeit formally a derivative of Roman antiquity's 'absolute' right of the father to take the lives of his progeny and slaves, the 'right of life and death' in 'its modern form' was 'relative and limited' (HS1 135–6; see also Lemke 2011: 35). Sovereign power, as already said, involved passing laws that mediated the sovereign's will and were supposed to be obeyed. Defensive wars aside, only when a subject rebelled, breaking the sovereign's laws, could the sovereign have the perpetrator killed (HS1 135). The law, Foucault adds in turn, always carries a weapon: anyone contravening it is, in response, certainly 'as a last resort', threatened with execution (HS1 144).

The theory of sovereignty envisaged 'rules' as products of the sovereign's volition (SD 38) and, Foucault specifies, based power on his corporeal being (SD 36). This resonates with the idea of individualisation at the summit of the sovereign power configuration. The subject's relationship with the sovereign was 'personal' (BP 45). Thus, 'a crime' – apart from constituting 'voluntary harm done to another' and 'society' – was a strike against the sovereign's 'will' codified in his laws as well as against the sovereign's 'rights', 'strength', and 'physical body' (AN 82, see also DP 47; Sheridan 1990: 141), against 'the sovereign in the very body of his power' (BP 46, see also 50n16). The distinction between those obeying and disobeying his laws and will simultaneously demarcated his foes (HS1 144, see also DP 50; Lemke 2011: 38–9).[8] By the same token, punishment contained the sovereign's own intervention on the offender's body (BP 45; see also Sheridan 1990: 140–1), his 'personal vendetta' (AN 82). The 'death penalty' was among his retorts to people who had assaulted 'his will, his law, or his person' (HS1 137–8, see also BP 50n16, DP 48; Sheridan 1990: 141).

A key function of punishing in this context was the 'reconstitution of power in its integrity' (AN 83, see also DP 48–9). Punishment had to assert power's inherent supremacy – the supremacy of the sovereign's 'right' as well as of his 'physical strength' (DP 49). Punitive 'excess' needed to outdo ostentatiously, in 'a sort of joust' between punishment and crime, the 'excess' of the latter (AN 83). The penal ritual was meant to terrorise; its terror could be experienced in public torture and execution (DP 49, AN 83).

Controlling Life

However, what had been strengthened by the 1800s in contrast to the right of death was 'power's hold over life' (SD 239; see also Lemke 2011: 33–6; Sheridan 1990: 191–3): a 'power to "make" live and "let" die' in contrast to 'the right to take life or let live' (SD 241, see also HS1 138; Lemke 2011: 36). Formulated in the broadest terms, 'political power' had taken charge of 'administering life'. Foucault traces two modes, distinct but connected, in which this type of power has been developing (HS1 139, see also SD 249; Lemke 2011: 35–8; Sheridan 1990: 192–3). Some of his theoretical considerations on power were outlined above. Yet much of his work is dedicated to analysing its manifestations in specific settings, for instance in the field of health and illness.[9]

Disciplining life

Since the 1600s, argues Foucault, disciplinary power has been functioning as the first form of 'power over life'. The objectives of this *anatomo-politics of the human body* have been mentioned: targeting the 'performances' of the body 'machine', training its capacities, enhancing 'its usefulness and ... docility' (HS1 139, see also SD 241–3, 249–50; Lemke 2011: 36; Sheridan 1990: 139, 148–52, 192, 219). Discipline chiefly established itself in – though it has not remained confined to – institutions like schools or workshops (SD 250; Lemke 2011: 37). Foucault's analysis of the operation of disciplinary power on the sick provides one illustration of its operation as power over life.

In the Middle Ages and beyond, he points out, the demarcation of people stricken with leprosy from the rest of their group entailed 'a rule of no contact'

(AN 43, see also DP 199; Davidson 2003: xxi). In fact, lepers were expelled from the group and its spaces to a 'vague' outer sphere (AN 43; see also Davidson 2003: xxi), where they merged into an undifferentiated 'mass' (DP 198). Moreover, these outcasts were subjected to juridico-political 'disqualification' (AN 43; Davidson 2003: xxi). Their expulsions were marked by funerary rituals: every leper was 'declared dead' and their belongings 'passed on' (AN 43). In this cleansing of the group (AN 44, DP 198), the power of deduction and death still quakes palpably (see also AN 48).

It is hard to overstate the importance of these considerations for Foucault's studies of power: Western societies, he argues, have known but 'two major models for the control of individuals', 'the exclusion of lepers' and, in stark contrast to it, 'the inclusion of plague victims' (AN 44; see also Davidson 2003: xx–xxii). When the plague befell a late seventeenth-century town, it was immediately sealed off (AN 44–5, DP 195). Yet neither was the space thus demarcated allowed to remain 'vague' (AN 45), nor were its inhabitants left to amalgamate into an undifferentiated mass. As is characteristic of disciplinary power (DP 143), the plague-ridden town was rigorously partitioned down to single streets (AN 45, DP 195). Each inhabitant was identified individually by name and told to stay in her or his house (AN 45–6, DP 195–7). Instead of being kept at a distance, the people of the 'plague town' were placed under close, all-encompassing, incessant 'surveillance'; regular visitations to all the houses, during which each resident 'had to present himself at the window', for example, enabled inspectors to conduct a whole 'review … of the living and the dead' (AN 45–6, see also DP 195–7; Davidson 2003: xxi). Every detail – 'deaths, illnesses, complaints, irregularities' – was documented and its record passed on to those deciding on 'medical treatment' (DP 196). Power did not simply distinguish 'two types or groups' anymore, but individualised, establishing a range of delicate 'differences between individuals who are ill and those who are not' (AN 46, see also DP 197–8; Davidson 2003: xxi). The aim of these operations, finally, was not to cleanse the group, but 'to maximize the health, life, longevity, and strength of individuals' (AN 46). Disciplinary power was functioning with the objective of making live.

Foucault associates the recession of the former in favour of the latter 'model' with the recession, in the 1600s and 1700s, of a 'negative', deductive in favour of a 'positive', productive power (AN 48; Davidson 2003: xx–xxii). Power's productive orientation manifested itself in several ways in the plague town – in the ambition to generate health and life, of course (AN 46), but also, for instance, in the 'accumulation of observations' and the 'formation' and 'growth of knowledge', which, in turn, supported the proliferation of power 'effects' (AN 48; see also Davidson 2003: xxi).

Normalisation in discipline

What is more, the setting of the plague town reveals a tendency of disciplinary power, briefly touched upon above, which is crucial for power over life according to Foucault: the tendency to normalise (AN 49; see also Davidson 2003: xxi–xxv; Lemke 2011: 39). The operations of disciplinary power, he observes, often involve the definition of a 'norm' in the form of 'an optimal model' with regard to a specific outcome, for example, 'the best movement for loading one's rifle' (STP 57; see also Lemke 2011: 47) or, precisely, a 'norm of health' (AN 47). The uninterrupted investigation of the plague town, he argues, had the aim of figuring out the extent of each individual's 'conform[ity] to the rule, to the defined norm of health' (AN 47). In fact, a key component of disciplinary normalisation is the comparison of individuals – their attributes, conduct, and performances – in view of a norm. This is closely interlinked with the 'differentiation' between them. On the basis of such operations, disciplinary power constructs hierarchies, 'in terms of value', of 'the abilities, the level, the "nature" of individuals' (DP 182–3, see also 193; Lemke 2011: 47; Sheridan 1990: 154). The schemes for grading and ranking individuals in the school and the military – 'hierarch[ies] of values and success' – constitute prime examples (PP 52). At the same time, discipline exerts 'pressure', even 'constraint', on individuals to measure up to the same norm (DP 182–3). Its various 'training' methods are among its principal means to bring about people's conformance with the 'model' (STP 57; see also Lemke 2011: 47). In this sense, Foucault points out with reference to Georges Canguilhem, norms are not devices of expulsion, but related to the 'qualification' of individuals and to 'intervention' for their 'transformation' and 'correction' (AN 50; see also Davidson 2003: xxi).

However, whilst all those who thereby turn out to be capable of such conformity count as 'normal', those who turn out to be unable to adapt are categorised as 'abnormal' (STP 57, see also 63; Lemke 2011: 47). Thus, disciplinary power does draw an 'external' boundary, namely the boundary separating the sphere of 'the abnormal' from the arena of individual 'differences' (DP 183). Every disciplinary apparatus, Foucault argues, has borders that demarcate a remainder of 'unclassifiable' and 'inassimilable' people: the 'feeble-minded' who cannot be taught in schools, for instance, or the 'mentally ill', the 'residue of all residues', who cannot be assimilated according to any of the disciplinary schemata (PP 53–4). That said, finally, disciplinary power always also crosses this line, devising ever further mechanisms for dealing with 'the irreducible', too, and for 'reestablishing' norms with respect even to them, as the various 'schools for the feeble-minded' illustrate (PP 54). The procedures of division and exclusion did not, then, simply disappear at some point; it is just that by the 1800s the dwellers of the zones thus created – for example, the mad of the asylum – had become targets of disciplinary operations (DP 199).

Regulating life

The second form of life power identified by Foucault has been developing since the mid-1700s as '*regulatory controls*'. This '*bio-politics of the population*' revolves around managing the 'species body' and 'the biological processes' unfolding on and in it (HS1 139): birth and death rates, for instance (SD 243), or population health, and 'all the conditions that can cause these to vary' (HS1 139, see also SD 249–50; Lemke 2011: 36–7; Sheridan 1990: 171–2, 191–3). Disciplinary and regulatory power, emphasises Foucault, 'are not mutually exclusive' (SD 250): they can operate simultaneously (SD 250–2), and regulation has been utilising, 'by sort of infiltrating', the disciplines (SD 242; see also Lemke 2011: 37–8). Nonetheless, they must be distinguished. Regulatory power generally operates from the 'State level', although it can be located in 'sub-State' – for example, medical – 'institutions', too (SD 250; see also Lemke 2011: 37–8). More importantly, whereas disciplinary procedures seek to disassemble the 'multiplicity of men ... into individual bodies', so that they can be better supervised, drilled, 'used', and possibly 'punished', the new '"biopolitics"' engages with that multiplicity insofar as it constitutes 'a global mass' (SD 242–3), the 'body' of the 'population', which is conceived 'as a biological problem' (SD 245, see also 249; Lemke 2011: 37–8). Regulation involves endeavours to secure 'knowledge' and 'control' of problems such as 'the illnesses prevalent in a population' and draining its 'strength', as illustrated by the institutional organisation of healthcare and the campaigns to instruct the population in hygiene in the late eighteenth century (SD 243–4; see also Lemke 2011: 37–8). Moreover, regulation includes attempts to deal with the impact of the natural as well as human-made 'environment' or 'milieu' on population life (SD 244–5). Notwithstanding the resonances between Foucault's outline of regulation and his conception of security (see SD 246, 249, STP 24n5, 49), there are differences between them, too. That said, Foucault's discussion of how security mechanisms function in relation to illness does seem to help illustrate not only how security more specifically understood, but also how the modality of power concerning the population at issue here, operates as power over life.

In the 1700s, Foucault remarks, smallpox was both the 'most widely endemic' illness and prone to 'sudden ... epidemic outbursts'. Characteristic methods for tackling it were variolisation and, later, vaccination (STP 58). Foucault draws attention to a transformation of the understanding of disease in this context. The conception of an 'overall relationship between a disease and a place' gave way to numerical analysis and the representation of the 'distribution of cases in a population' (STP 60). This enabled the calculation of the 'risk' of falling ill for every member of a specific demographic, for example, a two in three risk of catching smallpox for every newborn (STP 60–1). The computation of increased risk of morbidity for people in some demographics compared to others allowed for the identification of 'danger'; being a small child, for instance, was seen to be 'dangerous'. The term 'crisis', finally, was given to a fulminant growth in numbers involving a 'spread' of disease in a certain location – a spread that bore 'the risk, through contagion ..., of multiplying cases that multiply other cases' (STP 61). The concern with population phenomena characteristic of security, focused, as it was here, on biological processes in the population, is typical also of the perspective of regulatory power over life.

For Foucault the approach to smallpox of that period is instructive not only with regard to the outlook of power but also with regard to its exercise. Vaccination and particularly variolisation, he highlights, did not merely mean preventing the disease, but involved inoculating people to trigger a slight form of smallpox and, by dint of this slight form, to avoid 'other possible attacks' (STP 59). Comparing this approach with contemporaneous strategies for dealing with grain scarcity, Foucault designates it as 'a typical mechanism of security' (STP 59, see also 30–49, 341–7). For unlike 'juridical-disciplinary regulations' concentrated on prevention, securitising strategies, as mentioned, centred on 'finding support in the reality of the phenomenon' and getting it to interact with other components to avoid the unwanted phenomenon. Foucault is convinced that their parallels and similarities with securitising strategies of that period contributed to the acceptance of variolisation and vaccination as viable approaches (STP 59).

Normalisation in security

The securitising approach to smallpox illustrates how power operated on population life as well as revealing an important transformation – which Foucault, however, only sketches – in the 'procedures of normalization' (STP 49). Normalisation in the disciplinary context began by 'positing a model' as the 'norm', proceeded to attempts to make individuals 'conform' to it, and culminated in the distinction between those able and unable to as 'normal' and 'abnormal' (STP 57, see also 63; Lemke 2011: 47). By contrast, security apparatuses began by ascertaining what was de facto 'normal', including whole varieties of 'normality'. For example, in the 1700s it was widely accepted that the smallpox death rate in the overall population was about one in eight, whilst the rate among small children was much higher. From the 'more favorable' of the 'distributions' thus charted, a 'norm' was then derived (STP 62–3; see also Lemke 2011: 47). Normalisation in the context of security comprised all the endeavours to align the least favourable, 'deviant normalities' with 'the normal, general curve' (STP 62). In the disciplinary procedure, 'the norm' is 'primary' and (ab)normality defined in view of it (STP 57), whereas in the procedure of security, normality is primary 'and the norm ... deduced from it' (STP 63). Hence, Foucault retrospectively proposes to speak of disciplinary 'normation' (STP 57) in contradistinction to security's 'normalization' (STP 63).

The 'norm', Foucault holds, finally, 'circulates between' both modalities of power over life mentioned above: it is capable of aiding the disciplining of 'a body' as well as the regulation of 'a population' (SD 253). Moreover, 'normalization' is more important for the functioning of power over human life than the law (HS1 89). This power does not simply distinguish those obeying the law from the disobedient, who will be punished and even threatened with death. Instead, it revolves around 'measur[ing]', 'apprais[ing]', and 'hierarchiz[ing]' with regard to norms and around corresponding strategies for 'correcti[on]' and 'regulat[ion]'. Due to the extension of power over life, the role of norms and normalising procedures is becoming ever more – that of the law per se ever less – relevant for understanding how power operates today (HS1 144, see also 89; Lemke 2011: 38–9; Sheridan 1990: 192–3).

CONCLUSION

For Foucault, examinations of current social conditions must centre on the problem of power. Disciplinary power as well as security and government have become more, sovereign power somewhat less, important to such examinations. Foucault's work also suggests that the problem of power over life has become crucial to investigations of contemporary society. In fact, this may well turn out to be one of his work's most influential intimations about what sociology should be dealing with – the sociological literature on biopolitics is substantial and growing. What Foucault's argumentation implies equally strongly, though this is less often emphasised, is that, as a consequence of the development of that power, sociological inquiry will remain an absolutely indispensable endeavour for at least as long as questions of life matter in any way at all:

> … power … has, thanks to the play of technologies of discipline … and technologies of regulation …, succeeded in covering the whole surface that lies between the organic and the biological, between body and population.
>
> We are … in a power that has taken control of both the body and life or … of life in general – with the body as one pole and the population as the other. (SD 253; see also Lemke 2011: 38; Sheridan 1990: 192)

If power has taken charge of life in its entirety, if nothing of life lies outside its target field, then all life is now social life.

Abbreviations

AN: *Abnormal* (2003)

BP: *The Birth of Biopolitics* (2010)

DP: *Discipline and Punish* (1991)

HS1: *History of Sexuality 1* (1981)

PP: *Psychiatric Power* (2006)

SD: *'Society Must Be Defended'* (2004)

STP: *Security, Territory, Population* (2009)

Selected Further Reading

See Sheridan, A. (1990) *Michel Foucault: The Will to Truth*. London: Routledge, for discussions of Foucault's conception of power, and Lemke, T. (2011) *Biopolitics: An Advanced Introduction*. New York: New York University Press, for a solid introduction to the theme of biopolitics in the work of Foucault and a series of other thinkers.

The journal *Foucault Studies* contains a range of scholarly articles on many aspects of Foucault's work and can be found here: https://rauli.cbs.dk/index.php/foucault-studies/index

Notes

1   The family, Foucault mentions, is a domain of sovereign power (PP 79, cf. 115–16, 124–5, DP 215–16). Among the attributes of its power configuration that identify it as sovereign power is 'maximum individualization' at the summit: 'the father, as bearer of the name, and insofar as he exercises power in his name, is the most intense pole of individualization' (PP 80).
2   Equally, discourse can be an obstacle to power, 'expos[ing]' it and offering 'a point of resistance' (HS1 101; see also Sheridan 1990: 186).
3   Foucault points out that disciplinary mechanisms had been formed centuries earlier and gradually spreading since then (PP 40–1, 63–70), before progressively pervading Western societies – in complex processes he describes in some detail – from the seventeenth and eighteenth centuries onwards (PP 70–3, 79, 93, DP 209–28).
4   For more detail on the following key concepts of population, security, government, and governmentality than can be offered here, see Gudmand-Høyer and Lopdrup Hjorth (2009: 99–109, 124–30).
5   Senellart (2009: 388–9) summarises how this concept develops in Foucault's subsequent work.
6   For more detail on the following – and further – aspects of Foucault's reading of liberalism, see Gudmand-Høyer and Lopdrup Hjorth (2009: 110–15).
7   'Liberalism', argues Foucault, entails that 'one should always suspect that one governs too much' (BP 319; see also Lemke 2011: 46). Foucault's related considerations of *homo œconomicus* and civil society cannot be discussed here (see BP 270–313; Senellart 2009: 385).
8   'There was a fragment of regicide in the smallest crime' (AN 82, see also DP 53–4).
9   For a brief overview of the following considerations, see STP 9–11.

8

Jean Baudrillard: Terror, Death, Exchange

PART 1: THE SOCIAL RELATIONS OF LIFE AND DEATH

For the purpose of the particular analyses, previous chapters of this book discussed the respective sociologist's conception of contemporary social conditions before proceeding to discuss their investigations of the problem of life in those conditions. Jean Baudrillard's *œuvre* does not render these analytical steps easily separable. His considerations of the social world are too closely intertwined with his considerations of life and, especially, death. Whilst from Baudrillard's perspective life and death are never not matters of social relations, his most penetrating and striking inquiry into social relations engages throughout with the social relations of life and death. Of central importance to his critical examination of contemporary social conditions is his conception of societies centred on symbolic exchange, including, crucially, exchanges with the dead and the exchange of death. Baudrillard distinguishes such formations from capitalist society, a social order or system in which life and death are mercilessly real, 'death power' operates, and lifetime is frantically accumulated.

Symbolic Exchange

Baudrillard associates what he calls 'the *symbolic*' chiefly with whom he calls 'the primitives' (SED 131). 'The symbolic', he emphasises many years after introducing it into his work, does not mean the same as '"imaginary"', but, for him, 'is *symbolic exchange* as anthropology understands it' (PW 15, emphasis added). Baudrillard distinguishes his notion of 'symbolic exchange' sharply from 'commodity exchange', which is dominant in capitalism (PW 73). When he deployed the former 'concept', he recounts, he sought to launch 'a political critique of our society'. He sought to do so with reference to a notion that some may call 'utopian'; but this notion, he insists, 'has been a living concept in many other cultures' (PW 15).[1] Whilst 'symbolic exchange' at first concerned the 'economic' sphere, that is, 'goods[,] as in potlatch', it was 'the symbolic exchange of death' that eventually became a major theme of Baudrillard's *œuvre* (PW 21).[2]

Exchanging with the dead

In his earlier work, notably in *Symbolic Exchange and Death*, Baudrillard discusses symbolic exchange indeed in explicitly anthropological and overtly sociological terms. It is also here that he discusses symbolic exchange most elaborately with regard to life and death. In other cultures, unlike in our society, 'exchange', he argues, 'does not stop when life comes to an end'. For '[s]ymbolic exchange' continues not only among 'the living', but also with 'the dead', with rocks, with animals (SED 134; see also Butterfield 2002; Genosko 1998: 20–1, 31; Pawlett 2007: 57, 59). Baudrillard speaks of 'an absolute law' (SED 134). During an initiation rite of the Sara people in Chad reported by the ethnologist Robert Jaulin (1967), which plays a privileged role in Baudrillard's thinking in this context (see esp. Genosko 1998: 29, 31–3), 'young initiates ... are given and returned' between 'the living adults and the dead ancestors' (SED 134). First, 'the ancestral group "swallows ..." ... [the] young initiation candidates'. The candidates, crucially, thus 'die *"symbolically"* in order to be reborn... [T]he grand priests ... put ... the initiates ... to death, ... the latter are ... consumed by their ancestors'. Subsequently,

> the earth gives birth to them as their mother had given birth to them. After having been 'killed', the initiates are left in the hands of their initiatory, 'cultural' parents, who instruct them, care for them and train them (initiatory birth).

The candidates' 'death' triggers a continuous 'play of responses' in which – and this is key – death and life can be ritually given and taken away, so that 'death can no longer establish itself as end ...' (SED 131–2, see also 135–7; Genosko 1998: 31–2, 2006; Pawlett 2007: 60).

Indeed, according to Baudrillard these groups conduct exchanges with the dead such that the dead themselves exist as partners in exchange. In the above ritual, the 'death' of the young initiates 'becomes the stakes of a reciprocal-antagonistic exchange between the ancestors and the living'; it installs 'a social relation' which connects the living and the ancestors and in which they are 'partners' (SED 131; see also Genosko 1998: 20–1, 31, 2006; Tierney 1997: 63).

'Initiation lies at the basis of alliances amongst the living and the dead' (SED 134). Jaulin (1967: 245) describes a further occasion on which a husband, through an offering of a portion of meat, 'gives his wife to a dead member of the family', so that the dead man becomes alive again (SED 131). Through 'the nourishment [*la nourriture*], this dead man is included in the life of the group' (SED 131, trsl. modified).[3] In groups such as the Sara, 'the dead are there, different but lifelike [*vivants*] and partners of the living [*vivants*] in multiple exchanges' (SED 127–8, trsl. modified, see also 141–2; Butterfield 2002).[4] Baudrillard also draws upon Maurice Leenhardt's study of the Kanak people here (for more detailed remarks, see Pawlett 2007: 57–8). They, notes Baudrillard (citing Leenhardt, in fact; see Baudrillard 1976: 207n2), do 'not mistake the idea of death for that of nothingness' (SED 189n12).[5] In groups such as the Sara, a dead person can, insofar as the members of the group exchange with her or him, become a partner within the group and thus exist.[6]

Against nature

Whilst Baudrillard does not aim to explain practices of this kind, his work contains a hint at their context. In 'natural death', in 'decomposition', the 'flesh', he argues, stops being 'a sign', the dead body is losing 'its social force of signification' (SED 180; see also Pawlett 2007: 61). One can perhaps most readily imagine this process when thinking of a decomposing face's loss of countenance or the corpse's loss of posture. In Pawlett's formulation, 'putrefaction' is here but 'a formless squalor of signs signifying nothing' (2007: 61). During this precarious period, a 'group' comes to experience 'the terror of its own symbolic decomposition', of its impending inability to exchange signs, converse, and maintain its internal relationships (SED 180). In response to this terrifying experience, the group engages in 'thanatopraxis' (SED 181; Pawlett 2007: 61). This word, which has no entry in the *Oxford English Dictionary*, translates Baudrillard's 'thanatopraxie' (Baudrillard 1976: 274). *Larousse* defines 'thanatopraxie' as a '[m]ethod that permits to delay as long as possible the decomposition of the corpse by embalmment techniques' (s.v.). Leenhardt, notes Pawlett, reports that the Kanak people in fact 'hasten the decomposition of the corpse by the sprinkling of water over it, and obscure the signs of decomposition by embalming' (Pawlett 2007: 61). What is important is Baudrillard's suggestion that every social formation's 'thanatopraxis' can be connected to its urge to deflect the 'loss of signs that befalls the dead' (SED 181; Pawlett 2007: 61). In savage societies specifically, the living 'showe[r] the dead with signs'. This is to ensure their speedy move on to 'the *status* [*statut*] of death', to give 'the dead their difference' (SED 181, trsl. modified, emphasis added; see also Pawlett 2007: 61–2). The dead are thus retrieved from nature and decay, placed into a social position, and enabled once more 'to become partners and exchange their signs' (SED 181; see also Pawlett 2007: 62). The group's ability to converse and connect remains intact. Baudrillard also points to Palermo's famous catacombs, whose passageways are populated with 'disinterred corpses, meticulously fossilised ..., with skin, hair and nails' (SED 181). The bodies, he remarks, are clad – some in basic 'wrap', others 'in costume' – and hold a whole variety 'of attitudes – sardonic, languid, heads bent, fierce or timid' (SED 181–2). In the past, family and friends frequently visited this place 'to see their dead, ... acknowledge them, show them to their children ...' (SED 182; see also Tierney 1997: 63). Their 'society', too, was still able to converse, indeed 'associat[e] with [*frayer avec*]' its 'dead' (SED 182, trsl. modified).

Baudrillard's considerations are also clarified by his contention that the groups at issue here 'have no biological concept of death'. For these people, he holds, 'the biological fact' of 'death, birth or disease' – whatsoever 'comes from nature' and, for the members of modern society, has 'the privilege of necessity and objectivity' – is meaningless. It is that which 'cannot be symbolically exchanged'. The savages regard these as 'defunct, cosmic energies' that their collective could not master 'through exchange'. But those people, Baudrillard emphasises, 'know that death ... is a *social relation*, that its definition is social'. They see death's genuine 'materiality ... in its *form*, which is always the form of a social relation' (SED 131, see also 137; Genosko 1998: 31, 2006; Pawlett 2007: 60; Tierney 1997: 63). The initiation ritual is the installation of 'an exchange ... where there had been only a brute fact'. A 'natural' and 'irreversible death' is, Baudrillard argues, left behind for 'a death that is *given* and *received*' in exchange rituals and hence – and this is decisive – 'reversible in the social exchange, "soluble" in exchange' (SED 132, see also 147; Butterfield 2002; Genosko 1998: 29; Pawlett 2007: 60–1, 2016: 74; Wilcox 2003). Simultaneously, as those rites show, 'birth and death' cease to be in 'opposition': birth and death 'can ... be *exchanged*' for one another 'under the forms [*sous les espèces*] of symbolic reversibility' (SED 132, trsl. modified, see also 147; Pawlett 2007: 60, 62; Tierney 1997: 63).[7] In the realm of symbolic exchange, Baudrillard finds 'the reversibility of life and death'; here, death and life 'are, strictly speaking, exchanged' (PW 15–16, see also SED 159).[8]

It is worth raising two further issues in this context, although they require further clarification below. First, this 'act of exchange', this '*social relation*', that Baudrillard understands by the 'symbolic' does away with 'separated terms': with the separation between birth and death, which, as mentioned, can be ritually endowed and exchanged for each other, but also with the separation between '*soul and ... body*', for instance, or with that between '*man and nature*'. Thus, argues Baudrillard, 'the symbolic operation' finishes with '*the real*'; in other words, 'the two terms lose their reality principle' (SED 133, trsl. modified; see also Butterfield 2002; Genosko 1998: 28–9, 2006; Pawlett 2007: 60–2, 143, 2016: 35–6, 129, 133–4).

Second, Baudrillard problematises the concept of 'value' in this context. Value, he holds, moves in one direction following 'a system of equivalence'. The very notion of value, in turn, depends upon 'opposed terms between which a dialectic can then be established'. But 'in symbolic exchange the terms are reversible' – notably 'life and death', which 'are exchanged' for each other. The 'terms' are not 'separate' and do not enter into a 'dialectic', so 'the idea of value is cast into question' (PW 15). Baudrillard also comments on 'the exchange of goods' here, specifically on 'potlatch'. Potlatch involves 'a ... circulation of goods ... exonerated from the idea of value, a ... circulation which includes ... the squandering of things, but must never stop' (PW 16). What is characteristic of 'potlatch' is 'the sacrifice of value', which is tantamount to its 'negation' (PW 18). Both Baudrillard's point about reality and his point about value require elucidation with reference to his assessment of life and death in capitalism.

Life and Death in Capitalism

According to Baudrillard, a key difference between savage societies and modern, capitalist society is that the dead have been pushed ever 'further away from the group of the living'. Initially, they were shifted from the 'intimacy' of the household to 'the cemetery', which, however, was still located at the core 'of the village or town'. Within 'the new towns or the contemporary metropolises', by contrast, people make no 'provisions for the dead' anymore at all – not 'in physical space', not 'in mental space' (SED 126, trsl. modified; see also Gensoko 1998: 27; Pawlett 2007: 57). Graves expire nowadays, and the deceased are talked about ever less (SED 182). Unlike in previous societies, 'today', Baudrillard explains, '*it is not normal to be dead*'. Hence, unlike previous societies, 'we no longer know what to do with them'. What the dead are shown through being thus extradited is that they 'are no longer ... worthy partners in exchange'. The dead have been excluded from 'the group's symbolic circulation'. 'From savage societies to modern societies', Baudrillard contends, 'the evolution is irreversible: little by little, *the dead cease to exist*' (SED 126, trsl. modified, see also 127–8, 142; Butterfield 2002; Genosko 1998: 20–1, 27; Pawlett 2007: 56–7, 2016: 69–70; Tierney 1997: 63–5).

Unlike primitive societies, modern society has 'de-socialised death'. That is to say, modernity supports 'the illusion of a *biological* materiality of death' (SED 131, emphasis added in accordance with the French original; see also Genosko 1998: 28–9). Today, all measures are taken to ensure a death of natural causes *qua* 'impersonal expiry of the body'. Of course, since, following the severance of all ties with the dead, 'we no longer know how to inscribe [death] into a symbolic ritual of exchange', it is unsurprising that we 'experience our death as a "real" fatality inscribed in our body' (SED 166, trsl. modified; see also Pawlett 2007: 58–9). But thanks to the aura of objectivity it is now granted, 'the physical materiality of death' downright 'paralyses us' (SED 131). The 'biological death', 'objective and punctual', is 'irreversib[le]' – though this is, Baudrillard claims, 'a modern fact of science' and 'specific to our culture' (SED 158). Today, one finds 'no reversibility' anymore, neither in respect of 'life' nor in respect of 'death'. Instead, the latter is the former's 'opposite' (PW 16; see also Butterfield 2002; Pawlett 2007: 56, 58–9, 62, 2016: 69–70; Tierney 1997: 65–7). Whereas in primitive societies, 'the *splitting* of birth and death' was 'conjure[d] away' by rituals in which they were exchanged for one another, now 'life … is split in this way' (SED 132, trsl. modified). Thus, Baudrillard adds, 'life', too, turns into a 'biological irreversibility' in that it is destined 'to decline with the body' (SED 132). Baudrillard presents a configuration of several critical themes around these separations between birth and death and between life and death.

Reality and value

One of his most far-reaching assertions is that 'the separation of birth and death' constitutes the only basis of the very '*reality* of birth' (SED 133, trsl. modified). Likewise, 'the *reality* of life itself derives solely from the disjunction of life and death' (SED 133), and it is also this 'disjunction' that lies 'at the origin of the *reality* of death' (SED 147). Likewise, the 'reality' – the '"objectivity"', the '"materiality"' – 'of nature … derives solely from the separation of man and nature …'. Baudrillard speaks of the '*effect of the real*' and understands it as nothing but 'the structural effect of the disjunction between two terms'; and he conceives of 'our famous reality principle' as nothing but the 'generalisation of this disjunctive code to all levels' (SED 133; see also Butterfield 2002; Genosko 1998: 28, 2006; Pawlett 2007: 58–61). By contrast, where one term can be socially exchanged for another that is not its equivalent, such as death for life, the reality – the non-negotiable '"thing-ness"' (Pawlett 2016: 36, see also 133–4) – of both is in question. The life/death separation, Baudrillard emphasises, is the original model of 'all the disjunctions' underpinning the various 'structures of the real' (SED 133; see also Genosko 1998: 28; Pawlett 2007: 56).

Moreover, Baudrillard describes the current 'system' as one 'of values': in this system 'what is positive is on the side of life, what is negative is on the side of death'; in it, life and death are not reversible; in it, 'death' constitutes the 'opposite' and 'the end of life' (PW 16, see also SED 147; Butterfield 2002; Pawlett 2007: 56, 58–9, 62, 2016: 69, 106; Tierney 1997: 65–7). It is, Baudrillard specifies again, the life no longer exchanged for death, the 'life' from which 'death' has been 'removed [*ôtée*]', the '*residual* life', that 'can', henceforth, 'be read in the operational terms of calculation and value' (SED 130, trsl. modified). Within the modern capitalist 'system', not only does 'life' have '"reality"', it is also, in fact, 'live[d] … as a positive value' (SED 133; see also Wilcox 2003).

Death power

In comparatively brief passages roughly contemporaneous with Foucault's development of his distinction between the right of death and biopower (*bio-pouvoir*) (Foucault 1976) (see Chapter 7 of this book), Baudrillard outlines what he, giving it this English name, calls '*Death Power*' (SED 129; 1976: 200). The initial 'point of emergence of social control', Baudrillard claims, can be located in the breaking apart of 'the union of the living and the dead' and thus in the interruption of 'the exchange of life and death'. In other words, it can be located in the extraction of 'life from death' and in the imposition of 'a prohibition on death and the dead'. 'Power' installs itself exactly on this barrier separating death from life. The power of 'the castes of priests', in particular, fed on their 'exclusive control over relations with the dead' (SED 130, trsl. modified; see also Genosko 1998: 27–8; Pawlett 2007: 56–8) and on their monopoly upon 'manag[ing] ... the imaginary sphere of death' (SED 144, see also 127–9). But ultimately, says Baudrillard, all 'power' is founded 'on the manipulation and administration of death' (SED 130; see also Pawlett 2007: 64; Tierney 1997: 64). 'The power of the State' of modernity simply rests on its 'management *of life as the objective afterlife* [Baudrillard plays on the French term *survie* here, which also translates as *survival*]' (SED 144).

Economy of life

Finally, Baudrillard outlines the theme of political economy in this context. According to Baudrillard, 'the Church' initially implemented 'a *political economy of individual salvation*', which would eventually turn on 'the accumulation of works and merits', in particular. In this arrangement, 'the Kingdom' came to be situated beyond 'death', whilst death was now faced by each person alone, rather than communally. From the 1500s onwards, Baudrillard elaborates, Protestantism, for instance through dismantling 'collective ceremonials', was advancing the isolated person's 'anguish of death' (SED 145). More importantly perhaps, Protestantism, as Baudrillard adds with reference to Max Weber's (2001) famous sociological analysis of the protestant ethic, set in motion an 'immense modern enterprise of staving off death: the ethics of accumulation and material production, sacralisation through investment, labour, and profit, which one commonly calls the "spirit of capitalism" ...'. From 'this salvation-machine ...', Baudrillard concedes, 'intra-worldly ascesis is little by little withdrawn in the interests of worldly and productive accumulation'. Yet 'the aim' remains the same: 'the protection against death' (SED 145–6, trsl. modified; see also Palwett 2016: 69).

Traditional 'communities' having been dissolved, 'death', continues Baudrillard, is not 'divided' (SED 146) or shared – 'se partage' (1976: 224) – anymore. Death begins to reflect the properties of 'material goods' (SED 146). These goods, however, 'circulate ever less, as in previous exchanges, between inseparable partners' (SED 146, trsl. modified). Instead, they circulate 'increasingly', as is characteristic of capitalism, 'under the sign of a general equivalent', that is, ultimately, money. And just like, in capitalism, everybody stands 'alone before the general equivalent', everybody stands 'alone before death' (SED 146). Soon, the urge to eliminate 'death' by way of 'accumulation' – by accumulating value, notably 'time as value', and thus by pushing 'death' to the end 'of a linear infinity of value' – begins to operate as an essential component in the engine 'of the rationality of political economy' (SED 146–7; see also Butterfield 2002; Tierney 1997: 68).

> Even those who no longer believe in a personal eternity believe in the infinity of time as they do in a species-capital of double-compound interests. It is the infinity of capital that passes into the infinity of time, the eternity of a productive system which no longer knows the reversibility of gift-exchange, but only the irreversibility of quantitative growth. (SED 146, trsl. modified)[9]

Baudrillard sees similarly stark commonalities between the function of Christianity's 'ascesis' and the 'paradoxical logic' of contemporary 'security'. In ascesis, an 'accumulation of suffering and penitence' was to constitute 'a protective sarcophagus against hell'. Today's obsession with 'security' involves 'an anticipation of death in life itself'; life proceeds as though in a 'sarcophagus' behind 'protection' after 'protection', 'defence' after 'defence', as death lurks behind every corner of life (SED 178). Life turns into a 'book-keeping ... on survival', an accountancy of time gained, which has replaced 'the radical compatibility of life and death' under symbolic exchange (SED 178–9). With the termination of 'the *ambivalence* of life and death', of the latter's 'symbolic *reversibility*', not only does life turn into value, as already mentioned, but also begins 'a process of accumulation of life as *value*' (SED 147, emphasis added on reversibility in accordance with the French original).

Today, 'death' is unidimensional, merely 'the end of the biological journey', as though, sighs Baudrillard, 'a tyre' were deflating. Life is now a 'quantity'; 'death' is 'nothing' (SED 163–4; see also Pawlett 2007: 58, 63). A dead person has nothing left 'to exchange'. They simply vanish from the scene (SED 164).

The Breach of Suicide

According to Baudrillard, it is only when 'life' becomes 'life-capital', that is, becomes 'a quantitative evaluation', as 'living' turns into 'accumulation', that 'a biomedical science and technology' of life extension emerge. Crucially, this new ability to make 'the limits of life' retreat gives rise to the conception of a '"natural" death'. Here, a natural death means simultaneously a '"normal"' death, a death arriving '"at life's proper term"', a 'death ... subject to science' – to its capabilities at the present moment in time – and a death destined, ultimately, 'to be exterminated by science'. As though every individual had a '"normal expectancy" of life' and a '"contract of life"', each ought to be able to get to the end of his or her 'biological "capital"', to enjoy life "to the end" without violence or premature death' (SED 162, trsl. modified; see also Butterfield 2002; Pawlett 2007: 62–3; Tierney 1997: 67–8, 70, 76n19). Increasingly, 'society', deploying its scientific and technological means, is 'responsible' for every person's 'death'. But living to their 'natural death' is equally 'a *duty*' of every individual. Any death deviant from this 'natural' and simultaneously socially controlled death constitutes 'a *social* scandal' (SED 162; see also Pawlett 2007: 55, 64, 66, 2016: 70, 128). Whereas the savages' arrangements were such that death was 'given and received', in other words 'socialised through exchange', current arrangements are such 'that death is never done to anybody by *someone* else, but only by "nature"' under social surveillance (SED 166, see also 1976: 253).

What is thus of vital importance is that people's lives and deaths not be 'freely theirs'. In fact, death should not be prone 'to biological chance' either. All 'life and death' is to come under 'social control'. This objective reveals itself, for instance, in the maintenance, assisted by very expensive health technologies, 'of life as value'. But it is also manifest in the 'economic choice' to let a certain percentage of sufferers from a particular illness die (SED 174, trsl. modified; see also Genosko 2006; Pawlett 2007: 55, 64, 66; Tierney 1997: 68–9, 71–2). To illustrate his point, Baudrillard also cites an ad for seatbelts (SED 177) with the telling phrase '"Bouclez-la"' (Baudrillard 1976: 269), whose double meaning is similar to that of the English instruction '"Belt up"' (SED 177). 'Security', he argues, 'is another form of social control'. People must be deprived 'of the last possibility of *giving* themselves their own death' (SED 177).

In this context, Baudrillard draws attention to suicide.[10] In a passage written many years after *Symbolic Exchange and Death*, he describes 'suicide' as nothing less than 'the only political act worthy of the name' (IELP 131). *Symbolic Exchange and Death* offers several considerations in support of this contention. Insofar as any 'system' is comprehensively beaten simply by the inability to achieve 'total perfection', that is, as soon as the least thing eludes 'its rationality', every 'suicide' causes a tiny yet 'inexpiable breach' in a system of social death regulation. In short, 'in a highly integrated system', 'every suicide becomes subversive' (SED 175–6; see also Genosko 2006; Pawlett 2007: 64–5; Tierney 1997: 70–1).

Today, Baudrillard adds, every person constitutes 'a parcel of capital'. According to the contemporary 'law of value', people have no 'right to remove any capital or value' (SED 175). Consequently, they have 'no right' to self-destruction (SED 175–6). The 'suicide', who obliterates the bundle of 'capital' she or he disposes of, thereby 'revolts', namely against that very 'orthodoxy of value': taking one's life 'in a society saturated by the law of value' poses 'a challenge to its fundamental rule' (SED 176; see also Genosko 2006; Pawlett 2007: 65).

The contemporary 'system', Baudrillard sums up, 'exhorts one to live [*somme de vivre*] and capitalise life'. It is a tightly 'regulated' sphere – a sphere, he remarks, 'of realised death'. In it, the sole 'temptation is to normalise everything by destruction'. And to Baudrillard 'resistance' is becoming noticeable. This resistance is directed against the precept 'of accumulation, production and conservation' of the human being, wherein she or he is facing her or his already 'programmed death'. Suicide thus becomes a form of 'death ... played off against death' (SED 177, trsl. modified; see also Pawlett 2007: 65–6).

Baudrillard's formulations regarding the political, subversive quality of suicide would yet prove highly prescient.

PART 2: THE SOCIAL RELATIONS OF TERRORISM

Contemporary capitalism, Baudrillard diagnoses, supports vast endeavours of 'archiving the entire world' (SED 185, trsl. modified). The aim of these endeavours, he claims, is the world's being 'discovered by some future civilisation' (SED 185). In Baudrillard's view, 'political economy' itself is established with the intention of being 'recognised as immortal' by a society yet to come (SED 185–6). In fact, he points to 'the hieroglyphic schemes' of Paris's La Défense district and, not long after its 1973 opening, New York's World Trade Center – alongside the media's 'great informational schemes', for instance – to suggest that today's 'humanity' is already 'an object of contemplation to itself' (SED 186).[11] The entire 'system of political economy' is now a 'finality without end', an 'aesthetic vertigo of productivity'; and 'with its gigantic towers, its satellites, its giant computers ...', the system 'double[s] itself as signs' (SED 186). Understandably, the attack on the World Trade Center in 2001 immediately drew Baudrillard's sustained attention. For Baudrillard, contemporary terrorism is – and September 11, in particular, was – a conspicuous scene in which not only the problem of life and death but the problem of the social relations of life and death can be analysed further.

Towering Twins

In the aftermath of 9/11, during a philosophical discussion concerning the Manhattan atrocities, Baudrillard presented a 'Requiem for the Twin Towers' of the World Trade Center (ST 35–48). The piece draws heavily on – almost replicating – several formulations published a quarter-century earlier in *Symbolic Exchange and Death*.[12] The latter book reports Baudrillard's observation that New York City has, by dint of its architecture, always 'retraced ... the contemporary form of the system of capital' (SED 69, trsl. modified, see also ST 40). When capitalism was still 'competitive', it was delineated by a skyline drawn by 'great buildings ... confront[ing] each other in a *competitive* verticality' (SED 69, see also ST 38). Generally, every skyscraper has been exceeded by another, thus constituting an 'original moment of a system continually surpassing itself' (SED 70; see also Genosko 2006). In the 1970s, however, structures began to 'stand next to one another, without challenging each other any longer, like the columns of a statistical graph' (SED 69, trsl. modified). They embody a social 'system' that has become 'digital and countable', in which 'competition' has given way to 'networks and monopoly' (ST 38–9, see also SED 69). The Twin Towers, in particular, were 'identical', which '*signifies* the end of all competition' and 'of every original reference' (SED 69, see also ST 39; Genosko 2006). Each tower was its twin's 'model';

disregarding all other structures, they did not 'compare themselves to' and 'challenge' those others anymore (SED 70, see also ST 39–40). The towers indicated that a 'strategy of the model' rather than one 'of competition' would be dominant at the system's core (SED 70). What was hit in New York on that cloudless September morning in 2001, says Baudrillard, was 'the brain … of the system' (ST 41).

The Twin Towers, Baudrillard points out, were not only a material, but also, and more importantly, 'a symbolic object' (ST 43) – 'symbolic in the weak sense', to be sure, yet 'symbolic' still (ST 43n3). They symbolised 'financial power and global economic liberalism'. They 'were the emblem of [global] power' (ST 43–4, see also 47) and, 'in their very twinness', the consummate 'embodiments' of a world 'order' that, by the turn of the millennium, had become 'definitive' (ST 6; see also Butterfield 2002; Genosko 2006; Pawlett 2007: 144–5, 2016: 130). The hijackers, Baudrillard holds, pointed the aeroplanes specifically at 'the symbolic object' (ST 44). They demolished a highly 'prestigious' edifice – in fact, as he will shortly be shown to argue, 'a whole (Western) value-system and a world order' were wrecked along with it (ST 37; see also Pawlett 2007: 143–5, 2016: 129–30).

Globalisation and Terrorism

To make this explicit, Baudrillard sees the devastation of the World Trade Center on 9/11 as part of a 'violent protest against' the 'violence of globalization' (ST 41; see also Merrin 2005: 104, 112). 'Current terrorism …', he emphasises, 'is contemporaneous with globalization' (ST 87; see also Merrin 2005: 103–4, 111–12). The West has been fond of presenting specifically modern 'Western' creations – for instance 'human rights' or 'freedoms' or 'democracy' – as 'universal', as in harmony with 'all cultures and their difference' (PX 11–12, see also SO 155, ST 87–8). For a time, those values were proclaimed 'as mediating values' and, Baudrillard acknowledges, were somewhat successful at 'integrating singularities, as differences, into a universal culture of difference' (ST 91, see also PX 14, SO 158; Merrin 2005: 104).[13] However, the 'promotion' of a 'value … to universality' is perilous: 'universalization' has come to involve an 'indefinite extension' of 'values' that entails their 'neutralization'; the 'expansion' of 'human rights' or 'democracy' matches 'their weakest definition', warns Baudrillard (PX 12, see also SO 156, ST 88–9, 97–8).

From his perspective, it is actually 'the market' – the constant movement of capital and 'promiscuity of … all products' – as well as 'the promiscuity of all signs and … values' that are being 'globalized' (PX 12, see also SO 156, ST 89–90). The 'universal values' are increasingly illegitimate (ST 91, see also PX 14, SO 158). A now victorious 'globalization' removes 'values' as well as 'differences' (ST 91, see also PX 14, SO 158; Merrin 2005: 104).[14] Thus putatively 'universal values' are not able to fulfil their integrative role anymore. In the end, an omnipotent 'global technostructure' on the one hand confronts 'singularities' – which have been 'returned to the wild' – on the other (ST 91, see also PX 14, SO 158–9; Merrin 2005: 104). Indeed, the occident of today seeks to impose the 'law of equivalence' upon the various 'cultures' (ST 97). Global capitalism 'hounds out any form of ... singularity' (ST 94; see also Merrin 2005: 104, 112). For such 'singular forms', the sole options are 're-enter ... or ... disappear' (ST 97).[15] Vis-à-vis globalisation's simultaneously 'homogenizing' and 'dissolving power', in turn, 'heterogeneous forces' are rebelling around the world (ST 94, see also PX 15, SO 159; Butterfield 2002; Merrin 2005: 103–4, 111–12). Baudrillard sees here 'a rejection' of both 'the global technostructure' and 'the mental structure of equivalence of all cultures' (ST 95, see also PX 13–14, SO 157–8).[16] In fact, he deems 'singularities' able to frustrate 'the system' and its 'single-track thinking'. They can be 'subtle', for instance in 'art', but also 'violent', as, precisely, in the case of 'terrorism' (ST 96). Terrorism wreaks vengeance for 'all the singular cultures' that have vanished so the 'single global power' could be installed (ST 97, see also 9; Merrin 2005: 103; Pawlett 2007: 144, 2016: 130).

Humiliation and Terrorism

Yet Baudrillard unequivocally rejects any notion of 'a clash of civilizations or religions' (ST 11, see also 73, 97; Merrin 2005: 103; Pawlett 2007: 144, 2016: 130). For one thing, one might, he says, rather 'speak of ... the Fourth' – and, to be exact, the first truly worldwide – 'World War' (ST 11). The near all-encompassing 'single world order' is forced to tackle 'antagonistic forces', rebellious 'singularities', everywhere, including in its very midst (ST 12; see also Merrin 2005: 103–4, 112). Baudrillard insists that no 'world order' could avoid such conflicts: 'if Islam dominated the world, terrorism would rise against Islam' (ST 12). For another thing, this 'confrontation', whereby an equalising 'universal culture' and phenomena that still preserve elements of 'irreducible alterity' come to blows, is, he argues, 'almost anthropological' (ST 97). The latter adjective deserves underlining, for it simultaneously points to a dimension of globalisation and terrorism from which a further issue already thematised in *Symbolic Exchange and Death* resurfaces.

In *Passwords*, which was published shortly before the Manhattan attacks, Baudrillard calls into question the anthropological approach to 'potlatch', the narrow focus on its operation 'in primitive societies', and the idea that 'we are totally in market societies'. Suggesting that contemporary social relations, too, might call for an anthropological perspective, he confesses his readiness 'to believe ... that ... things are decided', now as ever, in the realm of 'symbolic exchange'. What Baudrillard emphasises here is that the specific 'form' of the 'challenge, of one-upmanship, of potlatch' continues to be 'fundamental' (PW 17–18; see also Merrin 2005: 104–5; Pawlett 2007: 55, 145, 2016: 131).

Correspondingly, Baudrillard holds that the antagonism that came to a head on 9/11 cannot be grasped without paying close attention to the problem of 'symbolic obligation' (ST 100). For in Baudrillard's eyes 'terrorism rests' to a great extent 'on the despair of the humiliated and insulted' (ST 104). Everyone else's 'hatred of the West', he claims, is fuelled not by 'deprivation and exploitation' but by the 'humiliation' they have suffered. They have suffered this humiliation, crucially, as the West has 'given' them 'everything', and they cannot return it (ST 100, see also 6; Merrin 2005: 104–5; Pawlett 2007: 140). And not only they: Baudrillard considers ours a similar position of 'always receiving' – possibly anything at all – 'through a technical system of generalized exchange and general gratification' (ST 102; see also Genosko 1998: 22–4; Merrin 2005: 105). Whereas the 'God' or 'nature' of previous societies could be presented with something in return, notably through 'sacrifice', in 'our culture' any 'counter-gift' has become 'impossible'. Making 'reciprocation' impossible – and this, again, is decisive – constitutes the foundation 'of all domination'. For Baudrillard, a 'unilateral gift' amounts to 'an act of power' (ST 101–2; see also Genosko 1998: 22–4, 2006; Pawlett 2007: 66). Experiencing such 'saturation' and 'protected', our Western 'existence' is simultaneously 'captive' (ST 103). An 'abreaction' to it, be it as 'open violence', including terrorist acts, be it as the 'self-hatred and remorse' we feel, is, Baudrillard claims, unavoidable (ST 103; see also Merrin 2005: 105). Everybody is averse 'to *any* definitive power' (ST 6, emphasis added) – 'they *did it*, but we *wished for* it' (ST 5; see also Butterfield 2002; Merrin 2005: 103; Pawlett 2007: 143–4, 2016: 34, 106–7, 129–30).

Terrorism and Its Ramifications

In Baudrillard's view, on September 11 the global system was not merely attacked, but hit hard. He points to several reasons for this. First of all, to the extent that 'the system' constitutes a 'single network', inflicting damage at even just one 'point' amounts to harming the whole system. Thus, a small number of 'suicide attackers', by striking but two sites, '... unleashed a global catastrophic process' (ST 8). More specifically, and crucially, they did so 'thanks to the absolute weapon of death, enhanced by technological efficiency' (ST 8; see also Merrin 2005: 103–4; Pawlett 2007: 143–4, 2016: 129–30). On the one hand, notes Baudrillard, 'the terrorists' have access to, and are using, 'weapons that are the system's own' (ST 20), such as 'stock-market speculation' and various technologies, to attack it (ST 19, see also 23, 27; Genosko 2006). On the other hand, what ultimately lends the attackers their 'superiority' is their successful deployment of those 'modern resources' together with a further, 'highly symbolic weapon', namely 'their own deaths' (ST 20–1; see also Butterfield 2002; Merrin 2005: 103–4; Pawlett 2007: 143–4, 2016: 129–30). Baudrillard, as is well known, had pinpointed the scandalous, subversive, rebellious quality of suicide as early as the 1970s (see e.g. Genosko 1998: 6, 21, 2006; Pawlett 2007: 64–6; see also above). The 9/11 attackers, using 'their own deaths' both 'offensive[ly]' (ST 16) and in conjunction with the weaponry of 'the system' under attack, rendered their suicides truly damaging (ST 20–1; see also Merrin 2005: 103–4).[17] Amidst Baudrillard's considerations of this attack and its ramifications, his spotlight on the symbolic sphere is once more vital.

Terrorism's symbolic relationship

Nothing is more damaging 'for global power', Baudrillard holds, than being 'humiliated'. Yet this is just what happened. Whilst the West had been humiliating the rest of the world throughout the late twentieth century, global power 'was humiliated' at the beginning of the twenty-first – and in a very similar fashion: the hijackers 'inflicted something on it ... that it cannot return'. Here, 'global power was defeated symbolically' (ST 101; see also Merrin 2005: 105–6; Pawlett 2007: 146). The 'excess of power' of the 'system', Baudrillard concedes, 'poses an insoluble challenge', but 'the terrorists respond with a definitive act ... not susceptible of exchange' either (ST 9). The New York attacks were a 'symbolic challenge' (ST 12; see also Butterfield 2002; Merrin 2005: 103–4, 106, 163n2; Wilcox 2003).

The objective behind terrorism, elaborates Baudrillard, is 'to radicalize the world by sacrifice' (ST 10). It is decisive within the terrorist act that the attackers throw 'their own deaths' at the 'system' to attack it. This 'system', as already indicated with reference to *Symbolic Exchange and Death*, adheres to 'an ideal of zero deaths'. This entails, of course, that attacks such as those in 2001 are intolerable to it (ST 16; see also Genosko 2006; Merrin 2005: 103–4; Pawlett 2007: 136–7, 2016: 106–7, 127–8). And indeed, the West is deploying 'means of deterrence and destruction' in response – although, since the West's adversaries are manifestly '"... as eager to die as the Americans are to live ..."', these measures appear trivial (ST 16).

Yet Baudrillard also draws attention to a further and, it seems, graver problem. The hijackers successfully moved the confrontation 'into the symbolic sphere'. What was important on the morning of 9/11 was the incursion not simply 'of death in real time ... but ... of ... a death which [was] symbolic and sacrificial'. Baudrillard goes as far as to suggest that on that day 'the system' was challenged or provoked 'by a gift'. Within the symbolic realm, crucially, a strict 'rule' applies, namely a rule 'of challenge, reversion and outbidding'. As a consequence of this, the only possible response by 'the system' is reciprocation, which is to say, 'its own death and ... collapse'. On Baudrillard's reading, the 'terrorist hypothesis' is precisely this: 'the system ... will commit suicide in response to the multiple challenges posed by deaths and suicides' (ST 16–17; see also Butterfield 2002; Genosko 1998: 6, 12–13, 22–3, 25–7, 2006; Merrin 2005: 103–4; Pawlett 2007: 64–6, 145, 2016: 36–7, 106–7, 130–1; Wilcox 2003).

However, in capitalist society, to repeat, 'death' is basically 'forbidden' (ST 94). The 'system' absolutely 'cannot exert' the 'symbolic violence ... of its own death' (ST 18). According to Western society's 'values', the terrorists' introduction of their 'own death into the game' constitutes 'cheating' (ST 23, see also 19). The West pursues a '"zero-death" strategy', that of a '"clean" technological war', which is no suitable response (ST 21; see also Genosko 2006; Merrin 2005: 83–4, 106–7, 112). Having obliterated this 'from its own culture', global power has not the slightest notion of 'the terrain of the symbolic challenge and death' anymore and can no longer act on that level (ST 15; see also Merrin 2005: 103–4; Pawlett 2007: 145–6, 2016: 130–1; Wilcox 2003). When, in the aftermath of 9/11, the United States were commencing military operations in Afghanistan, Baudrillard sensed that their goal would be simply to 'liquidat[e]' an 'invisible' 'target' (ST 26; see also Butterfield 2002; Merrin 2005: 83–5, 103–4; Pawlett 2007: 142–3, 146). Yet the terrorists' attacks, which require their 'death', do not follow an exclusively 'destructive logic'; they rather form part of a 'challenge', a 'duel', a 'personal' relationship with the opponent: the 'power' that 'humiliated you … must be humiliated' – must 'be made to lose face' – in turn (ST 25–6; see also Genosko 2006; Pawlett 2007: 142–4, 2016: 130). In the end, the West's answer to the terrorists' 'challenge' remained inferior. Neither 'bombing' the opponent 'to smithereens' nor caging them 'like a dog at Guantánamo', Baudrillard insists, will do. The West was bitterly 'humiliated' and fell short of 'humiliating the other' in response (ST 101; see also Butterfield 2002; Merrin 2005: 106–7).

The system's escalation

Still, 'the system and power' cannot extricate themselves from the 'symbolic obligation', and it is with this obligation that Baudrillard associates 'the only *chance* of their catastrophe' (ST 18, trsl. modified, emphasis added; see also Genosko 1998: 22–3, 2006; Merrin 2005: 26; Pawlett 2007: 64–5, 145, 2016: 37, 107, 131; Wilcox 2003).[18] In a remark in his late 1970s essay '… Or, the end of the social', Baudrillard describes the 'position' of a 'protagonist of defiance' (SM 70) or of the challenge – 'défi' in the original (1982a: 73) – as 'suicidal' (SM 70). By dint of 'the destruction of value', namely her or his 'own', the protagonist compels the recipient of the challenge to issue 'a never equivalent, ever escalating response' (SM 70; see also Pawlett 2007: 135–6, 2016: 44). In his closely related considerations of the German Autumn of 1977 – the hijacking of the Lufthansa airliner *Landshut*, which ended in Mogadishu with the pilot and most of the hijackers dead, and the deaths of members of the Red Army Faction at Stammheim prison shortly afterwards – Baudrillard describes 'the death of the terrorists (or of the hostages)' as an 'abolition of value' (SM 120). This brief text supports key components of his analysis of 9/11 (ST). Referring to the latter event, Baudrillard identifies a 'vertiginous cycle' in which the 'exchange of death' is 'impossible' (ST 18, see also SM 122). Within it, argues Baudrillard, as Merrin (2005: 104, see also 163n2; Wilcox 2003), too, has highlighted, the terrorists' 'death', though a minute 'point', generates a massive 'suction … Around this tiny point the whole system of the real and of power [*la puissance*] gathers' (ST 18, see also SM 120). It contracts or cramps momentarily (ST 18; SM 120), then activates 'all its anti-bodies' (SM 120), and, crucially, ultimately 'perishes by its own hyperefficiency'. The terrorists seek to provoke 'an excess of reality, and have the system collapse' underneath (ST 18, see also SM 120; Merrin 2005: 163n2; Wilcox 2003).

According to Baudrillard, Merrin continues, the terrorists' assault 'provokes a hyperreaction and reversal of the system, leading it to introduce the same repressive security measures as fundamentalist societies' (2005: 104, see also 163n2). Still drawing on his considerations of the terrorist activities of 1977 (SM 113–23), Baudrillard accentuates that after 9/11 one can observe the 'repression of terrorism ru[n] along the same unpredictable spiral as the terrorist act'. For Baudrillard, such 'unleashing of reversibility' constitutes the terrorists' 'true victory' (ST 31, trsl. modified, see also SM 115–16; Merrin 2005: 163n2; Pawlett 2007: 136–7). It can be seen in several of their attack's 'ramifications': in various recessions (ST 31; see also Wilcox 2003) and, most strikingly to Baudrillard, 'in the slump' (ST 32) – 'récession' in the original text (Baudrillard 2001) – 'in the value-system, ... the ... ideology of freedom, of free circulation'; that is, in the slump in the very ideology of which the West, as mentioned, has been availing itself for influencing 'the rest of the world'. What can be witnessed after September 11 is the realisation of 'liberal globalization' as, conversely, the institution of 'total control', the 'terror' of security, the 'maximum' level 'of constraints and restrictions' (ST 32; see also Butterfield 2002).

Collapsing Twins

In his 'Requiem' for the World Trade Center structures, Baudrillard once more reports his observation that New York's architecture has been delineating 'the present form of the system and ... its ... developments' with remarkable precision (ST 40). This observation leads him to read the Twin Towers' 'collapse' as an early indication of the eventual 'disappearance ... of the world system' such structures have embodied (ST 40–1). As he has just been shown to argue, on September 11 that system was, for various reasons, struck severely. Notably, shortly after the attack Baudrillard was already able to highlight the ensuing slump in the ideology of free circulation. As he reiterates in 'Hypotheses on terrorism' (ST 51–83), the attackers' triumph is their having aroused an 'obsession with security' in the Western world that amounts but to 'a veiled form of perpetual terror' (ST 81; see also Merrin 2005: 104, 163n2; Pawlett 2016: 107).

Simultaneously, the propositions in 'Requiem' resonate also with another point addressed earlier. Baudrillard treats the Twin Towers' 'collapse' as 'the major symbolic event'. It is evidence of the 'fragility of global power' (ST 43). In Baudrillard's eyes, as Genosko (2006), in particular, has emphasised, the towers in fact 'collapse[d] themselves'; their collapse 'resembles a suicide' (ST 43, see also 7–8; Merrin 2005: 103; Pawlett 2007: 145, 2016: 131). It was as if, Baudrillard specifies, the 'system, by its *internal* fragility', partook in 'its own liquidation', in 'terrorism' (ST 45, emphasis added, see also 7–8; Genosko 2006). In 'Hypotheses', Baudrillard provides the diagnosis of

> a society's obscure predisposition to contribute to its own doom – as illustrated by the high-level dissensions between the CIA and FBI which, by reciprocally neutralizing information, gave the terrorists the unprecedented chance to succeed. (ST 79)

Moreover, and consistent with one of the aforementioned claims, 'Hypotheses' not only classes the attackers' 'strategy of ... overturning power' among the consequences of the 'unacceptability of that global power', but also accentuates that both 'Islamist' extremists and others ('we') alike meet the 'global order' with 'rejection' (ST 73–4). According to 'Requiem' again, when 'the power of power' grows, so, inevitably, does 'the will to destroy it': the closer a 'system' comes to being all-powerful, 'the stronger' will be 'the rejection' – but also, and crucially, the '*internal* rejection' – it is met with (ST 45, emphasis added, see also 5–7; Genosko 2006; Merrin 2005: 103–4, 111–12).

CONCLUSION

In Baudrillard's sociological work, considerations of the social world are intertwined – possibly more closely than in any other *œuvre* discussed in this book – with considerations of life and death. This is true of his conception of societies centred on symbolic exchange relations, in which life and death are reversible and exchangeable, as well as of his critique of the capitalist system, in which life is accumulated and death staved off. In 1987, Baudrillard admitted that his distinction between these two formations disclosed a certain 'nostalgia for a symbolic order ... born out of the deep of primitive societies' (EC 80). Some of his writing may well convey nostalgia, but Baudrillard does not associate symbolic exchange exclusively with archaic or tribal societies:[19] his essays regarding the Manhattan attacks unequivocally identify expressions of the problematic of the social relations of life and death, including, crucially, the problematic of symbolic exchange, in the social relations that foment, in the acts that constitute, and in the processes that are triggered by contemporary terrorism (see also e.g. Butterfield 2002; Genosko 2006; Merrin 2005: 100–1, 113; Pawlett 2007: 55, 143–6, 2016: 33, 67, 126–31; Wilcox 2003). These phenomena still pester the global order over a decade after Baudrillard's death. Not only in this sense will his sociological inquiries into the social relations of life and death – his analyses of symbolic exchange relations no less than his account of the capitalist system – keep provoking and challenging sociologists in their critical examinations of social life in the twenty-first century.

Abbreviations

EC: *The Ecstasy of Communication* (1988)

F: *Fragments: Conversations with François L'Yvonnet* (2004)

IELP: *The Intelligence of Evil, or, The Lucidity Pact* (2013)

PW: *Passwords* (2003a)

PX: *Paroxysm: Interviews with Philippe Petit* (1998)

SED: *Symbolic Exchange and Death* (1993)

SM: *In the Shadow of the Silent Majorities or, the End of the Social and Other Essays* (1983)

SO: *Screened Out* (2002b)

ST: *The Spirit of Terrorism and Other Essays* (2003b)

Selected Further Reading

For a thorough and accessible discussion of many of the key domains of Baudrillard's social thought, including his conception of symbolic exchange and his analyses of terrorism, see Pawlett, W. (2007) *Jean Baudrillard: Against Banality*. London: Routledge.

An engaging discussion of Baudrillard's thinking with specific attention to the media is provided by Merrin, W. (2005) *Baudrillard and the Media: A Critical Introduction*. Cambridge: Polity Press.

The International Journal of Baudrillard Studies contains a wealth of articles on many aspects of Baudrillard's work. It can be accessed here: https://www2. ubishops.ca/baudrillardstudies

Notes

1 A few years before Baudrillard conducted these reflections, Tierney had asserted – somewhat less equivocally – that Baudrillard 'offers' the 'claims about symbolic exchange' in his 1970s work 'as a sort of counter-myth to the story ... moderns have been telling themselves about death ...', 'as a utopian alternative to modernity's more rigidly demar-cated stance toward death', but 'not ... as historical truths', and that their 'value ... lies' more 'in their ability to reveal and challenge certain features of modernity that have gone unnoticed' and less 'in their historical veracity' (Tierney 1997: 64, see also 69, 75n16; Butterfield 2002; Wilcox 2003).

2 For wider discussions of Baudrillard's notion of symbolic exchange, see for example Pawlett (2007: 66–9, 2016: 32–7). On the influence of Baudrillard's reception of Marcel Mauss's (2002) examination of potlatch and gift exchange on that notion, see Genosko (1998: 25–7); Pawlett (2007: 49–55).

3   According to Jaulin, the 'value' of the 'nourishment ... is, like the hunger of the dead man, symbolic of participation in the exchanges of consumption goods and thus of inclusion in the life of the group ...' (Jaulin 1967: 244).

4   When '[c]annibals ...', in turn, 'eat their own dead', they do so, Baudrillard claims, '... to pay homage' to the dead. Thereby, they seek to avoid that the dead, 'left to the biological order of rotting [*la pourriture*], ... escape from the social order and turn against the group ... This devouring is a social act, a *symbolic* act, that aims to maintain a tissue of bonds with the dead man ...' (SED 138, trsl. modified).

5   In the realm of 'the symbolic', where 'life and death are reversible' – as in the above rituals, for instance – 'death/nothingness does not exist ...' (SED 159, trsl. modified).

6   The flipside of this, continues the note citing Leenhardt (see Baudrillard 1976: 207n2), is that 'an idea similar to our "nothingness"' might be discernible from the Kanak word '*sèri*', which 'indicates the situation of the bewitched ... man ... abandoned by his ancestors ...', someone 'in perdition, out of society', who 'feels himself non-existent ...' (SED 189n12). In Mauss's (1979) essay on the idea of death in Australia and New Zealand, Baudrillard finds the comparable observation that in such societies death in this sense is, precisely, 'being removed from the [*être ôté au*] cycle of symbolic exchanges' (SED 134, trsl. modified).

7   Baudrillard describes 'initiation' as a 'symbolic hyperevent', in which 'birth and death lose their status as fatal events, as necessity ...' (SED 137). A 'sacrifice', too, designates, for the savages, the rejection 'of natural and biological succession, an intervention of an initiatory order, a controlled and socially governed ... anti-natural violence' (SED 165; see also Pawlett 2007: 63).

8   Baudrillard proposes ultimately to 'extend ... symbolic exchange to [the] broader ... level of forms. So the animal form, the human form, the divine form are exchanged according to a rule of metamorphoses in which each ceases to be confined to its definition, with the human opposed to the inhuman, etc.' (PW 16).

9   But 'communism', Baudrillard adds, also seeks to end 'death', and '... in accordance with the same fantastic schema of an eternity of accumulation and of productive forces' (SED 147, trsl. modified).

10 Baudrillard places particular emphasis on 'suicide in prison', which he deems 'an act of *subverting* [*détournement*] institutional death and turning it against the system that imposes it': the suicide 'invert[s] the authorities' and 'condemns society' (SED 175; see also Genosko 2006; Pawlett 2007: 65, 2016: 37; Tierney 1997: 70–1).

11 Here, Baudrillard develops Walter Benjamin's famous remarks from the 1930s on '*the aestheticizing of politics, as practiced by fascism*' (Benjamin 2003: 270). Benjamin's ideas have been important for Baudrillard's work (see e.g. F 6).

12 A number of commentators have highlighted similarities between Baudrillard's earlier writings, including earlier considerations of terrorism, and his writings on the 9/11 attacks (e.g. Butterfield 2002; Genosko 2006; Merrin 2005: 102–3, 163n2; Pawlett 2007: 134, 143, 145, 2016: 129; Wilcox 2003). On those earlier considerations, see, for example, Butterfield (2002); Pawlett (2007: 134–8, 2016: 126–9); Wilcox (2003).

13 'Singularities', Sandford suggests, means 'unique or unusual identities or approaches' in this context (in Baudrillard 2002a). Baudrillard counts 'species, individuals and cultures' among them (ST 9).

14 Following the fall of the Iron Curtain, the West, Baudrillard argued in the 1990s, was sending Eastern Europe Western 'technologies and markets'; 'the global' had won at the cost of 'the disappearance of the universal' *qua* 'value system' (PX 10).

15 Writing shortly after the US–UK invasion of Afghanistan, Baudrillard added that such 'wars ... aim ... to normalize savagery, to knock all territories into alignment[,]... to quell any refractory zone, to colonize and tame all the wild spaces, whether in geographical space or in the realm of the mind' (ST 98; see also Merrin 2005: 106, 111–12).

16 In the 1990s, Baudrillard proposed that the Balkan War be seen in the context 'of globalization' (PX 18). The 'violence' in Bosnia could be understood as a manifestation of a 'surge of vital energy, like hatred, against a "cleansing" in all fields at the global level', as a 'revolt against the world order' (PX 17–18). From this angle, 'the exacerbation of national, linguistic and religious sentiment, or of a sense of identity, is a form of singular resistance' (PX 18).

17 By contrast, as 'the Palestinian suicide attacks' had illustrated over the years, when terrorists launch exclusively 'their own deaths' at 'the system', 'they ... disappear ... quickly in a useless sacrifice' (ST 20–1).

18 Genosko proposes 'to read Baudrillard's account of 9/11 in the mode of the "as though/if"': 'the twin towers collapsed by themselves as though in a response in kind to the challenge of the suicide planes'; 'it was as if they were fulfilling an obligation to return something' (Genosko 2006). Whilst such a reading cannot be attempted here, it appears that reading the following considerations of Baudrillard's in that fashion could be possible. As might become clearer in a moment, this seems to be the case particularly in view of Genosko's spotlight on a passage from *Symbolic Exchange and Death* (SED 37). In that passage, Baudrillard 'claim[s] ...', according to Genosko, 'that the so-called "system ..."... turns on itself like a scorpion when faced with the challenge of death in the form of the counter-gift. Scorpions,' Genosko notes, 'do not, however, commit suicide but, on occasion, in a frenzy of stinging, fatally immolate themselves. In other words they are not fulfilling an obligation, even though Baudrillard used this example to make precisely the opposite claim' (Genosko 2006, see also 1998: 22–3, 46–7).

19 On the question of nostalgia, see also Merrin (2005: 18, 42); Tierney (1997: 62–3, 75n10, 75n14).

9

Emerging Sociological Themes and Concerns

The preceding eight chapters have discussed a range of very different socio-theoretical *œuvres*. It would be difficult to ascertain conceptions, arguments, or elements of analyses common to all eight thinkers. By contrast, it is possible to recognise sociological themes and concerns – dealt with in various ways, of course – shared by some of the thinkers in focus. This is the case both in respect of their endeavours to examine and critically interrogate social relations, contexts, and conditions and in respect of their investigations of specific phenomena associated with living in the contemporary social world. On the basis of the foregoing discussions, some – not all – of these themes and concerns can be, if only briefly, highlighted.

PART 1: THEORISING THE CONTEMPORARY SOCIAL WORLD

Social Conditions

One question raised by some of the socio-theoretical bodies of work under discussion here is whether the social conditions of the present should be characterised as a modern or as a postmodern society. One can discern at least three different responses from those writings: the contention that contemporary society is in a radical or second phase of modernity; the view that the current social – or at least cultural – conditions are postmodern; and the suspicion that the very notion of modernity must be problematised. The different interpretations of the radically modern, postmodern, or non-modern conditions reveal much about the respective theorist's understanding of the social world of today as such and aim to contribute to sociology's wider endeavours to grasp and explain that world.

According to Giddens, present-day social conditions ought not to be described as postmodern. However, he does observe 'the emergence of ways of life and forms of social organisation' that differ from those facilitated by 'modern institutions' (CM 52). Giddens argues that people living in contemporary society are living in a radicalised, extreme version of modernity. This form of modernity, he holds, is future-oriented, reflexive, and global (CM, RW). One of the key challenges for Giddens is how people harness the problems associated with radical modernity, for example, climate change (BLR, TW). Bauman, in his writings on liquid modernity, also focuses his analysis on modern conditions. Yet he provides a detailed portrayal of two different modernities, a portrayal centred on his distinction between 'solids' and 'liquids' (LM 1–2). As shown, Bauman draws this distinction with regard to many domains of the social world. Individualisation, modernisation, and transformations in the time and space dimensions of society occupy core positions in his thinking (LM, LL).

That said, Bauman's concept of liquid modernity is comparable to the conception of postmodern society. The concept of postmodernity is, of course, deployed in Lyotard's analysis of the contemporary condition. This analysis revolves around a specific notion of language games and draws heavily on observations of developments in twentieth-century science (PC). The assertion that 'language games' are 'heteromorphous' and that the agreement on any game's 'rules' is temporally 'limited' chimes, as he himself points out, with the insight that 'the temporary contract' is increasingly commonplace in various areas of 'social interaction' (PC 66). This insight, in turn, is reconcilable with Bauman's assessment – which is, however, much more overtly critical than Lyotard's diagnosis – of social relations in liquid modernity, for instance, with his identification of those relations that are creating growing 'uncertainty' for the individual at work (LM 147; see also Campain 2008: 202–3; Poder 2008: 106).

While Giddens and Bauman scrutinise what they describe as a radical stage of, and as a liquid, modernity, Latour seeks to offer an alternative approach to the theorisation of modernity per se. Latour does not suggest – as modernists do – that the contemporary condition is a second or radical modernity. Rather he seeks to problematise the very idea that we have ever been modern (WHNBM). According to Latour, 'modernity is often defined in terms of humanism'. However, he also argues that this 'overlooks the simultaneous birth of "nonhumanity"' (WHNBM 13). The very notion of the modern is, for Latour, contradictory. Instead of occupying a radical or second modernity, we are, he states, currently entering a non-modern world 'without ever having really left it' (WHNBM 130). Haraway also argues that 'the modern' will not be 'superceded or infiltrated by the postmodern' (PM 77). Along with Latour she maintains that to believe in the existence of 'something called the modern' has always been 'a mistake'. According to Haraway, we have never been at the start or end of things; rather we are always right 'in the middle' (PM 77).

Inequality and Capital

Attempts to understand social and economic inequality are of major significance for socio-theoretical interrogations of contemporary society. The discussions of inequality in several of the works explored above thematise forms of capital. As mentioned earlier, according to Bourdieu, it is capital that 'makes the games of society – not least, the economic game – something other than simple games of chance' (FC 46). In his analysis of solid and liquid modernity, Bauman problematises the current relationship between capital and labour. In solid modernity, he argues, 'labour' 'depended' on 'capital', but capital also on labour: they were permanently bound to one another (LM 145; see also Poder 2008: 101). In liquid modernity, the 'fulfilment' of the 'capacity' to work still hinges on an investment of capital (LM 121), but the 'reproduction and growth' of the latter no longer strictly on a long-term 'engagement with labour' in any specific location. Thus, those 'ties' are ever weaker (LM 149; see also Campain 2008: 202–3; Davis 2016: 66–7; Poder 2008: 106). This analysis of society, which includes, as shown, further considerations of contemporary power relationships and politics, is evidently strongly shaped by Marx's critique of political economy. Although Lyotard is highly sceptical of the potential political impetus of the class struggle – or rather, of class 'struggles' (PF 73) – today, Marx's scrutiny of the class relationship has influenced his conception of the system, too: the system follows the principle of '"good productivity"', an 'eminent case' of which is the 'exploitation' of labour power – the wages expended being lower than the 'value' gained – at the hands of 'capital' (PF 72).

The sociological contribution of some of the theorists whose works were discussed in this book lies not only in elucidating the role of economic capital but also in conceptualising other types of capital and incorporating these conceptions into their analyses. Bourdieu, for example, conceptualises different forms of capital, which he identifies as economic, cultural, and social, and which, when legitimated, are converted into symbolic capital and power. For Bourdieu, the distribution of cultural and economic capital is the main source of class differentiation in society (FC, D; Skeggs 1997: 8). Bourdieu extends his analysis to include a focus on embodied capital. The embodied nature of capital appears to underpin much of Bourdieu's work – from inheritance of cultural capital to the biological occupation of particular social and physical spaces. For Bourdieu 'embodied capital' is 'external wealth' that is then 'converted into an integral part of the person, into a habitus'. Embodied capital cannot be transmitted immediately (unlike money, for example) and is often acquired unconsciously (FC 48).

Baudrillard's critical examination of contemporary society accentuates the living's suspension of symbolic exchange relationships with the dead. On the one

hand, Baudrillard suggests that the multifaceted structures of social 'discrimination' of capitalist societies can be linked to the severance of social relations with,
to the expulsion from society's 'symbolic circulation' of, 'the dead' (SED 126; see
also e.g. Genosko 1998: 27; Pawlett 2007: 56–7, 2016: 69–70; Tierney 1997:
63–5). On the other hand, he has been shown to argue that in these conditions 'life'
has become 'value' (SED 133), 'a quantitative evaluation', indeed 'life-capital' (SED
162). Human existence has become 'accumulation', and this is the setting that has
given rise to the scientific and technological means of life extension (SED 162; see
also 147; Butterfield 2002; Pawlett 2007: 55–9, 62–4; Tierney 1997: 65–72;
Wilcox 2003). The rapid expansion of the biomedical sciences over recent decades
has meant that the notion of embodied or biological capital is becoming increasingly important to contemporary sociological discussions on inequality (Webster
2007). Both Baudrillard's and Bourdieu's account were prescient in this regard.

Power

Power – its distribution, exercise, and operation – is a key topic in much contemporary sociology. Out of all the theoretical works explored in the preceding
chapters, it is Foucault's *œuvre* that places the strongest emphasis on power for
conceptualising social conditions. His approach to power is distinct from many
prior sociological frameworks, though. This is partly because Foucault argues
that power cannot be owned and that it is not something that can be acquired
only by some members of, or groups in, society (SD 13–14, 29, HS1 94; Sheridan
1990: 139, 184–5, 218). To repeat, power is a relationship of unequal force, and
power relations cannot exist without resistance (HS1 93–6, SD 15; Davidson
2006: xvi, xxiin9; Sheridan 1990: 139, 184–5, 218). Moreover, Foucault
refuses to embed power in other dimensions of the social world. Whilst power
relationships are entangled with, for example, economic relationships, they are
the result of 'differentiations' in such other kinds of relationships but also their
'conditions' (HS1 94; see also SD 14; Sheridan 1990: 184, 219). Foucault's
analyses of power are supported by a comprehensive set of concepts, notably
by the concepts of disciplinary power, security, regulation, and government, but
also by the concept of sovereign power, against which those are demarcated.

However, power is an important theme also in other writings discussed above.
Drawing on Foucault's research on disciplinary power, Bauman traces a transformation in the power relationships between, *inter alia*, 'capital and labour': the
period of their '*mutual engagement*' and direct 'confrontation' is coming to a close,
as advances in technology are beginning to allow those who have power to exercise power without having to be in the same locality as the targets of that power
(LM 10–11; see also Campain 2008: 202–3). Understood in yet another way,
power is also an important dimension of the agonistic language games – in which
speaking *qua* moves and countermoves amounts to fighting – at the heart of
Lyotard's conception of the social (PC 10–11, 15–16; Malpas 2003: 20–3;
Williams 1998: 27–30). Absolutely nobody, Lyotard insists, 'is ever entirely
powerless over the messages that traverse and position' them (PC 15).

Social Relations

The concept of the social is usually positioned at the core of the discipline of sociology. Developing a conception of social relations has been central to many socio-theoretical endeavours to analyse the contemporary social world. Several of the theorists whose works were explored above problematise and extend sociology's understandings of the social. Both Latour's and Haraway's notions of the social are informed by science and technology studies. One of the distinguishing features of Haraway's social theory is her accentuation of the role of non-human actants and agents, namely animals and technology. According to Haraway, when discussing the concept of the social, social theorists tend to refer to the study of social relations and history. She, however, seeks to move away from locating the social solely in the context of human social relations (Gane and Haraway 2006: esp. 142–3). What Haraway seeks to make clear through the development of the concept of the cyborg is that one cannot attempt to theorise contemporary social conditions without grasping the relationships between humans and other, non-human forms. Latour, too, seeks to contribute an alternative socio-theoretical view to the concept of the social (RAS). Rather than seeking to use the concept of the social for developing social explanations, he focuses instead on exploring networks and associations, including those involving both humans and non-humans (RAS; de Vries 2016: 88).

Lyotard, in turn, argues that it is a conception of their linguistic dimension that – although this dimension may not exhaust the social – ought to be at the core of any attempt to analyse social relations and interactions. Once such a conception has been achieved, it becomes possible both: to rebut the claim that social relationships are disintegrating and collectivities are becoming but 'a mass of individual atoms thrown into the absurdity of Brownian motion' (PC 15), a view that has never sat particularly easily with many sociologists; and to trace current transformations of social relationships themselves, an endeavour that has been vital to the sociological discipline. What Foucault prioritises in his study of the social – also without asserting that these exhaust the social – are, as mentioned, relationships of 'power'. They crisscross in, and decisively shape, the social world (SD 24; Sheridan 1990: 139).

When discussing social relations between people, most of the socio-theoretical writings explored here and much sociology *tout court* tend to focus these discussions on relationships between the living. Through his work on symbolic exchange, Baudrillard emphatically diverges from this tendency. Sociology's understanding of social relations, he suggests, must be underpinned by a conception of the relationships between the living and the dead. In some cultures, '[s]ymbolic exchange' continues even 'when life' no longer does; that is to say, it operates not only among 'the living', but also between the latter and 'the dead' (SED 134; see also Butterfield 2002; Genosko 1998: 20–1, 31; Pawlett 2007: 57, 59). A key contribution of Baudrillard's to existing sociological perspectives of social relationships lies in this conception of symbolic exchange and of relations across the boundary of life and death. His remarks on societies centred on symbolic exchange, including exchanges *with the dead* and the exchange *of death*, may primarily evoke images of premodern social conditions. But they are, as has been underscored, of central importance to Baudrillard's critical delimitation and interrogation of contemporary social conditions, of capitalist society (see e.g. PW 15; Tierney 1997: 64, 69).

Social Change

Sociology often seeks to contribute to political debates about social transformation. Several of the theorists whose writings have been in focus above provide striking perspectives on the problem of social change. Haraway does so, for example, through the development of her concept of the cyborg, which, she argues, can be a source of inequality as well as a facilitator of social change. As mentioned earlier, the notion of the cyborg – with its possible mix of human/technology/animal – has the potential to challenge various 'dualisms' that have permeated 'Western traditions' (e.g. 'mind/body, culture/ nature, male/female') (CM 177). These dualisms, according to Haraway, have been key to the oppression of minority ethnic groups, women, nature, workers, animals etc. – to the 'domination of all constituted as others, whose task is to mirror the self' (CM 177). For Haraway, high-tech culture has the potential to challenge these dualisms in new ways (CM 177).

In contrast, Giddens develops what he calls a radical politics of the centre to address the problems posed by radical modernity (BLR, PCC, TW). A framework of radical politics should, according to Giddens, be guided by utopian realism, a critical theory 'without guarantees' (CM 155). This framework should, he says, relate to 'the four overarching dimensions of modernity' and be focused on countering poverty, environment degradation, arbitrary power, and violence (BLR 246).

Latour, in turn, seeks to break with what he refers to as the dominant 'emancipatory master narrative'. By questioning what it means to be modern, he seeks to tell a different story about our past, present, and potential future. He argues that if what it means to be modern is rethought, then the role of oppressed 'others' in history must be recast, too. They must be seen instead 'as companions in a long history that has collected humans and nonhumans in various assemblages and at various scales' (www.bruno-latour.fr/node/328). By reinterpreting the past in this way, he suggests that one would also need to rethink our future, thus potentially altering the course of change.

In the works of Baudrillard and Lyotard, the political question of social transformation is inextricable from the concept of the system. For Baudrillard, the capitalist system remains vulnerable to acts of defiance both tiny and massive. In particular, 'suicides' are 'political', and even one person's self-destruction can constitute a serious 'breach'. One of the reasons for this is that within 'a system' the failure to regulate even just a minute detail amounts to 'total defeat' (SED 175; see also Genosko 2006; Pawlett 2007: 64–6; Tierney 1997: 70–1). In his essays on 9/11, Baudrillard puts forward a multifaceted set of arguments to show, firstly, that the global system itself has created an environment conducive to such events, and, secondly, that such events can – as the New York attacks did – create deep and lasting damage to the system (ST). An important political conundrum highlighted by Lyotard's writings on postmodernity ensues from the fact that 'the system' – 'an alternative' to which, if not 'a "pure"' one (PC 66), would be at issue – has use for critical interventions, including those of intellectuals, and even for disturbances, including class struggles (PF 67–74; Palumbo–Liu 2000). Lyotard, as shown, searches for clues in contemporary science and art, but also in the kind of thinking and writing he is engaged in, for ways of resisting the more stubborn pressures of the system. Neither in the social world Baudrillard depicts nor in the society at the centre of Lyotard's attention do more conventional strategies for social change, for instance those attaching to democratic institutions or even those attaching to class conflict, seem to hold a great deal of political significance.

PART 2: LIVING IN SOCIETY

The stark differences between the conceptions and analyses of the social world of the present day in the bodies of sociological thought explored in this book are evident. Yet several sociological concerns, albeit approached in different ways, are shared by some of the sociologists whose works have been discussed. Among those are the questions of whether the contemporary conditions are best characterised as modern, postmodern, or not at all modern, how this society can be understood and critically interrogated in view of longstanding problems such as inequality and the exercise of power, how social relationships are to be conceptualised, and where the potential for, and barriers to, social change lie. Further, it is possible to highlight – though once more only selectively and briefly – concerns that some of the eight thinkers have in common – although, again, they tackle these in different ways – with regard to their investigations of specific phenomena associated with life and people's lives in the current social conditions.

Pluralities

Several of the theorists stress the need to develop a methodological approach that can account for and capture the plurality of perspectives and values present in contemporary social life. Of course, each theorist puts such arguments forward in their own respective manner. In his work on social suffering (WOTW), Bourdieu, for example, underscores the importance of juxtaposing different 'points of view' (the space for points of view) in research in order to illuminate what happens when different perspectives of the world 'confront each other' (WOTW 3). By adopting an approach that allows space for different points of view, Bourdieu seeks to capture all forms of suffering in contemporary social life. This may include extreme forms of suffering on an individual or collective basis as well as what he refers to as '*positional suffering*', which, as mentioned earlier, is often taken as the 'point of reference for criticism' (WOTW 4).

Latour also seeks to show that there is not 'one "outside world"', but rather 'a plurality' of 'worlds' that relate directly to the key 'institutions' that frame people's 'lives' (Muecke 2012). A comparative anthropological approach needs to be developed, according to Latour, which is based on establishing 'common ground'. This approach however also 'requires an instrument to make the differences among collectives emerge anew' (www.bruno-latour.fr/node/328). This must then frame the way problems in contemporary social life, such as the ecological crisis, are dealt with. In her work on partial perspectives, Haraway also argues that in order to offer 'a better account of the world', we must recognise the 'irreducible difference and radical multiplicity of local knowledges' (SK 579; see also Clough and Schneider 2001: 342). This focus on situated knowledges frames her approach to specific phenomena in social life, namely immunology.

These calls for acknowledging plurality in present-day social life also resonate with the work of Lyotard. He encourages the 'recognition of the heteromorphous nature of language games' and of the 'heterogeneous' nature of their 'rules' (PC 65–6). The system's 'decision makers' wish to treat the 'language games' taking place in society as 'commensurable' nonetheless (PC xxiv). One strand of Lyotard's investigations in response to the question 'how to live, and why?' (PF vii) concerns ways of resisting commensurability and exchangeability as a critical intellectual in one's own language game moves.

Suffering and Terror

It scarcely needs pointing out that suffering is a major characteristic of contemporary social life. It is also a substantive focal point in a number of inquiries into social life discussed above. Each of the theorists in question, however, illuminates and examines a different aspect of suffering, and these investigations reflect the theorist's own particular analyses of the contemporary social world. Bourdieu, for example, prioritises and explores the relativity of suffering. He draws on ethnographic data to analyse the ways in which suffering is part of daily life for many people (from the individual to the population level), focusing on a range of sociologically pertinent issues, including poor housing and unemployment, social and symbolic forms of exclusion, intergenerational and interethnic conflict, and urban dystopia (Couldry 2005: 355). Bourdieu continues to explore the transmission of cultural and social capital in his work on suffering in the context of the family and education and social and physical space.

Bauman problematises the liquid life partly because it involves continued suffering. Life is characterised by perpetual 'non-satisfaction' associated with living in the market (LL 80). But more problematically, it is also pestered by 'liquid modern fears' (LF 21). Bauman is able to contextualise non-satisfaction and liquid modern fears in the specific social relations and contexts that constitute liquid modernity. At the same time, he is able to remain critical, not only of those social conditions, but also of people's responses to, and attempts to act against, non-satisfaction and fear.

In his work on terrorism, Baudrillard establishes explicit links between suffering and globalisation. Whilst he does not seek 'to deny' the 'suffering and death' of the 'victims' of the devastation of the World Trade Center on 9/11 (ST 24), he seeks, on the one hand, to emphasise that these attacks were part of a 'violent protest against' the 'violence of globalization' (ST 41; see also Merrin 2005: 104, 112). On the other hand, he suggests that 'terrorism' is vitally fuelled by 'the despair' of those who have been 'humiliated and insulted' (ST 104) by being at the receiving end of the West's, the system's, stream of products without any possibility of reciprocation (ST 100–2; Genosko 2006; Merrin 2005: 104–5; Pawlett 2007: 66, 140). The social relations in which terrorist attacks are sparked, the attacks themselves, and their ramifications cannot, Baudrillard thinks, be understood without an understanding of how relationships of the gift, the challenge, and symbolic exchange manifest themselves today.

Life and the Ecological Crisis

Climate change has for several years been central to a global political agenda. As numerous scholars have argued, a continued warming of the world's temperature has the potential to 'transform human and animal life as it has been known' (Urry 2009: 87). Both Giddens's and Latour's analyses of contemporary social life address the problem of climate change and the current ecological crisis. Giddens's work on climate change incorporates components of his writings on radical modernity as well as of his writings on politics. As discussed earlier, his investigation centres on what he calls 'Giddens's paradox'. He argues that as many of the dangers posed by climate change are not visible in everyday life, people are often not compelled to do anything about them (PCC 2). 'Giddens's paradox', he holds, 'affects almost every aspect of current reactions to climate change'. It is why climate change is an issue that is often at the back of people's minds (PCC 2). While Giddens outlines the problem of climate change in his work on radical modernity (CM), he starts to map out a strategy to deal with environmental decay in his more politically focused texts (BLR, TW), which he then elaborates on more fully in his writing on climate change (PCC). Although some have argued that Giddens's work on climate change is less academic than his earlier conceptual work (James and Steger 2014), the message that he articulates in his book on climate change is consistent with his writings on radical modernity. He is keen to stress that the world we occupy now is one 'where hazards created by ourselves are as, or more, threatening than those that come from the outside' (RW 34).

Latour also takes the current ecological crisis as the background to his comparative anthropology, arguing at the start of AIME (8) that we need to choose between modernising and ecologising. In *Politics of Nature* (PON), Latour argues for new perspectives on 'political ecology' (de Vries 2016: 194), outlining 'the principles of the politics that he thinks will be needed' (de Vries 2016: 198).

In AIME, Latour seeks to develop 'a platform for the diplomatic exchanges that will be necessary, if ... ecological catastrophe [is] to be avoided' (de Vries 2016: 199). AIME does clearly extend Latour's work on actor network theory, shifting his focus from networks to modes of existence. The main purpose of the text, however, is to revisit the main questions he posed in WHNBM in order 'to offer the Moderns a clearer view of themselves' and other people (de Vries 2016: 199). According to Latour, once the moderns start reflecting on their own position, it then becomes 'possible to think of comparative anthropology as a diplomatic enterprise'. This is because 'the former Moderns ... are no longer cheating about who they are ... and what they want to achieve' (www.brunolatour.fr/node/328).

Life, Death, Bodies, and Power

Finally, several investigations of social life discussed in the preceding chapters unearth close connections between phenomena of life and living and the exercise and operation of power. Foucault's work has been decisive in this context. According to his famous conception, disciplinary power operates upon the individual 'body', notably its actions – broken down further into components such as movements or behaviours – and 'forces'; it is to serve to render the body docile and productive at the same time. The 'regulations of the population', by contrast, concentrate on 'the mechanics of life' within and 'biological processes' on 'the species body' (HS1 139; see also Lemke 2011: 33–8; Sheridan 1990: 139, 148–52, 171–2, 191–3, 219). Foucault distinguishes discipline, regulation, and security from the sovereign's right of death. He illustrates different modalities of power with reference to their manifestations in the treatment of the ill at different moments in European history: the latter right with reference to the treatment of lepers in the Middle Ages, the disciplines of the body with reference to the approach to plague victims in the 1600s, and security with reference to the approach to smallpox in the 1700s.

Foucault's studies have fundamentally shaped the ongoing analysis of biopolitics in the social sciences (e.g. Lemke 2011). Haraway, too, has developed a position on biopolitics, namely in her essay on the immune system (BPB; see also Munnik 1997: 112–14). This is implicit in the development of the concept of the cyborg in her manifesto and in her introduction to the term material-semiotic in her work on partial perspectives. However, Haraway uses her work on the immune system to illustrate that position more fully. Just as Foucault does, Haraway focuses on 'the body as a specific object of biopower'; however, she does this from what she calls a 'material semiotic' perspective, through which she 'deconstruct[s] the unitary character' of the body (Esposito 2011: 146). In contrast to Foucault, Haraway 'approaches the body' through a focus on its deconstruction and multiplication, which is prompted by the 'proliferation of technology' (Esposito 2011: 146). She continues to acknowledge the 'relations of power into which the management of the living being is inscribed' (Esposito 2011: 146). Simultaneously she also draws attention to the ways in which the connections between 'life' and other spheres such as the social or political are being 'radically redefined'. For Haraway, it is the increasing 'proliferation of technology' that is driving this change (Esposito 2011: 146). For other theorists, such as Giddens, the increasing proliferation of technology is just one part of a broader juggernaut of modernity, which is responsible for radically altering contemporary social life as we know it.

Many sociological analyses of power focus on power as it is exercised in relation to the living and life. This includes Foucault's analyses. He distinguishes from his concept of power as right of death several further concepts of power, such as those of discipline, security, and regulation, that he deems more pertinent to examining the key developments in its operation in the past three to four centuries. Baudrillard has been shown to extend the sociological understanding of power by virtue of his notion of death power (SED 129). What he emphasises is that 'social control' has arisen from the severance of the relationships of 'the living' with 'the dead', and that, in the end, all forms of power, including all 'power' over the living, are grounded in the control over the management 'of death' (SED 130; see also Genosko 1998: 27–8; Pawlett 2007: 56–8, 64; Tierney 1997: 64).

10

Conclusion

The conceptions of and arguments about social relations, contexts, and conditions explored in the preceding chapters, and the eight thinkers' attempts to analyse present-day society that those conceptions and arguments support, have made decisive contributions and posed serious challenges to sociology's project of understanding and critically scrutinising the contemporary social world. The foregoing studies have sought to highlight that each theorist's conceptions of and inquiries into wider social conditions are also intertwined with their own endeavours to analyse how those conditions shape, are manifested or expressed in, and receive influence from more particular phenomena. Being aware of – indeed unsettled by – most of these phenomena per se does not hinge on prior exposure to sociological research. Many, such as non-satisfaction or fear, are frequently part of immediate experience; others, such as climate change or terrorist attacks, can be heard and read about daily. What each theorist's work demonstrates is the potential of a specifically sociological engagement with such phenomena to provide critical insights that would not otherwise be available. The focus in this context has been on key components of the eight thinkers' investigations and analyses of phenomena that are in one way or another associated with the problem of living, of people's lives, of human life in contemporary social relations and conditions. Their critical interrogations illustrate what it can mean when sociologists explicitly or implicitly work with the idea that people live in society. They will continue to offer much to the sociological study of social life.

References

Adorno, T. W. (2000) *Introduction to Sociology*. Stanford, CA: Stanford University Press.

Adorno, T. W. (2008) *Philosophische Elemente einer Theorie der Gesellschaft. Nachgelassene Schriften IV: Vorlesungen, Band 12*. Frankfurt am Main: Suhrkamp.

Baudelaire, C. (1950) *My Heart Laid Bare and Other Prose Writings*. London: George Weidenfeld & Nicolson.

Baudrillard, J. (1976) *L'Échange Symbolique et la Mort*. Paris: Éditions Gallimard.

Baudrillard, J. (1982a) À *L'Ombre des Majorités Silencieuses ou la Fin du Social (suivi de) L'Extase du Socialisme*. Paris: Denoël/Gonthier.

Baudrillard, J. (1982b) *Der Symbolische Tausch und der Tod*. Munich: Matthes & Seitz.

Baudrillard, J. (1983) *In the Shadow of the Silent Majorities or, the End of the Social and Other Essays*. New York: Semiotext(e).

Baudrillard, J. (1988) *The Ecstasy of Communication*. New York: Semiotext(e).

Baudrillard, J. (1993) *Symbolic Exchange and Death*. London: Sage.

Baudrillard, J. (1998) *Paroxysm: Interviews with Philippe Petit*. London: Verso.

Baudrillard, J. (2001) 'L'Esprit du terrorisme'. *Le Monde*, 3 November 2001.

Baudrillard, J. (2002a) 'The despair of having everything'. *Le Monde Diplomatique*, November 2002.

Baudrillard, J. (2002b) *Screened Out*. London: Verso.

Baudrillard, J. (2003a) *Passwords*. London: Verso.

Baudrillard, J. (2003b) *The Spirit of Terrorism and Other Essays*. London: Verso.

Baudrillard, J. (2004) *Fragments: Conversations with François L'Yvonnet*. London: Routledge.

Baudrillard, J. (2013) *The Intelligence of Evil, or, The Lucidity Pact*. London: Bloomsbury.

Bauman, Z. (2000) *Liquid Modernity*. Cambridge: Polity Press.

Bauman, Z. (2003) *Liquid Love: On the Frailty of Human Bonds*. Cambridge: Polity Press.

Bauman, Z. (2005) *Liquid Life*. Cambridge: Polity Press.

Bauman, Z. (2006) *Liquid Fear*. Cambridge: Polity Press.

Bauman, Z. (2007) *Consuming Life*. Cambridge: Polity Press.

Beck, U. (1992) *Risk Society: Towards a New Modernity*. London: Sage.

Benjamin, W. (2003) 'The work of art in the age of its technological reproducibility [third version]', in W. Benjamin *Selected Writings. Volume 4: 1938–1940*. Cambridge, MA: Harvard University Press, pp. 251–83.

Birch, K. and Tyfield, D. (2012) 'Theorizing the bioeconomy: Biovalue, bio-capital, bioeconomics or ... what?'. *Science, Technology, and Human Values* 38(3): 299–327.

Blackshaw, T. (2008) 'Bauman on consumerism – living the market-mediated life', in M. H. Jacobsen and P. Poder (eds) *The Sociology of Zygmunt Bauman: Challenges and Critique*. Aldershot: Ashgate, pp. 117–35.

Bourdieu, P. (1977) *Outline of a Theory of Practice*. Cambridge: Cambridge University Press.

Bourdieu, P. (1984) *Distinction*. London: Routledge.

Bourdieu, P. (1997) 'The forms of capital', in A.M. Halsey, H. Lauder and A. Stuart Nells (eds) *Education: Culture, Economy, Society*. Oxford: Oxford University Press, pp. 46–58.

Bourdieu, P. (1988) *Homo Academicus*. Cambridge: Polity Press.

Bourdieu, P. (1995) Physical space, social space and habitus, Lecture delivered to the Department of Sociology, University of Oslo, May 15. Report 10. Oslo: Institutt for sosiologi og samfunnsgeografi.

Bourdieu, P. et al. (1999) *The Weight of the World. Social Suffering in Contemporary Society*. Cambridge: Polity Press.

Bourdieu, P. and Passeron, J.-C. (1977) *Reproduction in Education, Society and Culture*. London: Sage.

Bourdieu, P. and Wacquant, L. (1992) *Invitation to Reflexive Sociology*. Chicago, IL: University of Chicago Press.

Butterfield, B. (2002) 'The Baudrillardian symbolic, 9/11, and the war of good and evil'. *Postmodern Culture* 13(1). Available at: http://pmc.iath.virginia.edu/issue.902/13.1butterfield.html

Callinicos, A. (1999) *Social Theory: A Historical Introduction*. Cambridge: Polity Press.

Callinicos, A. (2001) *Against the Third Way*. Cambridge: Polity Press.

Campain, R. (2008) 'Bauman on power – from "solid" to "light"?', in M. H. Jacobsen and P. Poder (eds) *The Sociology of Zygmunt Bauman: Challenges and Critique*. Aldershot: Ashgate, pp. 193–208.

Clifford, J. and Marcus, G. E. (eds) (1986) *Writing Culture: The Poetics and Politics of Ethnography*. London: University of California Press.

Clough, P. T. and Schneider, J. (2001) 'Donna J. Haraway', in A. Elliot and B. S. Turner (eds) *Profiles in Contemporary Social Theory*. London: Sage, pp. 338–48.

Connor, S. (1989) *Postmodern Culture: An Introduction to Theories of the Contemporary*. Oxford: Basil Blackwell.

Couldry, N. (2005) 'The individual point of view: Learning from Bourdieu's The Weight of the World'. *Cultural Studies, Critical Methodologies* 5(3): 354–72.

Davidson, A. I. (2003) 'Introduction', in M. Foucault *Abnormal: Lectures at the Collège de France, 1974–1975*. New York: Picador, pp. xvii–xxvi.

Davidson, A. I. (2006) 'Introduction', in M. Foucault *Psychiatric Power: Lectures at the Collège de France, 1973–1974*. New York: Picador, pp. xiv–xxii.

Davis, M. (2016) *Freedom and Consumerism: A Critique of Zygmunt Bauman's Sociology*. London: Routledge.

de Vries, G. (2016) *Bruno Latour*. Cambridge: Polity Press.

Durkheim, É. (1982) *The Rules of Sociological Method. And Selected Texts on Sociology and Its Method*. London: Macmillan.

Elliot, A. (2001) *Concepts of the Self*. Cambridge: Polity Press.

Esposito, R. (2011) *Immunitas: The Protection and Negation of Life*. Cambridge: Polity Press.

Foucault, M. (1976) *Histoire de la Sexualité 1: La Volonté de Savoir*. Paris: Gallimard.

Foucault, M. (1981) *The History of Sexuality, Volume 1: An Introduction*. London: Penguin.

Foucault, M. (1991) *Discipline and Punish: The Birth of the Prison*. London: Penguin.

Foucault, M. (2003) *Abnormal: Lectures at the Collège de France, 1974–1975*. New York: Picador.

Foucault, M. (2004) *'Society Must Be Defended': Lectures at the Collège de France, 1975–76*. London: Penguin.

Foucault, M. (2006) *Psychiatric Power: Lectures at the Collège de France, 1973–1974*. New York: Picador.

Foucault, M. (2009) *Security, Territory, Population: Lectures at the Collège de France, 1977–78*. Basingstoke: Palgrave Macmillan.

Foucault, M. (2010) *The Birth of Biopolitics: Lectures at the Collège de France, 1978–79*. Basingstoke: Palgrave Macmillan.

Frank, A. W. (2001) 'Can we research suffering?'. *Qualitative Health Research* 11(3): 353–62.

Gane, N. and Haraway, D. (2006) '"When we have never been human, what is to be done?" Interview with Donna Haraway'. *Theory, Culture & Society* 23(7–8): 135–58.

Genosko, G. (1998) *Undisciplined Theory*. London: Sage.

Genosko, G. (2006) 'The spirit of symbolic exchange: Jean Baudrillard's 9/11'. *International Journal of Baudrillard Studies* 3(1). Available at: https://www2.ubishops.ca/baudrillardstudies/vol3_1/genosko.htm

Giddens, A. (1990) *The Consequences of Modernity*. Cambridge: Polity Press.

Giddens, A. (1994a) 'Living in a post-traditional society', in U. Beck, A. Giddens and S. Lash (eds) *Reflexive Modernization: Politics, Tradition and Aesthetics in the Modern Social Order*. Cambridge: Polity Press, pp. 56–109.

Giddens, A. (1994b) *Beyond Left and Right: The Future of Radical Politics*. Cambridge: Polity Press.

Giddens, A. (1998) *The Third Way: The Renewal of Social Democracy*. Cambridge: Polity Press.

Giddens, A. (1999) *Runaway World: How Globalisation is Reshaping Our Lives*. London: Profile Books.

Giddens, A. (2000) *The Third Way and Its Critics*. Cambridge: Polity Press.

Giddens, A. (2011) *The Politics of Climate Change* (2nd edn). Cambridge: Polity Press.

Goux, J.-J. and Wood, P. R. (1998) 'Introduction', in J.-J. Goux and P. R. Wood (eds) *Terror and Consensus: Vicissitudes of French Thought*. Stanford, CA: Stanford University Press, pp. 1–10.

Gudmand-Høyer, M. and Lopdrup Hjorth, T. (2009) 'Review essay: Liberal
    biopoloitics reborn'. *Foucault Studies* 7: 99–130.
Haraway, D. (1988) 'Situated knowledges: The science question in femi-
    nism and the privilege of partial perspective'. *Feminist Studies* 14(3):
    575–600.
Haraway, D. (1991) 'A cyborg manifesto: Science, technology and socialist-
    feminism in the late twentieth century', in D. Haraway (ed.) *Simians, Cyborgs,
    and Women: The Reinvention of Nature*. New York: Routledge, pp. 149–81.
Haraway, D. (1993) 'The biopolitics of postmodern bodies', in L. Kauffman
    (ed.) *American Feminist Thought at a Century's End: A Reader*. Oxford:
    Blackwell, pp. 199–233.
Haraway, D. (2004a) 'Introduction: A kinship of feminist figurations', in
    D. Haraway (ed.) *The Haraway Reader*. London: Routledge, pp. 1–7.
Haraway, D. (2004b) 'The promises of monsters: A regenerative politics for
    inappropriate/d others', in D. Haraway (ed.) *The Haraway Reader*. London:
    Routledge, pp. 63–124.
Hobbes, T. ([1914] 1947) *Leviathan, Or The Matter, Forme and Power of
    Commonwealth Ecclesiastical and Civil*. London: J.M. Dent.
Horkheimer, M. (1972) 'Traditional and critical theory', in M. Horkheimer
    Critical Theory: Selected Essays. New York: Continuum, pp. 188–243.
Horkheimer, M. and Adorno, T. W. (2002) *Dialectic of Enlightenment:
    Philosophical Fragments*. Stanford, CA: Stanford University Press.
James, P. and Steger, M. B. (2014) 'A genealogy of "globalization": The career
    of a concept'. *Globalizations* 11(4): 417–34.
Jaulin, R. (1967) *La Mort Sara: L'Ordre de la Vie ou la Pensée de la Mort au
    Tchad*. Paris: Plon.
Jenkins, R. (1992) *Pierre Bourdieu*. London: Routledge.
Kant, I. (1991) 'An answer to the question: "What is enlightenment?"', in
    I. Kant *Political Writings* (2nd enlarged edn). Cambridge: Cambridge
    University Press, pp. 54–60.
Kaspersen, L. B. (2000) *Anthony Giddens: An Introduction to a Social
    Theorist*. Oxford: Blackwell Publishers.
King, K. (1987) *The Passing Dreams of Choice... Once Before and After:
    Audre Lorde and the Apparatus of Literary Production, Book Prospectus*.
    University of Maryland at College Park.
Kirby, V. (1997) *Telling Flesh: The Substance of the Corporeal*. London:
    Routledge.
Klein, N. (2015) *This Changes Everything: Capitalism Vs. the Climate*.
    London: Penguin.
Kleinman, A., Das, V., and Lock, M. (eds) (1997) *Social Suffering*. Berkeley,
    CA: University of California Press.
Kunzru, H. (1996) 'You are cyborg'. *Wired*. Available at: http://archive.wired.
    com/wired/archive/5.02/ffharaway_pr.html
Lagrange, J. (2006) 'Course context', in M. Foucault *Psychiatric Power: Lectures
    at the Collège de France, 1973–1974*. New York: Picador, pp. 349–67.
Lane, J. (2006) *Bourdieu's Politics: Problems and Possibilities*. London:
    Routledge.

Latour, B. (1988) *The Pasteurization of France*. Cambridge, MA: Harvard University Press.

Latour, B. (1993) *We Have Never Been Modern*. Cambridge, MA: Harvard University Press.

Latour, B. (2004) *Politics of Nature: How to Bring the Sciences into Democracy*. Cambridge, MA: Harvard University Press.

Latour, B. (2005) *Reassembling the Social: An Introduction to Actor-Network-Theory*. Oxford: Oxford University Press.

Latour, B. (2013) *An Inquiry into Modes of Existence: An Anthropology of the Moderns*. Cambridge, MA: Harvard University Press.

Latour, B. (2015) *Face a Gaia*. Paris: La Découverte.

Latour, B. and Woolgar, S. (1986) *Laboratory Life: The Construction of Scientific Facts*. Princeton, NJ: Princeton University Press.

Leach, B. (1998) 'Industrial homework, economic restructuring and the meaning of work'. *Labour/Le Travail* 41: 97–115.

Lemke, T. (2011) *Biopolitics: An Advanced Introduction*. New York: New York University Press.

Lyotard, J.-F. (1979) *La Condition Postmoderne: Rapport sur le Savoir*. Paris: Les Éditions de Minuit.

Lyotard, J.-F. (1984a) 'Answering the question: What is postmodernism?', in J.-F. Lyotard *The Postmodern Condition: A Report on Knowledge*. Manchester: Manchester University Press, pp. 71–82.

Lyotard, J.-F. (1984b) *The Postmodern Condition: A Report on Knowledge*. Manchester: Manchester University Press.

Lyotard, J.-F. (1993) *Moralités Postmodernes*. Paris: Éditions Galilée.

Lyotard, J.-F. (1994) *Das Postmoderne Wissen: Ein Bericht*. Vienna: Passagen.

Lyotard, J.-F. (1997) *Postmodern Fables*. London: University of Minnesota Press.

Lyotard, J.-F. (1998) 'Terror on the run', in J.-J. Goux and P. R. Wood (eds) *Terror and Consensus: Vicissitudes of French Thought*. Stanford, CA: Stanford University Press, pp. 25–36.

Mackenzie, D. (1993) *Inventing Accuracy: A Historical Sociology of Nuclear Missile Guidance*. Cambridge, MA: MIT Press.

Malpas, S. (2003) *Jean-François Lyotard*. London: Routledge.

Marcuse, H. (2002) *One-dimensional Man: Studies in the Ideology of Advanced Industrial Society*. London: Routledge.

Martuccelli, D. (1999) *Sociologie de la Modernité*. Paris: Gallimard.

Marx, K. (1990) *Capital. Volume 1*. London: Penguin.

Mauss, M. (1979) 'The physical effect on the individual of the idea of death suggested by the collectivity (Australia, New Zealand)', in M. Mauss *Sociology and Psychology (Essays)*. London: Routledge and Kegan Paul, pp. 35–56.

Mauss, M. (2002) *The Gift: The Form and Reason for Exchange in Archaic Societies*. London: Routledge.

McRobbie, A. (2002) 'A mixed bag of misfortunes?: Bourdieu's Weight of the World'. *Theory, Culture & Society* 19(3): 129–38.

Merrin, W. (2005) *Baudrillard and the Media: A Critical Introduction*. Cambridge: Polity Press.

Michaels, M. (2016) *Actor Network Theory: Trials, Trails and Translations*. London: Sage.

Morgan, D. and Wilkinson, I. (2001) 'The problem of suffering and the sociological task of theodicy'. *The European Journal of Social Theory*, 4(2): 199–214.

Muecke, S. (2012) '"I am what I am attached to": On Bruno Latour's "Inquiry into the Modes of Existence"'. *Los Angeles Review of Books*. Available at: https://lareviewofbooks.org/article/i-am-what-i-am-attached-to-on-bruno-latours-inquiry-into-the-modes-of-existence/#!

Munnik, R. (1997) 'Donna Haraway: Cyborgs for earthly survival', in H. Achterhuis (ed.) *American Philosophy of Technology*. Indianapolis, IN: University of Indiana Press, pp. 95–118.

Murray, M. (2007) 'Xenotransplanation and the post-human future', in M. Sque and S. Payne (eds) *Organ and Tissue Donation: An Evidence Base for Practice*. Milton Keynes: Open University Press, pp. 152–68.

Norton, M. B. (2013) 'Review of AIME'. *Interstitial Journal: A Journal of Modern Cultural Events*. Available at: https://interstitialjournal.files.wordpress.com/2013/10/norton-latour.pdf.

Oakley, A. (1979) *Sociology of Housework*. Oxford: Basil Blackwell.

Palumbo-Liu, D. (2000) 'Fables and apedagogy: Lyotard's relevance for a pedagogy of the Other', in P. A. Dhillon and P. Standish (eds) *Lyotard: Just Education*. London: Routledge, pp. 194–214.

Parsons, T. (1970) *The Social System*. London: Routledge & Kegan Paul.

Pawlett, W. (2007) *Jean Baudrillard: Against Banality*. London: Routledge & Kegan Paul.

Pawlett, W. (2016) *Violence, Society and Radical Theory: Bataille, Baudrillard and Contemporary Society*. London: Routledge.

Poder, P. (2008) 'Bauman on freedom – consumer freedom as the integration mechanism of liquid society', in M. H. Jacobsen and P. Poder (eds) *The Sociology of Zygmunt Bauman: Challenges and Critique*. Aldershot: Ashgate, pp. 97–115.

Riesman, D. (1953) *The Lonely Crowd*. Garden City, NY: Doubleday Anchor.

Senellart, M. (2009) 'Course context', in M. Foucault *Security, Territory, Population: Lectures at the Collège de France, 1977–78*. Basingstoke: Palgrave Macmillan, pp. 369–401.

Sheridan, A. (1990) *Michel Foucault: The Will to Truth*. London: Routledge.

Skeggs, B. (1997) *Formations of Class and Gender*. London: Sage.

Skeggs, B. (2004) 'Context and background: Pierre Bourdieu's analysis of class, gender and sexuality'. *The Sociological Review* 52(S2): 19–23.

Sullivan, A. (2001) 'Cultural capital and educational attainment'. *Sociology* 35(4): 893–912.

Sullivan, A. (2002) 'Bourdieu and education: How useful is Bourdieu's theory for researchers?'. *The Netherlands Journal for Social Sciences* 38(2): 144–66.

Tierney, T. F. (1997) 'Death, medicine and the right to die: An engagement with Heidegger, Bauman and Baudrillard'. *Body and Society* 3(4): 51–77.

Urry, J. (2009) 'Sociology and climate change'. *Sociological Review* 57(2): 84–100.

Wacquant, L. (1989) 'Towards a reflexive sociology: A workshop with Pierre Bourdieu'. *Sociological Theory* 7(1): 26–63.

Wacquant, L. (2008) 'Pierre Bourdieu', in R. Stones (ed.) *Key Sociological Thinkers*. Basingstoke: Palgrave Macmillan, pp. 261–77.

Wacquant, L. (2015) 'For a sociology of flesh and blood'. *Qualitative Sociology* 38(1): 1–11.

Weasel, L. (2001) 'Dismantling the self/other dichotomy in science: Towards a feminist model of the immune system'. *Hypatia* 16(1): 27–44.

Weber, M. (2001) *The Protestant Ethic and the Spirit of Capitalism*. London: Routledge.

Webster, A. (2007) *Health, Technology and Society: A Sociological Critique*. Basingstoke: Palgrave Macmillan.

Wilcox, L. (2003) 'Baudrillard, September 11, and the haunting abyss of reversal'. *Postmodern Culture* 14(1). Available at: http://pmc.iath.virginia.edu/issue.903/14.1wilcox.html

Wilkinson, I. (2005) *Suffering: A Sociological Introduction*. Cambridge: Polity Press.

Williams, J. (1998) *Lyotard: Towards a Postmodern Philosophy*. Cambridge: Polity Press.

Willis, P. (1983) 'Cultural production and theories of reproduction', in L. Barton and S. Walker (eds) *Race, Class and Education*. London: Croom Helm, pp. 107–38.

Winner, L. (1993) 'Upon opening the black box and finding it empty: Social constructivism and the philosophy of technology'. *Science, Technology, and Human Values* 18: 362–78.

Winograd, T. and Flores, F. (1986) *Understanding Computers and Cognition: A New Foundation for Design*. Norwood, NJ: Ablex.

Wittgenstein, L. (1953) *Philosophical Investigations*. New York: Macmillan.

Index

CPSIA information can be obtained
at www.ICGtesting.com
Printed in the USA
LVHW060022260523
748075LV00008B/62

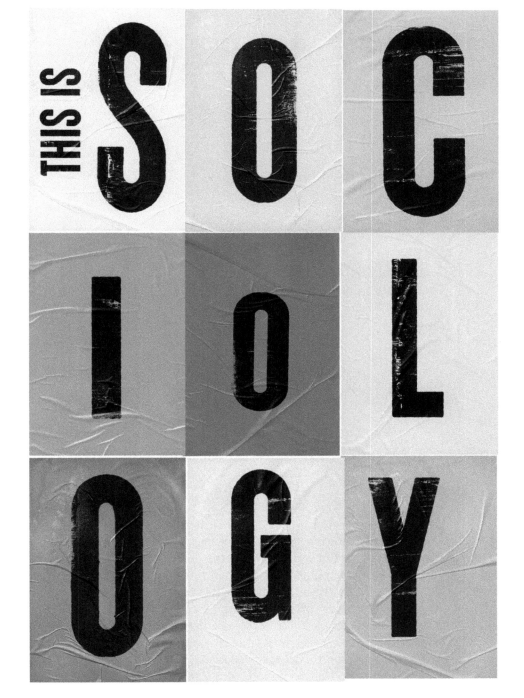

THIS IS **SOCIOLOGY**

A SHORT INTRODUCTION

DAN WOODMAN & STEVEN THREADGOLD

SAGE

Los Angeles | London | New Delhi
Singapore | Washington DC | Melbourne

Los Angeles | London | New Delhi
Singapore | Washington DC | Melbourne

SAGE Publications Ltd
1 Oliver's Yard
55 City Road
London EC1Y 1SP

SAGE Publications Inc.
2455 Teller Road
Thousand Oaks, California 91320

SAGE Publications India Pvt Ltd
B 1/I 1 Mohan Cooperative Industrial Area
Mathura Road
New Delhi 110 044

SAGE Publications Asia-Pacific Pte Ltd
3 Church Street
#10-04 Samsung Hub
Singapore 049483

Editor: Natalie Aguilera
Assistant editor: Ozlem Merakli
Production editor: Katherine Haw
Copyeditor: Fern Bryant
Proofreader: Emily Ayers
Indexer: Milo Kei
Marketing manager: George Kimble
Cover design: Francis Kenney
Typeset by: KnowledgeWorks Global Ltd.

Library of Congress Control Number: 2020951950

British Library Cataloguing in Publication data

A catalogue record for this book is available from the British Library

ISBN 978-1-5297-6882-4
ISBN 978-1-5297-6883-1 (pbk)

CONTENTS

LONG CONTENTS

ABOUT THE AUTHORS

Dan Woodman is T.R. Ashworth Professor of Sociology at University of Melbourne. He researches youth, young adulthood and generational change and is a co-Chief Investigator on the Life Patterns Project, a 30-year and ongoing study that has followed three generations of young Australians as they become adults. Dan is also co-Editor in Chief of *Journal of Youth Studies* and the current President of the Council for the Humanities, Arts and Social Sciences in Australia. He has been teaching first year sociology students at the University of Melbourne for a more than a decade.

Steven Threadgold is Associate Professor of Sociology at University of Newcastle. His research focuses on youth and class, with particular interests in unequal and alternate work and career trajectories; underground and independent creative scenes; and cultural formations of taste. Steve is the co-director of the Newcastle Youth Studies Network, an Associate Editor of *Journal of Youth Studies*, and on the Editorial Boards of *The Sociological Review* and *Journal of Applied Youth Studies*. His latest book is *Bourdieu and Affect: Towards a Theory of Affective Affinities* (Bristol University Press). *Youth, Class and Everyday Struggles* (Routledge) won the 2020 Raewyn Connell Prize for best first book in Australian sociology.

ACKNOWLEDGEMENTS

Dan: Thank you to all my students in the introductory sociology subject Understanding Society at the University of Melbourne, since I first taught the subject in 2012. Thank you also to my co-lecturers and tutors over the years, particularly Barbara Barbosa Neves, Megan Sharp, Mitchell Taylor, Nick Pendergrast, Nick de Weydenthal, Julia Cook, Danielle Nockolds, Isabel Jackson, Lachlan Ross and Amy Vanderharst. Thank you to Corinne for your support over the many years it has taken to write this book, including in its final stages during a pandemic and lockdown. And to my co-author Steve, who has been patient with me over the half decade we have been working on this project. This book is for my children, who are coincidentally four and seven. Watching you grow has been a privilege, even if it has slowed down my writing a little.

For Pearl and Louis

Steve: Thanks to all the students I have met in SOCA1010 since starting to tutor in it in 2005 at the University of Newcastle. They have been the motivation for writing this book. It has also been a pleasure to work with all the dedicated and enthusiastic tutors and lecturers in the course over the years, especially Megan Sharp, Matthew Bunn, Georgina Ramsay, Barrie Shannon, Jonathan Curtis, Jai Cooper, Adriana Haro, Mitchell Taylor, Vanessa Bowden, Joel McGregor, Nafi Ghafournia, Kearin Sims, Kathleen Butler, Penny Jane Burke, Pam Nilan, Terry Leahy, John Germov, Julia Cook, Julia Coffey, Emma Kirby, Stephen Smith and Mitchell Hobbs.

Dan and Steve: We would both like to thank Mitchell Taylor for his exceptional research assistance on the book, especially all his work finding much of the support material and compiling the glossary. Thanks also to Milo Kei for compiling the index. Thanks to Ashley Barnwell, Barbara Barbosa Neves, Megan Sharp and Julia Coffey, who provided feedback on early drafts of some chapters, and the anonymous readers of the manuscript selected by the publisher. Your feedback improved the book immensely. Thank you also to Natalie Aguilera, our commissioning editor at SAGE, for her belief in the different approach to introducing sociology that we have taken in this book and to our production editor Katherine Haw for seeing the project through to completion.

PREFACE

This Is Not All of Sociology

You are reading this book, so you probably want to know what sociology is. If we don't tell you, you will likely want your money back. Many books like this one will tell you that it is the study of 'society'. Stop there, job done, time for a snack... But wait, it is not that simple. Especially as there are debates within sociology about what a society is, and even whether 'society' actually exists. Sorry, you are going to have to read the rest of the book to really develop a sense of what sociology is. Even then we will only be giving you part of the story.

We were being a bit cheeky to call this book *This is Sociology*. Treat anyone, including us, with suspicion if they tell you something like that. There are many different approaches to sociology, and it is impossible for any single book to cover the whole discipline. We could have called the book 'What sociology is to Dan and Steve: A partial at best introduction to some sociological concepts from the perspective of two white guys from Australia'. Our publishers did not think this would sell well. Even textbooks with 40 chapters and 600 pages cannot really do justice to the breadth of sociology, and there are plenty of these if you have $100 plus to spare. We cannot cover all of this diverse, amazing and rapidly changing field. In reality, this is our brief presentation of sociology and the history and concepts that we think will give you a helpful introduction, tailored to how we teach sociology to our own students. It aims to introduce you to the key concepts you will need as you develop your ability to look at the world like a sociologist. We have highlighted these concepts in bold throughout the text and you will find a comprehensive glossary of all these terms at the end of the book. We hope some of you who read it are inspired to delve deeper into the many approaches to sociology and the different lenses they provide for trying to understand, and make better, our complex social worlds.

As well as introducing important concepts, we also introduce you to the thinkers who developed these ideas. While it is important to know these names, one of the things you will discover as you read is that important ideas emerge in particular times and places, and often through the interaction of many people developing a way of thinking, as people have tried to understand the changing social world around them. Like any major discipline taught in universities, from sciences such as physics and astronomy, to arts and humanities such as literature or painting, sociology's history and canonical texts are dominated by white European and American men. To tell the story of sociology and get an understanding of its history, those white males and the influential concepts that they developed need to be understood – many of their ideas are still of at least some use today. However, sociologists are increasingly recognising other writers from the past, who were – because of the biases they faced – not given the attention they deserved for their insights into social life. We have tried to highlight these contributions as well.

It is important to emphasise that sociology is changing, and the leading thinkers in the field today are much more diverse than when sociology was emerging. Things are improving, if too slowly. More recently non-white, non-male, non-gender-binary voices, and voices from the majority of the world beyond North America and Europe, have been making a major impact in sociology, and we introduce you to many of these thinkers in this book. Yet, there are still considerable institutional biases and marginalisations in sociology specifically, and academia generally. At the very beginning of what we hope will be your sociological journey we want you to know that sociology, like the social worlds it is part of, has its own problems of inequality and biases. One of the things sociology, at its best, can do is apply its own insights into these biases and how they emerge onto the discipline itself.

We hope that if our publishers let us write a second edition of this book in the future, sociology will be even more diverse. While the foundational concepts will still have value and we will still need to know how sociology emerged and changed over time, there will almost certainly be an even greater array of voices and perspectives in mainstream introductory sociology in the near future.

We always wanted this book to be small. Maybe when we started we thought it would be easier to write something short. We were wrong! It just meant tougher decisions to make about what to leave out. We also wanted to write a book that could introduce people to sociology – what has been for us a life-changing way to look at the world – that they could buy for the cost of a few coffees, not a week's rent. We also wanted it to be small enough to keep in your bag, or even your pocket. If you get into sociology as much as us, you might want to have the book handy: we think sociology can make for better, more informed, conversation (though, to be honest, sociological insights can be challenging to people's deeply held ideas, and this book is unlikely to make you more popular at parties).

To keep the book pocket-sized, and as engaging as we could, we've done a couple of things. Firstly, we have not used formal academic referencing in the body text of the chapters. In academic writing, referencing is the way writers note exactly where, in which book or other source, each idea they are discussing appears. If you study sociology, or any other subject, you'll learn more about the academic rules for referencing others. This is incredibly important for learning to write academically and making sure you fully attribute ideas, but it can make a text longer and less readable. In this book you will find we give you the names of the scholars associated with each concept in the text, and then at the end of each chapter you will find a list of the important writings from that thinker.

Secondly, we have moved some of the material you might find in a longer textbook off the pages and onto a website:

https://thisissociology.home.blog

We hope you check it out. The website contains an array of support materials beyond the glossary and key references we have included directly in the book. It includes:

- A set of discussion questions for each chapter to check and extend your growing knowledge of sociology.

- Recent articles on each topic, including studies that use the concepts we introduce to do new research into social life.
- Some of the best contemporary examples of sociological thinking in the areas we cover, not just from sociologists working in universities but from journalists and activists.
- Introductory videos and podcasts.

This is our version of sociology. We hope you enjoy it.

1

WHAT IS SOCIOLOGY?

There are almost more ways to do sociology than there are things to make you angry on the internet. Yet across this diversity, sociologists share a particular way of looking at the world. Sociologists use different **theories** – sets of developed and organised ideas about how social life works – and **methods** – systematic ways of collecting **data** about our social lives such as surveys, interviews, focus groups and different kinds of observation – to see beyond taken-for-granted understandings of social life.

Sociologists bring to light *hidden dimensions* of our lives. Maybe you have a friend who also likes to point out what they see as the hidden dimensions shaping our lives, directing you to websites that 'prove' we are ruled by a powerful clandestine elite; they may even be an alien race of lizard people in human disguise. This is no joke. Based on surveys about belief in different conspiracy theories, it seems that at least several million Americans believe that the government is controlled by these lizards. We think this is bunk (sorry to any believers, or reptilian humanoids, who are reading). Sociology and the theories sociologists develop have a strong relationship with data, while lizard queens do not. However, sociology also gives us a way of understanding why conspiracy theories develop. Conspiracy thinking can help people who feel they are being overlooked or condescended to feel that they know something others do not. While there is a sense in which people are manipulated into believing in conspiracies, these ideas are also a source of fun for many adherents (we will cover some of the pleasures of being part of social groups in the coming chapters, as well as the negatives that can emerge from them). More than this, in crucial ways, the theory of reptilian overlords and similar conspiracies exploit, and push to a particular extreme, a tendency to think about the world in a way that is exceedingly common.

People tend to position the causes of patterns in our societies as resulting from the deliberate decisions, attitudes and personalities of individuals, or sometimes a small group of individuals working in cahoots. There must be someone (or some lizard person) to blame and, given the size and complexity of the system being manipulated, they must be extremely powerful. Sociologists provide an alternative way to understand the hidden dimensions that shape our social worlds. The most powerful insights of sociology show that we are all a part of creating the patterns that influence our lives and are constrained by them. This applies to queens and presidents, to sweatshop workers and the homeless, and to those in between (like most of the readers of this book). This does not let the powerful off the hook, it helps us better understand how **power** works.

When things happen, particularly things that seem good or bad, we tend to think that people have either brought negative consequences on themselves through their choices, or that people have used their power to bring about such consequences for others to benefit themselves (and of course they would want to hide this). This way of thinking particularly characterises individualistic cultures, but to some extent is common around the world. Yet we also recognise that things happen outside of our individual power. In every culture, demands are made of people to fit in and there is some sense that – through fate, luck, divinity, or biology – we are not fully in control of our lives. In some cultures, it is much more common to realise, and even demand, that the individual will is subordinated to the group.

These opposing views are called, on the one hand, **voluntarism** – where we make decisions and no one can really force us to do anything – and, on the other hand, **determinism**, where we have no choice and are totally puppets on strings. Sociology takes seriously the question: How free are we to act? And the answer almost every sociologist comes to is 'not as much as many people think'. For example, in most cases only the very rich around the world can realistically send their children to the world's highest status universities, such as Oxford and Cambridge, or Harvard and Yale. Even if you gained the entrance marks, the costs of tuition are beyond most people. Even with a tuition scholarship, the costs of living near these universities in the UK and USA are beyond the means of most people. Could you or your parents afford those high-status options, even if you gained the entrance marks?

Learning to think through a sociological gaze can help you see that we are not as free as we think we are, and this is particularly important in cultures that valorise the notion of freedom of choice. Yet recognising these limitations on us is not what is most valuable about developing what the sociologist C. Wright Mills called the **sociological imagination**. This is a mindset that uses observation and theory to systematically link what happens in our everyday lives to the changing social contexts in which we live. It is a way to methodically make connections between individual lives and larger social contexts. For Mills, the value of sociology is to see that what seems like *personal troubles* – the issues and challenges we all individually face – are linked to how we have organised the ways we live together. This helps us recognise that much of what seems like a personal trouble is really a *public issue*, requiring a collective and political solution. For example, the person waiting for surgery has a private trouble, but if they die on a waiting list for that surgery or because they cannot afford it, there are broader public issues, such as a lack of hospital beds or access to affordable health treatment generally.

Mills was particularly interested in the way we understand employment. Youth unemployment is high in many parts of the world. Sociologists show that it has become harder to find work if you are a young person and that certain regions have much higher rates of unemployment than others. In fact, even if you have not yourself, you probably know a friend or family member who has struggled to find work. Often governments and newspapers focus blame on the apparent failings of the unemployed person as the main reason they are out of work, but sociologists show that the number of jobs available and the expectations employers hold of applicants have changed. There always seems to be many more unemployed or underemployed people than job vacancies. Jobs that members of a previous generation could get without finishing high school often now require it, or even a university degree. These days it's relatively common to see a job advertised as 'entry level', immediately followed by 'must have three years' experience'. This shows that unemployment is a public issue, with social explanations, as much as a personal trouble.

This sociological way of thinking can be difficult to learn because it is often counter to the way we have learned to think about how people act – it makes the normal seem strange – but it is worth the effort because it provides a way to think through seeming paradoxes or contradictions. This includes this division between our capacities to make choices and how our social environment shapes us in profound ways. Instead of voluntarism and determinism, sociologists use the terms **agency** and **structure**. We use agency to highlight how within the boundaries of our social context we can make decisions, and even act individually or collectively to change things. However, these actions happen under *constraints* of various kinds such as laws, traditions, religions, norms, morals and inequalities. More than this, however, it is also important not to think of our social contexts just as constraints. Our agency is also *enabled* by various elements of the situations we find ourselves in. A law to make killing other people in day-to-day life illegal is a constraint on murderers but allows the general population to live relatively more safely. Our world is often made of unintended consequences. Because the social world is complex and determined by a great many factors, our current actions shape our future action and the action of others in many ways we could not foresee and did not intend.

Understanding the way our lives are structured is central to the sociological enterprise. For sociologists, agency and structure are not opposed. We help perpetuate the norms and rules of the groups we are part of, and sometimes even create them. They constrain what we can do, but without norms and guidelines it is impossible to act.

For instance, think about a lecture theatre at a university. The organisation of space sets up specific ways of behaving that are reliant upon centuries of tradition. In most theatres there is a podium out in front for the lecturer to stand behind, symbolising authority and knowledge. There are almost always uncomfortably small chairs and flip tables, organised in rows for the students to act as audience. We both teach introductory sociology at our respective universities, and the university institution bestows a power on lecturers (which is very nice for us and makes teaching a class much easier). However, this power would not exist if you met us in a different context, such as on the sporting field or in a bar. Most of the time, our students sit and listen, or at least pretend to, and only raise their voices when we ask them a question. If someone does make a noise – their phone goes off or they come down to the front and interrupt – it breaks the social norms that everyone expects and requires an apology from the student or a joke from the lecturer to get the class back on track. In this one everyday situation, a sociological imagination uncovers an array of things – traditions, conventions, roles – that we take for granted, that we tend not to question, all of which could be very different under another set of social circumstance or norms.

The Sociological Imagination

The sociological imagination is a way of thinking that links our lives to the broader contexts in which they occur, connecting our personal experience to the settings and networks of others in which it occurs, through to the most impersonal and seemingly remote changes in the global economy. Developing Mills' ideas, contemporary sociologists have suggested that a developed sociological imagination asks four types of questions:

The Historical: Typical historical questions include: how has the past influenced the present? What can we learn from history about events or trends taking place today? How have events in the past influenced the contemporary way of thinking or acting? What historical experiences cause people to act the way they do?

The Cultural: Typical cultural questions include: how does our culture impact on our lives? What influence does cultural tradition have on our social behaviour and interactions? What influence do shared cultural values have on the way people act and think? What effects do particular cultural belief systems have on social trends? How and why do different cultures have different conceptions of what is 'normal'?

The Structural: Typical structural questions include: what role does social organisation play? How do various forms of social organisation and social institutions affect our lives? How does the state of the economy shape our life choices? How does class, race, ethnicity, gender, sexuality, age, and disability shape our life experiences and opportunities? How do these vary over time and between countries and regions?

The Critical: Typical critical questions are: why is it this way? How could things be otherwise? Who benefits from the way things are now? Is there a legacy of injustice visible in how contemporary society is organised? What 'alternative futures' are possible? What kinds of knowledge can provide a starting point for social change? What kinds of 'other voices' need to be heard in relevant debates about reform?

Let us use the sociological imagination to think about what we call the environment. Today there are severe problems facing humanity across the globe relating to mass extinctions and depleted fisheries, potentially dwindling oil supplies and climate change, soil degradation and food supply, and problems of dealing with waste and pollution. From a *historical* perspective we could ask: what has led to this situation? What developments and changes have been most responsible for creating these effects? From a *cultural* perspective we could ask: why have Western societies seen themselves as separate from nature and perceived it as a 'resource'? Why do some cultures understand themselves as part of the environment and why do they not see it as something to be dominated or exploited? What are the consequences of these differences? From a *structural* perspective we could ask: how do the laws and policies of governments affect environmental issues? What constraints are on corporations or individuals in how they can use their environments? What are the economic and social implications of environmental destruction? From a *critical* perspective we could ask: who is benefiting from this situation and who is not? How can we intervene to mitigate environmental problems to make a different future?

By the time you finish this book you will have been introduced to a range of concepts, theories and perspectives to help you develop a sociological imagination: to see the strange in what was once familiar and to understand how and why social change happens, or why things stay the same. We don't know what the case will be for you, but for many who study sociology, once they learn and understand some of the many aspects of sociological thought, it can profoundly change how they view the world and themselves. We think developing a sociological imagination is vital in a world of conspiracy theories and 'fake news', where algorithms and advertising dominate our social media feeds, and where information is everywhere but its reliability is hard to ascertain. As we were completing this book, a global pandemic hit (as we were almost finished, we only make occasional reference to it). The crisis has highlighted deep social inequalities and how they affect our lives, including who lives and dies, and has put into starker relief the dangers of misinformation. Sociology can help you understand these inequalities and also to sort through misinformation and to see where, how and why misinformation arises.

The Birth of Sociology and Its Discontents

Sociology emerged in the 19th century, the middle of a period of great change in how society organised the production of goods, the creation of knowledge and political systems. Up until that point, production of food, clothing and shelter had mostly occurred largely in and around the family home with the family unit working together to produce enough to survive, to meet the demands of the local ruler and then to barter or sell whatever was left. In parts of the world at this time, production was shifting rapidly towards factories in the emerging large cities. This was called the **Industrial Revolution**. **Capitalism** established itself as the dominant mode of organising this production. This is a system where the components of production are owned by private individuals or companies who don't directly do the work but employ others to use these components to produce goods that can be sold for a profit.

At the same time, entrenched ways of understanding the world and our place in it, particularly based on **religion**, were being challenged by an explosion of new ways of thinking. Particularly important was the consolidation of an approach to understanding and changing society and nature by systematically investigating how they worked using science and technology. This was called the **scientific revolution**. Finally, new ways of acting together collectively to deliberately shape society emerged about this time, particularly building on the idea that a people could democratically govern themselves. For example, in the American and French **political revolutions** with their rallying calls of 'liberty, equality and fraternity', or government by 'we the people'.

There are a group of thinkers who were working in the 1800s and early 1900s that are often featured as the 'founders' of sociology in books like this one. While the lists can vary a little, they always include the big three. Émile Durkheim (1858–1917), a French scholar, was interested in how a **functional** social order was created through the way social structures affect people's lives, whether they know it or not. The German Karl Marx (1818–83) charted the ways societies progressed through **conflict** and struggle centred on the economic organisation of society. You have probably heard of Marx, because his ideas inspired the communist revolutions of the 20th century. Another German, Max Weber (1864–1920), argued that social change comes from new ideas and the realm of human meaning as much as struggles over production. He was interested in how people orient their actions using shared symbols, such as religion, as the drivers of social life. Change, for Weber, can be driven as much by struggles to reinterpret these symbols as by changes in technology and the economy. From this perspective, society is a type of **symbolic interaction**.

Others are sometimes added to the list of founders: such as Auguste Comte (1798–1857) – a French philosopher who, although he may not have been the first to use the term, was the first to develop a systematic outline of the idea of 'sociology' as the scientific study of social life; Georg Simmel (1858–1918), another German, who focused on the social interactions of everyday life. Occasionally an early advocate of sociology in the USA is added to the list, such as Lester Ward, William Sumner, or Albion Small, who founded the *American Journal of Sociology* and the first department of sociology in the United States, at the University of Chicago.

You may be noticing something similar about all of these 'founding fathers'. They are all men. Photos of the founding figures of sociology at first glance can look like the finalists in a hipster beard contest. At the time these scholars were writing, and into the 20th century, it was very hard for women to be considered as serious figures or leaders in an academic field. In fact, it was hard for them to conduct and publish sociological work at all. However, despite these barriers, there *were* women writing important sociological work at this time.

It is increasingly common to add the names of Marianna Weber (1870–1954), the German partner of Max, and the British scholar Harriet Martineau (1802–1876) to the list of founders. They tend to be presented as early representations of a 'feminist' approach to sociology. There is truth to this, but it unfairly minimises their wider contribution to the birth of the discipline. Marianna Weber did develop a sociology built on the perspectives and experiences of women, but she wrote widely about Marxism, socialism and war. Martineau did advocate for sociologists paying more attention to women's lives, but this was part of a broader project to highlight the importance of everyday life, the private sphere, the **socialisation** of children through morals and manners to understanding cultural differences, and to furthering cultural understanding.

Martineau also deserves significant credit for introducing sociology to Britain. She translated Auguste Comte's multi-volume work, in which he developed the idea of sociology, from the original French into English. It was more than a translation, however. She condensed and clarified, and in some sections 'freely translated' Comte's books, in some ways creating a new work. Comte himself seems to have seen it as an improvement, because soon after Martineau's version was released, he seems to have begun to set it as the preferred text for his own students, instead of his original. In her own work Martineau also developed, among other contributions, an argument about the social basis of suicide.

Whether suicide is influenced by social factors is one of the most famous research questions in sociology – an important social problem and a particularly powerful way of thinking with a sociological imagination about what seems to be the most obvious sign of a 'private trouble' vis-a-vis 'public issues'. Émile Durkheim wrote a celebrated book called *On Suicide* in 1897. Through showing how patterns differ from place to place, he revealed that something that seems as personal as suicide can be linked to the social organisation of different societies. This book is considered ground-breaking in sociology for applying the sociological method to a topic that seems so intimately linked to private despair. It has been largely ignored that Martineau's book from 1838 on how to systematically observe cultural differences in morals and manners contains half a chapter on the social basis of suicide, including its different types and that the rate varies across countries that are Protestant and Catholic.

The founding fathers were also all white Europeans. Even if we now add in these 'founding mothers', we are left with a group that is a little less beardy but still quite pasty. Hence there have been efforts to give greater prominence in introductory texts to the pathbreaking work of African American sociologist William Edward Burghardt (known as WEB) Du Bois (1868–1963), who was born just after the end of the American Civil War, and became one of the first African Americans to gain a PhD, and the first from Harvard. Before his study at Harvard, he had studied in Berlin, alongside Max Weber (they were even pen pals for a while, sharing their ideas via letters).

Like Martineau, characterisations of Du Bois's work are often focused on his studies of the experience of African Americans. Yet his arguments about the central role that race relations was going to play in the 20th century were global in their scope. A compelling case has been made by the American sociologist Aldon Morris that Du Bois played an influential role in founding sociology in North America, but his significance within American sociology was underplayed until recently because of **racism** among sociologists. You'll learn more about Du Bois and these other early sociologists in the coming chapters.

Sociology has both challenged and reflected the biases of the world in which sociologists work. Sociologists are making efforts to expand the list of founders to recognise the diversity that has existed, despite the barriers, as the discipline was being formed. At its best, sociology is a critical pursuit, and it increasingly aims to be reflective about its shortcomings and lack of diversity in terms of who have been and are its dominant voices. But, like the societies it has emerged from, sociology has not escaped the pervasive impact of **sexism**, racism and other **prejudices** and has often needed to be pushed by critical scholars to address its own failing. Through the hard work of scholars, often from minority groups themselves, sociology has been improving in the 21st century, with a broader array of perspectives entering into mainstream sociology. It is still overly dominated by what sociologists call the **Global North**, or the **Minority World** (primarily Europe and North America), a problem we return to in Chapter 3 and throughout the book.

The Theoretical and Methodological Traditions of Sociology

Sociologists study the social world and have developed many different methods – the systemic procedures used to select, collect and then analyse data. These methods are often summarised by categorising them as either quantitative or qualitative methods. **Quantitative methods** include the many different types of data that can be counted, most commonly survey data collected by asking a selection of people selected to represent a particular group or groups a set of questions about specific topics, with responses generally including ticking boxes, such as yes or no, or agree or disagree. Particularly since we have started to interact with each other and shop online, and information on what we do with our online clicks is collected by the sites we use, the amount of this type of data has grown extraordinarily quickly. The rise of what has become known as **big data** has seen quantitative modes of gathering data about us and analysing it become the primary way of selling us stuff, and – some argue – manipulating our voting preferences and buying practices. Sociologists are also accessing this big data to understand social life but also often highlight the implications of these huge data-collecting online platforms that are coming to have as much influence and money as countries, if not more. **Qualitative methods** vary greatly, ranging from the simple question-based methods such as the one-on-one interview or focus groups (a type of guided conversation among several participants), to methods where research participants are asked to take photos, write a story, make some art or a film to help convey their thoughts, feelings and experiences. Within the category of qualitative methods, there are also more observational-based methods such as ethnography, where a researcher will spend a considerable amount of time in a workplace, school or region taking notes, watching what goes on, and getting to know the people and practices, and participant observation, where the researcher actually takes part in the thing they are researching.

While there are a variety of methods that come under each banner, one way of understanding the difference is that quantitative methods collect data that is or can be converted to numbers, to help us see the breadth of patterns in social life, while qualitative methods use text, talk and experience to try to get a deeper understanding of the meanings that people form and that inform their actions. Many research projects will use multiple methods and some sociological research uses both quantitative and qualitative methods to approach their research question in more than one way, to alleviate the weaknesses and buttress the strengths of each research approach.

Sociologists study the social world using different methods. In doing so they are making different assumptions about what exists in the world (referred to by sociologists and others using the philosophical term **ontology**) and what can be known about it (**epistemology**). Beyond this brief introduction, we do not focus on research methods in this book, or even give you all the most recent up-to-date data on the social world (there is a lot of great research out there – you can find some of it if you check out our website). Instead, we focus on the different theoretical approaches that have developed in sociology and the concepts attached to them. As you learn about these different concepts, you will similarly notice that different sociologists and different approaches to sociology make different assumptions of what exists and how we can know about it. Noticing this can help us understand what is included and what is left out of different approaches to studying social life and where they might be complementary and where they are contradictory.

The development of theoretical traditions in sociology includes functionalist, conflict, interactionist, feminist, and post-colonial perspectives. *Functional* approaches view society as primarily based on and needing **social order**. Norms, rules, morals and sanctions are essential to create a world in which we can live together. Individuals are socialised into social **roles** needed for society to function smoothly, and those who do not conform are labelled deviant. *Conflict* approaches instead see society as primarily an arena of struggle, where norms and rules actually favour some groups over others, creating social hierarchies and unjustifiable inequalities as much as social order. In this approach, people are often coerced into actions and even false beliefs by those in power. Functional and conflict theories, despite seeming to be in opposition, both focus on the big picture; *interactionist theories* instead focus on specific contextual social situations and interactions of people, showing how this affects our ideas, emotions and **practices**. Society from this perspective is founded on the way people use and manipulate symbols in their day-to-day interactions with each other.

These three approaches are roughly linked with scholars following the lead of Durkheim (functionalism), Marx (conflict) and Weber (interactionist), although as you will see in the coming chapters, their ideas were richer than can be captured with these simple labels. Early sociological work focused mostly on class, institutions and the economy. Through the 20th century, however, other approaches developed and scholarship considering gender, racial, and geographic hierarchies have become more prominent. **Feminist theories** became prominent as scholars highlighted the ways that published and popular ideas within society came from a largely male perspective, and that this was true within sociology as well as society generally. This kind of knowledge is not only from a male perspective but tends to operate against the interests of women. Feminist perspectives have been particularly critical of the functional tradition by showing how the norms and roles that many functionalists have promoted as the foundation of the social order are sexist. We will say more about these approaches throughout the book, particularly in Chapter 9.

Post-colonial theories highlight that this same body of official knowledge has been dominated not just by men but by European and American perspectives, excluding the point of view of the billions of other people living in the rest of the world. As we will see in Chapter 3, for instance, Durkheim presented ideas about religion that have been criticised from a post-colonial perspective for containing simplified representations of Aboriginal people in Australia that reinforced racist perspectives.

These more recent developments have emerged through scholars who were previously excluded, fighting to be heard. Feminists and **Majority World** (outside of North America and Europe) perspectives in sociology were not excluded through a deliberate conspiracy among a powerful group of sociologists/lizard people, although there are certainly examples of sexist and racist behaviour. The social structures and cultures of the time naturalised the idea of European and masculine superiority. It was hard for people not included in these groups to be published and, if they were, to be read and taken seriously. Sometimes the marginalised themselves were socialised to believe their own apparent inferiority. As these newer perspectives have risen to prominence, it has hopefully made sociology more **reflexive**, meaning it is able to reflect on itself, to turn the sociological imagination inwards on sociology, to make visible its assumptions and the ideas it was excluding. Like all members of society, sociologists have biases and prejudices but at its best the sociological imagination can help individual sociologists confront how their own views are shaped by their place in the world. There are many different theories and ways of collecting information in sociology. By acknowledging this diversity and learning from many perspectives, we hope that sociology as a whole is becoming more reflexive.

Sociological Questions

The sociological imagination can provide us with a way of seeing the world that questions what we think of as 'normal'. Sociology takes on some big questions, including: what is normal? What makes something 'deviant'? Is race real, and if not, why does the idea have such deep consequences for lives? What is ethnicity? What is gender and sex – is one biological and one social, or is it more complicated than that? What are the causes of sexual or domestic violence? What about violence more broadly and what kind of social structures create less violence? These can be challenging questions. Sociology challenges worldviews. The American sociologist Peter Berger famously (at least among sociologists) once said that the first wisdom of sociology is that things are not what they seem. Sociology questions things that are taken for granted. It can 'step on toes' but hopefully contribute to making things better.

Throughout its development, sociology has also been interested in how contours of inequality – tied to class, gender, race and ethnicity, ability and sexuality among other factors – affect people's life chances and opportunities, and in more general terms, how these ideas, and the social divisions they create, shape the formation of **identity**. Researchers interested in **class** investigate how our economic position in society impacts our opportunities and life chances; for example, how your parents' type of work, their **occupation,** and the school you attended affect your prospects; how our occupations and appearance relate to the notion of **status** (our standing in social hierarchies that can bring benefits and influence, or the opposite); and how our socio-economic position affects our tastes, morals and opinions. You will hear more about class and the other major fault lines in our society throughout the book and we look specifically at class in more detail in Chapter 7.

Gender researchers investigate how much of who we are is biological (nature) and how much is culture (nurture) and whether this binary is even meaningful; they question whether the toys we play with as children teach us how to 'perform' our gender roles or why some **sexualities** have been deemed 'normal' and others 'deviant'. Research that investigates gender inequality asks why women are still paid less at work while still doing most of the housework and looking after the kids. How does the entrenchment of insecure employment in many countries shape gender roles and the family? What does the rise of things such as anorexia, steroid usage or plastic surgery mean? We discuss gender in detail in Chapter 8.

Researchers interested in **race** and **ethnicity** have questioned whether race as biological differences between people of different ancestry actually (scientifically) exists and asked how and why culture and skin colour continue to be used to create marginalisation and **discrimination**. How has **globalisation** affected the relationship between different cultures? What is the difference between **biological** and **cultural racism**? What problems and discriminations do migrants and refugees face? How does the historical trauma faced by Indigenous communities affect their lives today? Do Western countries have '**Islamophobia**'? How does 'whiteness' manifest forms of privilege? We go into detail in Chapter 9.

Another key concept that underpins sociological analysis is power. Who has power and who doesn't? When is power legitimate? Is power a top-down phenomenon or does it exist everywhere? How does power shape who we are as individuals and, as individuals, do we have any power? What about when we act collectively? Does money equal power? Does knowledge equal power? Does the media have power to create what is 'normal' and 'true'? Are algorithms power? Do we control our technological gadgets, or do they control us or is there another way to think about the relationship between technology and society? We get into these kinds of questions and give at least some of the answers in detail throughout the book.

Conclusion

Sociologists do not speak with one voice any more than do psychologists, philosophers or journalists. Sociology is neither inherently 'left' or 'right' in its political orientation, although many sociologists have a strong concern for social justice and redressing social inequality. As a discipline, sociology does lead to questioning any overly individual explanations for success and failure. Sociology is a way of looking at things, more than a discipline that looks at a particular topic. It addresses as many human issues and topics as it is possible to find. Just about anything you can think of is, or has been, studied by a sociologist somewhere in the world! But whatever the question, sociological research involves the use of data and evidence, as well as concepts that help us understand what evidence to collect, what the evidence means and its wider significance. This allows us to bring to light many of the other causes of what feel like our individual successes and failures and to talk about ways of organising how we live together that are most likely to lead to human flourishing and a fair go for all.

Sociology also provides a counter to individualistic and biological accounts of social life and human behaviour by focusing on how society influences our lives and how social change occurs. There are social factors that shape what happens to us. People who do well out of how society is organised often do not want this questioned, but one of sociology's greatest insights is that in most cases these people did not need to actively conspire to create the world that benefits them. Society is like a conspiracy that does not need conspirators (sorry lizard people, you're out of a job). Or an even better way to put it: while there are great differences in the level of influence and control different people have, society is the outcome of the actions of all of us, without us even paying attention to what we are doing most of the time. As you read this book, you will see that it turns out that in important ways the conspirators in the making of society are all of us. This also means we could make it differently, even if – as we will see in the coming chapters – this might not be easy. Practising sociology means considering the relevance of sociological insights to your own life, using the sociological imagination to adopt a questioning stance towards what happens in your society and the decisions you make. By the end of the book, we hope you are asking new questions about almost everything, except why you picked up this book!

Key references for this chapter

Abrahamson, M (1978) *Functionalism*. Prentice Hall.

Allen, RC (2017) *The Industrial Revolution: A Very Short Introduction*. Oxford University Press.

Blumer, H (1986) *Symbolic Interactionism: Perspective and Method*. University of California Press.

Bourdieu, P and Wacquant, L (1992) *An Invitation to Reflexive Sociology*. University of Chicago Press.

Clark, G (2007) *A Farewell to Alms: A Brief Economic History of the World*. Princeton University Press.

Collins, R (1974) *Conflict Sociology*. Academic Press.

Comte, A (2009) *The Positive Philosophy of Auguste Comte*, 2 vols., trans. H Martineau. Cambridge University Press.

Du Bois, WEB (1996) *The Philadelphia Negro: A Social Study*. University of Pennsylvania Press.

Du Bois, WEB (1998) *Black Reconstruction in America, 1860-1880*. Free Press.

Durkheim, E (1951) *Suicide: A Study in Sociology*. Free Press.

Giddens, A (1984) *The Constitution of Society: Outline of the Theory of Structuration*. University of California Press.

Henry, J (2008) *The Scientific Revolution and the Origins of Modern Science*, 3rd edn. Red Globe Press.

Martineau, H (2002) *How to Observe Morals and Manners,* 3rd edn. Transaction Press.

Martineau, H (2005) *Society in America*, 4th edn. Transaction Press.

Mills, CW (1959) *The Sociological Imagination*. Oxford University Press.

Morris, A (2017) *The Scholar Denied: W. E. B. Du Bois and the Birth of Modern Sociology*. University of California Press.

Palmer, RR (2014) *The Age of the Democratic Revolution*. Princeton University Press.

Principe, LM (2011) *The Scientific Revolution: A Very Short Introduction*. Oxford University Press.

Robertson, J (2015) *The Enlightenment: A Very Short Introduction*. Oxford University Press.

Rossi, AS (1973) 'The First Woman Sociologist: Harriet Martineau (1802–1876)', in Rossi, AS (ed.) *The Feminist Papers: From Adams to de Beauvoir*. Northeastern University Press.

Simmel, G (1950) *The Sociology of Georg Simmel*. Free Press.

Ward, L (1897) *Dynamics of Sociology*. D. Appleton & Company.

2

THE FOUNDATIONS OF SOCIOLOGY

A sense that the social world was changing rapidly was one of the drivers of the emergence of sociology in the 19th and early 20th centuries. These changes seemed exciting to some but worrying to others. There was widespread fear that the speed of movement allowed by rail and then motorcar, the new technology of the telegraph and then telephone, and life in the growing urban centres of the world, would overwhelm the human capacity to handle novelty. This mirrors concerns today about the impact of growing global travel, the rise of megacities and lives spent increasingly focused on a constantly changing digital interface (our phones) that we can carry around in our pockets.

Your life is likely quite different from your parents' and grandparents' in some significant ways. At least some of our readers will be reading this book under duress, a necessary requirement of a university subject you have enrolled in. Attending university even until very recently was extremely rare – for most young people the possibility would not have even crossed their mind. Today in some parts of the world it has become the norm. In China, for example, the rate of growth in higher education has been particularly rapid, doubling over the past decade, and now about 20 per cent go on to university. Almost everywhere the change has been relatively rapid, across one or two generations. For the generation before, literacy was rare across much of the world. Globally, the numbers in higher education are now five times higher than in the 1970s. This means that if your parents or grandparents went to university, they were likely among a very small elite, and graduate success was almost assured. Now, the outcomes are more tenuous.

Technology has helped more people become literate and go on to higher education. Keeping up with technology is also one of the reasons that people study for longer. Literacy and technological know-how are important for many current jobs and the jobs that are being created. On the other hand, we worry that technology might destroy jobs. There are some claims, probably exaggerated but with a grain of truth, that almost half of the jobs that currently exist will be automated (taken over by robots) in the coming decades. Maybe the second edition of this book will be written by bots.

These changes are hopefully setting off your sociological imagination, prompting you to ask how new patterns of education are changing people's lives, including your own, and who might win or lose from these changes. In this chapter we will see how changes linked to technology, work and inequality drove the emergence of sociology, focusing on three people that in the previous chapter we labelled 'the big three': Karl Marx, Émile Durkheim and Max Weber. Throughout the book you will see how their foundational ideas still shape sociology. However, although all three are brilliant thinkers who shaped the discipline and whose ideas are worth understanding, sociology has been pushed in more recent years to recognise its own – and the big three's – weaknesses. In the next chapter we will cover these challenges to sociology and how its perspectives have broadened out.

Changing Societies and the Emergence of Sociology

Created by people striving to understand the political, scientific and industrial revolutions reshaping Europe in the 19th century, sociology has its origins in times of upheaval. Old hierarchies and ways of thinking about the world were challenged and even dismantled. New ways of thinking and new hierarchies were emerging in their place. Inequalities were reappearing in new guises, despite the efforts of many to build a more open and fairer world. Changes were emerging at this point in history that continue to shape our contemporary societies.

Very recently you've probably had to hand over money to a big company for a product, worked for a wage, had to fill out a difficult form, or had to rely on an expert or official to help you navigate our complex society. Marx, Durkheim and Weber can help us understand where these everyday occurrences of modern life came from and why they might be more than everyday annoyances but part of the foundation of our contemporary social world.

Capitalism and Revolutions

Karl Marx is a key figure in the development of sociology. He was a philosopher and activist, but probably wouldn't have considered himself a sociologist. The term was new during his lifetime, and he was part of a generation of scholars working before the emergence of the disciplinary divisions between philosophy, economics, political science and sociology that exist today.

Marx's ideas influenced the unfolding of 20th-century sociology probably more than any other as people built on and challenged his ideas. His grave in Highgate Cemetery in London is a tourist attraction. His tomb is also regularly damaged by vandals protesting his legacy. He is widely recognised as the key figure in the development of communism, a model of economic and social life that was claimed at least for a time by many countries during the 20th century, most famously China and the USSR. His image held pride of place on mural walls and was reproduced in statues in central city squares throughout the communist world. For this reason, Marx tends to be thought of as a theorist of communism. This is at best partly true. Marx was a theorist of social change, change driven by an emerging new **capitalist** economic system, an economic model built around the market and the separation of the producers of goods from the owners of the means through which the goods are produced. Marx was primarily a critical theorist of capitalism.

Marx saw the foundation of social life and the dynamic of social change in the way humans transform the world to survive. He argued that human history was at its foundation an ongoing struggle over control of this production process. History was an unfolding confrontation between groups with opposing interests and power in this process: between slaves and slave owners, lords and serfs (an agricultural worker bound by law to work on their lord's land), and, finally, paid workers and business owners. Each stage in this struggle had its own dynamic, a set of contradictions that had to be understood to see how that system of production would break down and a new system emerge.

Although he was German, Marx lived in France for a time and uses French words for the main classes of capitalism. As a young man he worked as a journalist and moved to Paris as radical ideas were relatively free from censorship there. He uses the term **bourgeoisie**, which originally meant city dwellers and came to stand for a class of business owners, to designate who can invest money to privately own factories and enterprises, also known as the ruling class. For Marx, new industrial technologies and a small but growing class of bourgeoisie put the pre-existing feudal system in Europe under pressure. **Feudalism** was a system where a class of lords ruled areas of land and the people who lived on it, on behalf of the king or queen, in return for sending the monarch taxes and soldiers.

The new type of capitalist production needed workers who were 'free' to sell their labour in the emerging cities; people with little power but not tied by law, as peasant serfs were, to the land controlled by their local lord. The growing power of the bourgeoisie led to the breakdown of the feudal order, and peasants became the **proletariat**, or the working class, dependent on undertaking a specific job earning a wage to survive, instead of supporting themselves off the land, and largely excluded from any hope of owning the means of production. Marx argued that these two groups were dependent on each other but had rival interests.

Marx believed that competition between capitalists to produce cheaper goods would put constant downward pressure on wages and force many smaller capitalists out of business, leading to concentration of money in fewer and fewer hands. Marx argued that this process would eventually lead to a **class consciousness** among workers as they came to realise their shared interests with each other and the way that the system was exploiting them. In these relations, capitalism therefore contains the seeds of its own destruction. Both the dynamics of capitalism and an emerging class consciousness would provide the foundations for a **revolution**, the overthrow and replacement of the existing system and government. The next stage of history, Marx believed, would be communist.

Marx did not have a developed theory of how this revolutionary transition would occur, and despite his fame as the theorist of communism, he had relatively little to say about what a communist society would look like, beyond sketching out some key principles like the common ownership of the means of production. This was not simply an oversight; he saw the end of capitalism as a freeing of human potential to shape their own lives, for their personal and the collective good. For Marx, not owning the products of our labour, and having a very narrow task in the production for which we are paid a wage, leads to **alienation**; workers become cogs in the production process, undertaking dreary and repetitive tasks to make only parts of products that are then shipped to stores where they cannot afford to shop. Workers are like any other thing playing a role in the system, rather than a human realising their creative potential through work.

To pre-empt too much of what such a future society would look like would be to deny humans this creative potential to shape their own future in a communist society. Marx did, however, believe that these future societies would be characterised by a shift from the time devoted to the **realm of necessity** (work that a worker needs to do to survive and reproduce) to the **realm of freedom** (time to pursue their creative potential). He also imagined that in a future society our work would be more varied and we could do one thing today, and another tomorrow – that we would work for a couple of hours in the morning, and tend the garden in the afternoon, and play music and have a drink in the evening, without ever becoming a worker, gardener, or musician.

Marx was right with many of his critiques of capitalism, certainly about the problems of growing unequal concentration of wealth, but he also got plenty of things wrong. He predicted that communist revolutions were likely to occur in the most advanced capitalist countries, such as Germany or England, as this was where industrial productive capabilities and the contradictions of capitalism were most developed. At points in the 19th and early 20th century it looked as if he was going to be right but instead the major revolutions happened elsewhere, for example in Russia and Eastern Europe and in Asia. Today, most of the countries that became communist in the 20th century have again transitioned, this time to versions of a capitalist system. Another famous sociologist from this early period of sociology developed ideas about continuity and change, in an implicit dialogue with Marx, which provide some clues as to why capitalism has not come to an end.

Culture and Social Change

Max Weber, like Marx, was trying to understand the changing society around him, and how this fitted in the grand scope of change over history. He followed Marx in his focus on power and the belief that capitalism was central to the new society he saw emerging. He departed from Marx, however, in two important ways, which made him doubt that a revolution was on its way.

Marx focused on **material** aspects of economic **production** – the concrete process of how we make things as the basis of societal forms and the driver of change. Weber argued that **culture**, shared ideas, was an essential and overlooked part of the emergence of capitalism and the modern world. Weber focused on showing how a new mindset arose with capitalism. This new mindset did not create the capitalist mode of production, but had an **elective affinity** with it, a mutually reinforcing association rather than a strictly causal relationship. As such, a new capitalist mindset, a 'spirit', facilitated the spread of capitalism. A chance resonance between new technological possibilities and a new attitude emerging from aspects of the relatively new Protestant Christian religions provided the combination through which capitalism could grow. When Weber emphasised these cultural factors, he was not denying that material changes were important, but aiming to provide balance to the overemphasis of these factors in the writings of Marx and others.

This cultural spark through which capitalism could take off was the notion of the **Protestant Ethic**, a valuing of hard work dedicated towards a **vocation**. This ethic emerged among European Christian **sects.** A sect is a group that breaks away from an established church, based on denying or changing key beliefs of the established group. The sects that Weber focused on had broken away from the Catholic Church. These 'Protestant' religions emphasised a personal relationship to God and minimised the role of the church in salvation. In one of these sects, Calvinism, a new core belief of predestination emerged. Whether or not you would be saved and go to heaven or be damned and go to hell was decided by God from the beginning of time, before you were born. As such, it was not up to individual choice to live a good and holy life, or up to the church to provide forgiveness to the repentant. In fact, there was nothing that could be done.

Weber argued that this belief had a paradoxical effect. For Calvinists, the stakes are very high – salvation for a select few, eternal damnation for the rest – but completely outside of their control. Weber argued that the uncertainty of (unknowable) predestination was psychologically impossible to live with. You might think that the response to this would be to say 'Stuff it, there is nothing that can be done anyway, so let's party'. Weber, however, thought it had almost the opposite effect. Believers anxiously turned to signs in their lives that they were among the elected who would be saved into eternal life. This evidence was understood as succeeding at the type of work the sect members pursued, combined with an asceticism, an avoidance of all indulgences, including any lavish **consumption**. So, no partying. These believers pursued their work as a calling, something that they should be highly dedicated to and well-trained in – reinvesting the money earned in the pursuit of even greater evidence of success, while turning away from spending, delaying gratification.

Calvinism combined two prohibitions: first, a prohibition on luxury; second, a prohibition on most charity. The latter element is especially important: because money can neither be spent nor given away, investment emerges as the logical choice. This drove a calculative attitude towards business affairs, and a cycle of reinvestment that combined with technological and material advancements to set capitalism on its way to becoming the modern economic order.

This **rationality** – not meaning reasonable but meaning taking a calculative attitude that measures and manages and adjusts to ever more efficiently pursue particular ends, such as the accumulation of more money – spread with this economic order and played a large part in building it. Alongside capitalism this rationality moved beyond the factory and business decisions into the running of governments and households, becoming embedded in ever more complex systems of organisations, rules, regulations and decision-making based on a 'rational process' that Weber called **bureaucracy**. We think of bureaucracy as common in the public sector, but for Weber this type of logic dominated modern society far beyond government.

Weber saw the emergence of the modern world as driven to a large degree by culture, a set of broadly shared attitudes and beliefs that began with the ideas of a small number of people. The world can be changed by ideas. The story of capitalism and the Protestant Ethic is a story of the way that **charismatic leadership** can replace the traditional authority of the previous religious and economic order, but that these ideas spread, becoming the rule-bound and law-based form of authority in which many of us dwell today. A world where we are constantly agreeing to terms and conditions written by lawyers and entering into contractual arrangements.

This culture was as much constitutive of modernity as the means of production, and Weber saw it unfolding with an irresistible force, becoming an **iron cage of rationality** in which we were trapped but to which we would become accustomed. He saw little chance that this modern form could be overthrown by revolution, or even changes to the ownership of the means of production. Instead, it would simply evolve into ever tighter sets of rules and guidelines. The way that bureaucratic arrangements came to dominate the systems that emerged after successful communist revolutions in the previous century suggests he may have been right. In a pessimistic moment he thought that this iron cage would dominate our lives until the last tonne of fossil fuel is used up.

Increasing Complexity and the Challenge of Belonging

Émile Durkheim, at about the same time as Weber in Germany, was developing in France another sociological understanding of the emerging modernity. Like Weber he was also in an implicit conversation with Marx's ideas about the economy. He was under no illusions about the potential failures and inequalities of capitalism. He believed, however, that if its alienating pathologies could be managed through state interventions to maintain **equality of opportunity** and to allow people to find the niche to which they were best suited, a highly developed **division of labour** (people doing different, specialised roles) could support a flourishing society. Others had previously noted the growing importance of the division of labour to the emerging economic system, but Durkheim systematically thought about its consequences for society in great detail. He understood the emergence of modernity as a shift from a **mechanical solidarity** to an **organic solidarity**. These very different forms of social cohesion are tied to a shift from a weak to a strong division of labour.

Social cohesion is the glue that holds together groups. In most human groups, Durkheim argued, people undertook much the same labour, each providing for their own basic needs, and engaged in much the same activity more broadly as all others in their social group. This leads to mechanical solidarity, a sense of togetherness based on sameness. However, most of us in contemporary societies are skilled in a very narrow set of practices, not directly related to our basic needs. People need others to collect the garbage, grow their food, make their cars and keep the power on. Helpless, most of us including the authors would not last long if social functions ceased, being unable to feed, clothe or defend ourselves. We may think of ourselves as independent, but those of us living in cities and working in the contemporary economy rely on others at least as much, if in different ways, to those living in nomadic bands of hunters and gatherers.

Durkheim, unlike Marx, did not think that the true nature of humanity was to pursue our multiple and varied interests any more than it was to have one specialised task our entire lives. Instead, he saw the challenge of maintaining solidarity, the bonds of social life, to be solved in different ways as societies transitioned from traditional to modern types. Modern types had their own form of solidarity tied to the division of labour, but this penetrated less into people's sense of self than the shared world view that accompanied living with others in smaller scale, rural 'traditional societies' defined by 'mechanical solidarity'.

Durkheim argued that other institutions were needed to support the economic integration provided by the division of labour. The division of labour needs, for example, the support of a legal system that instils trust in the enforcement of contracts, a **meritocratic** education system that leads to the best people for the position taking the right jobs, and a set of shared norms (including religious). Durkheim's notion of organic solidarity characterises society as a complex system with parts that work together to form a unified stable whole that continues over time. Durkheim's way of thinking about society, identifying the pieces needed to maintain social integration, provided a template for many future sociologists who focused on identifying the role of different social institutions in creating **social order**. However, Durkheim did not dismiss the importance of change. People who challenge norms and bring into being new possibilities for living life are essential, because social norms can lag behind needed social change. But – importantly – Durkheim believed change without regulation leads to social disintegration.

Remember, and we hope you do, as it was only a couple of pages back, Weber saw a risk of modernity becoming an iron cage of rules and regulations that we would all have to follow. Durkheim also saw this as a risk. Over-regulation is a danger in modern societies, if the rules are too rigid and people are not allowed to find the right niche for themselves. This can lead to **fatalism** (a sense of everything being outside of our control). However, Durkheim pointed out that modern life, particularly if social change is rapid, also creates a risk of under-regulation. Focusing particularly on the government regulation of the economy, Durkheim argued that a state of **anomie** (tied to feelings of uncertainty and frustration) may develop when people experience a rapid change in their economic or social position. A sense of normlessness can develop, and he worried that people living in modern societies can be left with a sense of floating around without any secure moorings from which to make decisions about the right life for themselves and what a good life means. Maybe you feel like that sometimes. We certainly do.

The Continuing Influence of the Classics

Sociologists continue to read and write about Marx, Durkheim and Weber today. They got a lot of the detail wrong but had the foresight to see the important changes that would come to change the way we live together. They based their theories in research studies they and others conducted but were able to see the broader significance of what could seem like small changes.

When Weber wrote about the rise of the bureaucracy and its centrality to the pursuit of **rationality**, few organisations had this form, and it was rare insight to see the significance it would hold. When Marx wrote about capitalism and the rise of the working class that would eventually be its undoing, there were few wage labourers, and even fewer capitalists anywhere in the world. He asked big questions about how best to link the economy, politics and society that would shape the century that followed. The division of labour which Durkheim saw as the foundations of a new type of solidarity was only sharply differentiated in a handful of places around the world. He also saw some of the consequences of this type of social glue being too strong or too weak. He argued that, at its extremes, anomie can lead people to take their own lives. Suicide, Durkheim argued, was a reaction to the stultification of not enough social change or individuality but also to its opposite, too rapid change. This idea is still used by sociologists today to understand seemingly high rates of social suffering in contemporary societies, even among people whose material circumstances appears to be very secure.

The rise of cities was a key ingredient in the big three's diagnosis of modernity. Durkheim's organic solidarity and the risk of anomie were the structures and problems of the city. Marx named the class that were the new drivers of history after a word that meant city dwellers. Weber wrote a book called *The City*, arguing that the existence and growth of the city provides the first step in weakening older orders of kinship and obligation that allowed capitalism and its modern bureaucracy and new forms of identity to emerge. The city helped to create modernity and modernity drove the growth of cities.

One of the most famous contrasts used by sociologists, proposed by German sociologist Ferdinand Tönnies in 1887, is between **Gemeinschaft** and **Gesellschaft.** These are German terms, so (for the non-German speakers reading) you now have a little German sociological vocabulary to go along with the French. They can be translated as community (Gemeinschaft) and society (Gesellschaft). Tönnies tied the first to life in a rural village setting, where kinship and shared traditions and aims unite people, relationships are direct, emotional and personal. Gesellschaft was city life, where people had a relatively removed relationship with those they interacted with, often mediated by money and negotiating to achieve separate aims. This distinction influenced Durkheim and Weber. Another influential German sociologist (yes, we know there are a lot of Germans, we'll say more about this in the next chapter) of the early 20th century, Georg Simmel, wrote about the necessity of a **blasé attitude**. This was partly about the need to not attend too closely or be too invested in events and other people, but was also about not being too spontaneous or unpredictable, as the requirement for negotiating the hustle and bustle of a growing metropolis and its economic life.

These sociologists wrote at a time when almost everybody in the world continued to live outside of cities. Today it is more than half of us who live in cities and we are quickly on our way to two-thirds of humanity living in cities. There are now almost 50 megacities in the world with over ten million people, and the number is growing rapidly, particularly in Asia. Today some sociologists remind us that regional and rural areas have important relationships to these big cities and have undergone important social changes themselves. Nevertheless, understanding this process of urbanisation is one of the essential tasks of sociology. The authors introduced in this chapter saw the coming significance of changes that have reshaped the world. This is part of the reason that their work became more influential over time, and continues to be read and debated today, when many of their contemporaries in the early (classical) period of sociology have been forgotten.

There was likely some luck in the way that these thinkers were able to pick out such significant emerging new forms, and of being in the right place at the right time. There was also their sociological imagination, an ability to see the changes unfolding in individual lives and particular places in their larger structural and historical significance. They saw constants over time in social life, struggles between classes, the need for social cohesion, and the impact of culture on social and economic life, and asked how these were taking profoundly new shapes in the period in which they lived.

The motivation to ask these questions, in new times, continues to draw people to sociology today. We are living in times of significant social change – the rise of information communication technology, the globalisation of economies, the huge movement of people all around the world, pandemics that rapidly transform everyday life and the looming threat of climate change. The social sciences need to continue to produce the concepts and frameworks that will enable an understanding of these transformations. Many of the most prominent names in contemporary sociology contribute towards this knowledge building. They argue that we are in the end of an earlier period of modernity and the contours of another social formation are emerging. The terms used include **risk society, post modernity**, second modernity, and late modernity, depending on the extent of continuity the author claims. Others use new metaphors, that a **liquid modernity** is emerging, characterised by global flows, or a **network society** driven by information communication technology. We will say more about these arguments in coming chapters.

Continuity and Change

Change is a constant of social life. C. Wright Mills wrote his book, *The Sociological Imagination* at the end of the 1950s, a time we think of today as a period of post-Second World War stability. Yet Mills writes of a society undergoing rapid change, where old **values** feel under threat and the future seems radically uncertain. This was in part because of the ever-present fear of nuclear attacks during the 'Cold War' between the USA and the USSR. It was also a time of great upheaval and new promise in the Majority World as the British and other Western Empires fell, changing the UK and Europe and the USA with it. For example, India won independence in 1947 and the Philippines in 1946 and the Cuban revolution began in 1953. As we've learned, Mills wanted to understand how the social structure of his society had emerged – its history – and what this meant for the kinds of people Americans were becoming and the type of history-making in which they would participate. He also wanted to know where the divisions in that society were and how it might be changing further in the future.

A full sociological account of any aspect of our lives is attuned to continuities as well as change. Pitirim Sorokin, a Russian born sociologist who became the first chair of sociology at Harvard, saw sociology as the study of **social statics**, factors that remained constant across time, and **social dynamics**, the engines of change. However, it is important to recognise that social continuity probably is not experienced as or best understood as static. When other things are changing around you, it often takes a lot of work to keep some things the same. You may have noticed that the constants we listed above that are found in the work of the foundational sociologists, who have been our focus in this chapter, are abstract – conflict and inequality, social cohesion and the interplay of material and cultural factors. The promise of sociology is to see the way these are being created or remade in new times.

You will often see sociologists claiming there has been significant social change. Sometimes this can seem like hyperbole. The best sociology is about understanding continuity and change. But often even those sociologists claiming we are entering a new type of social world are not proposing that everything is reversed, and that everything needs to be understood anew, but are using new language to open up the sociological imagination, helping avoid taking for granted what exists and attuning us to the way that, in a society, things often have to change just to stay the same. This is sociology's potential and what allowed the breakthroughs that characterised the work of Marx, Weber and Durkheim.

Conclusion

The 'big three' were important thinkers, and we will see a little more of them in later chapters, particularly when we focus on class. They were living through a period of rapid social change, but some of the major changes that would define the societies of the 20th century were only just emerging. They thought about these changes and the ways they related to the past in the way that C. Wright Mills came to dub the 'sociological imagination'. They attended to social continuities as well, as the best sociology continues to do. However, they did not see these continuities, for example economic inequalities, as static but part of unfolding processes and as being made and remade in new forms in modernity.

The developments with which we opened this chapter may have made a significant impact on your life: the push to increase levels of educational participation, the rise of new technologies, and related changes in the world of paid work that are affecting the way young people find jobs and careers. Some reading this book will have moved from a rural or regional area to a big city, or from one city to another city, or even internationally, for education or work. We are living at a time when many things are changing, and these changes are global in their reach. We turn to these contemporary changes in Chapter 4, but first we will look at how sociology has needed to change too. While holding onto their important insights, in the next chapter we look at how sociology has been facing up to the limitations of having a discipline built primarily around the ideas of three dead white men, who all came from the same part of the world. For the bot that (might) replace Dan and Steve to write a new edition of this book in 20 years' time, not only will sociology look different to today, but the story of its foundations might be told in a very different way as well.

Key references for this chapter

Durkheim, E (1915) *The Elementary Forms of the Religious Life*. George Allen & Unwin.

Durkheim, E (1933) *The Division of Labour in Society*. Free Press.

Durkheim, E (1951) *Suicide: A Study in Sociology*. Free Press.

Durkheim, E (1964) *The Rules of Sociological Method*. Free Press.

Hughes, JA, Sharrock, WW and Martin, PJ (2003) *Understanding Classic Sociology: Marx, Weber, Durkheim*, 2nd edn. Sage.

Marx, K (1963) *The Eighteenth Brumaire of Louis Bonaparte*. International Publishers.

Marx, K (1964) *Selected Writings in Sociology and Political Philosophy*. McGraw Hill.

Marx, K (1970) *The German Ideology*. Lawrence & Wishart.

Marx, K (1976) *Capital*. Penguin.

Marx, K and Engels, F (1983) *The Communist Manifesto*. Penguin.

Mills, CW (1959) *The Sociological Imagination*. Oxford University Press.

Morrison, K (2006) *Marx, Weber, Durkheim: Formations of Modern Social Thought*, 2nd edn. Sage.

Simmel, G (1950) 'The Metropolis and Mental Life', in *The Sociology of Georg Simmel*. Free Press, pp. 409-424.

Sorokin, P (1937-41) *Social and Cultural Dynamics*, 4 vols. American Book Company.

Tönnies, F (1955) *Community and Association (Gemeinschaft und Gesellschaft)*. Routledge & Kegan Paul.

Weber, M (1946) *From Max Weber: Essays in Sociology*. Oxford University Press.

Weber, M (1958) *The City*. Free Press.

Weber, M (1958) *The Protestant Ethic and the Spirit of Capitalism*. Charles Scribner's Sons.

3

CRITIQUING THE SOCIOLOGICAL CANON

Building a More Inclusive Sociology

In the last chapter we met some of the foundational figures in sociology. Marx, Durkheim and Weber are the trinity featured in almost all introductions to sociology, with others added alongside. If you bring up a picture of the three on your computer, you might notice they are not easy to tell apart: it is almost a game of 'spot the difference' between three white bearded men who would look at home working as a barista in a hipster café today. Marx is the one with the bushiest beard – there's less time for grooming when you are writing about the coming revolution whilst maintaining a robust drinking habit. Not only do they look quite similar, they lived very close to each other. Marx, Weber and Durkheim spent most of their working lives in England, Germany and France about 1,000 kms apart. Marx was a generation older and died before Durkheim and Weber – who were working at the same time and were about the same age – started their sociological careers. They could have hopped on an overnight train and met up near the French-German border to work through their differences over an artisanal croissant or bratwurst.

Most introduction to sociology classes and textbooks start with this standard story: The major foundational figures in our discipline were struggling to understand a changing world – modernity, and its constituents: industrialisation, the modern nation-state, urbanisation, alienation, conflict. This sounds a lot like Chapter 2. While it is mostly true that the institutional canon of sociology was formed around Durkheim, Marx and Weber, as *the* story of the foundations of modern sociology, many influential contemporary sociologists argue that this is a convenient misrepresentation that reflects institutional power structures rather than an accurate picture of all the work that was happening at the time.

Acknowledging the Past, Creating Different Futures

If we told you that there was one person who is often attributed as the founder of disciplines such as economics, sociology, and demography, was seen as one of the first social scientists, and was one of the most important philosophers of the Middle Ages, you would think that this person would figure prominently in sociology and economic textbooks all around the world. Yet, Ibn Khaldun has until recently been left out of the origin story of these disciplines, despite sketching out early theories of the division of labour and economic growth. He spent his life in North Africa and, like many key figures outside of Europe, Khaldun's influence is only recently being acknowledged. The foundations of sociology have a history of their own, and we can apply our sociological imagination to it. As we mentioned in Chapter 1, sociology aims to be a **reflexive** science, using its tools to understand itself as well as the societies it studies. After all, sociology is studying something of which it is part. There is no escape from society to take a view from outside but only tools to make the familiar strange. Sociologists cannot view the world like a natural scientist might a test tube – sociologists, and everyone else, are inside the tube.

The Australian sociologist Raewyn Connell has applied the sociological imagination to the story of the foundation of the discipline that we gave you in the previous chapter. She has gone back over early sociological textbooks from the beginning of the 20th century and shown that Durkheim, Weber and Marx did not dominate to nearly the same extent that they do in the way the history of the discipline is told today. While they now take a prominent place in most sociology textbooks, many early texts did not list them at all. Instead we find a much larger cast of characters, with the authors of those early textbooks often giving their own work pride of place as leading the discipline. We were kind of tempted to do that too, with our own research. But we knew our publishers would not let us and we thought our colleagues might, rightly, make fun of us.

As the 20th century unfolded, why did the writers of textbooks in sociology come to focus on Marx, Durkheim and Weber? It probably had something to do with it taking a while for the valuable work of lasting value to become clear. But it also had something to do with some of the early sociologists making claims which today look troubling. By surveying early work in sociology, and the contents of early textbooks, Connell suggests that the beginning of 'modernity', that is, the social, technological and political upheavals we outlined in the previous chapter, was not nearly as central a topic of early sociology as it is presented as being in textbooks written today. Instead, writers such as the philosopher, biologist and early sociologist Herbert Spencer were writing about the evolution of 'superior' societies. Spencer was working in biology and coined the term 'survival of the fittest' to describe the work of Charles Darwin, a term people often attribute to Darwin himself.

Spencer was not talking about a reality television show. He thought that societies were engaged in a process of evolution from inferior to superior forms and that ways of acting and organising society were passed down within a **race**. While this meaning of race as a group of people from a particular place with a common ancestry goes back many centuries, it was in the 19th century that the idea that there was a scientific way of categorising humans into different racial groups emerged. (As we'll see in Chapter 9, sociologists have since challenged and critiqued this concept.) Spencer argued that different 'races' were 'evolved' from different types of societies.

Sociology and Colonialism

You might be able to see that such ideas would prove popular in societies that thought they were themselves superior to others and had a right, even a 'duty', to colonise the world.

Spencer became more conservative as he aged, but throughout his life he was a fierce critic of war and imperial expansion. Nevertheless, he believed that some societies were superior to others and that interracial marriage and children should be discouraged because a child of two 'races', that have evolved to be distinctly different and properly suited to a particular type of society, would instead find themselves not properly suited to either. Towards the end of his life, in the late 19th century, Spencer was one of the most famous intellectuals in the world. Yet by the middle of the 20th century the person who was then probably the most prominent sociologist in the world, an American sociologist called Talcott Parsons, could quip that no one reads Spencer anymore.

So why did sociologists dispense with Spencer and the many others whose ideas populated the early sociology textbooks? Talcott Parsons was part of the reason (today hardly anyone reads Parsons either – but that is a story for a later chapter). In the 1930s, Parsons wrote a book synthesising the work of Weber and Durkheim (and a handful of others) to argue that sociology should focus on the way that social rules and values integrated people 'voluntarily' (meaning without force) into society. People learned how to follow the rules and play different roles as they were growing up, and that recreated the major institutions of society, which in turn provided stability for societies over time. We hope, after reading the previous chapter, you can see that the focus on values comes from Weber and the ideas about different roles underpinning institutions from Durkheim.

Raewyn Connell proposes that the reason sociologists gave Durkheim, Marx and Weber pride of place in the **canon** – the central texts that most sociologists count as sociology's foundational and important documents – is that they were not as explicitly evolutionary in their writing. This helped sociologists deny the colonial underpinnings of the discipline. **Colonisation** is the process of one **nation** invading and taking over the land of another to exploit it economically and often to replace the existing population. However, even these sociologists who have been canonised were products of their colonial times and places. Germany and France had both colonised other parts of the world during their lifetimes. The 'big three' were focused on what they saw as making Europe at that time special. Implicitly or explicitly, when early modern sociologists wrote about modernity, they meant 'Western Europe'. This did not mean they completely ignored the rest of the world. Modern life was assumed to be the present and the future. Pre-modernity was the past, but it could also be found in the present in the rest of the world that had not modernised in the ways the big three defined modernisation. The implicit assumption that Europe was modern and could be the focus of sociology, with the rest of the world demoted to making comparisons and contrasts, has shaped sociology for many decades – and many argue it still does.

As we saw in the previous chapter, Durkheim proposed that to belong to a group meant being part of something bigger than yourself, even if the way this solidarity was created changed between pre-modern and modern social types. He also believed that social groups found ways to communicate and represent this shared belonging, attaching it to symbols that represented this sense of belonging. To make this point, Durkheim focused on the religious life of the First Nations people of Australia, arguing that the sacred totem (usually an animal) that represents these people is a representation of the group itself. He argued that all forms of religion are representations of a sense of powers beyond us and that the major factor that creates this sense of something beyond come from being part of a society. However, he compared modern religious forms of Europe to what he called these 'primitive' or 'elementary' forms.

Australia is a **settler-colonial** state, meaning that the colonising British aimed to replace the existing people and their social structure with a new society of settlers. Durkheim drew on the research of other Europeans or settlers of colonial descent to write about Australia. He was criticised for this during his own lifetime, but this has been written out of the mainstream retelling of the foundations of sociology.

Durkheim was writing about 'primitive religion' as French colonial armies were fighting to make vast 'conquests' in North and West Africa and South East Asia. Modernity therefore was also about modern imperialism (extending a country's influence and resources through violent colonisation of other places). At the same time, colonialism never became a central topic of the writing of Durkheim or Weber. Marx had a little to say about colonialism in the history of capitalism but focused on 'developed' capitalist societies, as that is where he thought revolutionary change would come.

Colonised societies were a source of data to contrast to the 'modern' metropolitan centres of Europe (and North America) compared to the 'primitive' past and present of other parts of the world. In terms of the emergence of sociology as a discipline and the way that story is now told, what is largely forgotten is that the perspectives of the likes of Marx, Weber and Durkheim had an underlying focus on the difference between the 'civilisation' characterizing the major cities of Europe and the perceived primitiveness of everywhere else, past and present. This means that many of the fundamental concepts that they created to explain how societies work were only really based on their own (limited) perspectives. This does not make those ideas useless but means that sociologists need to ensure that they critically engage with them rather than take them for granted.

Critiquing the Dead White European Male Perspective

Today sociology has expanded from its beginnings and sociological research takes place across the globe. Yet many sociologists argue that this history continues to shape sociology today. The African philosopher Paulin Hountondji points out that colonialism installed a global division of labour in sociology and the social and natural sciences broadly, which has continued in the post-colonial era. The work of 'serious' theory and synthesis was undertaken in the major metropolitan centres of North America and Europe, while the rest of the world was just a place to collect data.

The Egyptian-French social scientist and historian Samir Amin also calls this a type of **ethnocentrism**, the tendency many of us have to judge the practices of other cultures using the standards of our own culture. In particular, Amin says that the type of parochial viewpoint that shapes sociology is **Eurocentrism**: this is the idea that history unfolds as a progression, from classical Rome and Greece, to Christian European feudal societies, through to the Industrial Revolution and modern societies. For Amin, this story leaves out the crucial role of, among others, the Islamic world of North Africa and West Asia, which is where, for instance, Ibn Khaldun lived. Hountondji argues that it also shapes the mindsets of those in colonised societies, even settler-colonial societies like Australia, Argentina and South Africa. Researchers there become oriented towards Europe (particularly the UK) and the USA, trying to publish with the major publishers in those countries and hoping to study or get jobs there. He calls this **extraversion**, as the real authority is imagined lying elsewhere.

The Malaysian sociologist Syed Hussein Alatas developed a similar analysis at the same time, calling it the **captive mind**, in which the influence of colonisation and an imitative attitude towards Europe and the USA stymies the emergence of independent perspectives that better fit the real conditions in non-European societies. His son Syed Farid Alatas has developed this idea of **academic dependency** further. Europe – where Weber, Marx and Durkheim developed their ideas, and now joined by North America – continues to impose rules about what counts as knowledge and what is seen as the appropriate ways to conduct research in the rest of the world. Building on Hountondji, Amin and Alatas, Connell has called the parochial set of ideas masquerading around the world as universal **Northern Theory**.

Connell uses her criticism of Northern Theory to advocate for a greater role for **Southern Theory**, that is, work from scholars based outside the main centres of the development of sociology in the 20th century, mostly but not exclusively from countries in the Southern hemisphere. Connell's work is part of a broader movement that is aiming to challenge sociology to properly take account of the history of global inequality that is founded in the history of colonisation. It is related to longstanding efforts to build a **subaltern** perspective (this is a Latin term meaning the unrepresented or 'lower' status). Ranajit Guha, an Indian-born historian, used the term subaltern to note the lack of representation and recognition of the non-elites in the study of post-colonial movements. He highlighted that ordinary people in India, and other colonised societies, played an important role as political actors in the struggle against colonialism. Alongside others, Guha founded the **Subaltern Studies Group** of South-Asian scholars, aiming to develop a perspective on post-colonial societies from the perspective of those who were previously unrepresented. This approach is sometimes called a perspective from below, focusing on the experiences of marginal groups, not leaders or elites.

Gayatri Spivak, another Indian-born scholar, highlights that while social scientists may want to hear these perspectives from 'below', the subaltern have only been able to speak on their own behalf through others or by adopting the style and rules of knowledge that were created by elites. She asks social scientists to be reflexive about who is claiming to speak on behalf of the subaltern.

Indigenous Sociologies

The New Zealand Maori sociologist Linda Tuhiwai Smith, alongside a growing number of sociologists, argues for the need for Indigenous and Global South theories and methods and for approaches that are developed in the **Global South**. Different scholars have taken different pathways to try to develop alternative frameworks. Akinsola Akiwowo, a Nigerian sociologist, has proposed using poetry (and other stories and myths) as a foundation for building new explanatory concepts in sociology from the traditions of different parts of the world. He developed his set of principles for interpretations from ideas in Yoruba poetry from Nigeria, poems recited at the consecration of new villages and settlements in Nigeria that contain statements of relationships between basic elements in human society. For Akiwowo, the purpose of developing such concepts is not only to use them in the place where they were conceived, but to provide an expanded set of concepts for use in social settings across the world. Enrique Dussel, an Argentinian-Mexican theorist, suggests that the next step is for modernity to be studied and theorised from outside of the centres of the northern metropole (outside of Europe and North

America), to create new concepts for studying the North from the perspective of the rest of the world.

Sociology has had a tendency towards what the Jerusalem-born Palestinian-American scholar Edward Said calls **Orientalism**, a way of thinking where the so-called 'Orient' (an old Latin word for the East) was seen as backwards, exotic, uncivilised and autocratic. For Said, this wasn't just bad scholarship. The 'Orient' was constructed as Europe's **Other**, uncivilised and bad, while the Occident (the West) was civilised and good. It was an 'us' and 'them' way of thinking about the world. Said shows how this was used as justification for people from the Occident to exploit, enslave and invade Asia and Africa. 'Western' knowledge of the 'East' was built around crude binaries that made the East seem less human than the West. Examples of this abound in popular culture such as the story of Aladdin or the endless portrayals of Muslims as terrorists in film and TV.

Gurminder Bhambra, a British sociologist, has traced how sociology has, until recently, avoided **reflexivity** about its own imperial history. It is now being pushed to do so and to account for a plurality of perspectives, from different parts of the world. Bhambra and others point out that these diverse perspectives must in some way be connected to avoid reproducing simplistic divisions between the East and West, North and South, powerful and powerless, that they have aimed to challenge. Despite the caveats introduced by their proponents, the Indian sociologist Sujata Patel argues that some articulations of Southern approaches recreate binary oppositions that obscure the social relations that shaped the experience of the colonised and colonisers and still shape the post-colonial world. The strength of **post-colonial studies** (which studies the legacies of colonisation) is attending to the interactions between the European nations and the societies that they colonised and how this continues to shape societies that are now independent. The interrelationship between them is the focal point.

Some of the most influential work under the banner of post-colonial study works against binary constructions, aiming to construct alternatives. The Argentinian, and now Ecuadorian-based theorist, Walter Mignolo, has developed the idea of **border thinking** as a key aim of decolonial approaches. Border thinking aims to conceptualise what it means to live at the border between cultures and structures, challenging the binary constructions of modern sociology, aiming to do so without replacing them with a new binary such as Global South and North.

Mignolo develops this concept of border from Gloria Evangelina Anzaldúa, whose writing focuses on thinking through the place of borders and their crossing in our societies: she uses the concepts of borderlands. Borders and their surrounds do not exist only as physical borders but also as social and cultural boundaries, and they can shape psychological borders and tensions that we have within ourselves, which she calls *neplanta*, an American Indigenous word for an in-between space, and what she calls **mestiza consciousness**. Mestiza (in Latin American Spanish) means a woman with mixed heritage, particularly Spanish and Indigenous ancestry, which was Anzaldúa's own heritage and shaped her biography growing up in southern Texas, near the USA-Mexico border. She uses corn as a metaphor for this consciousness that develops as a survival strategy. Corn is bred by crossing varieties over generations to be able to survive under a variety of conditions. Anzaldúa argued that this way of thinking can produce a dual consciousness that can embrace ambiguity and contradiction and she hoped to encourage this way of thinking to spread.

Double Consciousness

This idea of mestiza consciousness resonates with another famous idea in sociology, the **double consciousness** that was developed by the African American sociologist WEB Du Bois over a century ago. He used this term to register the sense of not belonging or not quite fitting in to two different social worlds. This was a common experience for those living under colonial rule, but Du Bois pointed out it was also the experience of some groups who were seen as the 'other' within the colonial centres of the world, such as African Americans living after slavery in the USA. However, he saw it less as a sense of resilience in a hostile environment than as a form of suffering. He wrote of this double consciousness as two 'warring ideals' that must be held together by individual strength of will.

Du Bois linked the racism that was experienced by African Americans to colonialism. **Racism** is prejudice or discrimination based on the idea that some groups of people with particular heritages are superior. Racism can be individual discrimination or it can shape the structures of a society (we cover it in detail in Chapter 9). Du Bois's research in the USA showed how a set of attitudes that assumed the inferiority of some 'races' supported both domestic inequality and the colonisation of other countries. By collecting new data in a systematic way about the experiences of African Americans, he was able to show that their outcomes were due to social structures, not to racial inferiority. The Peruvian-American sociologist Sylvanna Falcón has combined Du Bois's concept with Anzaldúa's, using the mestiza double consciousness to argue that race and gender are separate but have interacting effects at the borders, that can be productive of new forms of thought and of coping but have also led to suffering.

Just as the voices of social thinkers from outside of the Northern metropole have until recently been subsumed within sociology, so scholars such as WEB Du Bois and, as we saw in the first chapter, Harriet Martineau, have struggled to be accorded the central place in the discipline that their thinking deserved, as the internal structures of gender and race meant that their ideas were demoted or credited to others. Although Du Bois is well known, as briefly mentioned in Chapter 1, Aldon Morris has recently pushed sociologists to acknowledge that his role in creating sociology is far greater than is usually credited.

In the USA, the story of sociology's development is that it was in America particularly at the University of Chicago, that sociology was developed into a properly scientific discipline that went beyond the less scientific approaches used in Europe. While Durkheim and Weber were developing major conceptual approaches to thinking about society, the team at Chicago were developing a set of methods for studying social processes systematically using surveys, interviews and ethnographies. Morris argues that Du Bois used participant observation, interviews and census data to study African American experience in Philadelphia in 1899, long before other sociologists at Chicago, or elsewhere. For Morris, Du Bois was the until-now-unacknowledged founder of scientific sociology and one that used his rigorous research to try to change the world for the better.

Morris makes a strong case for Du Bois as the founder of scientific sociology. Patricia Lengermann and Gillian Niebrugge also make a strong case for Harriet Martineau. Her book about how to study morals and manners is based on her attempts to study the structures of American society using new methods. She argued for methods that were based on sympathy, trying to understand why others acted the way they do by putting ourselves in their position. She was also among the first to develop research findings using methods that were deliberately designed to create knowledge that could lead to social change, hopefully making a better world. Martineau was one of the earliest social theorists and writers on the methods of social science, and like Du Bois, she used what she learned in her travels and research in the USA to push for equality in American society, including the end of slavery and equality for women, and in her own country, Britain. Yet, until recently, she was unknown apart for the occasional acknowledgement as a translator of Comte's work on sociology. Today she is deservedly receiving more attention.

Conclusion

Sociologists are returning to the work of Martineau and Du Bois, and increasingly embracing post-colonial critiques. Complex ideas are important within sociology and many of the thinkers introduced in this chapter have pushed us not to think in terms of crude binaries such as us and them, developed and undeveloped. They have pushed us to be comfortable with 'border thinking', and not to resolve tensions by simplistic solutions based on either/or thinking. Many argue that sociology needs to recognise it is part of the societies in which it is undertaken and has a responsibility to contribute to those societies. It needs to be communicated simply and to multiple audiences wherever it can be, without becoming simplistic.

Sociology emerged at a time when there were even greater limitations on women and non-white people than today (we'll tell you more about today throughout the coming chapters). It also emerged from the centre of empires. France, Britain and Germany had colonies scattered across the world. There is still a central place for the theories of Weber, Marx and Durkheim and the other theories we cover in this book that developed in Europe and North America, but they must be used in a way that tries to overcome their parochialism.

Many of the sociologists we have introduced in this chapter are calling on current sociologists and the next generation to do sociology differently, to remould global sociology to speak from different perspectives, not just from a Western perspective but without failing to recognise the way that experiences and perspectives are connected across borders. This means that the dominant institutions of sociology need to make room and give others a voice, not speak for them.

Building new theories from other traditions also comes with challenges about how to deploy them in a reflexive way when applied in other times and places. The thinkers introduced in this chapter are pushing sociology to take up this challenge, to examine its past and include the voices that have been long excluded. Along these lines, Tuhiwai Smith asks for researchers to be attentive to the cultural values of the people that are the focus of research. This means more than a researcher who is an outsider being reflexive about their own assumptions and avoiding ethnocentrism if that is their background training. It also means that understandings of Indigenous and marginalised people developed by Indigenous and marginalised people themselves are integrated into the research in a meaningful way. This is important as sociology, like the societies it is part of, grapples with globalisation, which we turn to in the next chapter.

Key references for this chapter

Akiwowo, AA (1986) 'Contributions to the Sociology of Knowledge from an African Oral Poetry', *International Sociology*, vol. 1, no. 2, pp. 343-358.

Alatas, SF (2003) 'Academic Dependency and the Global Division of Labour', *Current Sociology*, vol. 51, no. 6, pp. 599-613.

Alatas, SH (1972) 'The Captive Mind in Development Studies', *International Social Science Journal*, vol. 24, no. 1, pp. 9-25.

Amin, S (1989) *Eurocentrism: Modernity, Religion, and Democracy: A Critique of Eurocentrism and Culturalism*, trans. R Moore and J Membrez. Monthly Review Press.

Anzaldúa, GE (1999) *Borderlands/La Frontera: The New Mestiza*. Aunt Lute Books.

Bhambra, GK (2007) *Rethinking Modernity: Postcolonialism and the Sociological Imagination*. Palgrave Macmillan.

Brinton, CC (1933) *English Political Thought in the Nineteenth Century*. Ernest Bean Ltd. [The 'who now reads Spencer' line is a quote from this text.]

Connell, R (2007) *Southern Theory: The Global Dynamics of Knowledge in Social Science*. Allen & Unwin.

Du Bois, WEB (1903) *The Souls of Black Folk*. Dover Publications.

Du Bois, WEB (1996) *The Philadelphia Negro: A Social Study*. University of Pennsylvania Press.

Dussel, E (1995) *The Invention of the Americas: Eclipse of 'the Other' and the Myth of Modernity*, trans. MD Barber. Continuum.

Falcón, SM (2008) 'Mestiza Double Consciousness: The Voices of Afro-Peruvian Women on Gendered Racism', *Gender & Society*, vol. 22, no. 5, pp. 660-680.

Guha, R (1982) 'On Some Aspects of the Historiography of Colonial India', in Guha, R (ed.) *Subaltern Studies*, vol. 1. Oxford University Press, pp. 1-8.

Hountondji, PJ (1995) 'Producing Knowledge in Africa Today', *African Studies Review*, vol. 38, no. 3, pp. 1-10.

Lengermann, P and Niebrugge, G (1998) *The Women Founders: Sociology and Social Theory 1830-1930, A Text/Reader*. Waveland Press.

Mignolo, WD (2013) 'Geopolitics of Sensing and Knowing: On (de)coloniality, Border Thinking, and Epistemic Disobedience', *Confero*, vol. 1, no. 1, pp. 129-150.

Mignolo, WD and Tlostanova, MV (2006) 'Theorizing from the Borders: Shifting to Geo- and Body-Politics of Knowledge', *European Journal of Social Theory*, vol. 9, no. 2, pp. 205-221.

Morris, A (2017) *The Scholar Denied: W. E. B. Du Bois and the Birth of Modern Sociology*. University of California Press.

Parsons, T (1949) *The Structure of Social Action: A Study in Social Theory with Special Reference to a Group of Recent European Writers*, 2nd edn. Free Press.

Patel, S (2000) 'Modernity: Sociological Categories and Identities', *Current Sociology*, vol. 48, no. 3, pp. 1-15.

Said, EW (1978) *Orientalism*. Pantheon Books.

Sarkar, S (1984) 'The Conditions and Nature of Subaltern Militancy: Bengal from Swadeshi to Non-Co-operation, c.1905-22', in Guha, R (ed.) *Subaltern Studies III*. Oxford University Press, pp. 271-320.

Smith, LT (1999) *Decolonizing Methodologies: Research and Indigenous Peoples*. Zed Books.

Spencer, H (1891) 'Progress: Its Law and Cause', in *Essays: Scientific, Political & Speculative*, vol. 1. Williams and Norgate, pp. 8-62.

Spivak, G (1988) 'Can the Subaltern Speak?', in Grossberg, L and Nelson, C (eds) *Marxism and the Interpretation of Culture*. Macmillan Education, pp. 271-313.

Walter, M and Butler, K (2013) 'Teaching Race to Teach Indigeneity', *Journal of Sociology*, vol. 49, no. 4, pp. 397-410.

4

GLOBALISATION

Living in a Connected World

You may be reading this chapter with a coffee in your hand. Unless you are reading in Kenya, Indonesia, Brazil or Colombia, it is likely your coffee beans were grown in another part of the world. The beans were likely processed in a third country, packaged in material from another, and branded and sold by a company based somewhere else again. The consumption of coffee began in North Africa and the Arabian Peninsula over 500 years ago, before spreading over the coming centuries around the world. Coffee, coffee culture and the coffee industry now shape the way people work, consume and interact all over the world. Like coffee, more recently the internet, mobile phones and forms of youth culture have spread around the world. As we saw in the last chapter, post-colonial thinkers have helped sociologists think about borders, but also about the way that borders are complex and porous, and how inequalities shape these connections. We will come back to this work in the second half of this chapter.

One of the most well-known terms used by social scientists (and everyone else) for these patterns of interconnection is **globalisation**. This is a broad term with many definitions, but most highlight the breaking down of national borders, the loss of personal and national control over global forces and growing economic and cultural interconnectedness. Sociology defined modernity, one of its foundational topics, in part through the rise of **states**. States are political communities with clearly defined borders and a single governing system with the power to police, defend and create laws over that territory. The concept of society, the object of sociological study, was mostly assumed to mean a country, such as France or the USA. Globalisation means that this no longer makes as much sense, as we will see. In this chapter we will introduce you to the long history of globalisation, but also to debates about the impact of a rapid increase in this interconnection in the past four decades, the most recent cultural, political, and economic wave of growing 'interconnectedness'.

Globalisation

The interconnections that shape our lives are not only about the trade of goods for consumption, but also about culture, politics and everyday life. As with coffee, it is possible to trace a long history of the spread of people and ideas. Cultural forms and customs have passed from one place to another, alongside the movement of people, throughout human existence. Hence, globalisation is not a new phenomenon – the level of interconnection across space has ebbed and flowed throughout history but it has intensified in the last century.

Göran Therborn identifies **waves of globalisation**. For millennia, major world religions aimed to preach and convert across the globe. Transcontinental **civilisations** were built around the major religions of Buddhism, Islam, Christianity and Hinduism in the period of 300 to 600AD. In the 1600s new connections (and suffering) were created by colonising European powers such as the Dutch, Spanish, Portuguese and English. Later, the proponents of major political ideologies aimed to spread their message across the world, with the Cold War between the Soviet Union and its satellite states on one side and the USA and its allies on the other an example of an ideological struggle between capitalism and communism. It was called the Cold War because there was no direct traditional armed conflict between the two, although both sides supported opposite combatants in other wars during this period. The most recent wave of globalisation began with the economic, social and technological changes that emerged in the late 20th century. The Cold War came to an end, new parts of the world such as China became stronger economic powers, the internet emerged, and corporations and markets aimed for worldwide influence.

Early sociologists were aware of the processes connecting different parts of the world and discussed them in their work. Marx and his collaborator Engels devoted parts of their writing to the compulsion driving capitalism to expand to ever new markets across the globe to avoid falling profits, while calling on the 'workers of the world' to unite to challenge the spread of capitalism. Weber saw the spirit of capitalism, which began in a small corner of Europe, exemplified most strongly in the early 20th century in the United States, particularly in the writings of Benjamin Franklin.

The early sociologists, however, mostly focused on individual countries as the natural container of a society. These tended to be **nation-states,** where a 'nation' as a common heritage (such as its history, traditions, ethnicity and language) overlaps with sovereignty – the right to political control of a designated territory. Most maps of the world are of nation-states and their borders. This form of social organisation was relatively new in human history when these sociologists were writing, coming into existence in a growing number of places. It was regularly produced by forces of colonialisation, replacing the constantly changing overlap of tribes and nations and other spheres of influence.

Even in the great kingdoms and empires of the past, the rulers often had very little control or influence over most of their subjects, with the village, town or region instead holding the place at the centre of social and political life. Sociologists were interested in contrasting the differences between these modern nation-states and other forms of social organisation that had a longer history. For many sociologists it was the nation-states, and the regions, cities and neighbourhoods within them, that were the container for society, and sociology focused on understanding individual societies within those borders.

Until sociologists turned properly to the most recent wave of globalisation, the relationship between different parts of the world was largely considered in terms of internationalization, the relationship between nation-states. In the past 40 years, however, sociological thinking has developed to focus on the processes that traverse the borders of states, and often break them down. The British sociologist Anthony Giddens calls this a runaway world, where it is difficult for people to manage the pace of change.

Liquids, Networks and Movements

Sociologists commonly claim that contemporary globalisation is like a wave, crashing down on previous social forms, not quite washing modernity away but leaving it radically reformed. The Polish sociologist Zygmunt Bauman calls the contemporary social system **liquid modernity**. Bauman uses the metaphors of solid and heavy versus liquid and light to characterise the impact of globalisation on people's lives. Modernity (and the associated colonial project that we introduced in the previous chapter) was about bringing solid 'rational' procedures to bear on greater expanses of space. 'Liquid' here acts as a metaphor for the new demands of flexibility and competition in all aspects of life, creating a permanent sense of impermanence that increases social suffering for those without the means to compete as the ground shifts beneath the feet of a burgeoning number of people, but leaves them with nowhere to go.

As we saw in Chapter 2, sociology developed in part among scholars trying to understand the changes going on around them in their own societies that were tied to the birth of modernity. Bauman and many others interpret contemporary capitalism as clearing away something that was already fragile and replacing it with something else. Modernity, in Bauman's view, was an obsessive project of replacing the old with the new, but also an obsessive urge for complete control and to fix things in place: think of Weber's metaphor of the iron cage. The new features of a global society wash away old certainties, creating new insecurities and risks.

The exemplary businesses of modernity – companies such as General Motors or the Ford Motor Company – had the biggest factories and made the most products. Indeed, the economy in the 20th century was often called a **Fordist** economy, after the production model developed at Ford. These companies' factories were the size of 20 to 30 football fields. Ford was the largest maker of cars in the world in the first half of the 20th century; it had a huge workforce and aimed to rationalise not only its production process, but the family and community lives of its workers. One post-graduation career path for sociology students during the height of the company was to join the 200 strong Ford Motor Company Department of Sociology!

This job was well paid but involved tasks that were akin to joining the secret police. You would monitor employees at home, checking their personal hygiene and the cleanliness of their house, check that their children were attending school and whether non-family members were living in the house, whether they were saving money in the bank, and if they were non-English speaking that they were learning English. You would also offer them classes and training to 'improve' themselves if they were found to not be at the required standard. If the employees passed the inspection, they were eligible for higher pay.

Globalisation shifted the pressures and opportunities on businesses towards a **post-Fordist** model. Fordist companies developed long-term plans to expand, to buy more hardware, and build bigger factories, firms and networks. In Bauman's view, liquid modern companies don't want to take up space; in fact, the worst thing is to be stuck in one place, responsible for workers or for a tax bill. While space matters less, speed matters very much. The most successful liquid modern companies, according to Bauman, will move and move quickly. Today, capital travels light and tries to make space irrelevant.

Another influential metaphor in contemporary sociology is that global social structures are an information network. The importance that information processing and networks would hold for the future was predicted in the early 1970s by the American sociologist Daniel Bell.

Bell saw signs that the US would evolve into a **post-industrial economy**, where manufacturing would become peripheral to the economy as knowledge work and service sector jobs increased in number. Those who could create, recombine and apply information would be the drivers of the society that emerged within what Bell called the **information age**. While largely cynical about changes in American society, Bell hoped that the expansion of information and communication technology would give rise to a large middle class of knowledge workers with greater autonomy over their working lives. He has been proven partly true. Digital technologies and knowledge work is an increasingly large part of the economy and some of this work is very well paid, but in many countries the middle class is being squeezed by insecure work and precarity, and many knowledge workers are not paid well at all, including many who work in universities.

Catalonian sociologist Manuel Castells argues that this information age is underpinned by a **network society**. The development of Information Communication Technologies (ICTS) and information-communication networks (such as the internet) are vital to the network society. The network society spans a set of 'post-industrial' nations with large service sectors and, as such, it is global. Manufacturing does not disappear. Information communication technology facilitates a network structure of **production** and **consumption**; manufacturing can move from one place to another, producing products for companies with head offices in one place, financial departments, research and development all happening elsewhere, and allows the products to be rapidly shipped and consumed anywhere.

The liquid modern or networked society, as a set of global connections, is reshaping time and space. The exemplar companies of the global liquid modern and networked world are those such as Apple, Amazon, Google, Netflix, Facebook, Airbnb, Airtasker and Uber. These companies have a global reach but often don't make their own products. Instead, their product is often an online platform for interaction that can be used anywhere, or they sub-contract the labour to another company. Their employees could be anywhere with a good internet connection, and their offices can be wherever taxes are lowest. If their product is an actual material thing, it is usually made in sometimes exploitative working conditions in factories in China or South-East Asia. While Ford was interested in every aspect of its employees' lives, the most successful contemporary company will avoid employing people at all if possible. Instead, production will be outsourced to others (like Apple does), or those that appear to be working for the company are instead categorised as freelancers or contractors, like Uber drivers in many countries or Airbnb hosts.

There are significant overlaps between the metaphors of the network society and liquid modernity. Liquids don't hold their shape and are prone, unless contained, to movement. Anyone who has sailed across or swam in the sea knows that this movement does not mean that liquids are without structure or force. They can easily sweep people away. Castells adds another layer to thinking about the structure of these flows: they are shaped like a network; flows occur between *nodes,* points where different flows intersect, and are processed and can be redirected.

The British sociologist John Urry attempted to combine the two metaphors in his sociology of **mobilities**, focusing on the movement of people, ideas, cultures and things around the world. He contrasts global fluids and globally integrated networks to distinguish different structures of mobility. Networks are stable and relatively predictable sets of networked nodes, such as multinational entities, for example McDonalds, or the Red Cross/Crescent. Fluids are less predictable, unplanned and relatively uncontrolled, for example the internet (created by the military and scientists but quickly taken over by a multitude of users for millions of different purposes), political turmoil and movements of refugees escaping conflict.

Beyond the Modern State

Many contemporary sociologists argue that the mobility and flows of the current wave of globalisation mean that the nation-state is no longer the obvious container for society. For instance, the German sociologist Ulrich Beck argues we now live in a world **risk society,** in which the power of the state weakens. As we covered in Chapter 2, the rise of science, technology and growing production capacity, a belief in progress and political control of the future, are key changes early sociologists used to characterise modernity. We continue to see gains in economic growth, new and better technology, and new connections across the globe, and this makes our life better in many ways. Yet the processes that drove modern progress have led to *unintended consequences* that no one foresaw at the time these processes were put in motion, producing new global risks that escape the control of nation-states and their borders. In other words, Beck proposes that new and sometimes invisible but profoundly consequential risks for the earth and human life emerged from the success of modern production, technology and politics. These risks include smog, climate threats from using fossil fuels, the potential for nuclear accidents such as in Chernobyl and Fukushima, the rapid global spread of pandemic viruses such as SARS or COVID-19, and the way global interconnection and new capacities for mobility potentially facilitate terrorist attacks and financial disasters on a scale never before seen. For Beck, nation-states cannot control these risks, and we live in a 'laboratory where there is absolutely nobody in charge'.

Living in a risk society creates **ambivalence** towards the idea of science and progress and our ability to control the future, but nonetheless we must try, and it is to science and politics that we must turn to do so. This sees us leading anxious and uncertain lives as it is difficult to trust experts when there seem to be constant contradictions in the information delivered in the media. One week a glass of red wine or a small amount of chocolate is good for you, the next week it leads to cancer or heart disease.

However, for Beck, it will not be nation-state politics, or even international politics between nation-states, that will be able to provide the solutions to this problem, but new political approaches responding to global political challenges, such as climate change, that cross or ignore such borders. For Beck, coalitions of activists need to work around these borders. As sociology grapples with studying the social beyond nation-state societies, Beck calls for **methodological cosmopolitanism**. He argues that contemporary sociology has been built around a **methodological nationalism,** but most of the key social processes shaping the environment, politics, inequality, culture and individual lives increasingly escape nation-state borders, and this is what sociology needs to study.

Globalisation and Place

Globalisation is sometimes presented in a positive light: hyper-mobility, flows of capital, people and ideas. Alternatively, it can be presented in a negative light by focusing on the spread of economic and cultural **homogeneity**, the suffering inflicted on workers by mobile capital, and the exploitation by the global elite of the global poor. In both the positive and negative descriptions, place often appears to be fading in significance. For example, the key nodes in the network society and the power brokers of liquid modernity could be anywhere, and they can move rapidly to wherever is most beneficial for the time being.

Of course, sociologists recognise that not everyone is allowed or able to move around the world freely, with free mobility being for the very **privileged**, which we discuss in detail in Chapter 7. While many sociologists share the view that we are living through a period of rapid globalisation, some scholars argue that the declining significance of place and the importance of mobility have been overstated. There is no denying that our everyday lives are permeated by ideas, economic forces, and institutional structures that originated elsewhere, but this process can be resisted, and global forms are creatively appropriated in different places.

Roland Robertson uses the idea of **glocalisation** to highlight this interaction between the global and the local. For example, hip-hop developed in the inner-city Black communities of the major cities of the USA with young people in poor urban areas, itself drawing on other cultural influences as it has spread around the world. French hip-hop, Brazilian hip-hop or Australian hip-hop will draw significantly on US hip-hop, but add something from local music traditions, or tell local stories and address local issues. Spanish hip-hop, for example, draws on flamenco and salsa beats, and addresses issues such as the rights of immigrants from Africa without official papers.

The Dutch American sociologist Saskia Sassen provides one of the most nuanced multi-layered analyses of place in the context of globalisation. She argues that the global flows highlighted by sociologists such as Bauman and Castells are in fact highly dependent on place, both people and the material infrastructure. The engine of globalisation is centred on particular places, **global cities** (such as London, New York, Shanghai, Dubai and Singapore). Companies and stock exchanges need central locations and a vast infrastructure to coordinate their most complex tasks. Sassen argues, in a seeming paradox, that it is this embeddedness that gives globalisation its hyper-mobility.

Sassen's conceptualisation of globalisation also encompasses much more than the emergence of an information society. There is a great amount of manual, often physically demanding and dirty work (janitorial, low-end service work, construction) that is done in places to allow the rise of the new global information economy. This work is poorly paid and often done by immigrants, especially immigrant women in the service sector. Sassen's own research has found that up to 50 per cent of workers in 'leading sectors' of the global economy, such as finance, are actually low-wage earners. The rise of two-income professional households in these global cities has also led to an increased demand for low-paid service workers such as maids and nannies – domestic tasks that were once left to 'housewives' are relocated to the market and are often performed by immigrant and migrant workers (more on this in Chapter 8). Greater access to employment has, in the past, offered some empowerment to immigrants, and women. Sassen argues, however, that this type of work produces a class of workers that are isolated and effectively invisible. The rise of both a knowledge economy and a low-paid service sector at the same time is leading to a growing polarisation of income and opportunity in these global cities, and between these global cities and other parts of the nation-states in which they are found.

Global cities are also restructuring inequality across borders. Struggling to pay back high debts, many countries in the Global South are dependent on emigrant women for the remittances they send home. Sassen calls the way that these economic shifts give rise to these flows of people and money **survival circuits**. The demand in global cities for low-paid workers and the material need in some countries in the South help fuel a new intensity in human movement, including people trafficking. Not all these workers move to the North by choice, or at least informed choice. This trafficking is made easier by more legitimate global flows. The same infrastructure designed to facilitate cross-border flows of trade and knowledge make possible 'unintended' flows of people.

Countries Still Matter

Even the state, often considered the 'loser' at the expense of globalisation, continues to shape people's lives in profound ways. Many people are not able to be mobile around the world and many others are mobile against their will, and potentially trapped at the borders of other countries. Global flows of migrant labour can be understood in part by focusing on the interaction between global cities, such as Hong Kong, and nation-states that have become dependent on remittances to maintain the national economy and pay international debt. States and globalisation have a complex dependent but sometimes contradictory relationship, but countries still matter. If we look at politics around the world, the state appears to be having a resurgence, with politicians in Brazil, Hungry, Britain, India, Russia, and of course the USA claiming that they are making their particular nation great and powerful again, or for the first time. These political movements are usually done in the name of protecting their country from the perceived negative effects of globalisation processes, often looking to return to an over-romanticised vision of the past.

Craig Calhoun highlights that those calling for sociology to focus on globalisation and abandon methodological nationalism often devote significant attention in their writing to nation-states, the way state borders become more difficult to control, but also the response to this, which is sometimes successful and often brutal. Jan Nederveen Pieterse, one of the most influential theorists of globalisation, does not see globalisation as coming at the expense of the state but as changing the state. The most successful states are using the potential of globalisation to influence trade deals and global treaties to their own benefit. States continue to play key roles in international treaties on climate change or refugees and remain a central target of lobbying by transnational coalitions pushing for change, from international health charities to global terror groups.

Calhoun and Pieterse are not simply saying that states still matter, but that a convincing sociology of globalisation must be more complex than asking for a concurrent focus on the local and global. They argue that to make sense of the role of place in our contemporary world, sociology needs to attend to many different scales and types of units of analysis, often concurrently, including transnational movements of people but also to how nation-states continue to try to control those flows. Further, flows within states between the urban, suburban and rural have profound effects on people's lives and opportunities. Nation-states still influence our lives, and the global world we live in, but there are now a greater number of alternative actors, including global corporations, transnational financial flows, international institutions and transnational charities, wielding influence over our lives.

Inequality in Global Context

Sociologists who focus on global patterns highlight stark economic inequalities across the globe. A critique of the way sociologists have approached class (see Chapter 7) is that many focus on what happens within countries, yet inequality is driven by global forces beyond the nation. Maybe it is primarily in the international system that we should focus to understand economic inequality.

From the earliest sociologists to those active in the second half of the 20th century, the dominant approach to global inequality was focused on the relationship between nation-states, comparing the **wealth** or average income of countries to each other. **Modernisation theory**, associated with the American sociologists Talcott Parsons and Seymour Martin Lipset, was an influential approach to international relations between nations in the mid-20th century and again among some after the end of the Cold War. During the Cold War a common way of dividing the nations of the world was to talk about the First World (Western nations usually friendly towards the USA), the Second World (made up of the communist states), and the Third World (of so-called 'undeveloped' nations). Proponents of a modernisation theory approach saw a strong connection between economic development (specialisation, the division of labour, markets) and other markers of progress, education and urbanisation, and a 'free press'. As such, they argued that 'First World' institutions were necessary for a functioning and flourishing democracy to emerge in the 'Third World'. The Third World and its people were poor, it was argued, because they had not yet developed the right system to be rich.

Proponents of modernisation theory, such as Parsons and Lipset, were not blind to the global inequalities or the challenges facing the United States but were largely optimistic about the ability of its institutions to cope with disagreement and respond to these challenges. Modernisation of the economy and other key social institutions in the image of the USA provided a model that other nations could, and likely would, follow.

Fernando Henrique Cardoso, a Brazilian sociologist and politician, is one of the most famous critics of modernisation theory. He had a successful academic career in which he developed an influential strand of **dependency theory** during the 1970s and 1980s, in opposition to modernisation theories. His political activism and academic writing against the then dictatorship in Brazil drew him into politics, culminating in his presidency of the country from 1995–2003. Responding to the influential view of modernisation theory that the impoverishment of most Latin American countries was evidence of too little capital investment and the continued influence of feudal relationships, Cardoso and others argued that Latin American and non-Western nations were placed in a state of dependency in the international economy. These nations were dependent on Western capitalist nation-states for technology and processed goods, in return for their raw materials. Many saw this as dooming most of the world to a state of underdevelopment. Although Cardoso saw some avenues for development within a relationship of dependency, mimicking the economic structure of the USA was not possible.

On a similar note, Immanuel Wallerstein used Marxist ideas about exploitation to understand this unequal dependency between nations. He saw not three different 'worlds' but a single world system made up of nations in the core, periphery and semi-periphery. There were different cultures and even economic structures in different countries, but there was no communist world, as there was and is only one world system and it was capitalist. There were instead communist nations trying to survive within this capitalist system. Countries in the core, and particularly the capitalist class within them, can exploit workers in peripheral nations for cheap labour and cheap production. These are the national equivalent of Marx's bourgeoisie class. The nations in the periphery are like Marx's working class, dependent on the core countries but exploited by them, providing not only raw material but cheap production and cheap labour. At the semi-periphery (a category that was largely ignored by dependency theory) are nations in the middle, like Marx's petty (or petite) bourgeoisie, or small business owners, exploited by the core, but in turn exploiting the periphery.

Wallerstein's **world systems theory** and dependency theory highlight the malignant connections between the histories of different nations. These scholars stress that to understand why some nations are rich and appear to have stronger and stable institutions, we need to look beyond the nations themselves to the international system. The nations of the Third World were not 'undeveloped' because they had yet to follow the right model laid out by the First World, but First World nations' development had held other nations in poverty. This was exacerbated by the huge debts countries owed institutions such as the World Bank – organised via the International Monetary Fund (an international organisation set up by European and North American countries at the end of the Second World War to regulate the international monetary system of lending and debt repayment) – loans that were made to 'help' the developing world become more like the developed. Susan George called this 'a fate worse than debt', as it left developing economies trapped to service the repayments that they could never pay off.

World systems theory takes a historical perspective on the relationship between nations. Global trade, access to new consumer goods, and being able to access new tastes, experiences and ideas seems to improve the quality of our lives, but it has also created suffering and violence. This is not new. The 16th through the early 20th century saw a wave of increased interconnection driven by **colonisation** (as discussed in Chapter 3). Invasions where one group comes to control another have a very long history, but around the 16th century new technologies, such as better ships and navigation, deadlier weaponry and new ideologies, led to a rapid expansion of the capacity of some European nations to control other societies. It also propelled the expansion of slavery, the ownership of people, and control over where they work and live.

In the previous chapter we introduced several sociologists and social scientists that argue sociology has a parochial bias towards theories created in the major centres of the North. While sociology does have the capacity for reflexivity, and is embracing approaches developed across the world, the dominance of voices from Europe and North America remains a major challenge. In this chapter, as with previous chapters, we've regularly told you where the ideas we have been presenting and the scholars these ideas are associated with come from, particularly which country. Ironic, you might think, in a chapter dealing with arguments about the declining significance of the nation-state. This shows the cultural significance of the state to the way we think about peoples' identities. It is interesting that these authors do not come from one place and have often been mobile themselves. Most are from 'global cities', even Sassen herself, who coined this term, is a Dutch-born New Yorker. You have probably noticed in this chapter we have a lot of Europeans and North Americans. We also mentioned the important work of a Brazilian thinker who has had global reach with his ideas – but he was also the President of Brazil – possibly showing that the threshold for gaining global attention is indeed quite a bit higher for people from some parts of the world, relative to others.

Post-colonial, dependency and world-systems approaches to sociology have shown that modernisation theory was one-sided and overly optimistic. Few sociologists today talk about the developing or Third World, conscious of the false hierarchy and parochialism of these terms. More common today is the term Global South and Global North, or Minority and Majority World. The Minority World in this case is what has been referred to as the West, the First World or the Developed World. While those terms seem to place it at the top of a hierarchy, they actually make up a small proportion of the global population. These theories also show that focusing on relations between places complicates national theories of class inequality, which we will discuss in Chapter 7. Some Marxist-inspired theorists have argued that the reason the revolutionary potential of the working class in places such as Britain, Germany, Australia and the USA was never realised is that they were benefiting from the exploitation of working people in other parts of the world. The Marxist theorist and later Communist Party leader Vladimir Lenin called these privileged workers in colonising countries the labour aristocracy.

To understand the current wave of globalisation and the backlash against it means we need a global sociology that does not continue to impose a vision of 'Northern Theory'. Post-colonial scholars have stressed the cultural impact of this unequal world system, shaped by colonisation as well as the current wave of economic globalisation. Writers, including those we introduced in the previous chapter such as Edward Said and Gayatri Chakravorty Spivak (both of whom lived in a 'global city', New Yorkers again, but with ties by birth to Palestine and India), argued that the development of 'modern institutions' in other countries would not necessarily benefit these countries but be driven by what Herbert Schiller called **cultural imperialism**. Schiller used this term to highlight the way that some nations were pressured, bribed and sometimes seduced into adopting institutions and values like those in the minority world, but this rarely led to economic riches, but cultural loss and often economic exploitation.

Increasingly scholars of globalisation from Europe and America are acknowledging that they have not paid sufficient attention to the colonial and post-colonial history that shaped the emergence of the international world and now our globally connected world. Yet, even when they do this, Gurminder Bhambra argues that there is a tendency among sociologists to treat only those who were colonised as needing to be understood in terms of their colonisation and their relationship to former colonising nations. Instead, she proposes, the relationship to globalisation of all the countries of Europe, North America and all colonising and **settler-colonial** states also needs to be understood as a type of post-colonialism. This history helps us understand the multicultural states that exist today, and the anxieties about multiculturalism that have driven much of the backlash to globalisation in former colonising nations. As modelled by Mignolo and Anzaldúa, whose ideas we introduced in the previous chapter, to understand the global present that we live in, including the fractured politics within and across state borders that we face, a strong sociological imagination will require '**border thinking**', understanding in nuanced terms the ways that borders change over time, can both connect and exclude and that many lives are lived at these intersections. Importantly, it is not just the borders of countries that sociologists need to understand but also the divisions that exist within states, and even within each person's thinking as they live with, reinforce or challenge existing borders.

Conclusion

It is not just your coffee beans that seem to be moving more freely and rapidly around the world. You may have bought this book on Amazon, a global platform accessible anywhere, or be reading an electronic copy online. If you are studying sociology at university you may share a class with students from many different parts of the world. Offering education to students from other places is one of the biggest export industries in some countries, including Australia, New Zealand and Britain. You may also live in a part of the world where the papers are full of news and opinion about the flows of economic and lifestyle immigrants, the *push/pull factors* driving people to leave their countries of origins, of the risk of global financial meltdowns, about the importation of drugs, of global pandemics or computer viruses. These 'risks' are the social issues, brought about by a new wave of globalisation, that relate to both public issues and private troubles.

We live in a world that has seen the spread of technology that would appear to those living two or three generations ago as something from an alien world. But we also live in a world where the number of displaced people and refugees today is the highest it has been since the Second World War. There are more people in prison now than ever before, and a return to levels of economic inequality unseen since the 1800s. For many, globalisation is ushering in a new type of social structure, one where borders matter less for the privileged but more for the not-so-privileged.

In this chapter we have introduced you to central sociological ideas about globalisation, noting that the authors of them are often based in 'global cities' in Europe and North America, although they also have ties to other parts of the world. These contemporary scholars suggest that the borders of nation-states are becoming more permeable, less powerful, but not necessarily less consequential. Sociology emerged partly around questions to do with the rise and consolidation of the nation-state, which came to stand in for 'society' as most sociologists thought about it, arguably underplaying for too long the colonial ambitions of the states they studied. This framework missed important social dynamics of connection, exploitation and exclusion and has not kept up with social change. Indeed, this rapidly changing world appears to be causing a backlash in many countries against globalisation, although this backlash is, ironically, globally connected. We will discuss aspects of these social movements in Chapter 10. While sociologists often investigate local questions, sociology as a discipline is increasingly and necessarily global in its imagination.

Key references for this chapter

Bauman, Z (2000) *Liquid Modernity*. Polity Press.

Beck, U (1992) *Risk Society: Towards a New Modernity*. Sage.

Beck, U (2006) *Cosmopolitan Vision*. Polity Press.

Bell, D (1974) *The Coming of the Post-Industrial Society*. Harper Colophon.

Berman, M (1982) *All That Is Solid Melts into Air: The Experience of Modernity*. Verso.

Calhoun, C (2007) *Nations Matter: Culture, History, and the Cosmopolitan Dream*. Routledge.

Cardoso, FH and Faletto, E (1979) *Dependency and Development in Latin America*, trans. MM Urquidi. University of California Press.

Castells, M (1996) *The Rise of the Network Society*. Blackwell.

Giddens, A (2002) *Runaway World: How Globalisation Is Reshaping Our Lives*. Profile Books.

Lipset, SM (1959) 'Some Social Requisites of Democracy', *American Political Science Review*, vol. 53, no. 1, pp. 69–105.

Marx, K and Engels, F (1983) *The Communist Manifesto*. Penguin.

Parsons, T (1966) *Societies: Evolutionary and Comparative Perspectives*. Prentice Hall.

Parsons, T (1985) *Talcott Parsons on Institutions and Social Evolution: Selected Writings*, ed. LH Mayhew. Chicago University Press.

Pieterse, JN (2009) *Globalization and Culture: Global Melange,* 2nd edn. Roman and Littlefield.

Robertson, R (2012) 'Globalisation or Glocalisation?', *The Journal of International Communication*, vol. 18, no. 2, pp. 191–208.

Sassen, S (2001) *The Global City: New York, London, Tokyo*, 2nd edn. Princeton University Press.

Schiller, H (1976) *Communication and Cultural Domination*. International Arts and Sciences Press.

Therborn, G (2000) 'Globalizations: Dimensions, Historical Waves, Regional Effects, Normative Governance', *International Sociology*, vol. 15, no. 2, pp. 151–179.

Urry, J (2007) *Mobilities*. Polity Press.

Wallerstein, I (1974) 'The Rise and Future Demise of the World Capitalist System: Concepts for Comparative Analysis', *Comparative Studies in Society and History*, vol. 16, no. 4, pp. 387–415.

Wimmer, J and Quandt, T (2006) 'Living in the Risk Society: An Interview with Ulrich Beck', *Journalism Studies*, vol. 7, no. 2, pp. 336–347.

5

SOCIAL SELVES

In the previous chapter we looked at shifts that have moved the focus from the nation-state as the object of study in sociology to global relations and the increased interconnectivity of countries, cultures, and people. Sociology has historically and continues to be important for producing knowledge about the 'big picture', so-to-speak, the broad shifts in social, political, and technological changes that affect how people live their day-to-day lives. In this chapter we turn to thinking about how the individual fits into this big picture. From an early age we are encouraged to make the right choices and make plans for what we want to be when we grow up. Cultural norms and institutions encourage 'normal' ways to live and behave. On a day-to-day basis we interact with our families, our workmates or fellow students, media images and social media feeds, legal systems and health experts, and the built and natural environment. When it comes to social interactions and relations, we tend to remember the cringe-worthy thing we said in front of a new acquaintance, the anxiety of talking to someone we find attractive, or the time we had to speak publicly. These interactions can indeed be hard but our foundational skills for navigating the social world are, for most of us and much of the time, able to be taken for granted to the extent that we are rarely even aware of them. In this chapter we will see that how we think about ourselves and how we think about and interact with others is central to how societies function and are maintained.

In the first chapter we introduced you to the concepts of structure and agency, which sociologists use to think about how we act, individually and with others. In this chapter we look at this question in more detail. Sociologists are interested in **social action**, the way our choices and behaviours are shaped by society, but this does not mean we are determined by society. Our actions are constrained in various ways but, in a fundamental sense, our ability to act at all and to have meaningful choices is dependent on our social context. Sociologists are not only interested in our 'big' actions, such as leading a protest movement (see Chapter 10). They are just as likely to be interested in everyday interactions and things that feel routine, such as how the way that a classroom is set up affects learning, or how the use of smells, music and colours affects what and how much we may buy in a shop. Our everyday actions and habits, which we learn as we grow up, might seem like they are very personal but they reflect wider cultural and structural norms and are the glue holding together our social world, while also helping to shape unequal outcomes on a wider scale.

Humans Are Social Animals

Few sociologists deny biology plays a role in human life, just as few biologists or psychologists would completely disregard social influences. There are increasingly examples of sociologists, biologists and neuroscientists working together, for example on the way different social contexts impact on stress hormones. Nevertheless, sociologists tend to focus on illuminating how social structures and processes affect human behaviour. **Socialisation** is the long process in which we absorb norms, values and perspectives and make them our own. It is how we learn to behave and communicate and is, in many ways, what makes us human.

The tensions between biological and cultural and social influences speaks to what has become known as the **nature/nurture debates** that we elaborate on further regarding gender in Chapter 8. When it comes to thinking about how humans develop throughout their lives, it is important to avoid biological determinism, that we are solely the products of our genes or DNA, and cultural determinism, that we are solely products of **socialisation**. For instance, genetics can tell us about a person's ancestry and about their possible health outcomes. People can be identified as having genes that are linked to instances of some cancers, diabetes, and heart disease. However, it is important to consider that genes do not determine a life outcome but are only a precondition for it. Simplistic genetic thinking and biological determinism have a long racist history and have even been the foundation for acts of **genocide** (see Chapter 9).

Environmental factors do contribute to whether certain diseases develop. Yet, as the relatively new field of epigenetics shows, our genes appear to be affected by the environmental conditions and lifestyle choices of our parents and grandparents. Stressful situations such as famine, sickness, and high stress appear to lead to some genetic markers that are passed on to the next generation. This means that environmental factors experienced by your parents can mark your biological make up.

The interrelation between nature and nurture is well illustrated by twin studies. Twin studies show that we are not born a 'blank slate' but are influenced by the genetic background we inherit from our parents. Studies show, for instance, that if one identical twin has schizophrenia, there will be a 45 per cent chance that the other twin will develop the same condition. But this obviously means that 55 per cent comes from other (including likely many social) factors. Both genetic inheritance and social environment are involved in making us who we are.

Another example of this interaction is the rare cases in which a child or young person is discovered who appears to have grown up outside human society, with examples including neglected children who spent most of their time alone, or even with dogs or cattle instead of humans. You might imagine someone like Tarzan or Romulus and Remus, the mythical founders of Rome who were raised by a wolf. These figures are presented as having all the attributes we associate with human beings, such as language and complex thoughts and personalities. Instead, these children often appear more like the animals that they were raised alongside, lacking language, but able to move and bark remarkably like a dog, for example.

These 'wild' children are sometimes discovered to be hoaxes; but there are real examples of children who have faced extreme neglect and are missing some of the attributes most of us take for granted. Who we are, our abilities and our personality, are in part biological, but this biology only unfolds within specific social circumstances and its influence shifts over time based on our experiences. The behaviour of these 'wild' children points to something interesting about human biology: we are very good at learning from those around us and taking on their traits, even if they are not human. Human biology is primed to make us the most social of animals.

The Self and Identity

Charles Horton Cooley was an American sociologist in the 19th century who realised that the processes that make us 'individuals' are most profoundly social. For Cooley and the other sociologists we discuss in this section, the **self** is an outcome of a social process in which we learn to see ourselves as an individual with a unique set of attributes through our interactions with others who have expectations and opinions about us (in a way, our **social identity**). The self is closely related to the concept of **identity** – our understanding of the qualities that make us who we are (and who others are) has been central to how sociologists think about the self. Cooley developed a theory of how we come to understand ourselves, the '**looking-glass self**'. Our self-concept is acquired through the reactions of others. Our observation of other people's reactions provides a 'mirror' in which we come to know ourselves. Other people's responses tell us whether we are likeable, naughty, popular, or smart. We will like or dislike this reflection and make the necessary adjustments based on how we want to appear to others.

George Herbert Mead was a colleague of Cooley's for a time and was influenced by him to develop his theory of the **generalised other**, our sense of how others around us think about us. Our socialisation begins with imitating our **significant others**, such as our parents, siblings and grandparents. We then move on to play, where we dress up and imagine ourselves as others, like a superhero, firefighter or doctor. The next step is to engage in organised games with others, which is possible only because we begin to learn roles and rules. Finally, we learn to have a general (and differentiated) sense of how we are seen by others. For Mead, our sense of self is like a dialogue between a more impulsive part of us he calls the **I**, and a social **me** that develops over time. Yet, importantly for Mead, we should not think of the I as the self that exists before the generalised other. We are born into society and are given the language and reference points of that society and start having social experiences from birth, before we can have an individual consciousness. We are part of a community of others before we are anything else.

One of Mead's students, Herbert Blumer, labelled this way of thinking about how self and society are a product of relationships as **symbolic interactionism**. He used the term symbolic to emphasise that language and the meanings we convey to each other are at the heart of this process. Talking to each other makes us who we are, and through talking we create shared meanings and representations (symbols) of the world. For Blumer, societies are the outcome of this process of creating, using and redefining shared meanings, norms and expectations.

Building on this **interactionist** approach, Erving Goffman, a Canadian-American sociologist, drew on metaphors from theatre to develop his **dramaturgical** theory of the self. Playing **roles** in society and the ways we are socialised into roles is central to sociological understandings of the self, but it is an idea that has a far longer history. The famous English playwright William Shakespeare penned the often-quoted line, 'All the world's a stage, and all the men and women merely players; they have their exits and their entrances, and one man in his time plays many parts'. Goffman argued that we take on social roles like actors on a stage.

For Goffman, we aim to present ourselves in the best possible light, calling this **impression management**. We are alert to the norms of specific social situations. For instance, we act differently socialising with friends than we do at work, or with our parents. We regulate ourselves with those different norms and expectations in mind. Our self-identity is performed for a social audience to foster trust, respect and dignity – we want to be liked – and to maintain a coherent sense of self. Goffman looks behind the mask we present in day-to-day life to think about the ways we regulate our practice to fit the social setting, and to avoid being judged negatively by others. In a sense, we are all in on the act, trying to make the performance a success. We will often overlook small slip-ups in how others are performing the role they are trying to occupy in that moment. In other words, and continuing with the performance metaphor, if someone forgets their lines a little, unless we have an incentive to catch them out, we let it slip or may not even notice. Interaction does involve regular attempts to regulate and sanction each other. Think of all the small everyday expressions such as rolling your eyes, sighing loudly, or giving someone a dirty look, and how being on the receiving end of these makes you feel. Yet to varying degrees almost all of us are invested in allowing social performance to go on as it allows us to get on with our lives.

Goffman saw the performance of these roles taking effort. It can be tiring to maintain the performance. He used the metaphor of **frontstage** and **backstage**. The frontstage is all the performances we put on; the backstage is where you can relax a little (think of singing with a hairbrush in front of the bedroom mirror at home by yourself or getting to the point with a partner where you are so comfortable together that you may fart in front of them). The backstage is also the place (maybe in front of the bathroom mirror) where you get ready for your frontstage social performances.

In a sense the backstage is where you act like yourself without pressure of judgement, but this is not exactly what Goffman meant. While it may be a time when a performance is not being delivered, Goffman was not convinced any role could represent our 'true' self, or whether we actually have a true self. Like others in this interactionist tradition, he argued there was no true self outside of interaction. He thought that some people sincerely believed their social performances, while others consciously feel that their actions are not real or authentic. Most of us are somewhere in between in the way we feel about our actions, realising we are influenced by others but feeling some of our actions are close to our 'authentic' selves. For Goffman, in the end, all actions across this spectrum are a type of performance, but this doesn't mean we are just playing parts written for us. We are all actors together on a stage that presents us with the rough outline of scripts, props and a setting, but which also asks us to continually improvise. In some scenes we know our lines well and can function smoothly; in other scenes we may fluff or forget our lines, creating feelings of embarrassment and sometimes exclusion.

Difference and Deviance

Humans are a diverse bunch, which we and many others think is one of the wonderful things about humanity. Though the processes of interaction, we learn to see ourselves in relation to other people, and come to understand our identity in terms of where we are from, our gender, our community and how we are similar to and different from others. Yet, as we mentioned in Chapter 3, Edward Said and others have shown how ethnic background and other markers can be used to label some identities as 'other'. This is an example of a larger set of social processes through which some of the differences between people are labelled as abnormal, weird or 'deviant'.

There are many sociological theories that try to explain why some people come to be labelled as deviant – in violation of norms – and the most influential in sociology in this area through the 20th century have largely come from the symbolic interactionist tradition. There are also some approaches called **voluntaristic theories** that see all humans as rational decision-makers that know the difference between right and wrong. Therefore, any criminal or deviant behaviour is explained as the result of bad choices. In these theories, strong inner and outer controls make people follow norms and rules. Socialisation into shared social norms is important, but imperfect. Hence **social control** – formal and informal means of enforcing norms – is needed to make up for failing self-control. For many sociologists, this way of thinking about **deviance** downplays any acknowledgement of different life chances, discrimination and inequalities. What may seem like an irrational choice, based on poor self-control from one perspective, can seem totally sensible from another. More importantly, many get away with not following the rules, especially if they are privileged.

All of us have almost certainly deviated from the accepted norms in our society, and most of us have probably at some point broken the law. Let's face it, you probably broke some norm today – maybe you picked your nose, didn't wait your turn, crossed the road illegally or, more seriously, failed to do your sociology reading for class. Most of the time these actions have very little impact on how we think of ourselves or others think of us. However, sometimes these transgressions come to be attached to an identity and have a profound effect on a person's life. The American sociologist (and at one time professional jazz musician) Howard Becker developed **labelling theory** that argues deviance is always relative to time and place and to *who* is committing the act. For instance, the middle-class lawyer taking cocaine at a party is perceived very differently from a person on the street using methamphetamine. They are both committing the same act – taking illegal drugs – but their social and economic circumstances result in very different treatment.

For Becker, we cannot understand deviance just by looking at the actions of the person who transgressed a norm. He argues that we can only understand deviance by acknowledging that it is created by the people who make the rules and laws, who then get to label anyone who breaks them as deviant or criminal. The powerful and privileged as a social group get to make the rules and norms; those who do not fit the norms or follow the rules are labelled as **outsiders**. Therefore, deviance is not the act itself, but the result of the application of rules by the powerful over the 'offending'. Often the powerful are 'offending' too in various ways but are not under the same surveillance as individuals or groups who are disadvantaged or marginalised.

Once a deviant label is applied, especially if it is applied at an early age, it becomes part of a person's self-identity through the socialisation processes we outlined above. The transgressor is then treated as deviant. If we are told we are deviant, and treated like we are, we may eventually embrace the label that is forced upon us, self-identifying as an outsider, or even as a criminal. In other words, labels can become what another sociologist, Robert Merton, coined a **self-fulfilling prophecy**.

Structure and Agency

The classical sociologists had different starting points for thinking about how society functions and how it is linked to our social selves. For Durkheim it was essential to treat values and norms as their own independent reality – not the same, but just as real as rocks or trees. He called shared values **social facts** and claimed that the way to understand them was to see the relationship between current and historical social facts, not by looking at what individual people believed and the choices they made.

Marx was similar in his beliefs. The truth of human life had its foundation or **base** in the structure of economic production within a society. The ideas in people's heads were **superstructure**, different but derived from and dependent on the foundation of the base. In other words, what we believe is fundamentally what the system of production requires us to believe, what Marx called **ideology**. Weber, influencing the birth of the interactionist perspective, focused more on the subjective meaning of social action to individual agents. The ideas in people's heads for Weber are not fully determined by the mode of production; they are certainly influenced by it, but Weber gave more scope for ideas to influence norms and social change. These two views about where to start sociological analysis created two different ways to understand the link between society and the individual, which we first introduced you to in Chapter 1: approaches that start with a more bird's-eye macro view of social systems and how these systems interact to shape individual lives, and interactionist approaches that start with a more micro view of individuals and their interactions and how these coalesce into larger patterns and structures.

In the 1930s, the American sociologist Talcott Parsons aimed to connect macro and micro approaches, bringing together the notion of social fact (or structure) and human action (or agency). While they started from opposite positions – social facts and individuals in interaction – Parsons argued that Durkheim and Weber were heading towards a position that bridged the two by focusing on **values**. Parsons recognised that we can think about what we do and give reasons for it. We 'act' rather than just 'behave', and we can reflect on our actions and make choices. We act voluntarily, in the sense that we are not directly coerced. We try to achieve our goals and live a life we consider good. This is our agency at work. But, importantly, this voluntary action is shaped by norms, values and 'common-sense' that are socially created. He argued that tracing these normative frameworks and the role they played in maintaining a functioning **social order** was the key to sociology. How do we come to adopt these norms that guide our action? Through socialisation. We learn them as we grow up, as Cooley and Mead had already recognised.

Parsons understood socialisation as two phases, with those developing his work adding a third. While we are babies and young children, we undergo primary socialisation where our families, particularly our parents, are the main influence. However, in complex modern societies, Parsons argued that primary socialisation is not enough. Secondary socialisation occurs in later childhood as peers and social institutions such as schools influence learning. Others have then argued that tertiary socialisation occurs during adult life as we move out into the labour market and away from the family home and school. Re-socialisation can occur when people are confronted with new information and experiences, resulting in changes in norms and values, such as going to jail or war, or moving to another country. Parsons's later work headed further towards structural functionalism; in fact he is one of the names most associated with it. From this perspective, norms are functional for society and for how necessary institutions are reproduced.

There have been recent efforts to rethink socialisation to better recognise the activity of the individual. Social psychologists, and some sociologists, today talk about self-socialisation to recognise the active part we play in our own development. They argue that some specific messages in our social contexts have more influence than others: we choose to copy some people and not others, and we direct our efforts towards some activities that appeal to us but avoid others. At its best, this way of thinking about socialisation does not privilege agency over structure but tries to move beyond that simple dichotomy of object and subject. Creativity and improvisation constitute institutions and structures, and vice versa. We constantly improvise but don't improvise alone. This insight has been at the heart of more recent efforts, after Parsons, to rethink the relationship between structure and agency.

Hans Joas, a German sociologist, argues that humans' need for structured creativity was the real synthesis that Durkheim and Weber were converging on. He has a similar view to Goffman, who felt that socialisation had to be 'just enough' to allow us to respond with others to novel situations, to improvise, individually and collectively. Everyday life involves a constant series of improvisations, based on the situation and the responses of others among many different options. We cannot be socialised to the point where we will always know exactly what to do, like a robot, but we are socialised to be creative in our actions, imitating what we see and have learned and remember, and build on those foundations.

Beyond the Binary

Among contemporary sociologists, it is common to see agency and structure, self and society as not really needing to be bridged, as they were never really separate but instead **co-constituted**. As we mentioned in the opening of the chapter, the way our social interaction is structured is a central feature of what allows us to live our lives. There is a lot you can usually rely upon in your interactions. You can assume, without giving it any worry, that if you sign up for sociology that your lecturer will give the lecture on self and society as promised in the syllabus, not decide to talk for two hours on her trout fishing expedition to Alaska (complete with photos) instead. You can take it for granted that if you order and pay for a hamburger at your local restaurant that is what you'll receive, the chef won't suddenly decide he is a performance artist instead and substitute your burger for a one-hour one-person show featuring puppets and miming.

We assume and are usually not disappointed by the basic social performances of those we interact with, even if we might find ourselves regularly disappointed by people in other ways. It allows us to buy consumer goods, food, and travel, to go to work and take a university degree. Many sociologists today, instead of looking at the link between self and society, focus on the formal (institutions and organisations) and informal (groups and norms) ways that our interactions with each other are organised.

All groups are organised in a similar way at an abstract level. There are rules and guidelines that constrain our actions, but this has the paradoxical effect of making any of the actions we undertake possible as they provide the resources for interacting and coordinating with others. Without these shared understandings that allow us to synchronise action with others, we would find acting impossible, yet the way our lives are organised or structured in this way is fundamentally the routine patterns that exist because of the way we act. In other words, self and society, structure and agency, are not opposite forces acting in the world but 'two sides of the one coin' – they are co-constituted.

Arguably the most influential sociologists for shaping contemporary approaches to thinking about the co-constitution of self and society is Pierre Bourdieu, a French sociologist who worked from the 1960s to this death in early 2002. His work shows how dispositional ways of acting he called **practices** are foundational to social life but are also the foundation of inequalities (which we turn to in more detail in coming chapters). He highlights how socialisation is largely about the routinisation of social life, where we do not need to consciously think about most of the things we do. Bourdieu highlights that the process by which we are socialised into our society is not just cognitive (about shaping our minds) but affects the way we feel and sense the world, the way we carry our bodies and the spaces in which we feel comfortable. The word many sociologists use for this for this is **embodiment**, incorporated into our physical selves. The term that Bourdieu uses for these embodied dispositions is the **habitus**, which drives our practices (we return to this in more detail in Chapter 7). Another influential theorist of the 20th century, also working in France at the same time as Bourdieu, was Michel Foucault. He helped transform the way we think about embodiment and the self by linking it to power.

Power

The study of **power** has been a central tenet of sociology since the beginning of the discipline. Max Weber defined power as the ability of an individual or group to realise their will and control the action of others to achieve this. In other words, it is about the relationship between self and society: Weber says you are powerful if you can get your own way, even if you have opposition. This definition applies from the interpersonal to the global level. It captures the way you may be able to influence your friends to go to a Bangtan Boys (BTS) concert even though they would prefer to go to see Billie Eilish. It also captures the interactions between nation-states, such as the way the leaders of some nations that are big polluters can pressure other leaders not to adopt or push for high targets for carbon emission reductions.

In Europe in the 1960s and 70s, a new school of thought labelled **post-structuralism** emerged that critically engaged with these ideas to provide a decentred, less 'top-down' way of thinking about power. In this conception of power, rather than some people having power and others being powerless, post-structuralism illustrates how power is present in all social situations and makes us particular kinds of selves. The various approaches to the self we have so far introduced, under the label symbolic interactionism, had been the primary way in which sociologists thought about the self, but had less to say about power. Michel Foucault put this new understanding of power at the centre of how sociologists understand the relationship between self and society.

Foucault opens *Discipline and Punish*, one of his most influential books, with an evocative and disturbing description of an execution in Paris in 1757. The man executed, Robert Damiens, had attempted to kill the King of France. His punishment was to be publicly tortured, then drawn and quartered: literally hacked to pieces and torn apart using the pulling strength of horses. Foucault saw this as an example of **sovereign power**, a term he uses to characterise the general regime of power operated in pre-modern Europe that can be summed up with a king or queen proclaiming, 'off with their head'. Sovereign power here is the legitimate use of force, even violence and death, to enforce authority.

Compared to the brutal spectacle of public execution, the rise of the modern penal system that tries to rehabilitate prisoners seems like progress. Yet Foucault is not so sure. The sovereign (in the case of Damiens, represented by the King of France) had complete control over the life of the subjects in their territory, at least in theory. In practice, however, it was very difficult to know what was going on; technology to monitor the population did not exist, nor did systems to collect detailed information. The sovereign system of power was inefficient, so life for most went on largely without the powerful having direct control or knowledge. Foucault argues therefore that the sovereign turned to spectacular and heinous displays of power over the body of subjects when their power was challenged. Attempts to create a sense of the overwhelming power of the sovereign through such executions often went wrong. The condemned would sometimes shake in fear at their fate, and sometimes the crowd gathered for the execution would mock and boo them on their way to death, but other prisoners would mock the king or queen and their executioners, dancing and otherwise performing for the crowd on the way to the gallows. Often the crowd would not jeer but cheer for the condemned.

Foucault compares sovereign power to a **disciplinary power** that has developed throughout recent centuries that is especially connected to the development of different forms of technology. This newer form of power focused on instilling routine, discipline, training and surveillance, drawing on academic and 'expert' knowledge about how people could be shaped. The same type of monitoring, training and disciplining that emerged in the modern era, according to Foucault, did not just characterise prisons but also the army, workplaces of modern society, and even the schooling system (which sits alongside the family as one of the major institutions of socialisation). Today, we can think about social media as facilitating a new kind of monitoring.

Foucault highlighted how the workings of power become embodied. Training at school and outside school aimed to turn people into **docile bodies**, fit to take their place on the factory floors, in caring roles in the family, and in the frontlines in modern wars, reproducing norms, implicitly shaping or even actively shaping others and the next generation to play similar roles. In other words, all of us are trained to monitor ourselves and others. Disciplinary power drew on new techniques and scientific knowledge that could monitor people and track their progress, and through this develop more precise techniques to reach the preferred outcome. An exemplar of this disciplinary type of power is the teaching you likely went through during your schooling: an imposed curriculum that teachers across schools would follow, textbook-driven teaching, and testing that aimed to rank you against your classmates, and often against students from other schools. Just as important is learning about turning up on time, wearing the uniform, deferring to authority and other forms of discipline.

Another example of this connection between technology and bodies is the rise of prescription drugs. For instance, drugs are prescribed to help individuals with mental health issues such as anxiety or depression and can make a great positive difference to some people's lives, but if increasingly large swathes of the population are diagnosed with mental health issues, what exactly is being cured here? Individual problems? Or are our social systems, and the increasing precarity they create, drivers of these problems? Are these medications a 'solution' to economic productivity problems relating to maintaining a healthy and disciplined work-force in the face of insecurity at least as much as about improving the quality of individual lives?

Foucault investigates in his work how the new ways of understanding the world that emerged in modernity did not necessarily enhance freedom. They created the foundation for a new formation of power and surveillance of people through defining, classifying and 'improving' people, an intense surveillance of individuals and whole populations that wasn't possible before technologies emerged that could be used to control not only crime, but fertility, hygiene, physical and mental health and even people's sense of self. From this perspective, instead of progress from brutality to enlightenment, there is a steady shift from an inefficient to an efficient type of power that governs our actions, and even the types of people we can become.

Bodies and Power

Foucault traced this process though the history of **sexuality**. Sexuality is not the same as sex or gender. Sexuality describes desires, orientations, practices, and identities. He showed how sexuality has been heavily regulated by a variety of means including legal, religious, medical and psychological. Foucault referred to these expert bodies of knowledge as **discourse**. The identity of 'homosexual' was created through discourse around homosexual practices, push-ing it 'out of the shadows' of the private sphere to be placed under the microscope of experts that wanted to discover the 'truth' about sex and sexuality. This also enabled this discovered 'abnormal' behaviour to be seen as something that needed to be 'fixed'. Religious experts called it a sin. Legal experts made it against the law. Psychiatric experts diagnosed it as a form of deviance and administered shock therapy to try to 'cure' it. And so on. Yet, the effects of power are not straightforward, or held only by one group. Once this group were named and identified through the label of homosexual, the foundation was set for people to organise politically as a group against their own marginalisation. So, for Foucault, wherever there is power, there is **resistance**.

Foucault's work, indeed, the process he describes, has helped shape the development of an approach to thinking about society called **queer theory**, that has been used to theorise diverse sexual practices and orientations, how sexuality plays an important but ambivalent and fluid role in our sense of self, and how queer people can come together politically across difference. The term 'queer' was reclaimed from its former use as an insult to become a widely used and politically empowering term for broad and diverse sexual orientations.

An important figure here is Judith Butler, who brings together ideas from Foucault, Goffman and others to think about how gender and sexuality is not natural but made through these social processes. Like Foucault, she highlights the way things that seem natural are actually brought into existence through human action and socialisation, including a tendency to link types of sexual behaviour to gender and to identity, such that people sexed as male are assumed until proven otherwise to have a male identity and be sexually interested in women. This doesn't mean that people outright deny the possibility of other combinations of these factors, but that this combination, which Butler calls the **heterosexual matrix**, underpins what is considered normal. Even people who have come out as gay constantly have to rene-gotiate who knows and what assumptions people make about their identity and their partner whenever they meet new people or are in new environments. We say more about some of the key ideas in Butler's approach and queer theory in Chapter 8.

The Self and Technology

Foucault wrote about the creation of 'docile' selves, schooled for repetitive work, in the context of mid 20th century Europe. In his later work and that of others who have built on his ideas, it is argued that a new regime of power is emerging. Some elements of this new form of power are similar to disciplinary societies: we are still under surveillance, like in the prison or school, and still learn to internalise this surveillance. But we also perceive that we are 'freer' than in previous centuries. In new economies, the docile body needed for the factory floor became less efficient for the economy. Being willing to retrain, balance different commitments and be flexible is now more important. We need to learn to be mobile, entrepreneurial, employable selves. Surveillance is now mobile, security cameras proliferate around our cities and we are always contactable and tracked through the phones we carry in our pocket, linked into a worldwide web of online connection. Social media and apps collect our every click as sellable data as we interact with others and go about our lives. From a Foucauldian approach, the development of this technology leads towards living in a metaphorical **panopticon**. The panopticon refers to the style of a jail designed by the British philosopher Jeremy Bentham and his brother Samuel (an engineer and architect), where the guard tower is in the middle of the complex and able to observe all the cells, built facing inwards in a circle around the tower. While the tower guard can see into every cell, the view into the tower is obscured for the inmates, which means that the prisoners come to feel like they are always being watched, even if they are not, so they regulate themselves accordingly. Many sociologists today use this concept to analyse the saturation of technology, especially digital communication, algorithms, and social media.

In the previous chapter we discussed the way that networks and the rise of the World Wide Web are central to understanding global society. These same changes impact on the types of selves created within networked societies. When the internet was going mainstream, Manuel Castells recognised its potential to not just reinforce an emerging networked society but create **networked selves**. In the 1990s and into the 2000s, social researchers were often positive about the impacts of the internet and digital technology on the self, with some categorising the web as a playground in which we could experiment with identity, more easily find our tribe, explore our sexual and other identities, and even create second or third selves liberated from the constraints we faced 'in real life' (IRL) or 'away from keyboard' (AFK).

Digital technology has spread and along with it the extent to which the internet shapes our lives, both positively and negatively. Particularly since digital connection went mobile with the emergence of smart phones, the distinction between online and 'IRL' has become blurry. Nathan Jurgenson, an American-based sociologist who works for the company that makes Snapchat, argues that calling online life 'virtual' and the rest of our life 'real' is an unhelpful dualism. Much of our life is now tied up with being online. Instead, he proposes the concept of **augmented reality** and **augmented selves**.

Augmented means 'added to', and what has been added to our lives by networked technology is both good and bad. Contemporary sociologists tend to be ambivalent about its impacts. Digital technologies have freed up identity in all kinds of ways, but new forms of digital surveillance have also been amplified to become arguably the centre of economic growth and social life and we actively participate in the functioning of this new type of power. We constantly confront unrealistic images of others, read (and sometimes share) information and advice of dubious quality, and hand over vastly more personal details to others than ever before. The terms and conditions we tick off on when we sign up to a new app allow a whole new range of techniques for shaping our behaviour.

When you download a new app on to your phone you are opening up new possibilities for yourself, to access new music, to get special discounts, to enhance your dating life, or to track your exercise. But it also allows your actions to be shaped. Cookies track your purchases, the social media sites you use track the stories that you read and use it to sell targeted advertising. If you visit a site about pregnancy, an ad for contraception or nappies may pop up on your feed. Look up infertility and your local IVF clinic will soon be sending you targeted advertising. Your phone's GPS records your location, sharing the data with many of the apps you have downloaded onto your phone. This could help the police to track you down (sometimes you'll be grateful, other times maybe not). Increasingly governments are legislating to force your mobile phone company to pass on data about the websites you use.

The Australian sociologist Deborah Lupton highlights that we can also track ourselves in new ways, using apps to track how many steps we take, how many calories we eat, and how many friends we have. She calls this 'self-knowledge through numbers' the **quantified self**. Tracking ourselves can become addictive. Do you ever catch yourself checking how many people have shared or liked your Facebook post or Instagram photo every few minutes? Living in our technologically networked worlds gives us new ways of engaging with others and understanding ourselves. But as we track ourselves, we are also being tracked. What we might think of as personal data is being collected in never before possible quantities and used for business, government, and research, most often without our knowledge. And our actions are shaped in new ways. This is a form of power that we seemingly volunteer to participate in, without too much thought of the current and future consequences.

The influence of technology on the types of selves we become goes beyond connection to the internet becoming ubiquitous. It also has a longer history predating digital technology. Artificial limbs, wearing glasses and the contraceptive pill have all reshaped the self. Donna Haraway theorises that people are increasingly what she calls **cyborgs**, which are 'boundary creatures' that break down previous seemingly solid divisions. Some of these practices in which we use technology to reshape the body may improve our lives and health, such as wearing glasses, receiving a pacemaker or a hip replacement. But they may also lead to health problems or other issues: solarium, liposuction, plastic surgery, extreme diets. More ambivalently, our 24/7 tethering to our phones is also a 24/7 tether to work and shopping. Yet, for Haraway, such 'boundary' selves also open up positive possibilities for transforming powerful influences that shape our lives. Jack Halberstam points out, for example, how the transgression of gender norms becomes possible with sex reassignment surgery, an agency unimagined less than a century ago.

This is the social context in which the French sociologist Bruno Latour argues that binaries between agency and structure but also between nature and society are misleading. He proposes that believing that nature and society were separate was a category mistake – they are always intertwined – but this way of thinking of nature as separate was essential to the constitution of the entire modern world view and had the effect of facilitating human social activity that both fundamentally reshaped the natural environment while also allowing people to discount the impact it was having. For Latour, on the one hand, we need to properly recognise the way that human agency has created new intertwinements of the natural and social (climate change is an example of such a hybrid); on the other, we have to also recognise **non-human agency** in social life, including technological objects that mediate our lives in unplanned and unexpected ways, and things we might consider 'natural'. The large-scale bushfires that regularly disrupt and reshape social life in Australia, and which feel particularly close to home for the authors, and global pandemics such as COVID-19, are examples of these non-human actants.

Individualisation and Hybridity

Sociologists characterise our contemporary world as full of new uncertainities, possiblities and tensions that bring older ways of doing things into question. For some sociologists, including the British scholars Margaret Archer and Anthony Giddens, this has led to a greater opportunity to monitor and reshape our actions, plan our futures and pursue lives that realise our values. These scholars use a term we have already introduced, reflexivity, for this way of thinking about our lives and taking action on the basis of it.

German sociologists Ulrich Beck and Elizabeth Beck-Gernsheim have developed a different understanding of reflexivity and what it means for contemporary selfhood. They characterise lives during the middle of the 20th century as like a Russian (Bubuska or 'Grandma') doll, the type of doll where many increasingly smaller versions of the same doll are found within a larger doll. Our different social roles and identities were, in this earlier era, more closely nested inside one another, like these dolls. Different expectations that men and women were socialised into fitted with and presupposed a particular set of dominant social arrangements. For example, a married heterosexual couple who would have children fitted with a model of full-time paid employment where the man would be the primary 'breadwinner', while the women would care full-time for children in the role of 'housewife'. The economy assumed this family model was the norm, where the wife/mother would see to the needs of the household, while the minimum wage for adult men was meant to be enough for a family to survive and save for the future (we'll say more about this family structure in the chapter on gender).

This meant that choices were limited, but that the rules for how to play our social roles were clear and these roles tended to fit together. For the sociologist Richard Sennett, despite the obvious inequalities of this type of society for women and many others, it provided a foundation on which the future made sense to people; they felt their society and their own lives were 'progressing', and that their lives made sense, providing an opportunity to buy a house, provide for their children and build a savings nest-egg for their future.

For sociolgists such as Beck and Beck-Gernsheim, these securities are reducing for many people. Social change is pulling these Russian dolls apart, and new social arrangements presuppose that the individual is responsible for designing and staging their own lives. This idea appears to resonate with Goffman's view of the actor playing different roles and staging their own life, first proposed a generation before Sennett and the Becks. However, to continue with the theatrical metaphors, this new show is less a Shakespearean play (comedy or tragedy) and more the performance of an improvised circus act. Modern lives are no longer like Russian dolls but like tightrope walkers and jugglers. Instead of roles holding together, they are contradictory, or seemingly lacking reference to other roles you play in your life.

Beck and Beck-Gernsheim call this process **individualisation**. While it is still true that we are socialised to know what acceptable life choices are 'for the likes of us', there have also been growing freedoms and opportunitues for people, though not to the point of equality of choice. At the same time, everyone now has new individual responsibilities to juggle the inconsistencies and contradictions of contemporary life. Individualisation can lead to novel experimentation with identity. Equally, however, our capacity to act can be exhausted in the effort to keep juggling these multiple demands, struggling for compromises that can combine seemingly contradictory role demands. In fact each new experiment in doing so creates a set of new contradictions, tensions and 'decisions'. For instance, there are now more opportunities for women to pursue education and careers, but this has led to pressures for women to 'do it all', especially as men have not taken up equal domestic and child-rearing duties. The result is increasing uncertainty. Improvisation within realistic possibilities becomes a habitual way of being, but it also leads to insecurity, uncertainty and anxiety, all of which may be contributuions to the rise in diagnoses of mental illnesses discussed above.

How new is this process of individualisation? Beck and Beck-Gernsheim suggest it has emerged in recent decades. However, you may have noticed that this thinking about complex identities resonates with the notions of border-crossing we discussed in Chapter 3. The same can be said of Haraway's claims for the emergence of 'boundary creatures' or Latour's highlighting of the limitations of thinking about self and society, and the natural and social, in binary terms. Gloria Evangelina Anzaldúa's concept of borderlands was developed to think about juggling social and cultural boundaries. Her work on **mestiza (mixed) consciousness** prefigures contemporary theories of individualisation, without the risk of being misunderstood as a theory of individualism. Theorising the juggling of two worlds was also part of the foundational thinking of the African American sociologist WEB Du Bois well over a century ago.

Post-colonial theorists have focused on theorising the self in the context of the experience of structural transculturation for the colonised, in the context of immigration, or as the legacy of slavery. This often leads to suffering – Du Bois spoke about 'souls' ripped in two – but contemporary scholars also celebrate the sense of self that the post-colonial theorist Homi Bhabha calls **hybridity**. Bhabha suggests that having a hybrid self becomes a personal resource for creatively managing a fluid world. Theories of individualisation were developed largely separate to this important strand of theorising about the relationship between self and society in a changing world, reflecting the new norms of Europe, the USA, Australia and New Zealand for some groups of people. But they appear to have a longer history for people outside of North American and Europe, and for minorities within these places.

Conclusion

Attempts to understand the link between individual and society is one of the constitutive aims of sociology. But it is also one of the most conceptually difficult. The most famous early sociologists seem to think of self and society as a dualism and begin with and even favour one side of this dualism over the other. From the mid-20th century efforts have been made to bridge the two. Yet the debate is not over (it very rarely is in sociology). Some sociologists still argue that the most compelling descriptions of society make an analytic split between structures (which enable and constrain our action but cannot directly act) and humans (who can act individually and collectively). Many others see structure and agency as two moments in a larger set of processes and social practices, which might be full of contradictions and tensions. Here structure and agency are not a dualism, opposite and opposed forces in the social world, but co-constituted.

Symbolic interactionists showed us that our sense of self is built by interacting with the opinions, expectations and judgements of others around us. These expectations are often based on simplifications and **stereotypes**, including related to gender and race, which we will discuss in coming chapters. Sociologists who have focused on these practices have shown that these interactions provide the framework in which we have the capacity to act, but that we do so in an unequal society and our actions often (implicitly or explicitly) help to reproduce these inequalities.

Other sociologists have recently proposed that we should make a more radical break with our frameworks for thinking about self and society, in which technology (things) and people are intertwined, the division between the natural and the social dissolves, and non-humans are given agency. The critique of sociology for its parochialism that we introduced in Chapter 3 holds for how sociology has tended to think about the relationship between self and society. As you will see in further detail in coming chapters, some of the most influential contemporary approaches conceptualise social structures that are hybrid, inconsistent and intersect with each other in unexpected ways. This has implications for how we understand conceptions of the self. Sociologists working within post-colonial, feminist and Black frameworks have led this reconceptualisation. We will say a lot more about this in coming chapters, but first we will say more about how culture shapes our lives, particularly through the media.

Key references for this chapter

Anzaldúa, GE (1999) *Borderlands/La Frontera: The New Mestiza*. Aunt Lute Books.

Archer, M (2012) *The Reflexive Imperative in Late Modernity*. Cambridge University Press.

Beck, U and Beck-Gernsheim, E (2002) *Individualization: Institutionalized Individualism and Its Social and Political Consequences*. Sage.

Becker, HS (1963) *Outsiders: Studies in the Sociology of Deviance*. Free Press.

Blumer, H (1969) *Symbolic Interactionism: Perspective and Method*. University of California Press.

Bourdieu, P (1990) *The Logic of Practice*. Stanford University Press.

Butler, J (1990) *Gender Trouble: Feminism and the Subversion of Identity*. Routledge.

Castells, M (1996) *The Rise of the Network Society*. Blackwell Publishing.

Cooley, CH (1922) *Human Nature and the Social Order*, rev. edn. Charles Scribner's Sons.

Durkheim, E (1964) *The Rules of Sociological Method*. Free Press.

Foucault, M (1995) *Discipline and Punish*, 2nd edn., trans. A Sheridan. Vintage Books.

Foucault, M (1998) *The History of Sexuality*, 3 vols., trans. R Hurley. Penguin Books.

Giddens, A (1990) *The Consequences of Modernity*. Polity Press.

Goffman, E (1959) *The Presentation of Self in Everyday Life*. Anchor Books.

Halberstam, J and Livingston, I (eds) (1995) *Posthuman Bodies*. Indiana University Press.

Haraway, D (1985) 'A Manifesto for Cyborgs: Science, Technology, and Socialist Feminism in the 1980s', *Socialist Review*, no. 80, pp. 65–108.

Joas, H (1996) *The Creativity of Action*. University of Chicago Press.

Jurgenson, N (2011) 'Digital Dualism versus Augmented Reality', *The Society Pages*. http://thesocietypages.org/cyborgology/2011/02/24/digital-dualism-versus-augmented-reality/ (accessed 5 February 2020).

Jurgenson, N (2012) 'When Atoms meet Bits: Social Media, the Mobile Web and Augmented Revolution' *Future Internet*, vol. 4, no. 1, pp. 83–91.

Latour, B (2005) *Reassembling the Social: An Introduction to Actor Network Theory*. Oxford University Press.

Lupton, D (2016) *The Quantified Self: A Sociology of Self-Tracking*. Polity Press.

Marx, K (1977) *A Contribution to the Critique of Political Economy*. Progress Publishers.

Mead, GH (1967) *Mind, Self, and Society from the Standpoint of a Social Behaviourist*. University of Chicago Press.

Merton, RK (1948) 'The Self-Fulfilling Prophecy', *The Antioch Review*, vol. 8, no. 2, pp. 193–210.

Parsons, T (1949) *The Structure of Social Action: A Study in Social Theory with Special Reference to a Group of Recent European Writers*, 2nd edn. Free Press.

Parsons, T and Bales, R (1955) *Family, Socialization and Interaction Process*. Free Press.

Sennett, R (1998) *The Corrosion of Character: The Personal Consequences of Work in the New Capitalism*. W.W. Norton.

Zuboff, S (2019) *The Age of Surveillance Capitalism: The Fight for a Human Future at the New Frontier of Power*. Public Affairs.

6

CULTURE AND MEDIA

Culture is the name given to the symbols, language, gestures, norms, values and rituals that we use to understand the world. If your family has immigrated, or you have ever moved for education or work, or even if you've travelled abroad for holidays, you have probably had the experience of finding at least some of the practices of those around you disorienting or perplexing. Things like the cuisine and eating practices or attitudes towards personal space vary from place to place. Cultural shock can be visceral. While we do not know of anywhere today where people walk around freely burping in each other's faces, even the extent to which natural bodily functions need to be controlled or hidden varies from place to place. Because culture is the background to our lives, other ways of doing things sometimes just do not feel 'right'. But engaging in other cultures can also be one of the most exciting things we can do. It can help us see our own culture in a new light. In other words, engaging with cultural difference can hone our sociological imagination. Sometimes we have a sense of reverse culture shock when we return home after travel; things that we used to take for granted now seem strange, helping us see our home culture in a new light. Cultural norms go beyond establishing everyday expectations about regulating bodily functions or what are the things we find acceptable to eat. Analysing cultural traditions and knowledges not only 'makes the normal look strange' but can also highlight deep differences in the way knowledge is produced and valued. For instance, as we mentioned in the previous chapter, Western cultures, especially following the Industrial Revolution, have tended to see 'nature' as separate from 'culture'. Many Indigenous cultures around the world do not make this distinction, living life as if what is called 'the environment' in the West is a taken-for-granted element of their culture, not separate from it. For some sociologists, this separation of nature and culture in the West has contributed to the huge global problems we now face in terms of climate change, food production and waste. This chapter looks at sociological ways of thinking about cultures, including how the media (as a central aspect of and shaper of culture) and consumerism help shape everyday life and broader social outcomes.

Thinking about Culture

We saw in the opening chapters that early sociologists were interested in the way human social life was changing. For many of these sociologists, culture could bring about change or provide stability. For Durkheim, culture was an essential ingredient in all types of societies. For instance, in the form of **religion** – organised cultural practices and worldviews linking us to the supernatural – culture represented and reinforced the bonds of solidarity that were the glue in 'mechanical' social groups. In 'organic' societies, a new dependence on each other's different roles becomes another type of glue, but this does not mean shared culture loses its value. While less directly linked to religion, Durkheim worried that shared culture and rituals were needed to smooth over the new challenges raised by a complex **division of labour** and increased individual difference in 'organic' social formations. Without these rituals, society might fragment too much, which resonates with some of the concerns of sociologists who write about individualisation, which we discussed in the previous chapter.

The American sociologist Robert Bellah calls the type of secular culture that develops in this context of an organic society with a complex division of labour a **civil religion**, a term that he took from Rousseau. Societies are still full of their own rituals and rich with meaning, even if these rituals and meanings no longer claim a direct link to the supernatural. In the context of the USA, you can see how Bellah could argue that people in his country treat the Declaration of Independence, the Constitution and the Bill of Rights as quasi-sacred documents. The inauguration of the President of the USA shares symbolism with the coronation of monarchs. Maybe your country has similar rituals, or national holidays, that seem to have elements that are quasi-religious.

If you support a sports team or have seen your favourite band play live, you may have even had what felt like a quasi-religious experience there too. Durkheim thought that when people engage in worshipping a divine form, they are also unconsciously worshipping their society, as they embrace a sense of being part of something much bigger than themselves. This sense can be in the background much of the time but can at points become much stronger. One of the reasons groups develop religious rituals, Durkheim argued, was to bring people together to share in the same actions and feelings.

Durkheim thought taking part in these types of events could release powerful emotions that he called **collective effervescence**. Think of that electric feeling when everyone is singing along to your favourite song, or your team scores the winning goal. It would not feel the same if no one else cared. Durkheim argued that this effervescence was connected through rituals to certain symbols. In mechanical social forms, this feeling was particularly associated with a totem that represented a sense of the divine but also represented members of the group. For instance, Durkheim used the example of Indigenous Australian nations connected spiritually to the eagle. Bellah's framing of civil religion helps us understand how at least some citizens of the USA seem to think about themselves as eagle people as well. Maybe your team's mascot, your football jumper or your favourite band t-shirt marks out your sense of belonging to something bigger as well.

As we have already covered earlier (Chapter 2), for Max Weber, culture played an even more important role as the driver of change. His sociology traced out the emergence of modernity through a shift from authority embedded in tradition such as religion to a new form of rational and legal authority. This shift was driven by culture, through religion. Weber thought that a paradoxical effect of the **Protestant Ethic** in bringing about this cultural shift is that, as the attitudes it encouraged are embedded in bureaucratic and secular forms, it would lead to a decline in religious thinking over time, what he called **disenchantment**.

Marx gave less of a role to culture in driving change but believed that shared culture in capitalist societies helped to reinforce the status quo. He famously (at least among sociologists) called religion the 'opiate of the people'. He was acknowledging that religion can help people cope and carry on in the face of suffering, but also highlighted that it distracted them from their real situation. For Marx, culture in general supported capitalist **ideology**, a superstructure built on the foundations of the way economic life was ordered. In other words, cultural meanings reinforced the interests of 'capital' (the wealthy owners of land and companies).

The Culture of Capitalism

In the first half of the 20th century a critical sociology of culture developed building on Marx's ideas while trying to understand why the revolutions he foresaw did not eventuate, at least not in the places and contexts in which he predicted. Antonio Gramsci recognised that capitalist systems are often supported even by those who appear to be losing out within that system. Gramsci was a social theorist, political activist and even member of parliament, engaged with the Communist Party in Italy. Arrested by the regime of Benito Mussolini in 1926, Gramsci continued to develop his theory of power from an Italian prison, writing on scrap notebooks that were later smuggled out of prison at great risk by his sister-in-law, Tatiana Schucht.

Gramsci used the term **hegemony** to describe the way that those in power could convince others that their interests were in the national and general interest, so their rule seemed legitimate. The powerful did this in part through understanding what dominated class groups wanted, and that it was a good idea to continually make some concessions to them as long as they were insignificant for the overall class structure. Gramsci argued that a revolution would only occur where earlier efforts to build a widespread counterculture had been successful. Even if culture was a superstructure to the capitalist system, cultural change had to be the foundation of a revolution.

As we saw in the previous chapter, we learn our culture through socialisation. The French social theorist Louis Althusser added to the concept of hegemony a discussion of how people come to embrace the ideology to which they are exposed. People are exposed to ideas from multiple directions – from the state, schools, churches, voluntary associations, media organisations and even trade unions. While these institutions appear to conflict, they tend to have a shared common interest in maintaining the status quo. To be counted as a member of a society, driven by an implicit fear of exclusion or mockery, people accept the common-sense of those around them. While the state may use violence or at least its threat to maintain power, a shared common-sense – which as we covered in the previous chapter is what allows us to go about our everyday lives – is what really buttressed the power of the capitalist state.

This sociology of culture inspired by Marx was further developed by a group of German scholars known as the Frankfurt School due to their connection to the Institute for Social Research, in Frankfurt. While the group began their work in Frankfurt, and some finished their life there, many were forced to flee due to the rise of Nazism. Two of the central figures attached to this school, Theodor Adorno and Herbert Marcuse, made it to the USA, which influenced their thought about the prominent place of mainstream consumer culture in the power dynamics of society. Another member of the school was not so lucky. Walter Benjamin

– whose work among other things helped highlight the ideological role of the idea of 'progress' in buttressing inequality – committed suicide at the France–Spain border after his group of refugees were held up in their crossing.

The Frankfurt School members argued that **popular culture** – the most popular or generally available cultural forms in a society – play the central role in reducing the revolutionary potential of the working class. After the Second World War, where others saw the relative harmony within Western nations as the 'end of ideology', Herbert Marcuse called this a **manufactured consensus**. Specific post-war economic factors and technological improvements made production easier and facilitated a general rise in consumption. This made people feel that life was getting better. Yet these conditions also led to power becoming more centralised as technology developed at a rapid rate and facilitated the removal of power from democratic control and growth of bureaucratic rule by elites; expertise was given power over meaningful democratic participation.

Adorno, writing with Max Horkheimer, argued that pop culture was central to creating this consensus. In 20th-century societies it was for the first time possible to create cultural products in an industrial manner. Pop music, radio, movies, magazines and books were produced like a production line where even if there were superficial differences in style, for Adorno and Horkheimer they were largely interchangeable. They argued there was very little meaningful variety in popular culture but that it was designed to be pleasing, with the illusion of individual taste. For instance, most pop songs go something like intro-verse-chorus-verse-chorus-bridge-chorus-end. Most of the highest grossing films of all time are superhero movies or sequels. How many versions of TV shows like *CSI*, *Law & Order*, or *The Real Housewives* are there?

Popular music, TV and movies are part of a bigger consumer cultural machine based on a deceptive sense of choice. They called this the **culture industry** and argued that the sameness and shallowness of the cultural forms it created helped to destroy the revolutionary potential of the working class by creating a superficial sense of choice, what Adorno called **pseudo-individualisation**. Think about when you are in a supermarket and there is a whole row of washing detergents, which are basically the same product in different coloured boxes. Or the endless sequels, prequels and remakes in the film industry. Really, how different is each iteration of the iPhone? Are these examples of real choice?

Marcuse makes the distinction between **false and true needs**, where everyday life is depoliticised, people's ability for critical thought is stunted, and we become one-dimensional people. The mass media, particularly the advertising industry, shapes the way that people engage with society and shapes their sense of what they 'need'. We are pushed towards making 'choices' in a pre-packaged culture that valorises consumption and we are less able to think deeply about politics, ethics, morality and equality. Algorithmic social media and the mining of big data take these processes even further, to levels that even Marcuse probably could not have imagined.

For Marcuse, the 'bastardisation' of language has been central to this overall process. He argued that the language for critical thought, let alone analysis and action, was disappearing as language had become debased and actual meaning sanitised (he was thinking about advertising or corporate ways of speaking, through euphemism, hyperbole or empty terminology). The diminishing of our ability to speak clearly means that dissent is short circuited; we don't have the right language for criticism or for expressing horror. The euphemisms of war are prime examples of this: 'collateral damage', 'friendly fire', 'smart bombs'. If someone on the red carpet at a celebrity event like the Oscars can have their ballgown described in the media as an 'atrocity', how can we maintain a language to describe real atrocities such as war crimes and genocide?

Critical Sociology and the Media

The media, how it creates content, how we respond and who owns and controls the major outlets is a well-established area of research for sociologists attempting to understand how culture shapes morality, language and, therefore, how we relate to each other. For instance, most news networks and TV stations claim objectivity, that they just report the facts, but generally, multinational media corporations have been shown to favour the interests of big business and conservative governments. For instance, in the UK, USA and Australia, there has been concern about the influence and dominance of media outlets owned by Rupert Murdoch on the democratic process, understanding climate change and on the spread of Islamophobia. This fits with Marcuse's claim that the media manufactures consensus, misinforming and distracting the populace to make decisions and behave in ways that are actually to their own economic and existential detriment. For example, crime and deviance are a constant presence in the media but they may be deliberately focusing our anger on the wrong places. The way news media frames a story is a subtle way that bias creeps into reporting. For instance, when Hurricane Katrina occurred around the Gulf Coast of the USA in 2005, reporting of white people wading through the floodwaters to take food from supermarkets was reported through the lens of survival. When it was African Americans, they were framed as 'looting'.

A British sociologist named Stanley Cohen examined the way the media can frame particular issues through a process he called **moral panic**. He focused on young people, who are often carrying the symbolic weight of hopes and fears for the future within social groups. He noted that moral panics are rarely created out of thin air, but have a basis, however tenuous, in events. Something happens, for example a fight between two groups of young people, but the scale of the event and its likely recurrence is wildly exaggerated by the media and the police. Cohen did not say that this was a deliberate exaggeration but did note that a successful moral panic draws readers and viewers for the media, and extra resources for the police.

Cohen analysed the media coverage of a famous 'riot' between two groups of young people called the Mods and Rockers on Brighton beach in the UK, in 1964. He showed that the apparent threat from these groups was largely created by the way police responded to a group of working-class young men, with police threatening and goading a group of young people who dressed spectacularly and frequented the streets, and by media sensationalism about the group, so that it seemed to the young people involved that turning up to fight was the right and fun thing to do.

While based on exaggeration, moral panics are not completely made up. They are another example of a **self-fulfilling prophecy**. There is media exploitation via sensationalism, dramatisation and escalation, along with stereotyping. Predictions of the 'deviance' support calls for increased enforcement of existing laws and the creation of new legal constraints. The initial reaction then has a **polarisation effect**, as the so-called 'offenders' do not like the way they have been represented and react with further 'deviance', which dovetails with further, often inaccurate and frenzied, reportage. The latter step in effect confirms the stereotype for the general community. Here, the initial, usually conservative and ill-informed social reaction is 'proven' by the 'deviant's,' own reactions to the original misconception.

Moral panics might also be changing in our globalised world, particularly with the rise of digital technologies. When Stanley Cohen was doing his foundational study on moral panics, it was a time of newspapers and TV news bulletins. In introducing the concept, he noted that moral panics appeared in society intermittently. Some suggest that we now live in a permanent state of media-encouraged panic. Recent work on Islamophobia is a good example of this. Angela McRobbie and Sarah Thornton, two British sociologists of culture, argue that while moral panics may have once been an unintended outcome, or at least unconscious, they now seem to be the explicit goal for journalists, aiming to create sensation and garner clicks to websites.

More recently, a key problem in our engagement with the media, both the older forms of news and TV but also the newer developments of how we access information through the internet and social media, is how to know what is real information and what has become known as 'fake news'. An irony here is that at a time where we have access to more information than ever before at our fingertips through our mobile phones, we do not have more certainty on what is true or real. In fact, this information overload may lead to more misunderstanding, disinformation and manipulation of what we think than ever before.

French sociologist Jean Baudrillard developed ideas about this in the 1960s and 70s, arguing that even in that time of much simpler media it was difficult for people to tell what was real and what was fake. The media tends to rely on the spectacular because it is an industry relying on profit, and more people are likely to watch if there are explosions, violence, or sport. For example, a news story on a car crash where no one is injured may not be reported on, but if there is a video of the crash it will make the news just so the spectacular footage can be played. For Baudrillard, the media at the time he was writing was creating its own reality, with the spectacular taking over from the 'real'. Baudrillard uses the example that, on election night, many more people will watch a football match being broadcast than the coverage of the election. These changes towards the spectacular correspond with ever more media in our lives. Baudrillard argued that there is so much media in our lives that it has become impossible to know what is real and what is fake. A classic example is when CNN in the USA in 1991 crossed to Kuwait to get a report of what was happening in the 'Gulf War', and the reporter turned around on live TV to reveal that he was watching TV news to get the information to report back to America. This example looks quaint today compared to algorithmic social media feeds, election manipulations and presidents firing off tweets that rarely seem to relate to reality. Where the media once 'reflected' society, for Baudrillard we now live in a hall of mirrors where information just bounces around with no connection to a 'reality' outside of other media.

But importantly, unlike the Marxists who argue that this situation creates ideology rendering people as dupes, Baudrillard argues that this is actually what people want, that we crave spectacle and that maybe, instead of a revolution, what we are all collectively taking part in is what he called a 'fatal strategy'. Deep down we may want to see revolutionary change, as it is the ultimate spectacle, but rather than 'go to the barricades', which takes considerable risk and effort, we will just consume more and more until our social systems and environment are overloaded and it all comes crashing down. At the time, many thought Baudrillard was being playfully ironic, but looking around at climate change-induced bushfires and hurricanes and a reality-TV US President, maybe Baudrillard, who died in 2007, was ahead of his time.

The Global Culture of Consumer Capitalism

Baudrillard postulated that we may consume ourselves to death. As the critical theorists recognised, sustained resistance to the culture of capitalism seems to be difficult, even if classical Marxist theory thought that it was likely. Drawing on Weber, the American sociologist George Ritzer has characterised the spread of this culture around the world as **McDonaldisation**. He sees the principles that drove this hamburger chain of fast-food restaurants as coming to dominate not just the economy but also the culture, not only of the USA, but of the world.

McDonaldisation is not just about eating American-style hamburgers, or even consuming American products and culture. It is driven by a push for ever greater 'efficient' systemisation, control over the workforce and production process. It is not only our eating that has been transformed using these principles but the media, health care, cultural products and even education. Education from primary school to university increasingly looks the same from Kuala Lumpur to Chicago, with similar pedagogies, classroom layouts, assessments and subject contents.

Weber claimed that modernity was characterised by a relentless drive towards 'rational' efficiency in every aspect of our lives. Ritzer draws on this to point to four main interlinked components of McDonaldisation: efficiency, calculability, predictability and control. These processes may lead to what Ritzer calls the 'irrationality of rationality'. For example, as health systems become increasingly rationalised in the economic sense, their funding is cut, staff numbers decrease, and doctors and nurses have to do more with less. This can mean that waiting lists for surgery lengthen and emergency units are closed, basically ensuring the unnecessary death of some people.

Ritzer acknowledges certain benefits and conveniences from McDonaldisation. Yet, like Weber whom he draws upon, Ritzer sees this rationalisation becoming an **iron cage** that would provide a seductive sense of control while also becoming ultimately dehumanising and destructive of important cultural differences. As the search for standardisation across the globe comes into tension with the connection many have to their local culture, there are often small accommodations to the local context, but these are relatively minor. McDonald's restaurants, for example, often adapt some local cuisines into their menu, serving noodles in Asia, non-beef burgers in India, and the 'McOz' burger (with beetroot) in Australia.

French sociologists Luc Boltanski and Eve Chiapello have recently highlighted the way that the culture of capitalism is dynamic and, also building on Weber, argue that a 'new spirit of capitalism' emerged over the last decades of the 20th century. Remember that Weber saw the spirit of capitalism becoming an inflexible bureaucratic structure. Boltanski and Chiapello propose that fewer of us in countries that have moved away from manufacturing factory work are constantly watched by a supervisor. Instead, even if we are employed by others, we're encouraged to think and act like an 'entrepreneur' and hustle to reach our targets in different ways. We seem to have a relative 'freedom' at work, with more and more people even working at home, but many of our jobs are less secure, and if we are not successful in our 'entrepreneurialism' we can more easily lose our job. This also relates to art and creativity.

As Angela McRobbie shows, the demand to 'be creative' instils a performance of creativity at work that aligns with the market demands of cheap labour, flexibility, internships, and individualised entrepreneurialism. As more and more jobs demand you to be creative and embrace aesthetics and media production, Boltanski and Chiapello argue that the 'artistic critique' of capitalism has been co-opted and folded back into its very logic. For instance, graffiti was once scrawled on the walls in cities as a form of defiance by marginalised people, but now that aesthetic has been co-opted and appears in advertising. 'Do-It-Yourself' was once the motto of punk scenes around the world who strived to escape the culture industry by making their own records or holding gigs in squats or car parks. Now 'DIY' is more associated with renovating a house, especially in reality TV shows.

This work on the new spirit of capitalism was undertaken in the late 20th century. Today it is more difficult to argue that we are subject to less surveillance at work than in the past. The rise of digital data collection, social media and smart phones seems to have given a new shape to work and non-work culture as we move towards what has been called **platform capitalism**. Platforms are digital tools that connect different groups together using data, dominated by Facebook and Google, Amazon and Uber. Working or studying at home does not necessarily lead to more free time or fewer meetings, but more time spent on Zoom or Microsoft Teams. These companies rely on collecting data about us and using this to connect people together and people with services or advertisers.

New technologies bring new opportunities in terms of keeping in touch with people, working with others across distances, finding information, and connecting with values and cultures. But they also potentially destroy privacy, exposing us to the influence of hackers, data theft and algorithmic bias and providing new ways for us to be tracked and our actions manipulated, including by employers and advertisers. Increasingly this seems to mean that more people will work for people as a service provider through the platform, driving their taxis or delivering their products, without having the rights of an employee, in the so-called '**gig economy**'. A culture that claims to be celebrating entrepreneurism and freedom is actually promoting surveillance and insecurity.

Culture and Autonomy

You may have noticed the critical approaches above seem to follow Marx in giving the economic structure the defining role in shaping culture, even as they look to show how cultural factors intervene to stop otherwise inevitable structural changes flowing from capitalism. Or follow Weber in arguing that economic rationalisation that may have originally had cultural roots now overwhelms cultural differences. At the same time as **critical theory** approaches were reshaping the sociology of culture, in America, sociologist Jeffrey Alexander was developing a different approach building on Durkheim, what he called a *strong* version of the turn towards culture in sociology. Alexander acknowledged that many sociologists had studied culture in the past but argued that others, including the Frankfurt School, tended to reduce culture to the effect of something else, the class structure of society, or the effect of the institutions making up society. He called this the sociology of culture and called instead for a **cultural sociology** that recognised culture as central to all social life and an autonomous, fundamental aspect of what makes us human.

In the late 1960s many countries experienced social upheaval linked to clashes over morals and values, with some groups challenging the norms of their society. The American sociologist John Milton Yinger called the groups making these challenges a **counterculture**. These struggles helped sociologists see culture as not just a reflection of society, but capable of changing society. In Britain a number of sociologists, including Richard Hoggart and Stuart Hall, developed approaches focused on investigating how people produce and interpret culture, not just receive or inherit it.

Even if the culture industry helps create particular dominant meanings, we cannot take for granted how people interpret the culture they consume. **Semiotics** is the name for the academic approach that attempts to uncover the meanings, myths and connotations present in the consumption of symbols and images, such as the way a punk-Mohawk, appropriated from Native Americans, has connotations of aggression or rebellion that go beyond just being a haircut. Cultural items are encoded with particular myths and meaning. But Stuart Hall highlighted that individuals then must decode these meanings; they need to read the myths and meaning built into an object, and then interpret them from their own perspective. Hall calls the creation and then interpretation of meaning in texts **encoding** and **decoding**. For instance, for some people a pair of Nike shoes may symbolise coolness or athleticism. Some may associate the shoes with specific people such as Serena Williams or Michael Jordan. These kinds of readings are what Nike would want, and they spend millions of dollars encoding their products to try to do so. But others may decode the Nike shoe as symbolising sweatshops and exploitation, criticising the ways the shoes are produced. In this one everyday example of a popular shoe brand, we can see how cultural products can be a tool of ideology, or be used to resist and to uncover that ideology.

Hall, with Hoggart, led the Centre for Contemporary Cultural Studies (CCCS) at the University of Birmingham, sometimes referred to as the **Birmingham School**. Scholars associated with the centre focused on understanding the multiple subcultures that exist alongside a dominant culture, showing how subcultures are related to age, class and ethnicity, and, more recently, gender. Along with Alexander in the USA, these scholars led the push for cultural studies to become a central part of sociology.

The Birmingham School developed a theory of **subculture** building on earlier approaches to thinking about differences within a dominant culture. Sociologists working in the USA in the first half of the 20th century had studied 'gangs' in large cities to understand the sociological foundation of these groupings, countering influential understandings of gangs as a collection of individuals with psychological failings. Instead, sociologists such as Frederic Thrasher, E. Franklin Frazier and William Foote Whyte argued, in different ways, that youth gangs were collective responses to 'disorganised' social structures linked to rapid social change, immigration and the legacy of slavery. Gangs provided a way for young people to create a sense of coherence, to have 'fun', and even a route to meet their basic material needs when other legitimate avenues to do so were not available due to racism and inequality.

Another American sociologist, Albert Cohen, developed and popularised the concept of subculture in the mid-20th century, again in relation to understanding young people in gangs. He drew on these earlier ideas but also developed and challenged Robert Merton's **strain theory** of gangs (and criminal activity widely). Merton saw gangs as part of a broader culture. Gang members valued the same cultural products as the rest of society but had their access to them limited by prejudice and inequality, so pursued illegal means to access them. Cohen argued instead that gangs were the result of the emergence of a new set of values when people came together due to shared circumstances and a particular set of unmet needs. They were not just using different means to reach the same ends, but were a separate culture with different aims, contained within a 'mainstream' culture.

The Birmingham School linked this theory of subcultures back to a critical theory focus on class. They were heavily influenced by research on working-class youth subcultures in London by Phil Cohen. (Phil is not related to Albert or to Stanley Cohen, who developed the concept of moral panic – it can be hard not to confuse your Cohens when learning about the sociology of subcultures!). Phil Cohen combined an understanding that subcultures were formed in opposition to mainstream culture, with the argument that a second relation was with the class culture of the members' parents (we discuss class in detail in the next chapter). The cultural response of young people who are part of youth subcultures are neither the pursuit of illegitimate means towards mainstream goals nor a unique set of cultural values. Instead, Phil Cohen argued that young people use culture to symbolically or 'magically' overcome the inequities faced by their working-class parents through creating an oppositional style.

Affiliates of the Birmingham School – including Dick Hebdige, Paul Willis, and Angela McRobbie – used these ideas to rework the concept of popular culture as a product of the dominant ideology. They identified certain groups taking part in 'positive mass consumption', where spectacular youth practices and forms of pleasurable consumption are an opportunity for subordinated groups of young people to resist dominant norms. This is often done through the practice of **bricolage**, which involves 'tinkering' with cultural products and icons – borrowing, combining, recombining, discarding, altering, embellishing, inventing, synthesising – to create something new. Examples include culture jamming, skateboarding in carparks, graffiti, and sampling in music.

You can see that the Birmingham School had a much more positive attitude towards popular culture than the Frankfurt School. They illustrate how popular culture can be as much an opportunity for creativity and critique as a place of distractions and consumption. Yet, a major critique of subcultural understandings argues that youth cultures might not necessarily be a symbolic challenge to the wider culture as the Birmingham School interpret them to be, but a way of creating a measure of autonomy to live within it.

Culture and Identity

Culture is more than the dominant or contested ideologies of the powerful. It is more than high and popular cultural production and consumption. It includes our sense of self and how our understanding of the groups we are part of shapes us. This is called our **cultural identity**. Culture also includes the way we walk, the way we talk and even our posture (which, in our case, isn't great, given how long we spent hunched at the computer working on this book). In other words, culture is more than symbolic meaning and material cultural products, it is embodied in the ways we speak, move and behave. This can give us a sense of self but is also used in the process of creating **distinctions** between groups.

We are pretty confident that you don't need to be told not to roll your earwax into a ball and flick it at someone at a dinner party, or to be told not to pick your nose and eat it. The intervention of our parents and others while we were very young teaches us these basic cultural norms. It seems obvious that an earwax fight over dinner is not ok, but it has not always been so obvious. Arguably the most famous early work in the sociology of culture was by the German sociologist Norbert Elias. In the 1930s, Elias wrote a book tracing the history of changes in what was culturally acceptable behaviour in Europe over 1000 years, from about 800 to 1900 AD. Elias used many examples from books meant for the education of high-status members of society during the Middle Ages, explicitly giving advice and rules for actions that we now take for granted as inappropriate.

While it may now go without saying, 500 years ago there were books counselling against blowing your nose on the tablecloth, picking your teeth with the sharp end of a knife over dinner, and against spitting, defecating, urinating and scratching your testicles in public (okay, maybe there are a few who still need to be reminded about this one). Elias quotes from an etiquette guide from 1477 that gave the following sage advice: 'Belch thou near to no man's face with a corrupt fumosity, for that swerves from courtesy.'

You might see these kinds of guides as part of an effort to build a better society, more aware of the comforts of others. Today we might need similar guides about etiquette for using mobile phones. Elias is not so sure these guides are so benign. He sees this **civilising process** as an effort by powerful groups in society to use culture to separate themselves from others. In the elite strata of European society, so-called court society based around the households of monarchs and nobles, the rules for behaviour became increasingly extreme. An extraordinarily complicated set of rules for court behaviour developed and needed to be learned, so that by the 19th century very complex rules governed who ate first, the way food was eaten and with which numerous pieces of cutlery. These ever more complex rules governing behaviour were part of efforts to build a sense of superiority over others, as the earlier rules (such as not flicking earwax at each other) spread beyond nobility to broader society.

After reading the above, you might be daydreaming about being a rich noble in the 15th century. While you might have to deal with the occasional unwanted belch, you are probably picturing a life of plenty. But you almost certainly own more things, have a greater variety of food and access to more information than even kings and queens of centuries passed. These rulers would have had vastly more than their subjects, but consumer goods were time-consuming and expensive to produce, putting limits on even the richest. Until around 1400 and the first printing presses, all books were individually produced, mostly written out by hand. Only the wealthiest would own a book and only a very limited number of texts would have been considered worth the effort (we hope you're enjoying reading this one and find it useful but are willing to concede we might not have made the cut if someone had to copy the whole thing out by hand). Now most of us can access many billions of texts instantly on the smartphone in our pockets. This is one of the new affordances of our digital society.

One of the first sociologists to highlight consumer culture and its role in identity processes was Thorstein Veblen. Writing about the North American 'new rich' who had made their money in the expanding economy at the end of the 19th century, Veblen argued that they were using their new-found wealth to engage in what he called **conspicuous consumption**, aimed at demonstrating status by showing the capacity to spend and consume. Veblen had in mind status-related goods and activities, like owning a yacht and the right clothes and equipment to go with it. From this perspective, it is not really a love of sailing that drew people to such purchases, but a desire to display their wealth and prestige, including through their access to free time for leisure that poorer people simply do not have.

Veblen focused on the newly wealthy class of Americans, but it is not only the wealthiest that do this. For people across the globe and in different cultures, in wealthy and poor countries or neighbourhoods, there is evidence of efforts to stand out relative to those around us using consumer goods as evidence of success and cultural superiority. As consumer culture expands, as well as concern about the impacts of overconsumption, the way we consume or actively avoid consuming things has become an increasingly central part of our identities.

Culture, Difference and Hybridity

We wrote above that we were pretty confident that you don't need to be told not to pick your nose and eat it. What would you say if we told you that there is evidence that picking your nose and eating it might have positive health effects? A study has shown that doing so might improve your immune system. Why would a society have a taboo against something that might be good for you?

In Chapter 5, we discussed Foucault's work around **discourse** and the construction of what is 'normal' and how some practices and even some identities can come to be labelled as abnormal, weird or deviant. Norms and rules are important. A set of shared expectations allows us to live together and achieve more than we could on our own. This is why many of us find the breaking of implicit or explicit rules threatening, at least to some extent, and most support some form of legal institutions, including police, law courts and prisons, to intervene in the more serious types of deviance. Yet, what counts as normal, deviant, disgusting or illegal is not given or natural but varies across cultures, and people within a culture can disagree.

Some people are disgusted by eating dogs, where others are disgusted by eating pigs. Some countries have laws where they kill their own people with the 'death penalty' and some have outlawed that practice. Not everyone agrees on what is right or wrong, but not everyone has an equal say in defining deviance. As we saw in the previous chapter, some people get labelled as deviant when others do not, even if they engage in the same practices. In other words, negative identity labels come to be associated with some people. Labelling not only affects individuals. A group can also be labelled a threat to social values. Hopefully you are making a connection to the above discussion of moral panics, and the decisive role that the media plays in this process.

Sociologists have shown that a person's cultural identity can have multiple affiliations at once. Self-identity can relate to where we are from, our generation, our ethnic background, class and gender or any other collective that we think of as having elements of culture that are its own, including the subcultural groups we discussed above. It is clear we can each have multiple cultural affinities. This also means that many of us find a way to weave together seemingly incompatible cultural affiliations.

Remember that Weber thought that the Protestant Ethic had the (ironic) unintended consequence, when it was institutionalised, of disenchanting the world (diminishing religious thinking). While many societies do seem to be relatively secular (non-religious) compared to the past, the Canadian social theorist Charles Taylor points out this is not a world where religion and enchanted thinking have disappeared. He defines secularity as a context where one religion does not dominate, and religious worldviews as a whole do not dominate the way we live anymore. In the previous chapter and above we discussed the rise of digital communication technologies, which are reshaping culture alongside identity. It has put huge amounts of new information literally in our hands (on our phones) available at the click of a button. This can help break down traditional cultural authorities. But no single authority takes its place. Instead secularisation or a lack of faith might become, according to Taylor, just one possibility among many, which people might need to choose between or juggle. For Taylor and other sociologists, we inhabit a context of curious new hybrid cultures of faith, consumer culture and non-religious thinking that we can draw on in our own lives.

In previous chapters we introduced the idea of **hybridity** and **border thinking**. This can be helpful in understanding this mixing but a note of caution is required. Power is central to thinking about culture, just as it is to thinking about the self and identity. Even if most of us juggle some contradictions and have multiple cultural belongings, this does not mean that we are treated equally in our lives. Someone living near their hometown in England that has a grandmother from Spain and is really into both football and punk music is not living a hybrid cultural identity in the same way as someone juggling multiple minority identities while trying to find work in a foreign city. We will cover this in some detail in the coming chapters.

Conclusion

Culture is at the heart of how we live our lives. It is embedded in what we wear and consume, what we like, our values and our language. It shapes profoundly what we understand as good or bad; moral or immoral; normal or abnormal; and even what can be considered art. Culture provides the common source of meaning we need to live our lives with others and to build an identity. But we do not just take culture as it is given to us by our parents or by the media; we actively produce and interpret culture depending on needs and desires. Engaging with culture is a wonderful part of being human. But as we show in other chapters, cultural elements map onto nationalism, how we define deviance and difference, and are experienced very differently depending on one's class, gender and ethnicity. Culture therefore plays a central role in how the world is made unequal.

In this chapter we have seen how many 20th-century scholars of culture drew on a Marxist lens to understand popular culture, using this to present us as **cultural dupes**, naively following what those in power want us to do and even what they want us to enjoy. The general approach these scholars developed, called **critical theory**, aiming to understand the deep barriers to building a better world for all, and how these barriers can be overcome, continues to animate the work of many sociologists even if they do not agree with the idea of the cultural dupe. And the ideas of these critical theorists continue to influence how sociologists think about mass media.

We saw alternatives to this critical approach, including scholars who turned for inspiration to some of Durkheim's very last works, where he focused on how religion and culture helped cement the feeling of belonging to a group. Drawing on accounts of the rituals of Indigenous Australian groups, Durkheim proposed that taking part in a group can lead to a sense of collective effervescence, an excited feeling of being part of something bigger than ourselves.

Today we would include quasi-religious experiences such as dancing at a club or going to the stadium to cheer for a team alongside traditional religious experiences as examples of this collective experience.

We also saw the way in which a dominant culture might face a counterculture, or subcultures that have been understood as having different values to the wider culture. Examples of subcultures include punks, goths, mods, rockers, riot grrrls, ravers, even football hooligans. More recently there are Bronies (Adult Fans of My Little Pony), Roller Derby and many other groups us 40-something authors have no idea about. Some of the readers of these books – maybe even you – might be into these cultures or heavily involved in one or more communities formed around them. You might think they are a bit of fun, or more subversive than that, a type of political resistance to the mainstream.

However, as the Birmingham School in their work on subcultures highlighted, and as before them the critical theorists had already recognised, resistance within capitalism is difficult. The culture of capitalism has proven remarkably capable of incorporating different values, including values that seem antithetical to capitalism. Resistance is appropriated, as capitalism itself changes.

McRobbie and other feminist sociologists have highlighted issues with the Birmingham School approach to subculture and their theorizing of how subcultures can be understood as a form of class resistance. The (mostly) men who developed the approach tended to focus on young men involved in the most spectacular types of youth culture (think punks with mohawks, piercings, torn clothes and spectacularly loud music with offensive lyrics). The types of subcultures that might give women a more central role, and may develop less spectacular practices while still creating new or oppositional norms, were ignored in this approach.

The types of subcultures the Birmingham School scholars had in mind also seemed to preclude a sense of belonging to the mainstream culture or other subcultural groups concurrently for members of a youth subculture. In this chapter and the previous, we have seen how our sense of belonging and our sense of self are deeply social and complex. You can love sociology (and hopefully like this book), while being a keen participant in Roller Derby or a regular at K-Pop gigs. Our cultural affiliations are multiple, but this does not mean that we are all treated equally or that nothing more can be said about how culture and cultural identities are linked to inequality. In the coming chapters we turn in detail to how sociologists approach gender, race and class.

Key references for this chapter

Adorno, T (1991) *The Culture Industry: Selected Essays on Mass Culture*. Routledge.

Alexander, JC (2003) *The Meanings of Social Life: A Cultural Sociology*. Oxford University Press.

Althusser, L (2001) 'Ideology and Ideological State Apparatuses', in *Lenin and Philosophy and other Essays*, trans. B Brewster. Monthly Review Press, pp. 85–126.

Bellah, RN (1967) 'Civil Religion in America', *Journal of the American Academy of Arts and Sciences*, vol. 96, no. 1, pp. 1–21.

Boltanski, L and Chiapello, E (2005) *The New Spirit of Capitalism*. Verso.

Cohen, AK (1955) *Delinquent Boys: The Culture of the Gang*. Free Press.

Cohen, P (1972) *Sub-cultural Conflict and Working Class Community. Working Papers in Cultural Studies, no. 2*. University of Birmingham.

Cohen, S (2011) *Folk Devils and Moral Panics: The Creation of Mods and Rockers*. Routledge.

Durkheim, E (1915) *The Elementary Forms of the Religious Life*. George Allen & Unwin.

Durkheim, E (1933) *The Division of Labour in Society*. Free Press.

Elias, N (1978) *The Civilizing Process*. Urizen Books.

Gramsci, A (1971) *Selections from the Prison Notebooks of Antonio Gramsci*. International Publishers.

Hall, S (1993) 'Encoding/Decoding', in During, S (ed.) *The Cultural Studies Reader*. Routledge, pp. 507–517.

Marcuse, H (1991) *One-dimensional Man: Studies in the Ideology of Advanced Industrial Society*. Routledge.

Marx, K (1970) *Critique of Hegel's 'Philosophy of Right'*, trans. A Jolin and J O'Malley. Cambridge University Press.

McRobbie, A (2016) *Be Creative: Making a Living in the New Culture Industries*. Polity Press.

McRobbie, A and Thornton, SL (1995) 'Rethinking "Moral Panic" for Multi-Mediated Social Worlds', *The British Journal of Sociology*, vol. 46, no. 4, pp. 559–574.

Merton, R (1938) 'Social Structure and Anomie', *American Sociological Review*, vol. 3, no. 5, pp. 672–683.

Ritzer, G (2009) *The McDonaldization of Society*. Pine Forge Press.

Taylor, C (2007) *A Secular Age*. The Belknap Press of Harvard University Press.

Thrasher, FM (1936) *The Gang: A Study of 1313 Gangs in Chicago*. University of Chicago Press.

Veblen, T (1899) *Theory of the Leisure Class: An Economic Study in the Evolution of Institutions*. MacMillan.

Weber, M (1946) *From Max Weber: Essays in Sociology*. Oxford University Press.

Weber, M (1958) *The Protestant Ethic and the Spirit of Capitalism*. Charles Scribner's Sons.

Whyte, WF (1943) *Street Corner Society: The Social Structure of an Italian Slum*. University of Chicago Press.

Yinger, JM (1982) *Countercultures: The Promise and Peril of a World Turned Upside Down*. The Free Press.

7

CLASS

If you have been reading this book through from the beginning, it might be time to sneak off to the fridge for that snack that we mentioned right at the start. Most of us do not grow our own food, so it is likely that the snack will be bought from a shop. Most of us do not know how to make our own clothes or to build a house. If you are like us, you wouldn't last long without buying key necessities from others. Some of us feel we could not 'survive' without our smart phones, or access to the latest music and fashion. These things are far from being necessities but have come to feel like they are. Without supermarkets, malls and the internet, many of us would quickly find ourselves at first bored, and then hungry and shabbily clothed.

In terms of survival and flourishing, humans rely on the skills of other humans, ever more complex technology, and a system for producing and distributing the things we need that is now global in scale. Our access to the goods and services produced in this great network of production is not through altruism, charity or reciprocity. Today we are part of a global capitalist system of private ownership and gain access to most of the things we use through a **market economy**, where what is available and at what price is driven by competition between private businesses.

In Chapter 2 we described one of the central questions that shaped the emergence of sociology as how capitalism as an economic system shaped societies and relationships. It is still a central question today. Sociology was born in the wake of what Karl Polanyi called the **great transformation** in how we produce and consume. A large part of this transformation was new ways of making goods, where the emergence of mechanical and chemical production processes allowed **production** on a much grander scale than previously possible, in factories and mines, shipyards and mills. The emergence and spread of these new production processes is called the **Industrial Revolution**. After the Second World War, as consumer culture expanded due in part to the increased disposable income of the middle classes, the notion of **consumption** became an important area of analysis as well (as discussed in Chapter 6).

Our *relationships to each other* in this production process, in the market economy, and in the way we consume goods and services are the foundations of what sociologists call **class.** Sociologists define class in different ways, as we will see in this chapter, but all the definitions refer to how access to wealth or income impacts on access to education, jobs, health, and the possibility of having a life free of material deprivation. In other words, our economic resources shape our life chances relative to others, which sociologists call **socio-economic**

stratification. Increasingly, class is also analysed in cultural and symbolic terms as well as focusing on how much wealth, income or **economic power** people have. This highlights how tastes, morals and values that are produced through class relations reinforce economic stratifications.

Do We Need Economic Inequality?

Some sociologists have argued that differences in stratification in terms of income and wealth may be good for society to help it function. In Chapter 2 we showed how Émile Durkheim believed that growing specialisation and difference between people's role in production, what he called the **division of labour**, could be beneficial for a society. Yet, Durkheim did not believe that large levels of material inequality were particularly functional and hoped that sociology could help shape the social world to decrease economic inequality, particularly through informing the creation of universal education systems and industrial regulations. He saw government intervention as essential for providing **equality of opportunity** and for making sure that people found the most appropriate role in the production process.

Some sociologists who have followed in this functional approach have, however, tried to develop a theory of the function of economic inequality. Kingsley Davis and Wilbert Moore believed that economic inequality is a **functional necessity**. They argued that some positions in the division of labour are more important to society's functioning and reproduction than others, and these important roles must be filled by qualified people. These jobs are also seen to be more difficult and carry greater responsibility. To motivate people to take on more difficult roles that require greater skills and training, the market or some other mechanism must offer them greater rewards.

The argument for the functional necessity of inequality has been challenged by others because the evidence suggests that economic reward is not distributed in this **meritocratic** way. CEOs of medium-sized enterprises often earn much more than prime ministers and presidents. Teachers, nurses and garbage collectors, seemingly essential to the functioning of society, are paid much less than professional football players, or most other professionals for that matter. There is significant evidence that the equality of opportunity Durkheim saw as essential to a successful modern division of labour has not been achieved. Wealth and family background, not ability, is a greater predictor of university access in most parts of the world. Meritocracy meets a **class ceiling**, as many studies show that those who take up the most important positions, or even those most likely to gain access to important professions, come from privileged backgrounds.

Wealth and Privilege

Class is not just about disadvantage – it is about advantage and privilege as well. **Wealth** is defined as income from investments, ownership of productive assets, salaries, bonuses, shares and property. But wealth is difficult to accurately measure because of offshore banking and trust funds. Many wealthy people disguise their true worth; unlike welfare recipients, they have the power to do so. There is a group of extremely wealthy global citizens that Leslie

Sklair called the **transnational capitalist class** who hide immense sums of money. It is estimated that about one quarter of all global wealth is hidden, more than the annual GDP of the USA. It was widely reported in 2018 that the richest eight people in the world now own as much wealth as the bottom 50 per cent of the world's population. Despite constant media stories about 'self-made millionaires', much wealth is passed down from generation to generation and is not 'earned' in the way that the self-made stories portray.

Political proponents of neoliberal capitalism argue that rising wealth for the privileged few is good for everyone due to what has become known as the 'trickle-down effect': when the living standards of the very rich rise, they bring everyone else up with them. Critics say that this is an ideology that hides the reality of the consequences of inequality. Wealthy 'Global North' countries do have higher standards of living based on economic growth. But this ignores power relations within and between societies, between capital and workers, between the included and the excluded, and the exploitation of workers in the 'Global South' (discussed in Chapter 4). Many recent studies show that there is a social cost of increasing inequality in income and wealth, both within and between countries. This is reflected in health and mortality outcomes (lower life expectancy, higher rates of addictions, depression, stress, work injuries, obesity); higher rates of social problems (higher crime, lower rates of literacy and trust); and the unsustainable impact on the environment (not everyone can consume at the same rate as the industrialised countries as there are not enough resources). We will come back to wealth at the end of this chapter.

Class Conflict

Most sociologists of class highlight how patterns of socio-economic stratification are the result of exploitation and power inequalities that are not natural or necessary. As we saw in Chapter 2, Marx saw capitalism as a system of struggle, with the primary division between the **bourgeoisie** and the **proletariat**. The bourgeoisie or ruling class own what he called the means of production. Marx proposed that the seeming production of profit from money invested, or from exchanging money and goods, is an illusion: it is actually the product of other people's labour, that of the proletariat or working class. Workers are paid less for their time than the value they produce in that time, even accounting for all the other costs of production. It is this unpaid time that creates **surplus value**, the source of profit. A good example of this is in the COVID-19 pandemic. While media presents economic growth and profit as resulting from the apparent innovations and entrepreneurialism of the genius owners of businesses and companies, as soon as large sections of the population stopped going to work, productivity and economic growth plummeted. It is the labour of everyday workers that drives economies and profit.

So why do employees put up with all this apparent exploitation? Firstly, they are dependent on a wage. The working class is everyone who must work for wages because they have no other choice. They do not necessarily need to work for any particular owner (depending on the availability of jobs), but they must work for someone, or they will starve. They are 'wage slaves' in that all they own to sell is their labour. A less than full rate of employment also stops workers from rebelling by establishing a **reserve army of labour**, the unemployed who could take the current employees' jobs. Marx also referred to what he called the **petty**

bourgeoisie, the 'middle class', such as small business owners and managers, as a social group who were in some senses exploited but also the enforcers of exploitative conditions on others. This category was marginal to his analysis as he saw it shrinking as a small number moved up to become capitalists proper, while most would eventually sink into the working class.

Marx's original theory of class relations was ironically idealistic in the sense that he foresaw a system that would create so much inequality and **alienation** that it would lead to revolution, and to what he proposed as a better social system: communism. More recent theorists influenced by Marx point out that capitalism has not progressed by giving workers subsistence wages as Marx predicted; it has progressed by rewarding them with the joys and spectacles of consumption, but this produces its own problems. Most of us do not feel we are proletarian workers – we did not all become miserable impoverished factory workers – and fewer and fewer people, at least in the Minority World, do manual labour. Many readers of this book will now or one day own cars, live in nice houses and apartments, and shop and have holidays, despite being part of what Marx saw as the working class. Many working-class people in countries such as Australia, the UK and the USA self-identify as 'middle class'. This is especially the case as the categories of working-class jobs that have increased in number are in the service industries – not making things anymore, as that production has moved to the Majority World, but serving coffee, cleaning houses and working in call centres.

Class and Culture

Other theories of class can help us see why the class structure and the potential for the rise of a working-class revolution are more complicated than Marx suggested. Recent theories of class often draw on developments made by Weber, which emphasised cultural aspects of class. Where Marx focused on production, Weber brings in consumption as a disseminator of class inequality. Many possible factors make up what Weber called the **market situation**, which includes the relationships between labour power, inheritance of property and business, acquisition of skills and education, organisation of unions and professional accreditation, and gender, race and ethnicity, religion, and age.

Weber argued that there were more than two classes, because there were more than two market situations:

- propertied classes (ruling class, owners of property, factories and companies);
- the intelligentsia (professionals, highly educated 'white collar' workers, professionals such as doctors and lawyers);
- the petty bourgeoisie (small businesses, family farms, self-employed tradesmen, shopkeepers);
- the working class (which itself was divided between well-organised occupations such as miners and skilled trades, and factory workers, casual workers);
- the unemployed.

Although almost all of us are forced to work for a living, some of us are paid more or have better conditions because of particular qualifications or because of unions negotiating pay and conditions for us. Some workers manage other workers. In other words, quite a lot of us fall somewhere in between being completely controlled by owners and bosses on whom we rely to get paid and being completely in control ourselves.

Importantly, Weber introduced the idea of **status** into class analysis as a distinct form of stratification, to highlight the importance of interactions and relationships with each other, and therefore how class needs to be thought about beyond the economic. Status involves who you identify with, what people think of you, and what you think of others. It is often associated with a person's job, where white collar professional workers such as doctors and lawyers are seen to have more status than blue collar manual workers such as tradespeople or cleaners. Further, people make distinctions between the 'nouveau riche' and 'old money' or between the dignified, 'respectable' working class and the undeserving. You can be highly educated and living in poverty. You can be very wealthy and like football and beer rather than opera. This will all affect your social standing (Weber used the term 'honour') and your access to future economic opportunities. For Weber, status similarities were more closely linked to shared consciousness than market situation alone.

Weber also introduced the idea of **party** to help highlight how the ways we associate and organise with other people is closely linked to class but has some independence in that a party, in Weber's terms, will organise around a specific goal. People can organise politically around status groups and values independently from their market position. Here, the complexity of voting intention at elections can be understood; people only imperfectly vote along their economic interests, and often seem to vote against them.

While Marx theorised economic determinism, Weber built on and contested this understanding of class, providing instead an analysis of life chances and power related to but not reducible to market situation. Both continue to influence the sociology of class today. Since Marx and Weber developed their thoughts about class, many sociologists have tried to combine and clarify elements of these two approaches to develop more sophisticated ways of measuring class. Class means a lot of different things to different people (and different sociologists), but if we can agree on a way to measure it, we can see how stratified a society is and how much social mobility is possible in people's working lives or across generations. To categorise people's class position, many sociologists have focused on **occupation**, the category of job a person has. Probably the most well know schemes for measuring class were developed by John Goldthorpe working in the Weberian tradition in the UK and Erik Olin Wright working in the Marxist tradition in the USA. They both built models to focus not just on ordering different jobs into a hierarchy based on status and income, but attempted to merge income, status, autonomy and power at work into one measure.

Cultural Capital

The way sociologists think about and measure class has become more sophisticated, but many sociologists believe these scales still miss something essential to understanding the mechanisms of class relations. Probably the most influential contemporary theory of class was developed by Pierre Bourdieu, a French sociologist who we introduced in Chapter 5 for his model of the way self and society are intertwined in the **habitus**. Like Marx, he gives primacy to material relations, but like Weber, he brings to the fore concerns for status and how cultural formations have relative autonomy from and influence on economic position. He adds cultural and symbolic dimensions, only indirectly related to paid employment, into our understandings of class.

For Bourdieu, people are symbolisers, as much as they are producers or consumers. Social relations take place in different contexts that have their own rules, norms and common sense. He uses the concept of **field** to understand these different contexts, in that we do not participate in all of society at once. It is impossible. Fields therefore are specific social contexts that have their own set of rules and stakes that people compete over. Major examples are education, the labour market, legal systems, media, science, and politics – what other sociologists may call institutions.

Fields have their own **illusio**, that is, the emotional investment in competing for the rewards and stakes of a field. Bourdieu does not mean that these rewards are an illusion but that they are socially constructed as humans must create meaning in their lives, and then invest themselves in those meanings, otherwise we would be faced with nihilistic existential horrors! For example, in the field of art, one may be trying to make an anti-capitalist statement rather than pursuing money and fame, although sometimes the two can cynically go together. Fields are not completely independent of each other and economic logics shape all fields to some degree. But they have their own logic as well. In the arts it can be a normal thing not to want to make money as it might be seen as 'selling out', in a way that would not make sense in other fields.

For Bourdieu there are two distinct systems of social hierarchisation. The first is economic, in which position and power are determined by money and property, the economic capital one owns. The second system is symbolic, where positions are determined by how much cultural or symbolic 'capital' a person possesses. **Cultural capital** consists of capacities that enable one to be successful in a specific field. The already privileged tend to possess or are at least familiar with this type of cultural knowhow because they have influence over what is socially defined as normal, legitimate, tasteful, cool or moral within important fields. They have also had the greatest opportunities to develop this knowledge as they were growing up. People with more cultural capital have the ability to make the world in their own image.

Cultural capital includes having good institutional credentials, owning the right things, considered high status in that field (whether it's clothes or computers, or – we'd like to think – this book in the context of sociology), knowing technical terminologies, and understanding how to 'act' in a specific social situation.

In other words, ideas of taste are used within social groups to create **distinctions** between people. One of Bourdieu's most famous quotes is 'taste classifies, and it classifies the classifier'. You might feel like the type of music you like is objectively the best but, according to Bourdieu, tastes are not objectively better or worse than each other, but we define ourselves and we limit or are limited by our tastes. Imagine you meet someone who tells you they like Justin Bieber. You will then instantly make assumptions about them based on what you think of Justin Bieber. If you are a fan, you are more likely to feel an affinity with the person; if you are not a 'Belieber', you are less likely. Importantly, though, your opinion of Bieber in that moment is also a way to categorise you. When you make categorisations, they also categorise you. For Bourdieu, people's tastes – their likes and dislikes – are related to their class position, and people use taste in deciding whether people are like them or not.

You surely feel more comfortable in some social situations than others. Bourdieu uses the notion of habitus, which we introduced in Chapter 5, to help us understand why. As a reminder, habitus is our personal way of seeing and sensing the world. Bourdieu liked to use sporting metaphors. If we metaphorically treat life as a game, habitus is the 'feel for the game'. Some people have learned to perform well and feel comfortable on the field, without having to consciously think about it. In fact, if you start to think too much about what you are doing while playing, your performance will suffer. We learn this sense of comfort as we grow up. Our feel for the game is heavily influenced by where we live, what our parents do, what school we go to and so on. You are likely to be better at the game if your parents were players and coaches, your friends all played, and the game was commonly played where you live. If you did not have this upbringing and find yourself playing a game with those who did, their superior 'feel for the game' might lead you to decide quickly that the game is not for you.

Networks and Social Capital

Our habitus affects our ability to 'fit in' and 'get on'. It links to the distinctions we make with 'taste'. Exclusive brands and classy restaurants; dress codes and membership of clubs; particular kinds of décor, food and atmosphere are used to create hierarchies. As we've discussed, some have the embodied skills and knowledge to feel comfortable in these places; others do not. Those less privileged often exclude themselves, because 'that's not for the likes of us'. This reinforces class systems because the already privileged are the ones to define what is good or bad, legal or illegal, tasteful or vulgar, which is actually reinforcing their own world view. This solidifies networks of people with the same taste. Bourdieu and other sociologists refer to the resources such networks provide as **social capital**. Many sociologists point out that different types of networks provide different resources. The American sociologist Mark Granovetter famously suggested that for getting a job it was the **strength of weak ties** that matters. Having a large network of acquaintances is how many people hear about job opportunities, get someone to recommend them to that employer, and often land the job when the boss finds out that they have a network in common. Relatedly, some social scientists distinguish between **bonding social capital** and **bridging social capital**. Bonding social capital is that provided by tight connections to close others – think family or family-like connections. Bridging capital is more like Granovetter's weak ties, in this case ties that link you in with other groups or places (a different neighbourhood or ethnic group) to which you are less closely aligned.

You might be thinking that some of your closest friends might not be much help in getting a job, you might even think some are more of a bad influence on you. If your networks tie you into obligations, expectations or even opportunities that lead to you getting arrested, for example, or mean that you have to turn down a great job, these can hardly be thought of as a positive. One of the benefits of using Bourdieu's framework for thinking about social capital is that it might help us see the dark side of connections and networks as they are often exclusionary. We can see that even social capital that does benefit the individual might be at the expense of others and that social capital, along with cultural capital, gives some people unfair advantages that go beyond differences in income and wealth.

Why Does Fitting in Matter?

Whether or not they have the 'feel for the game' shapes the way people reach high positions in important fields (art, legal, academia, politics, business, science, media and others). We can also use these ideas to think about who feels at home in higher education, something with clear consequences for people's futures.

The British sociologist of education Diane Reay has used Bourdieu's concepts to look at the experience of young people transitioning to an elite university. She undertook a study of the experiences of people who were the first in their family in tertiary education or from a working-class background who attended one of the most prestigious universities in England. The field of higher education, and this university in particular, is an unfamiliar field where their habitus should not fit. Bourdieu suggested that such experiences would be uncomfortable but could transform the habitus, creating a habitus that felt split or divided against itself. The students did experience what the authors call the 'shock of the elite'. Part of the shock was a lack of social fit, as the researchers were expecting. They were not expecting the degree of anxiety about academic performance given the level of achievement in high school that the participants needed to gain entry to such a university in the first place. Reay and her colleagues suggest the participants lacked the background to feel and narrate an assured sense of belonging intellectually.

Reay's work suggests, however, that the shock of a new field can be overstated and that participants found a comfort in acceptance of academic effort that they had not necessarily found in secondary school. The students felt less like a fish out of water at university than at school, as where their academic achievement was rarely recognised or understood. Because of the lack of fit with others at secondary school, the participants seemed to have started early in their lives to develop strategies for dealing with feeling like a 'fish out of water' through what sociologists call reflexivity (as we introduced in earlier chapters).

They partially accepted the idea of meritocracy in accounting for success, while at the same time recognising the stratified experience of advantage based on background. The participants thought of their university as not the 'real world' and were critical of it for this, but nonetheless directed their reflexive energies at conforming to middle-class educational norms. They did not, however, experience a wholesale escape from their previous life, but made an active effort to hold on to parts of their older self in an effort to avoiding getting lost in the elite 'unreal' bubble (for example, wanting to do particular types of professional work to help others). Reay and colleagues argue that their research participants were engaged in acts of invention that were not needed by their middle-class counterparts. The students had managed tensions between habitus and field since early in childhood. In this context, reflexivity itself becomes a type of disposition.

Everyone experiences social discomfort at times where they do not feel that they fit in. But for those in denigrated or disadvantaged social positions, they can experience these distinctions as a form of social suffering. Bourdieu argues this can be damaging in a similar way to the suffering caused by physical violence, calling it **symbolic violence**. As we saw in the example above about attending an elite university, our educational institutions are created to fit with some dispositions, while others are forced to learn to be someone else to navigate these places. Many people from the working class avoid going to art galleries, not necessarily because they do not like art, but because they feel they do not have the technical expertise to view the art 'properly'. Symbolic violence is also disseminated through language, where some people can use words better than others, but also in the way that people with more cultural capital get to define how words are used. For instance, the way the term 'ethnic' is used in the media to apply only to minorities, not just different cultural groups. In Australia, refugees have been referred to as 'queue jumpers', which misrepresents their actual situation, implying that there is an actual queue to join, and places a negative value assessment on them.

Bourdieu shows how the processes of socialisation provide us with a way of seeing, feeling and sensing the world, but as with the example of working-class students at an elite university, we shouldn't think that this means our lives are totally determined by who our parents are and where we grow up. Humans create meaning in their lives and invest themselves in that meaning. This is part of what it means to be human. Bourdieu highlights, however, that this sets the foundation for social struggles that are more than just economic. Bourdieu brings status to the fore in understanding culture, where taste, morals and values become a way of making hierarchies and classifications, and where cultural capital is central to success in whatever fields we participate in.

Cultural Formations of Class

This work on taste and dispositions has been key to developing understandings of the relational, symbolic and cultural aspects of class, where the different ways we interact with different people is how class is made and reproduced on a daily basis. For instance, there is an array of terms used to describe the 'wrong' kind of white poor people across the globe who are positioned as having bad taste and morals. You may have heard or even used some of these yourself and they vary from place to place, for instance, chav (UK), redneck and white trash (USA) and bogan (Australia). Another term used to describe people is hipster, for those with more middle-class interests and associated with well-kept moustaches and beards, obscure music, obsessions with coffee or artisanal beers, crafting and other retro-oriented practices. Terms such as chav, bogan and hipster have become quintessential ways of talking about and positioning people in relation to consumer cultures.

When written about in newspapers, magazines or on the internet, hipsters are criticised, but it tends to be in a comedic or ironic way that sees the term often used quite playfully. On the other hand, through processes of symbolic violence, the figures of bogan or chav have rapidly become a key and voiceless cultural folk devil. They both enable distinction to be performed while eschewing the very notion of class. Why is this the case? Well, those writing these stories are people with positions in the media and tend to be from middle-class backgrounds that have a lot of cultural capital. Their own values, morals and cultural tastes will cross over a lot more with the hipster than they will with the chav, redneck or the bogan. Therefore, when writing about those below them in status – people not like them – it tends to be more pejorative, expressing disgust. When writing about people similar in status and with similar tastes, the writing is more analytical and empathetic even when it is gently making fun of a group. This small example shows how in day-to-day practices and communication, class is present in how people relate to each other, even if it is not something that is talked about openly.

British sociologist Imogen Tyler has called the figurative usage of these kinds of labels, along with racial and gendered stereotypes such as 'pramface' single mothers, 'gypsies' and asylum seekers as **revolting subjects**, positioned by those in power as revolting (in the sense of provoking disgust) to elicit political responses, but, importantly, once these labels are applied, those who suffer the symbolic violence can use the label to organise and revolt against this kind of marginalisation.

These relations of disgust connect to the notion of distinction. Many studies show how people relate to each other, or don't, through their likes and dislikes. For instance, research shows that heavy metal is one of the most hated genres of popular music but is one of the most liked by working-class men. The noise and aggression are off-putting for an apparently discerning disposition but attractive to young men to express disaffection and frustration. Across an array of studies on the lives of young disadvantaged women and on an audience's reception of reality TV, Beverley Skeggs and colleagues have shown the classed nature of value and moral judgements that are often directed towards young disadvantaged women. '**Femininity**' in this sense is still framed from a middle-class perspective, which Stephanie Lawler calls the **disgusted subject**. What she means here is that middle-class women often tend to define themselves as what they are not and show condescending even disgusted attitudes towards women who don't have the means to keep up with latest fashions, go to 'good' schools, or replicate middle-class 'helicopter parenting'.

Recently, the distinction between high culture (opera, literature, art galleries, theatre) and popular culture (films, TV, pop music, games) seems to have become less marked as all people across class groupings appear to be engaging with the same types of pop culture. However, *how* people consume is as an important marker that people use to make class distinctions as *what* people consume. For instance, Skeggs and colleagues found that their research participants seemed to be performing a version of themselves in their interviews where middle-class participants were likely to feign embarrassment about watching the shows, even though they knew a lot about them and seemed to actively enjoy them. This ironic distance is a reflexive performance to show how a person of good taste 'knows' that reality TV is trash but can still enjoy it and be critical. These middle-class women juxtaposed their own consumption against how they perceived others would consume the shows uncritically, positioning other reality TV fans like a cultural dupe (as discussed in Chapter 6) as a way of distinguishing oneself within popular culture consumption.

Globalisation and Class

Throughout much of the 20th century, sociologists were mostly concerned about class within a specific nation-state. But how can we understand class in a globalising world? As shown in Chapter 4, whether by democracy, design, seduction or force, since the end of the Second World War many countries that were on the periphery of the world system and former colonies of Western nations have created economies and patterns of consumption similar to those in the **Minority World**. While inequality between countries is still stark, on some measures it has flattened and even slightly improved in the past 15 years. This is driven by countries like China and India entering the world economic system. The **Majority World** nations of the Asia-Pacific are about to be home to the majority of the world's middle class. Yet overall global inequality appears to have increased because of growing differences between people within countries. There is still a huge citizenship premium; the poorest 10 per cent of

Australians, Americans or Germans are still richer than all but the very wealthiest people in India. It remains unlikely but increasingly possible to be socially mobile, and even to make a lot of money in the Majority World, but across the Minority and Majority World the gap between the richest and the rest within countries appears to be growing.

There are many new ways of thinking about class and inequality globally, and many of them draw on the concept of networks discussed previously. Manuel Castells uses the terms net-workers, the networked and the 'switched off', where capitalism is now about the production and control of information, rather than controlling the material means of production. Zygmunt Bauman metaphorically compares global tourists and vagabonds (those who can freely move and do, and those who are forced to move and suffer the consequence), showing how global capitalism produces billions of 'wasted lives' and 'collateral casualties of consumer-ism', where the ground constantly moves below their feet (metaphorically), but they have nowhere to go. Similarly, John Urry has shown how mobility is a new way to think about inequality, that is, some people are able to move around the world much more freely than others based on what he calls **network capital**, which is having the right documents, skin colour and connections. Loïc Wacquant has detailed the development of huge inequalities within rich nations where 'urban outcasts' experience 'advanced marginality' in ghettos that are emerging even in wealthy countries, which respond by criminalising poverty.

These new ways of thinking about inequality globally, challenge sociologists to think about economic inequality anew. In the chapters following this one, we will say more about gender and race and how they shape inequalities. Foreshadowing these chapters, it is worth noting that many sociologists believe an understanding of the working of capitalism and the creation of classes cannot be complete without understanding gender inequality and racism. Such analysis has a long history, particularly tied to scholars building on Marx, but from within a feminist or racial lens.

In attempting to understand racism in the USA, the American sociologist Oliver Cromwell Cox challenged a prevalent understanding of racism as an example of a common tendency towards favouring the in-group, our own community or ethnicity, or as a type of individual prejudice. Instead, racism could only be understood through understanding its role in capitalism. For Cox, colonialism and slavery were part of the way capitalism created its dynamic accumulation. For Cox, slavery was not a moral failing within a particular culture, like that of America in the 1700s. At its heart, slavery and the racism that justified it was about finding enough labour to exploit the potential to make money from the significant natural endowment of America.

As we saw in Chapter 3, early sociology did not properly confront racism and colonialism. Of the thinkers now seen as foundational for sociology, Marx was arguably the most explicit in his acknowledgement of colonial exploitation and at points spoke about its relationship to capital accumulation. However, his foundational model of relations of production moving through four stages, from primitive societies to ancient slave societies to feudal societies and then, in certain parts of the world, to capitalist, meant that he had to see slavery as a holdover from a previous economic form, slowly being replaced by a logic built around capitalists and workers that would eventually homogenise the working class. Cox and others argued that racism and then ongoing antagonisms between groups of workers that had come to see themselves as in opposite racial groups was not an older type of social interaction on its way out but used and encouraged in the growth of a capitalist system.

Relatedly, the Italian scholar Silvia Federici challenges Marx's claim that primitive accumulation (the first stage of building wealth, before feudalism and capitalism can be established, which is based on the more powerful taking things) has been superseded by capitalism where exploitation is based on who owns the means of production and the power to underpay people for their work. Instead, she argues capitalism cannot survive only through taking surplus from paid labour. It still relies on labour that it does not pay for at all. She focuses on the role of women in reproducing society, including the work of reproducing the next generation, and their oversized role in care and maintenance of the family group. The outcome of this is not just that women do work that is not paid that is at the heart of maintaining the economic system, it also affects women's opportunities in paid work. The British sociologist Sylvia Walby shows how men dominate the jobs with the highest remuneration while women are much more likely to be found in part-time and low-paid work. Walby argues that this context of unequal care responsiblities pushes women to 'choose' part-time work or no paid work at all.

For Federici, the growth of capitalism has only been possible because the web of inequalities it produces are naturalised and obscured through culture, turned into understandings of naturalised differences between different types of bodies that are classed, raced and gendered. In her influential book *Caliban and the Witch*, Federici looks closely at historical documents about the witch hunts of the 17th century to argue that they were not the vestiges of a previous religious and patriarchal order that would be overturned by capitalism, but an effort to use culture and violence to push women into the new role as the unpaid reproductive labourers of the emerging capitalist system. Caliban, a central character in Shakespeare's play *The Tempest*, is used to highlight the portrayal of colonised people. In the play, Caliban is the dark-skinned son of a witch. Federici, Cox and others have argued that straight theft, the taking of things of value based on treating some people as less human than others, plays a more important role in capitalism than even its greatest critics had realised.

Today, wealth is seemingly ever more polarised. Casualised labour and job insecurity are increasingly the norm and owning a home is becoming out of reach, even for some in the middle classes in many countries. Patterns of work that used to be characteristic of the labour market in the Majority World are becoming widespread in the Minority World. Guy Standing has developed an argument for what he calls the **precariat**, a new global class of people who are faced with casual, short-term and underpaid work, if they can get any work at all. This is exacerbated by the rise of the so-called **sharing** and **gig economies**, where companies like Uber, Airbnb and Airtasker do not consider their workers employees but contractors, while ever more people are reliant on credit to get by.

French economist Thomas Piketty has shown that the assumption that as economies grow there would be less inequality is not the case, but in fact the opposite seems to be true at least within countries, with the Minority World countries currently having levels of inequality not seen since the late 1800s. Piketty argues that unless something is done we will be returning to a world where the super-rich form an even more out of touch elite, their children will inherit more and more, concentrating wealth regardless of the performance of the economy.

Conclusion

What is the impact of class today? Some sociologists have claimed that class is a less useful concept than it used to be, pointing to the apparent embourgeoisement of the working class, and the decline in **class consciousness** and class-based politics and the growing recognition of other powerful inequalities within social groups. Another critique is that class is an analysis that happens within countries, yet inequality is now driven by global forces over which individual nation-states have little control. While it is hard to measure and can be defined in different ways, quantitative research consistently shows that economic inequality is increasing, and qualitative research shows that many people bearing the brunt of rapid social change are impoverished, economically and emotionally. This economic inequality is also closely intertwined with cultural and social processes that help buttress class differences.

As noted, we will say more about how sociologists think about race and gender and other dynamics of discrimination and inequality in the coming chapters. In this chapter we have focused on the way the allocation of resources in our economy shapes our lives and creates what sociologists call class dynamics. In the final sections of the chapter, we have focused on globalisation and feminist and colonial critiques of class theories focused on the division between classes within a particular country. The British sociologist Satnam Virdee has argued recently that sociology must give colonialism the central place in our theories of contemporary society that it deserves, but in turn we cannot ignore that capitalism and class have their own dynamic that have some independence from colonial logics and through which colonialism also needs to be understood.

Related to the importance of **border thinking** we described in earlier chapters, Virdee argues that colonial dynamics unfolded across the world, and cultures, languages and people were destroyed as other nation-states were created, not just as Europe colonised other parts of the world but within Europe as well. For Virdee, there are different modalities of racism. Colour and colonialism are central to these dynamics, but they cannot be reduced to this. He points out that a risk within postcolonial frameworks is that Europe and whiteness are homogenised. This limits our ability as sociologists to understand the multiple routes through which inequalities, economic and otherwise, are made. To understand racism without understanding how these processes are related to capitalism is, for Virdee, to risk underestimating the material but also shifting force of racism in the past and in our contemporary moment. Understanding class, and how it is entangled with race and gender but not reducible to them, is a vital way of understanding how the world works. We pursue this further in the coming chapters.

———————— Key references for this chapter ————————

Bauman, Z (2004) *Wasted Lives: Modernity and Its Outcasts*. Polity Press.

Bourdieu, P (2010) *Distinction: A Social Critique of the Judgement of Taste*, trans. R Nice. Routledge.

Bourdieu, P and Wacquant, L (1992) *An Invitation to Reflexive Sociology*. University of Chicago Press.

Castells, M (2000) 'Towards a Sociology of the Network Society', *Contemporary Sociology*, vol. 29, no. 5, pp. 693–699.

Cox, OC (1959) *Caste, Class and Race: A Study in Social Dynamics*. Monthly Review Press.

Davis, K and Moore, W (1945) 'Some Principles of Stratification', *American Sociological Review*, vol. 10, no. 2. pp. 242–249.

Federici, S (2004) *Caliban and the Witch*. Autonomedia.

Friedman S and Lauriston, D (2020) *The Class Ceiling: Why it Pays to be Privileged*. Policy Press.

Goldthorpe, JH (2000) 'Social Class and the Differentiation of Employment Contracts', in *On Sociology: Numbers, Narratives, and the Integration of Research and Theory*. Oxford University Press, pp. 206–229.

Granovetter, M (1973) 'The Strength of Weak Ties', *American Journal of Sociology*, vol. 78, no. 6, 1360–1380.

Lawler, S (2005) 'Disgusted Subjects: The Making of Middle-Class Identities', *The Sociological Review*, vol. 53, no. 3, pp. 429–446.

Marx, K (1987) *Capital: A Critique of Political Economy, Vol. 1*, trans. B Fowkes. Penguin Books.

Picketty, T (2013) *Capital in the Twenty-First Century*. Harvard University Press.

Polanyi, K (1944) *The Great Transformation*. Farrar & Rinehart.

Putnam, RD (2000) *Bowling Alone*. Simon & Schuster.

Reay, D, Crozier, G and Clayton, J (2009) '"Strangers in paradise"? Working-class students in elite universities', *Sociology*, vol. 43, no. 6, pp. 1103–1121.

Skeggs, B and Wood, H (2012) *Reacting to Reality Television: Performance, Audience, and Value*. Routledge.

Sklair, L (2000) 'The Transnational Capitalist Class and the Discourse of Globalization', *Cambridge Review of International Affairs*, vol. 14, no. 1, pp. 67–85.

Standing, G (2011) *The Precariat: The New Dangerous Class*. Bloomsbury Academic.

Sweetman, P (2003) 'Twenty-first Century Dis-Ease? Habitual Reflexivity or the Reflexive Habitus', *The Sociological Review*, vol. 51, no. 4, pp. 528–549.

Tyler, I (2013) *Revolting Subjects: Social Abjection and Resistance in Neoliberal Britain*. Zed Books.

Urry, J (2007) *Mobilities*. Polity Press.

Virdee, S (2019) 'Racialized Capitalism: An Account of Its Contested Origins and Consolidation', *The Sociological Review*, vol. 67, no. 1, pp. 3–27.

Walby, S (1986) *Patriarchy at Work: Patriarchal and Capitalist Relations in Employment*. Polity Press.

Weber, M (1978) *Economy and Society: An Outline of Interpretive Sociology*. University of California Press.

Wright, EO (1985) *Classes*. New Left Books.

8

SEX, GENDER AND SEXUALITY

There is a good chance you are reading this book for a class at university. As we noted at the beginning of Chapter 2, a generation ago university attendance was much rarer than today. Men also vastly outnumbered women in universities until recently. However, women now outnumber men in universities throughout much of the world. This is one way in which the lives of women have changed radically over the past half century. There has been significant progress, but these changes have not been uniform across all places, or even within universities. Some areas of study still have more men than women, for example in computer engineering, and these areas tend to have higher graduate salaries. In the growing number of places where women are now more qualified than men, they are still paid less on average than men, even for doing the same job. The new opportunities in education for young women *en masse* have not flowed into equity in employment participation rates or remuneration.

There has been considerable progress in terms of equality for women, particularly since the mid-20th century. Yet there is a long way to go before anything like equality could actually be claimed as being a reality. International research is almost unanimous in identifying gender-based inequalities at work, in the home, in public life and media representation. These hierarchies and inequalities in status between men and women are also seen by sociologists as helping to underpin violence in our societies. This chapter outlines some of the fundamental concepts we need to understand one of the most predominant and ongoing of social inequalities, highlighting both the significant changes that have occurred over time, and the way men and women continue to live unequal lives.

Sex and Gender

One way to think sociologically about gender and how it is constructed is to distinguish it from sex. '**Sex**' denotes the biologically referenced categories such as male, female or intersex, including primary and secondary sex characteristics. **Gender**, including **femininity** and **masculinity**, is instead used to signify cultural traits that are associated with each sex. Simone de Beauvoir, a French philosopher, provided the most influential formulation of the power of these gender norms in her book *The Second Sex*. She argues that 'One is not born, but rather becomes, a woman'. What this means is that the effects of gendered socialization are so powerful, and shape us so profoundly, that they appear as if they could only be natural. But they are not.

Sociologists of gender focus on how our socialisation as gendered people shapes belonging to groups with particular norms and values that are encouraged and even enforced, and how we often come to think of these norms as natural. Sociologists continually point out that if differences between the genders were as 'natural' as some claim, then social groups would not need to work so hard to produce these differences, through clothing, hair and other forms of bodily presentation, and to police them. If such differences were indeed based on nothing but sex categories, the time and energy spent worrying about their transgression would make little sense; it would be like legislating to stop meerkats from forming rock bands. Gender theorists question why there is so much anxiety about policing gendered behaviour if the differences are 'natural'. The answer is that they are not just biological but deeply social as well.

Sociological approaches to gender such as this unfold in the context of long-running nature/nurture debates. Some emphasise 'nature', arguing that who we are is based on our biology, our genes or our hormones. Others emphasise 'nurture', illustrating how are we impelled to learn to take on 'normal' roles and traits through socially and culturally constructed means of custom, habits and knowledge. Today, most scholars across disciplines will acknowledge a role for and interaction between nature and nurture, biology and culture. Sociologists tend to emphasise nurture, not denying biological differences, but seeing them as working in tandem with social and cultural factors.

Whatever the features of our biology, the impacts of this are heavily mediated by the way we are treated by those around us, that is, in our social interaction. The different treatment of boys and girls starts from birth. 'It's a girl' or 'it's a boy' is one of the first things proclaimed about us in many cultures, before we even have a name. This can be seen in the rise of so-called 'gender reveal' stunts and parties. A consistent body of research has shown that our parents, aunts and uncles, and even complete strangers will behave differently towards us – give us greater autonomy, be rougher or gentler in their interactions, stricter or more lenient, and often give us very different toys – based on our assigned sex, treating us differently from the moment we are born. In fact, thanks to technologies of ultrasound the sex of a baby is often known well before the baby is born, and there is some evidence that people act differently towards the mother and are more or less likely to direct comments directly towards the foetus (talking to the baby in-utero), based on whether they are assigned male or female, even before birth. There is no 'natural' reason to give boy children toy cars and girl children Barbie dolls or dress them in blue or pink. This is how we begin to be made into gendered selves.

Gender Roles and the Family

While it is likely impossible to find a sociologist who believes differences between the genders are entirely natural, some influential sociologists have defended the existence and even importance of a strong separation of roles between men and women. Talcott Parsons, arguably the most influential sociologist of his time in the mid-20th century, argued in a defence of the status quo between women and men at that time. In the American society that Parsons was analysing, he maintained that there were important instrumental and expressive differences built around gender lines and that the functioning of society should be built around the nuclear family. He saw the **expressive role** of wife/mother caring for the family as largely complementary to the one of the husband/father who provided for the (**instrumental**) financial needs of the family. In his view, such complementary roles held the nuclear family together and provided for the socialisation of children (to one day take up such roles themselves). Engaging with Parsons, the American historian and sociologist Christopher Lasch saw the nuclear family, and the caring role it can play, as providing a moral foundation even in a dysfunctional society. Writing in the 1970s, he saw rampant consumerism, individualism and competition as leading to fragmentation, and a culture of narcissism, with self-centredness and short-term wants putting pressure on relationships and social institutions. The nuclear family could, however, provide a type of 'haven in a heartless world'.

Lasch and even Parsons did not think that biology *caused* gender roles to emerge. Lasch thought fathers could play a caring role in the family and Parsons believed that while women were in a sense predisposed towards an 'expressive role' through childbirth and breastfeeding, that this predisposition was greatly heightened in societies with a nuclear family, as the role of caregiver is more discrete. He also saw the division as facilitated by the way young boys would learn to identify with their fathers and girls with their mothers, helping to prepare them for their own later occupation of these same roles. For Parsons these institutions and roles were not wholly natural but were valuable to the smooth functioning of society and fitted with the preferences people held and were socialised into in modern societies. This perspective was challenged by many other sociologists and has been largely discredited. De Beauvoir, along with decades of feminist sociological research since the mid-20th century, has highlighted the **sexist** assumptions that underpinned this theory of different roles. These functionalist claims have been thoroughly critiqued in sociology, but such ideas still exist in society broadly.

Gender Inequality

As far back as Simone de Beauvoir's work on the 'second sex', feminist sociologists have been highlighting that the division of roles for men and women is not neutral or complementary but part of reproducing and reinforcing a broad and long-lasting system of **patriarchy**, a society ruled by an elite group of older men over younger men and all women, that serves the general interests of men. Patriarchy literally means the rule of the father. Carole Pateman argues that many theories that emphasise society as a type of **social contract** that benefits all of us ignore an implicit agreement (a contract in this sense) between men to share power over women that lies at the heart of modern societies. Sylvia Walby has shown how patriarchy continues to pervade all the major social institutions. Women overall have less political power and are more likely to suffer physical, sexual and verbal abuse from their partner on top of being paid less, and being underrepresented in public forums such as politics, news media and the culture industries, and having an unequal share of household and caring responsibilities. For Walby such **gender-based violence**, violence connected to the norms and power differentials that have been attached to gender, are ubiquitous in society. Walby argues that sociology in the past did not pay enough attention to this, seeing violence as an issue for other disciplines or, if they did focus on violence, looking at violence in 'public' or directly perpetrated in the name of the state or groups. Yet as Walby highlights, the direct perpetrator is in many cases not a stranger but a family member, intimate partner or friend.

Sociologists who analyse patriarchy do not argue that every man is in a dominant position over every woman in each circumstance. It is always possible to find examples of women doing well in patriarchal societies; a queen or president or prime minister who is a woman may still hold powerful positions in a patriarchal society. The point is that in patriarchal settings the activities and traits associated with men and masculinity are considered superior to things that are categorised the domain of women or categorised as feminine. These beliefs are institutionalised in rules and expectations that favour men. With this in mind, sociology itself is not immune to gender-based critique. Ann Oakley argues that sociological modes of thinking, its methods, concepts and objects of study made it one of the most sexist academic disciplines in the 20th century, as it posited the male orientation on the world as the orientation of sociology.

Critiques of the patriarchy, and the way it makes women into a category of people with fewer rights, was a catalyst for the second-wave feminist movement (we say more about these waves later in the chapter). This second-wave brought a broader agenda than what was then called first-wave feminism, which had pursued formal legal equality in voting and property rights. **First-wave feminism** was exemplified by the movement for **suffrage** (including the suffragists and suffragettes), who fought for voting rights for women in the late 19th and early 20th century. One of the leaders of the women's suffrage (right to vote) movement in the United States was sociologist Jane Addams. She believed that sociological ideas should be used to change the world and was an engaged activist. Firstly, Addams helped provide leisure activities, housing and education to new immigrant women in Chicago. This contributed to founding modern social work. Then, as a leader of the international peace movement before and after the First World War, Addams highlighted the impact of conflict on women and children. For this work, in addition to her push for the right to vote, she was awarded the Nobel Peace Prize. This is a good example of where a lot of courage and hard work, and a little sociology, can take you.

Performing Gender

Second-wave feminism emerged after the Second World War and lasted roughly from the beginning of the 1960s through to the beginning of the 1980s. The feminist writing at this time illustrated the way that everyday experiences helped to shape gender, highlighting inequalities deeply embedded in the nuclear family, household division of labour and rights at work, and protection from harassment in public. As more and more women have moved into the workforce, sociologists have also highlighted the interaction of paid employment, unpaid household labour and care. Arlie Hochschild traces changes in the labour market in America and argues that the rise of 'service jobs' has made **emotional labour** more important in the workplace. This includes hospitality and retail employment, personal care and nursing, and counselling. One of the primary examples she gives is the work of flight attendants. These workers must manage their own emotions constantly, even when faced with unreasonable demands, while being paid to keep customers calm and happy in cramped conditions and through what is sometimes a bumpy ride.

Such management of the emotions of the self and others has long been associated with women, and increasingly people are being paid to do this work. The 'feminisation' of paid employment is one of the factors that has been reshaping gender in recent decades. This has opened up employment opportunities to more women, but this work is often underpaid and demanding. Managing your own and other people's emotions is draining. While more women have entered the paid work force, men have not shown an equal propensity to contribute more unpaid domestic labour. This leads to many women facing what Hochschild calls the **second shift**. Despite success in the labour market, the social expectation is still that women are responsible for the role of wife, mother and housekeeper. So, highlighting the limitation of thinking about gendered work through the lens of 'preferences', after a day or night of paid employment that often involves contributing some form of emotional labour, many women come home to a second shift of domestic labour.

Yet these unequal gender rules do not necessarily create great lives for men either. Many men cannot live up to the idealised 'masculine' traits that characterise patriarchal societies. Any man who cannot live up to this ideal is likely to view himself as inferior and incompetent. Raewyn Connell calls the most valued form of being a male **hegemonic masculinity**, bringing together cultural myths and stereotypes such as the hero, the leader, the stud, and the warrior, where men are represented as physically strong, rational, and emotionally distant. There is strong social and cultural pressure on males to achieve the presentation of a legitimate masculine heterosexual gender, and other forms of masculinity are devalued. The standard conventional norm of female behaviour is what Connell calls **emphasised femininity**, which includes a focus on caring and beauty, being emotional, and submission to men. The cultural myths and stereotypes that emphasise these conventions are the princess, the mother, and the virgin.

These stereotypes are built upon a set of simplistic binaries – strong/weak, rational/emotional – that help sustain gendered norms and attributes. In terms of sexuality, for instance, in many places it is accepted that men are seen to be 'active' while women are supposed to be 'passive'. Thinking with such binaries means that many possible practices and people are left out. These myths and stereotypes create pressures to conform to them and many of us work hard to try to meet these expectations, because to do so leads to social acceptance. Yet these binaries are unrealistic and impossible to live up to.

Erving Goffman, who we introduced in Chapter 5, studied the performance of identities as people work to present themselves in a way that fits with social norms, and the **stigma** of a failed identity. Writing about life in the mid-20th-century in the USA, he argued that in essence there is only one non-stigmatised identity: a young married white man, who is heterosexual, urban, a father, has a college education and is good at sport, is in full employment, and is of a 'normal' height, weight and complexion. As you can see, this list does not apply to many people and is quite unrealistic. But this is the norm that young men are meant to aspire to.

The American sociologists Candace West and Don Zimmerman write about gender as a performance. They add the concept of **sex category** to the sex/gender distinction. Sex category is the biological sex that people assume you are, separated from the sexual characteristics by which you are assigned a sex, or the way you identify as a gender. We are pushed to perform the right displays tied to these categories, and some of us are asked to do more than others to meet the societal expectations of how we are meant to 'do' gender.

Judith Butler, who we first introduced in Chapter 6, has been hugely influential in the way we now think about gender, theorising what we now call gender **performativity**. She famously argues that gender roles rely on the constant repetition of stylised acts over time, which socially constructs the 'essential' basis of gender. This gender performance is not really voluntary; you have to perform something to be recognised by others, and we are all 'taught our lines' or 'know the script' from early socialisation and subsequent social interaction. This allows people to perform a role accordingly in masculine or feminine ways.

By the 1980s, feminist theorists started to question the sex/gender distinction. Moira Gatens, an Australian feminist theorist, argued that it was based on too strong a distinction between mind and body, as if our body did not affect who we are or that our body was neutral and natural. Butler builds on this to argue that sexual difference is also the outcome of performances. The act of naming your sex that happened at birth was not itself a neutral act but itself a normative act: picking out your genitals as a defining feature of your existence, assuming that sex falls naturally into two categories, and that this will mean that your body, if you are a 'normal' boy or girl, will unfold in certain sexed ways.

Iris Marion-Young provides an example of the way that seemingly biological differences between sexes have a significant social overlay. She focuses on observations of how young women and men learn to throw a ball to argue that the way some of us might come to 'throw like a girl' does not have a biological basis. Young notes that girls have tended to be encouraged towards more sedentary and indoor play. They are less encouraged to engage in sport and develop particular skills, but her central argument does not come down to many girls simply having a lack of practice at throwing. Instead, it is that girls and boys are socialised and habituated into having a different bodily conduct.

Men learn to freely move through space, and to assume a right to take up space, while women learn the opposite. Men can throw their whole body into the action of throwing a ball, while women learn to feel that this is unnatural. We likely need men to learn to be less confident in space. Men learn from an early age that they can and should take up space, for example when they sit with their legs spread, colloquially known as 'man-spreading', often to the discomfort of the person trying to occupy the seat next to them on public transport. Women are more likely to learn to sit with their legs crossed taking up less space.

We mentioned above that we start treating people differently based on their assigned gender from birth. The American sociologist Karen Martin showed the process of making bodily differences is enacted in preschool classrooms in a **hidden curriculum**, which is the rules and values schools teach that are not explicitly policies or lessons. Children are made into boys and girls with bodily differences through differently enforced rules for sitting, talking, moving and dressing. This process continues throughout schooling and beyond.

Yet how men and women are socialised to use their bodies and move through space is shifting. For example, there are more and more professional women's sports leagues and TV broadcasts that are changing the way young women are encouraged to develop particular skills. However, if you read the comments on social media, women athletes and the women journalists and broadcasters who report on this sport must deal with continual sexist backlash – often from men who in almost every case likely cannot perform the sports as well as the women they are criticising. These men, and on occasions women, are exhibiting **misogyny**, a cultural attitude of prejudice towards women because they are women. Misogyny is the ideological accompaniment to a patriarchal society.

One of the structural factors that provides the grounds for us to challenge the gendered rules we face is that the performances of gender we are impelled to do inevitably fail. The perfect performance is seemingly impossible to pull off. Butler emphasises that this impossibility opens some opportunities for playing around with the edges of what is normal or not. Some people deliberately reject hegemonic masculinity or emphasised femininity, despite the stigma this may create, and through doing so open new possibilities and reduce this stigma. For instance, from Butler's perspective, a woman may not want to 'pass' as a man if she decides to dress in masculine coded attire. She is not 'imitating' men but creating a whole new gender category that is both resisting the dominant **discourses** and creating new ones. When someone coded as one sex imitates what is expected of the gendered performance of the other in an exaggerated way, it can bring to the fore the ways that *all* the accepted traits of gender are a kind of performance.

This sociological work on the *making* and the *doing* of gender can make it seem as if there is no choice but to play our gendered roles. However, these sociologists also show that there are possibilities for change to emerge and for resistance in people's performances. Indeed, things are changing. Male and female, man and women, are no longer the only recognised sex and gender categories. Intersex and transgender are long established scientific categories which are now rapidly gaining social recognition and legitimacy. 'Sex' itself is recognised as more than a hard binary, but it is still the categories of male and female which dominate common understandings of 'normal'.

Gender and Difference

Feminist debates have grappled with how to fight for women's rights if it is recognised that gender is complex and fluid and that there is likely no essence to gender that necessarily unites women across their many differences. This important point goes back a long time. In a published speech from the 1850s Sojourner Truth, an African American who had escaped from slavery and became a campaigner for both abolition and women's rights, asked 'Aint I a woman?'. She was highlighting that ideas about women circulating at that time never included Black women and that Black men often sided with white men when it came to questions of women's rights. Between then and now a whole tradition of **Black feminism** has emerged from scholars such as Audre Lorde questioning whether the tools developed by white feminists can make positive change for other women.

Patricia Hill Collins traces out this history of **Black feminist thought** in a book with that name, arguing that the actual lived experience of Black women must be central to such a tradition, but the world is too complex and categories too entwined with the social processes that created them to argue that it is only Black women who can contribute to the tradition. This tension recognises differences within categories that deeply shape our lives, and the way they have been used to shape and maintain inequalities, while also trying to avoid essentialising (naturalising) these differences. Managing such tensions is a challenge for the sociology of gender and really for sociology as a whole. We will discuss race and gender, and their intersections, further in the next chapter.

Race is only one of the factors that separate the experiences of different women. Others include levels of education and class. As we have noted, women's participation in education and employment has rapidly increased in the last few decades, not only transforming the lives of many women, but transforming education systems and labour markets as well. In some ways it is women who are seen as the poster children for a seemingly growing educational meritocracy, and the benefits of hard work. Media representations and advertising use the figure of the girl who can do everything as a new form of collective fantasy, where trendy lifestyles and upwardly mobile careers are becoming seen as the norm.

At the same time, the increasingly precarious and globalised labour markets in many places and areas of employment, especially the knowledge and service sectors, rely more and more on flexible young female workers who work casualised and irregular hours with low pay. The new shiny representation of what Anita Harris calls 'can-do' girls distorts the ways young women have been conceptualised as the ideal subjects of this new globalised precarious labour markets. The example presented of the 'can-do' girl is usually very privileged, has relatively wealthy parents, lives in the right place and has the right connections. But the unruly young woman, who does not know how to dress and how to 'behave', represents the opposite fantasy to the successful young woman, where class and ethnic stratification are obscured. Angela McRobbie has discussed what she calls post-feminist symbolic violence, where it seems to be acceptable to ridicule poor or working-class people in TV shows like *What Not to Wear*, where middle-class 'experts' come into the lives of working-class women to tell them all that they are doing 'wrong' (resonating with our discussion of revolting and disgusting subjects from the previous chapter).

McRobbie, Ros Gill and many others describe what they call **post-feminism**, which is a claim that feminism has done its job and is not needed any more. People taking this line both celebrate and repudiate the achievements of previous forms of feminism under the guise that the political work is done and that women are now empowered, and any further changes might risk 'going too far' and disadvantaging men. Such claims that women have been empowered rely on neoliberal values and a misplaced notion of meritocracy, where if women just work hard, and make the correct choices, they will have no problem achieving their ambitions. Sheryl Sandberg, the Chief Operating Officer of Facebook and tech billionaire, famously told women that they needed to 'lean in', to work harder, and wealth and success would be theirs. Think about whether you have seen any portrayals of women along these post-feminist lines. The women used as examples tend to be white, wealthy, traditionally attractive and are often celebrities.

As we saw in Chapter 3, sociologists have also been challenged not to assume that sociological thought from the 'North' can be applied across the world. Alongside Black feminist thought discussed above, a 'Third World' and then **post-colonial feminism** emerged that challenged claims of a united experience of gender and gender inequality across place from authors such as Indian sociologist Chandra Talpade Mohanty. Mohanty argues that many feminist traditions are of limited applicability outside the contexts of their formation. She moved from proposing a focus on the uniqueness of **Third World feminisms** to arguing for the possibilities of a transnational linkage between different feminism and feminist struggles in the context of global economic processes.

As we have seen, sociology thinks with concepts, and many sociologists aim towards having a global dialogue with other sociologists and all those interested in thinking sociologically about their lives. However, too often the concepts promoted do not fit the experiences and social patterns to which they are applied. In response to Mohanty and other writing at the time, a New Zealand-based feminist and post-colonial scholar, Radhika Mohanram, showed how the idea of a Third World, post-colonial (multicultural) feminism can fail to capture the experiences and structures shaping the lives of Indigenous women. As we saw in Chapter 3, it may often be more productive to think of sociological categories in terms of relations and, in some cases at least, to focus on borders and **border thinking**.

In Chapter 3 we introduced Gloria Evangelina Anzaldúa's concepts for thinking about borders and their crossing, including *neplanta*, an indigenous term for the space between, and mestiza (mixed heritage) consciousness. Such concepts are designed to focus on relationships and to embrace ambiguity. Such border thinking is essential across contexts for thinking sociologically about gender, and how it intersects with race, class, mobility and migrant status. Since the 1970s sociologists have been challenging the prototypical image of the refugee and the ambitious young man as the prototype of the migrant. Mirjana Morokvasic argued in the early 1980s that economic changes across the world were making young women from countries that were peripheral in the global economy the ideal migrants from the perspective of employers. She argued they would be increasingly in demand, and vulnerable. This has been shown to be true.

As a greater number of households in the Minority World and in the more privileged parts of the Majority World have both partners working, the pressure rises to either better share household labour, do less housework, or pay someone else to do it. Also, as more women are earning post-school credentials and have entered fields from which they were once excluded, domestic tasks that were once left to 'wives' are relocated to the market and are often performed by immigrant and migrant workers. For example, the rise of two-income professional households in the USA, Hong Kong and Singapore has led to an increased demand for low-paid service workers such as maids and nannies, and often these employees come from poorer neighbouring countries like Mexico, Malaysia and the Philippines, as discussed in Chapter 4 in regard to Saskia Sassen's concept of **survival circuits**.

Sexuality and Bodies: Queer and Crip

It is important to consider sex, gender and sexuality as different things. Sexuality is not the same as sex or gender. Sexuality describes desires, orientations, practices, and identities. As Foucault's famous work shows (see Chapter 5 where we discussed sexuality and power), sexuality has been heavily regulated by a variety of means including legal, religious, medical and psychological. The **Kinsey Scale** has been one prominent way of thinking about sexuality as more than a binary. The Kinsey Scale provides the following range: 0 = exclusively heterosexual; 1 = predominantly heterosexual, incidentally homosexual; 2 = predominantly heterosexual, but more than incidentally homosexual; 3 = equally hetero and homosexual; 4 = predominantly homosexual, but more than incidentally heterosexual; 5 = predominantly homosexual, but incidentally heterosexual; 6 = exclusively homosexual. While prominent, it too has been criticised as being too simplistic to capture the complexity of human sexuality.

Butler and other queer theorists suggest the links between sex, sexuality and gender can be considered as largely arbitrary. The sexual roles attributed to people based on their assigned sex or gender are socially constructed and not reducible to biology. Gender and sexual identities are often fluid and unstable, where people can and do experiment and change their orientations throughout their life. The American scholar Eve Sedgwick proposes the metaphor of the **closet** to understand the broader social structures of Global Northern societies in which people are understood along a small number of axes (for example their gender and sexuality) that are assumed to line up in particular ways. For Sedgwick, as highlighted by many queer theorists, people are different from each other but also have affinities to each other in many ways far beyond those sociologists tend to focus on.

Relatedly, **crip theory** has been developed by Robert McRuer and others through engaging with **queer theory** (first introduced in Chapter 5). Critical disability theory has a longer history as an approach to studying the way disability is a social and political phenomenon at least as much as an identity or embodied state, but crip theory (the name building on the reclamation of 'crippled' by people with a disability) is a more recent and more radical challenge to ways of thinking about disability, linking it to a matrix (like Butler's heterosexual matrix) of bodies, actions and identities that are either normal or 'deviant' from a norm. Echoing Sedgwick, Ellen Samuels talks about the assumptions and the challenges of 'coming out' about hidden disabilities but also the way that 'crip' approaches can challenge the ways we understand what bodies can do. For crip theorists, the point of theorising and activism about disability should not be acceptance or tolerance but transgression of norms and deconstruction of the 'abled' body.

The development of queer theory in the work of Butler, Sedgwick and others, such as Jack Halberstam and José Esteban Muñoz, has done much for the sociological understanding of sex, gender and sexuality and is increasingly being used to think about all kinds of actions that destabilise simplistic social norms. Similar to Butler's analysis of performing gender, Halberstam argues that when the strictures of sexuality 'fail' there are opportunities to highlight differences, transgress social norms and live a creative life. Halberstam proposes 'Gaga feminism', using the example of Lady Gaga as a way of expressing sexuality and gender outside of mainstream norms. Muñoz proposed the idea of disidentification to think about how queer people of colour need to negotiate a world in which they are constantly marginalised and face dangers just by being in public. Disidentification involves tactically reworking the presentation of self as a survival strategy, where one needs to constantly situate oneself both within and against norms, expectations and stereotypes.

While **heteronormativity** – the belief that heterosexuality relating to the male/female binary is the default – still dominates public perceptions, the rise of **social movements** (see Chapter 10) about sexuality-related discrimination and violence has seen much political progress. Contemporary LGBTQI and queer activism has seen the removal of many legal restraints on the sexuality of consenting adults and the growing legal acceptance of gay marriage. Despite this progress, non-heteronormative identifying people still face considerably higher rates of discrimination and violence than straight **cisgender** identifying people.

Gender Today

We started this chapter talking about how life at university had changed in many parts of the world, particularly the gender mix of the students. The experience of gender and sexuality has changed significantly in the past generation in many parts of the world. Much of this progress has been hard won by social activists in the feminist movement. Increasingly blatant sexist discrimination is illegal, and many young women are doing very well in education, employment and often rightly feel more empowered in their relationship decisions.

British sociologist Catherine Hakim has developed what she calls preference theory. She argues that gender inequality remains rife, but in the contexts where women do have meaningful choices, most women prioritise a mix of commitments to combine caring for a family and paid work, making both significant priorities. She argues that in contexts where it is a meaningful option, only about one in five women are 'work centred' and make employment their overriding priority and often never have children. About the same number are 'family centred' and choose not to work or work only a little for much of their adult life to focus on caring. Noticeably, in this framework, men's preferences are assumed to be work centred and, more importantly, very few people even consider the question of how men might make a choice between care and making work their priority. Until very recently, and often still, it is taken for granted that work is men's priority, and it is women who will have to work out how they balance care and work. This highlights that we still live in an unequal society, even in contexts where it appears that women have been given more 'choice'.

There is evidence that younger generations are further reworking the **gender order**. The American sociologist Barbara Risman, with colleagues, has recently studied the attitudes towards gender of young people. This builds on her lifetime's work of outlining what she calls the gender order of society (the social structure of gender), as she argues this is equally important if not more so than understanding gender as an identity: gender as a social structure visible throughout our lives, from our everyday interactions to the political structure and economy we live within. Interviewing one hundred young people, Risman created a typology of ways young people are changing or helping to reproduce gender structures. She calls the four approaches she identifies: straddlers, true believers, rebels, and innovators.

The innovators said that they were not bound by gender, mix and match traits that tend to be categorised as either feminine or masculine, and did not feel they were constrained by gendered expectations. Rebels went even further, not just playing around with and combining gendered expectations but rejecting them outright. They saw that these norms existed but wanted to dismantle them. They often identified outside of the traditional gender labels, as **genderqueer**. Doing so was not easy as they faced social sanctions for their challenge to a wider gender order still built around a binary. Straddlers were inconsistent in their actions and reported contradictory beliefs. As an example, some reported that they felt they mixed 'masculine' and 'feminine' traits and were proud of this, yet at the same time would report that they believed it was women's role to be caring and that a real man should be tough. While this group seemed uncertain in their beliefs and sometimes contradictory, they shared with the rebels and innovators a recognition that gender expectations were changing, and that further change was needed. The true believers were outliers compared to the others, supporting the need for gender norms and, highlighting the paradox mentioned at the start of this chapter, seeing them as needing to be actively defended yet also based on evolutionary biological differences that made the gender order natural and immutable. It is important not just to see 'true believers' as hold-outs or a throwback to earlier times. They are remaking 'tradition' in a context where their beliefs no longer have the complete normative power they once did, even if they remain powerful.

Despite these ongoing changes, discrimination continues. Women continue to be paid less and men's violence continues to shatter the lives of women. Governments respond with draconian new laws in response to the threat of terrorism yet fail to respond to the continual deaths of women killed by the significant men in their lives. The successful women versus failed women narrative identified by McRobbie, Harris and others can be understood as a reshaping for new times of the longstanding good women/bad women dichotomy, what the Australian scholar Anne Summers once referred to as 'damned whores or God's police'. Today this manifests in 'slut shaming' and rape culture, as well as the need some feel to police 'at risk' young women.

Yet, even if they are not disappearing and often seem to be gaining strength, even old prejudices are being remade. Recently, there has been the rise of a more subtle, complex and ironic sexism. It is defined as a form of self-aware objectification of women, using paradox, irony and mockery. It is reasoned 'acceptable' because the middle-class performers of type of 'hipster sexism' (remember we mentioned hipsters in the previous chapter) are usually conscious of the sexism, but because they are educated and understand classical sexism is antiquated and intolerable, making sexist remarks or performing sexist practices is therefore meant to be ironic, satirical and 'edgy'. Jokingly calling friends sluts, skanks or bitches is a prime example. Popular culture examples that have been criticised for hipster sexism include charity date auctions, the TV show *Girls* and the Harmony Korine film *Spring Breakers*, among many others. Much advertising today depends on this reflexive form of nudge-nudge wink-wink kind of imagery where overtly sexualised images are used but presented in an ironic way. When Katy Perry 'ironically' shoots foam from her bra in the *California Gurls* film clip, mouses are clicked and advertising is sold.

Conclusion

A focus on diversity and individualism arose among feminist scholars and activists in the 1980s and 1990s. This was called **third-wave feminism**. In the contemporary context that includes continuities but also profound changes such as the rise of social media and the related rise of new online social movements and the 'alt right', some argue a **fourth wave of feminism** has emerged, focused on challenging body shaming, rape culture and pushing for rights in the 'me too' era.

Yet, these 'wave' labels have tended to be coined by journalists, not academics. They are used by academics, but they should be treated with caution, particularly considering the critiques we have introduced you to in this chapter. In the context of thinking about waves of gender theorising in Black feminist studies, for example, the American sociologist Kimberly Springer has argued that there was no third wave of Black feminism, nor second wave, because of the complex and ambiguous relationship the theorising of Black women's experience has had with the feminist movement as a whole. For Black feminist thinkers the influence of foremothers of Black feminist thought has had a heightened salience for research over time, with the connections across generations often more important than the disconnection.

The British sociologist Rosalind Gill challenges sociologists to do gender research and use theories that can hold together the seeming re-emergence of (new) feminisms concurrently with new types of, and intensifying, misogyny. The sociology of gender aims to trace continuity and change while remaining focused on differences and inequalities. Research such as Risman and colleagues' study of how young people are responding to the gender order highlights the range of different ways of doing gender and feminist politics that are now circulating and are sometimes in tension with each other. Thinking about waves of feminism and how academic and non-academic feminists have developed and contested ideas across the generations can be valuable. Like other areas of sociology, particularly areas most focused on activism, there is a pattern of new cohorts of scholars and activist learning about and using, sometimes arguably misusing, the ideas of their feminist 'foremothers', simultaneously identifying and disidentifying with them.

One of the challenges in researching gender is that overly clear-cut categorisations risk erasing important experiences and difference, such as the way 'boy' and 'girl', 'woman' and 'man' tend to remain clearly distinct, erasing the many identities that fit in-between. For more and more young people (and some older people as well) these distinctions do not fit with their experiences and dispositions.

Key references for this chapter

Beauvoir, S (1971) *The Second Sex*. Alfred A. Knopf.

Butler, J (1988) 'Performative Acts and Gender Constitution: An Essay in Phenomenology and Feminist Theory', *Theatre Journal*, vol. 40, no. 4, pp. 519-531.

Connell, RW (2005) *Masculinities* (2nd edn). University of California Press.

Gatens, M (1996) *Imaginary Bodies: Ethics, Power and Corporeality*. Routledge.

Gil, R (2011) *New Femininities: Postfeminism, Neoliberalism and Subjectivity*. Palgrave Macmillan.

Goffman, E (2009 [1963]) *Stigma: Notes on the Management of Spoiled Identity*. Simon & Schuster.

Hakin, C (1998) 'Developing a Sociology for the Twenty-first Century: Preference Theory', *British Journal of Sociology*, vol. 49, no. 1, pp. 137-143.

Halberstam, JJ (2012) *Gaga Feminism: Sex, Gender, and the End of Normal*. Beacon Press.

Harris, A (2004) *Future Girl: Young Women in the Twenty-First Century*. Routledge.

Hill-Collins, P (1990) *Black Feminist Thought: Knowledge, Consciousness and the Politics of Empowerment*. Routledge.

Hochschild, AR (2003) *The Second Shift: Working Parents and the Revolution at Home*. Penguin Books.

Lasch, C (1977) *Haven in a Heartless World: The Family Besieged*. Basic Books.

Martin, KA (1998) 'Becoming a Gendered Body: Practices of Preschools', *American Sociological Review*, vol. 63, no. 4, pp. 494-511.

McRobbie, A (2009) *The Aftermath of Feminism: Gender, Culture and Social Change*. Sage.

McRuer, R (2006) *Crip Theory: Cultural Signs of Queerness and Disability*. New York University Press.

Mohanram, R (1996) 'The Construction of Place: Maori Feminism in Aotearoa/New Zealand', *National Women's Studies Association Journal*, vol. 8, no. 1, pp. 50-69.

Mohanty, CT (2003) *Feminism without Borders: Decolonizing Theory, Practicing Solidarity*. Duke University Press.

Muñoz, JE (1999) *Disidentifications: Queers of Color and the Performance of Politics*. University of Minnesota Press.

Oakley, A (1985) *The Sociology of Housework*. Basil Blackwell.

Parsons, T and Bales, R (1955) *Family, Socialization and the Interaction Process*. Free Press.

Pateman, C (1988) *The Sexual Contract*. Polity Press.

Risman, B (2018) *Where Will the Millennials Take Us?: A New Generation Wrestles with the Gender Structure*. Oxford University Press.

Samuels, E (2003) 'My Body, My Closet: Invisible Disability and the Limits of Coming-Out Discourse', *GLQ: A Journal of Lesbian and Gay Studies*, vol. 9, no, 1, pp. 233–255.

Sassen, S (2002) 'Global Cities and Survival Circuits', in B Ehrenreich and AR Hochschild (eds) *Global Women: Nannies, Maids, and Sex Workers in the New Economy*. Henry Holt, pp. 254–317.

Sedgwick, EK (1990) *Epistemology of the Closet*. University of California Press.

Springer, K (2002) 'Third Wave Black Feminism?', *Signs,* vol. 27, no. 4, pp. 1059–1082.

Summers, A (1975) *Damned Whores and God's Police: The Colonisation of Women in Australia*. Penguin Books.

Walby, S (1990) *Theorizing Patriarchy*. Basil Blackwell.

West, C and Zimmerman, DH (1987) 'Doing Gender', *Gender and Society*, vol. 1, no. 2, pp. 125–151.

Young, IM (1980) 'Throwing Like a Girl: A Phenomenology of Feminine Body Comportment Motility and Spatiality', *Human Studies*, vol. 3, no. 2, pp. 137–156.

9

RACE AND ETHNICITY

As you look around your classroom, the bus, train or street, you will likely be able to immediately distinguish a mix of racial backgrounds around you. Race can *feel* like one of the essential facts of our identity and can be one of the first things that we notice about each other. Yet race is not the natural category that it appears and is not a biological fact. Race refers to using physical, biological and cultural characteristics to distinguish one group of people from another. In the middle of last century, scientists found that the biological differences once thought to clearly define race do not exist. This does not mean that there are not genetic differences that vary across regions of the world, but research shows that these are minor, the boundaries are blurry and that there are often greater differences between people of the same 'race' rather than between racial groups. Yet this biological construct of race has deep historical consequences and still profoundly impacts our lives today.

The process of **racialisation,** categorizing ourselves and others by physical features, particularly the colour of our skin, but also other features like the curliness of our hair, is a foundation for **racism**: prejudice or discrimination based on race. How did race come to be so significant in our lives, and the basis of discrimination, if its genetic basis is so insignificant? The American sociologist William Sumner argued that humans are essentially group forming and that this led to a tendency to favour the in-group. He used the term **ethnocentrism** to capture a tendency to favour others who share our **ethnicity**, a broader concept than race used to capture how a group is marked out, or marks itself out, on the basis of a way of life, religion, language, nationality, traditions and customs. However, ethnicity is often tied to race, and the two are often used interchangeably (and often incorrectly) in everyday life.

Sumner's writing was important for highlighting that understanding discrimination and the creation of **stereotypes**, a term he developed that is still in common use today, requires a focus on the group doing this discrimination and stereotyping, rather than the group being discriminated against and stereotyped. The concept of in-group bias helps understand otherwise surprising research findings from sociology. People will claim to have negative attitudes to other racial and ethnic groups, even if the researcher makes up some of the groups. Most famously, in a mid-20th-century study of prejudice by Eugene Hartley, white people in the USA reported negative attitudes or prejudice towards Black and Jewish Americans, but also towards completely made-up groups such as the 'Danerians', and 'Pirenians'. Most participants who answered they disliked the real groups also said they disliked the made-up groups.

While it is hard to actually discriminate against a group like the Danerians, who do not exist, these survey participants displayed **prejudice**, which is the pre-emptive judging of a group or individual. **Discrimination** is the unfair treatment of that individual or group. Prejudice and discrimination are about the identity of a group and its members, casting people as insiders or outsiders.

Structures of Racism

Many sociologists make power central to their definitions of racism. Not everyone who is prejudiced has the power to discriminate in a meaningful way. Racism is tied up with history and how it is embedded in the contemporary patterns and institutions of our lives. People often trace the notion of institutional or structural racism to a book by two thinkers and activists associated with the Black Panther Party in the USA. Stokely Carmichael (who later changed his name to Kwame Ture) and Charles Hamilton were wanting to draw attention to a type of racial inequality that can be harder to spot but more significant than explicit racism. They gave the example of the impact of lack of access to adequate housing and health care in many primarily African American neighbourhoods and the way that this led to a higher infant mortality among Black babies. It is hard to think of a more consequential impact of racism.

More recently, Camara Phyllis Jones, an American epidemiologist (someone who studies social or population patterns of health), has used the allegory of a gardener to further articulate the effect of structural racism on individuals. The very same plant seed will flourish if grown in rich and well-cared-for soil, particularly if it is further well-tended by an attentive gardener, but not in poor and neglected soil. In this allegory, the unequal soil conditions include the initial historical insult of slavery, related social norms, and contemporary structural barriers, such as poor public transport and access to basic facilities. The gardener, refusing to act as it should to improve outcomes but blaming the seed, is the government.

While these works have helped popularise the notion of structural racism, an important earlier foundation was the work of WEB Du Bois, whose work we discussed in Chapter 3. His study of African Americans in Philadelphia was the first systematic sociology of its type. He combined his own new research with census data to create striking visual illustrations of his findings (you should check out his hand-drawn data visualisations). He showed how the lives and opportunities of Black Americans were not curtailed by the inferiority of Black people but by the unequal opportunities they were given by the social structure. In Australia, Maggie Walter has shown how structural inequalities are behind stark patterns of Indigenous health and education inequalities in this country. Until these structures are changed, programs or initiatives focused on individual behaviour will only make a small positive difference at best and risk reinforcing cultural prejudices that individualise blame. These structures of inequality, in Australia and elsewhere, have a long history.

Racism: From Biology to Culture

This practice of racialising people when combined with power (see Chapter 5) is the driver of racism. As we discussed in Chapter 3, sociologists in the late 19th century and early 20th century often provided support for racist views. Racism has a long history, running back far before the 19th century, but it took on a new impetus and power through this period into the early 20th century as it was reinforced by the growing influence of science, including sociology, even if many of the 'scientific' claims were dubious. Throughout the 19th and parts of the 20th century racism was normalised and justified on scientific terms, what is called **biological racism**. This was also an exercise in ethnocentrism, where categories were produced that ranked races in a hierarchy that was claimed to be natural, almost always positioning the creator's own group at the top.

Social Darwinism and biological racism went on to provide an intellectual foundation for **eugenics**. A philosophy that believes that humans can identify socially and biologically 'fit' and 'unfit' individuals, eugenics promoted interventions to improve the 'fitness' of society. Used to justify the forced sterilisation of people deemed unfit to reproduce, including people with a disability, eugenics was used in Nazi Germany as a justification of the **Holocaust**, the genocidal murder of Jews on the basis of their race and other persecuted groups, including those who were gay, disabled, or Roma.

Zygmunt Bauman uses this extreme manifestation of racism to show that the Holocaust is not 'anti-modern'. The Holocaust appears like an act of irrationality that represented a step back to a barbarous past. Yet it was pseudo-scientific thinking about race, combined with a modern 'search for control' through **scapegoating** – blaming a group for outcomes for which they are not responsible – further combined with techno-scientific rationality that 'efficiently' facilitated murder on an industrial scale. Efficient here relates to examples such as the decision to use gas rather than bullets for executions because it was cheaper and the use of IBM technology to keep track of and facilitate the process. Genocides have not been consigned to the dustbin of history since the Nazis, with recent examples of genocide in the 1990s by Bosnian Serbs towards Bosnian Muslims or by Hutu towards Tutsis in Rwanda.

After the Second World War, instead of drawing on dubious claims of biological inferiority or incompatibility between groups, what British sociologist Paul Gilroy calls **raciology**, the focus has turned to 'social' claims of 'cultural differences'. Gilroy also describes what he calls a **post-colonial melancholy**, where straight white men in particular feel threatened by social progression achieved by feminism, LBGQTI and racial equality movements such as Black Lives Matter and want to return to a romanticised past where they were unquestionably dominant.

Gilroy and French social theorist Etienne Balibar highlight the emergence of a **new racism**. Arguments about racial inferiority and superiority can sound absurd to many contemporary ears; instead, populist politicians and newspaper commentators speak of the need to maintain the **cultural identity** of the host nation or ethnic group. Instead of claiming natural superiority, they argue that there is a way of life and culture 'under threat'. Gilroy gives the example of a shift in racist rhetoric aimed at people in Britain of Caribbean descent. While arguments of cultural incompatibility have long existed, this **cultural racism** has shifted to the centre while claims of racial inferiority have diminished, if not completely disappeared.

With this new definition of racism focused on culture, it may make sense to think of discrimination of groups that are not tied to existing racial formations as experiencing racism. Recent events such as the first Gulf War, the September 11 attacks on the USA, the wars in Iraq and Afghanistan, the 'Bali bombings', and the terror attacks in London and Paris have seen a rise in vilification of Muslims and people of Arab descent in most Western countries.

This **Islamophobia** follows a pattern where discrimination tends to rise in times of crisis and uncertainty – with events such as 9/11 seeing millions of people labelled as dangerous threats even if they also vehemently disagree with and express horror at what happened. Similar claims to those identified by Gilroy are made today about refugees from Africa and the Middle East: it is claimed that because they do not share the same national history or customs, they find it difficult to 'fit in'.

In settler-colonial countries like Australia and the USA, such claims about history, culture and ethnicity seem particularly difficult to sustain because, excepting a relatively small population of Indigenous peoples, most are the descendants of relatively recent immigrants. This highlights the way that ideas about ethnicity and national character are substantively fictions. Benedict Anderson defines the nation as an **imagined community**. National identity is usually based on a collection of overly general stereotypes and dubious historical myths that overstate **homogeneity** (sameness) within a country and reflect a distorted representation of the nation's history, usually writing out anything negative, uncomfortable or shameful.

For instance, what does it actually mean to be an 'Australian'? The stereotypes point to being blonde with blue eyes, having a BBQ at the beach after going surfing. Or being in the bush and playing cricket. Or soldiers dying gallantly at Gallipoli in Turkey during the First World War. Note *everything* that this leaves out! Left out of this myth most noticeably is an articulation of the 60,000-year history of Aboriginal Australia, and the devastation brought by colonialism. Australia is far too diverse – culturally and geographically – to be able to be represented by a defining image or story. Yet people constantly try, such as the lionisation of solders at Gallipoli. How then can others be expected to become 'Australians', to 'fit in', when there is no clear picture of what it means, and the pictures that are presented are remarkably white and male?

It can be challenging to respond to this type of new racism, because it often draws on language that has been used to fight against racism and argue for multiculturalism. Often, nothing *overtly* racist is said: instead, there is discussion of the need to 'preserve' culture, to value 'identity', 'custom', 'tradition' and 'difference'. While fear of 'diluting' the 'white' race has long been part of racist discourse, historically the focus was on how other groups were racially inferior. Instead of constructing claims about the weakness of other racial and ethnic groups, a hallmark of new racism is the claim that Anglo-ethnicity and a 'Judeo-Christian' heritage is weakened and under threat in the context of economic and cultural globalisation and a multicultural society, such that the threat is imagined as not external but increasingly from within. As the Australian anthropologist and social theorist Ghassan Hage points out, this type of newer **paranoid nationalism** that claims to be under threat from within can appeal to working- and middle-class people who have become more precarious in current economic conditions, those who feel left out of their national community in the context of economic and cultural globalisation. They are vulnerable to romanticised fantasies of a country's past and primed to project their fears onto anything deemed culturally alien, particularly within their country's borders.

The importance of understanding power and recognising the legacy of past injustices and current inequalities to understanding racism points to the illegitimacy of the concept of reverse racism, which is a term used by those who claim that white people also face racial discrimination. Sociologists use racism to describe the prejudice and discrimination that is supported by social privilege and power. The dominant group, the group with greatest privilege and status in a society, is the source of racism. Minority groups are singled out for unequal treatment. The dominant group is not necessarily the numerical majority – for example, in colonial situations, or where a particular ethnic group has historically monopolised control over major institutions.

Racism can exist outside of North America and Europe – for example, racism exists in many countries in Asia where one ethnic group has significant social and political power. Within countries like the USA, white people may be occasionally discriminated against by an individual or groups, but they do not face systematised disadvantage that is the legacy of historical racism and do live in a system in which white people are systematically advantaged. For 'reverse racism' to exist in the systematic way sociologists define racism, the world would need to look very different, and not have the colonial history that it does. A member of a minority group can be prejudiced against the dominant group, but when this comes from a position of relative powerlessness, most sociologists would not call it racism.

Racism without Racists?

In a book called *Racism without Racists*, the Puerto Rican sociologist and recent president of the American Sociological Association, Eduardo Bonilla-Silva, links structural racism to the notion of 'colour blindness'. He argues that as concepts of biological inferiority were debunked, or at least as people kept them to themselves, people started to say things like 'I don't see colour'. The idea that everyone is now equal, or that racism has now been overcome if people ignore colour, functions to buttress an unequal status quo in which **whiteness** is still advantaged. Writing in the context of the USA before the election of President Trump, Bonilla Silva wanted to know how racist patterns were still so prevalent in a country where almost everyone proports to not be racist. The answer was that oppressive policies and institutional racism can go unchecked in a country that refuses to acknowledge colour as significant.

Racism as a process of racialising has always had a cultural aspect and claims of biological difference never completely disappeared. While there has been important sociological work on the rise of cultural racism, a focus on biology may even be reemerging in some respects. As Alondra Nelson has highlighted, the science and study of the genetics of ancestry has not diminished in the decades since eugenic thinking was at its peak. The science of DNA has become big business. DNA testing is used to personalise medicine based on ancestry, to prove people innocent and guilty, and to make sense of where we come from. In some ways the science has improved, but genetic testing is often used beyond what is scientifically legitimate. It partly reinforces claims of group difference, while also leading to fine-grained individual accounts of mixed ancestry. The science of DNA is intertwined with our society in complex ways, and how people use it can be empowering or disempowering. For example, the North American First Nations scholar Kim TallBear has spent her career looking at the role of science and technology in justifying and enabling colonisation but also at the way that new DNA technology is used in complex ways today in claims to sovereignty and Indigenous governance.

Internalised Racism

At the beginning of this chapter, we presented arguments that people tend to favour members of groups to which they feel they belong and see their group as having more favourable traits. However, distinguishing between dominant and minority groups highlights the power dynamics within which this occurs, and a minority group often feels split between two worlds and can take on the attitudes of the dominant group. We hope you remember in Chapter 3 we introduced you to WEB Du Bois's notion of the 'double-consciousness'. Frantz Fanon, a Martinique-born social theorist, psychologist and revolutionary in the struggle for Algerian independence from the French, spoke of this experience of inadequacy but also dependency and even love for the dominant group's culture as wearing a **white mask**. The concept of **whiteness** has been used by sociologists to highlight an invisible norm against which others were seen as inferior, a norm which minority groups may take on themselves.

Kenneth and Mamie Clark conducted a famous study of racial identity in the 1940s that highlighted this process of seeing self-identity through the eyes of the dominant group. They tested the preferences of young children in the USA for dolls that were either brown or white in colour. Both African American and white children showed a preference for the white doll. When asked which doll they would like to play with, which was the 'nice' doll and the 'bad' doll, and which doll was the nicer colour, the answers between the two groups of children where similar, only differing substantially when they were asked which doll looked like them. The Clarkes presented this as evidence of **internalised racism**. The Clarkes' evidence, along with the evidence of other social researchers, played an essential part in the civil rights campaign to end legal discrimination in the USA. This study was used as key evidence in the 'Brown vs the Board of Education' trial in the USA that led to the end of segregated schooling. After 'Brown vs the Board of Education', schools in the USA became less segregated. However, today they are again almost as segregated as they were in the early 1960s. The language of race is no longer explicit in justifications; instead, there is discussion of 'school choice' and supporting educational 'excellence'.

Everyday Racism

There is also recent evidence that direct discrimination based on race continues in employment. Studies replicated across several countries where the dominant group is white shows that (fake) job applications from (fake) candidates with identical qualifications are more likely to lead to an invitation to an interview where the application is from a name that is ethnically associated with whites. In the USA, Black names are anywhere between 50 and 500 percent less likely to get a call back than the general population. These studies undercut the claims of reverse discrimination mentioned above.

This discrimination highlights the way that class and race can interact. One of the more controversial claims in sociology in the USA is William Julius Wilson's that the significance of race is in decline. Wilson's argument is complex, and he is not downplaying the continuation of discrimination. He argues, however, that the life chances of African Americans have more to do with their economic class position than their everyday experiences of racism in interactions with white people. Wilson highlights that the average economic position of Black

Americans is a legacy of slavery, racism and housing segregation, and **redlining** (residents of certain areas being ignored for jobs or denied services, such as bank loans, based on the racial make-up of the area).

Others do not agree that the day-to-day interactions between whites and Blacks are declining in their significance for shaping life chances. The American sociologist Elijah Anderson talks about the stereotypes that inform these interactions using the notion of the **ghetto** as 'iconic'. The ghetto is a metaphor that in the USA, through its saturation in popular culture and the media, has become so widely recognised and stylised that it can be considered 'iconic', and more-or-less everybody is familiar with the stereotype of crime, violence and vice-filled neighbourhoods attached to it. It acts as an implicit assumption about the place where African Americans come from, a deeply embedded stereotype. Black Americans are presumed in their interactions with others to be 'ghetto' until they disprove it and work to build mutually trusting relationships. Stereotypical assumptions about people and their background are embedded in even ordinary everyday interactions. Overcoming these stereotypes is like an additional form of labour for some people and not others. Similar relations affect the life chances of Indigenous people and racialised minorities generally.

Race and gender theorist Peggy McIntosh uses the metaphor of an **invisible knapsack** to talk about **privileges** that remain firmly tied to whiteness. Many of the advantages of whiteness can be ignored by white people as they are taken-for-granted. People who are not white cannot take them for granted, and hence see them clearly. Some of the examples that McIntosh gives are that if you are white you are never asked to speak for all members of your racial group, and you never feel that your success or failure will be seen as either a credit or discredit to your race. You will never be told you performed well or spoke well 'for a white person'. This burden even falls on racialised sociologists. Stuart Hall called this the Black person's burden and noted that when he was interviewed by the media, and this was very often, he was 'expected to speak for the entire Black race on all questions'.

White privilege relates to the phenomenon of **passing**. Cheryl Harris talks about the way that her light-skinned grandmother, living in the mid-20th-century USA, would travel from her predominantly African American neighbourhood in Chicago into the central business district each workday and pass from one world into another. At work she was not racialised, and this gave her economic benefits and new opportunities. She did not get asked if she was African American at work. She could come to learn about the lives of her colleagues outside work, but she could not share the details of her own. As long as she kept on this 'mask', no one thought to question her because it was implicitly understood that the high-end department store where she worked would not have employed a black person.

Passing is a feature of life in all white majority countries. Harris points out that it remains common, much more so than the occasional story of trying to pass as racialised when otherwise not. Passing has not faded into history and is a clear retort to claims that the age of diversity programs and affirmative action has made it a disadvantage to be white. Whiteness for Harris is like property – it gives certain rights and privileges.

Non-whites face constant slights, insults and discriminations that white people do not experience. In 2015 a study in Australia showed that bus drivers were twice as likely to allow white passengers to ride for free over non-white passengers and, reinforcing the salience of the concept of internalised racism, even non-white drivers favoured white passengers. Often those delivering these minor insults are not always aware of their behaviour, or the assumptions they are making. It is internalised stereotypes that can drive implicit racism. These types of interactions are examples of what Chester Pierce calls **micro-aggressions**. Pierce, a North American scholar writing after the successes of the civil rights struggle in the USA, used this term to highlight the shift away from overt racism to everyday interactions more subtly underpinned by racism. The micro-aggressions discussed by Pierce and McIntosh might be relatively subtle but are cumulative.

The other side of white privilege is what the American sociologist Robin DiAngelo calls **white fragility**, a reticence to talk about race and a defensiveness when presented with evidence of the structural privileges of being white. People with these privileges are often not even aware of the benefits they get and can be reticent and get upset and defensive when made to face up to them.

Intersectionality and Hybridity

Sociologists who study micro-aggressions show the myriad ways racialisation continues to shape people's lives. They do, however, agree with Wilson on the importance of acknowledging differences *within* groups and how different structures in society intersect to shape life chances. The most widely used term for this is **intersectionality**, coined by Kimberlé Crenshaw, an American legal scholar who discussed the way that multiple structural inequalities and types of discrimination shape the lives of minority groups, particularly black women.

Crenshaw developed this idea through a specific legal case study where gender and race met. She looked at the discrimination case brought by Emma DeGraffenreid and other Black women against the General Motors Company. At GM, Black people were hired in the manufacturing side of the business, building the cars, and this was overwhelmingly male. Women were hired in administrative support roles, another part of the business that was almost exclusively white. While this type of gender and race segregation across parts of the business is of itself a problem, for Black women the discrimination was particularly stark; they found it almost impossible to get a job at the company. Race discrimination laws and gender discrimination laws at the time were not well equipped to protect Black women, where the two types of discrimination intersected.

The intersections of class and race are also visible in the use in popular culture and among some young people of racial stereotypes to be 'edgy' – using irony or satire to hide or blur racism – or the **cultural appropriation** of cultural artefacts. As traditional forms of vulgar racism are increasingly unacceptable (though certainly not disappearing) in middle-class social circles that tend to consider themselves 'woke', the well-educated now seem to be able to use racist remarks as an apparent form of satire, such as the use of the n-word by white people to greet each other. This **hipster racism** (similar to hipster sexism discussed in Chapter 8) highlights middle-class ironic racism and cultural appropriation, as in pop music videos such as Gwen Stefani's deployment of Japanese Harajuku Girls or Lily Allen's use of Black female dancers in her video *Hard Out Here*.

Being a member of an ethnic group, or being an insider or an outsider, is complex. It can be claimed by oneself or ascribed by others. There is **identity politics** in this regard, where mechanisms of defining and deciding who is 'in' and who is 'out', who is normal and who is abnormal, who has rights and who does not, become visible and contested within a social group or movement. Some conservative critics claim that sociologists interested in intersectionality are obsessed with identity politics, about minutely separating groups into smaller and smaller enclaves and shouting down anyone who does not fit into that group who tries to make a comment about it. Sometimes the term intersectional is used this way, particularly on social media, but this is not how it tends to be used in sociology, a point made by Crenshaw herself.

The term intersectionality has also moved far beyond its Black feminist roots to be a term used to think about the inequalities experienced around class, disability and sexuality, among many others. Yet, for most sociologist at least, we cannot just add up the different identities someone holds to work out how oppressed they are. Intersectionality in the approach that builds on Crenshaw's is not primarily about identity but the interaction of different structures in our society and the way institutions do use identities to include and exclude, and how they can have compounding effects in particular cases.

While intersectionality is not primarily about identity, how people identify and are identified in a racialised world have implications for how we think sociologically. The **standpoint theory** approach was developed in opposition to the view that the oppressed, because of their subordinate status, were not free or empowered enough to be objective. Standpoint theorists point out that those who thought they were being objective, for example about the inferiority of others, were talking from the perspective of the powerful. Standpoint theory builds on the fundamental sociological insight that we cannot study society from outside but are always, in some senses, inside, and this shapes what we can see.

For Patricia Hill Collins, the insights of members of subordinate groups are an essential lens on that experience and, as a group of 'outsiders' within their own society, they can develop valuable knowledge about the broader social structure. Within this framework, knowledge is not a collection of facts but foundationally about the perspectives through which these facts can be understood. For Collins, this means that Black feminist knowledge is a particularly important lens for thinking about American society, as it is knowledge from the perspective of the outsider within. In Australia, the Indigenous sociologist Aileen Morton Robinson has demonstrated how the assumption of whiteness shaped the feminist movement and the way it represented women and feminist issues. These scholars have shown that whiteness has been the default standpoint and that this needed to be brought into critical reflection. Hill Collins and Morton-Robinson's work, among others, has inspired a greater focus on what has been called **whiteness studies**, in the sociology of race and gender and social sciences broadly.

Morton Robinson has helped pioneer a critical Indigenous perspective in sociology. Similarly, Maori sociologist Linda Tuhiwai Smith, whose ideas we introduced in Chapter 3, argues for **Kaupapa Maori** (Maori principles or values) in sociological research, an approach that recognises that research and knowledge building is fundamentally a collective enterprise. In this framework a researcher must establish an equal footing with the community in which they are conducting the research, making others in the community co-researcher with them, negotiating each part of the project as it develops. This is part of a larger project of developing an **Indigenous standpoint** approach to research.

Sociology can help people become more empathetic and better understand the lives of others. It is not just people who share a particular experience who are able to understand that experience but all sociology, by insiders and outsiders, requires **reflexivity**, understanding that research is inherently collective because it is always working on and developing ideas with others, including research participants, whether we acknowledge this or not. The perspectives we use are necessarily influenced by the world of which we are part. If you are writing about the experiences of inequality in relation to a particular structural inequality or the intersection of such structures, the perspective from the standpoint of those living that experience needs to be made central. The sociological imagination aims to see how structures emerged over time and are changing in relation to people's lives and the way they act. This means that sociologists attend to the way borders between insider and outsider are not natural but always made and remade. As we saw in Chapter 3, a particularly valuable perspective on the contemporary world might be one from the borders.

In developing the Indigenous standpoint approach, the Indigenous Australian scholar Martin Nakata uses the term the **cultural interface** to recognise the complexity of the social connections of Indigenous people, including to the broader settler-colonial society. He focuses on the deep connection he and his family have to the Torres Strait (islands and sea at the North Eastern tip of Australia) and the Indigenous community there, where he is from, despite living most of their lives in other places. Identity is about connection to a place, not just being in a place, and is not singular.

Nakata argues that the day-to-day experiences and struggles at this interface are a starting point to think about borders, dualities and their limitations, but just a starting point. It is essential for researchers using standpoint approaches to also be reflexive about their assumptions and the limitations of their knowledge. Here he is connecting with the line of arguments for working across theoretical traditions introduced earlier; the comparative view from the 'interface' allows a scholar to reflect on the assumptions embedded in different ways of knowing and create new productive engagements with different perspectives. As we have turned to these Indigenous approaches, it may have occurred to you that up until this point almost all the work on race we have covered in this chapter comes from scholars from North America, Britain and Australia. Many are themselves racialised, but few are from outside these major Northern hemisphere hubs, or from Asian backgrounds. This is changing as sociologists are moving beyond what American scholar Juan Perea calls the **Black/white paradigm** in the study of race focusing on a binary of two primary groups.

WEB Du Bois famously said at the beginning of the 20th century that the defining problem of the 20th century would be the **colour-line**, by which he meant the social divide between whites and Blacks. To update this for today, it is possible to say that the sociological problem of the 21st century is to understand the many complex and porous colour-lines and how they relate to racism. Building on the work of Mignolo and Anzaldúa and others on the complexity of borders, many sociologists highlight how people today often identify with multiple ethnicities and are recognised by others as rightfully able to identify in this way.

For instance, a young woman who is second generation immigrant to the USA may identify with aspects of both the dominant ethnic culture of the USA and her own family's cultural background. What she says and does, and how she presents herself, could be contingent on where she is: at home with her family where Mexican elements of her identity may come to the fore. Or out in public space where she may associate herself more with aspects of these cultural surroundings. She may even accentuate American aspects of her identity at home to annoy her parents as an act of teenage rebellion.

This is increasingly the norm for millions of people all around the world as mobility increases. Yet, holding these multiple identifications is not straightforward. The Australian sociologist Ien Ang uses her own life to think through these issues. She was born in Indonesia before growing up in the Netherlands and now works in Australia but has Chinese ancestry and is often assumed to be Chinese, despite growing up elsewhere and not speaking Chinese. Ang notes that she has different ways to define herself in different situations, but she is also placed by others in shifting categories. Stuart Hall among others, highlights the way it has become possible in Britain to maintain a diasporic identity, tied to a shared history with people now spread widely around the world (Jamaican, Jewish, or Irish, for example), while identifying as British. Ang, however, argues that the notion of **diaspora** too easily falls into a similar trap of the Black/white binary but just adds another layer; in her case, Chinese (including the diaspora) or not Chinese but with a second identity (British/Australian) added on top. Instead, she proposes using the notion of hybridity.

Hybridity emphasises the blurry nature of identity work around the notion of ethnicity and the ways people may have multiple and even shifting ethnic identities depending on the social context. Homi Bhabha (an Indian-English scholar now based in the USA) has theorised situations like this as a state of 'in-between-ness', fully belonging neither 'here' nor 'there', but in an emerging **third space.** The Argentinean social theorist Néstor García Canclini links hybridisation not just to identity but to whole cultures, noting that human history contains no pure cultures, just an ongoing process of borrowing and creative reworking. As we have highlighted throughout this chapter, however, sociologists must attend to the power imbalance between minority and majority groups to understand race and ethnicity, and to recognise the blurry line between hybridisation and cultural appropriation.

A Super Diverse World?

We opened this chapter by noting that, depending on where you are reading this book, if you look around you, you probably see people from a variety of different backgrounds. We saw in Chapter 4, that there have been increasing flows of people and cultures around the world. In many ways we live in what the British sociologist Steven Vertovec calls a **super diverse world**. He wants to capture not just how many places are made up of a growing mix of small to large communities with different ancestries and immigrant histories, but that within each of these communities there is growing diversity. We must be careful whenever we talk about a group with a shared ancestry as if it is a homogenous whole, whether Kenyan-Australians or Irish-Australians or any other.

So, what are the effects of living in such diverse contexts? The French-Canadian sociologist Michèle Lamont shows that such conditions make actions to bridge cultural differences everyday events. This is practical or **ordinary cosmopolitanism**. The British sociologist Paul Gilroy sees around him the seeds of a new **convivial culture**, where interaction across differently racialised groups becomes commonplace, and an often fun celebration of difference. He sees a generational difference in Britain with this conviviality most embraced by the young, while older Brits, particularly of Anglo ancestry, tend towards feeling melancholic about growing diversity and overly nostalgic for a less diverse past.

Indeed, the sociologist Stuart Hall, who we have mentioned already and was one of Britain's foremost public intellectuals of multiculturalism, was circumspect when discussing whether his and other sociologists' work on multiculturalism had made much of a direct impact on changing Britain, arguing that any change towards a convivial attitude was much more due to **multicultural drift**: spending time in cultural environments that were increasingly diverse led people to see that racialised others, in Hall's words, 'weren't going to eat you, they didn't have tails'.

Other sociologists also working in Britain (and elsewhere) are ambivalent about whether younger generations are more convivial. Les Back, another English sociologist working in London, has shown that a disavowal of racism towards some groups by white young Londoners and the **contingent inclusion** of young Black Londoners could go along with deep hostility towards other racialised groups, in this case young Londoners from South East Asia. Anoop Nayak has undertaken similar ethnographic work in a smaller mostly 'white' town in the UK, showing that the taken-for-grantedness of whiteness as a racialised category starts to break down in the face of cultural flows, such as K-Pop, hip-hop and the popularity of NBA basketball. Yet this only leads to an **ambivalence** about whiteness. Elements of Black culture, particularly tied to music and sport, were valorised by the young English people Nayak spoke to as better than 'white' culture while racialising **essentialisms** were reinforced, such as some groups being seen as more naturally rhythmic and athletic. At the same time negative racialised language was used to talk about the poorest white people living within their neighbourhoods.

The world is changing rapidly, as are the ways that people are racialised. These processes are complex, but it is essential to recognise that even in highly diverse contexts, racist attitudes that did seem to be weakening, or were at least being relatively hidden, appear to be growing in strength and driving political outcomes. While progressive movements such as Black Lives Matter have seen millions of people hit the streets to protest police violence, at the same time there is a growth in racist and reactionary movements such as the so-called Alt-Right, Proud Boys and other openly white supremacist group. In many parts of the world, racist violence seems to be on the rise, alongside evidence of continual conviviality. In this chapter we have outlined many forms of racism, some relatively subtle. While this subtlety is important to understand, the consequences of racism are not subtle. In the USA, Black men are at much greater risk of being shot by police. In Australia, Indigenous people make up a hugely disproportionate percentage of the prison population, are much more likely to die in custody, and have much shorter general life expectancy. Ash Amin, a British Indian scholar, asks why in the face of the seeming achievements of multiculturalism and politics of diversity has racism proved to be so persistent, even resurgent. Sociologists are trying to understand why and hopefully help to push back against the rising hate against racialised others.

Conclusion

For sociologists, race and ethnicity is one of many sources of self and social identity and a social structure, along with gender, sexuality, class, age, disability and so on. Ethnicity is not 'fixed' and is often conflated with nationality, religion and citizenship. It is shaped through social, cultural and political processes. This involves norms, traditions and religions along with appropriation, re-mixing and jettisoning various elements of those very things.

Politically, these categorisations work to decide who is included and excluded, that is, they produce and maintain culturally symbolic boundaries, in all manner of social situations that usually recreate the dominance of already powerful groups.

In this chapter, we have seen how racialisation takes place at the institutional or structural level, in everyday interactions, and can be internalised. Racialisation is a social process, but sociologists must be reflexive about how race matters to people in their everyday lives in complex ways. Some white sociologists jump from recognising racialisation processes and the structures of racism to saying that race is *just* a social construction. From one perspective this is true, but the way that historic actions have created and influenced race relations has shaped the way cultures have developed among groups. Being part of these cultures matters deeply to people.

It took us a while to write this book, as lives and other responsibilities got in the way. As we have been writing, we have seen the study of genetics explode and claims about the biological basis of difference and often also inferiority return to the mainstream. Particularly following the Holocaust, arguments of racial (biological) inferiority seemed to have lost much of their influence. When we started drafting this chapter, we wrote that few people today would dare to publicly support eugenics or even social Darwinism. We, like Bonilla-Silva, thought that probably the most pressing issues were racism without explicit racists, and the difficult-to-pin-down hipster racism or colour-blind racism. Yet today we are not so sure. With the rise of far-right racial politics, whether it was previously weakened or just hidden in many countries, and the growing influence of biological thinking, old and new racisms may be recombining in dangerous contemporary forms. At the same time, we take hope in how new forms of multicultural conviviality seem to exist and even grow alongside this racism.

The work of sociologists who study race and ethnicity has at times been used to bolster racist arguments, but sociology has also been at the forefront of challenging biological and cultural **essentialisms**. This is the idea that associates specified races or ethnicities (or genders or classes) with an 'essence' that defines their very being. It is the way many learned to see the world as we grew up, but using a sociological lens highlights that it is not a useful way to think about difference and can mask power relations within our social worlds. Rather, sociologists show how these differences are *made*. This is not to say that people are not different or have different customs and beliefs. But many of the differences we ascribe to other groups are based on inaccurate and over-generalised myths and stereotypes, and are often exaggerated, incorrect or without evidence. Sociology needs to be doing this work of tracing and challenging racialisation processes more than ever.

Key references for this chapter

Amin, A (2010) 'The Remainders of Race', *Theory, Culture & Society*, vol. 27, no. 1, pp. 1–23.

Anderson, E (2012) 'The Iconic Ghetto', *The Annals of the American Academy of Political and Social Science*, vol. 642, no. 1, pp. 8–24.

Ang, I (2001) *On Not Speaking Chinese: Living between Asia and the West*. Routledge.

Back, L (1996) *New Ethnicities and Urban Culture: Racism and Multiculture in Young Lives*. St Martin's Press.

Balibar, É (1991) 'Is There a Neo-racism?', in Balibar, É and Wallerstein, I (eds) *Race, Nation, Class: Ambiguous Identities*. Verso, pp. 17–28.

Bauman, Z (1989) *Modernity and the Holocaust*. Polity Press.

Bhabha, HK (2004) *The Location of Culture*. Routledge.

Bonilla-Silva, E (2010) *Racism without Racists: Color-Blind Racism and Racial Inequality in Contemporary America* (3rd edn). Rowman and Littlefield.

Booth, AL, Leigh, A and Varganova, E (2012) 'Does Ethnic Discrimination Vary across Minority Groups? Evidence from a Field Experiment', *Oxford Bulletin of Economics and Statistics*, vol. 74, no. 4, pp. 547–573.

Canclini, NG (1995) *Hybrid Cultures: Strategies for Entering and Leaving Modernity*. University of Minnesota Press.

Carmichael, S and Hamilton, CV (1967) *Black Power: The Politics of Liberation*. Random House.

Clark, KB and Clark, MP (1947) 'Racial Identification and Preference among Negro Children', in Hartley, EL (ed.) *Readings in Social Psychology*. Holt, Rinehart, and Winston.

Crenshaw, K (1989) 'Demarginalizing the Intersection of Race and Sex: A Black Feminist Critique of Antidiscrimination Doctrine, Feminist Theory and Antiracist Politics', *University of Chicago Legal Forum*: Vol. 1989, no. 1, pp. 139–167.

DiAngelo, R (2018) *White Fragility: Why It's So Hard for White People to Talk About Racism*. Beacon Press.

Fanon, F (1989) *Black Skin, White Masks*. Pluto Press.

Gilroy, P (2005) *Postcolonial Melancholia*. Columbia University Press.

Hage, G (2003) *Against Paranoid Nationalism: Searching for Hope in a Shrinking Society*. Pluto Press.

Harris, CI (1993) 'Whiteness as Property', *Harvard Law Review*, vol. 106, no. 8, pp. 1707–1791.

Hartley, E (1969) *Problems in Prejudice*. Octagon Books.

Hill-Collins, P (1990) *Black Feminist Thought: Knowledge, Consciousness and the Politics of Empowerment*. Routledge.

Jones, CP (2000) 'Levels of Racism: A Theoretic Framework and a Gardener's Tale', *American Journal of Public Health*, vol. 90, no. 8, pp. 1212–1215.

Lamont, M and Aksartova, S (2002) 'Ordinary Cosmopolitanisms: Strategies for Bridging Racial Boundaries among Working Class Men', *Theory, Culture & Society*, vol. 19, no. 4, pp. 1–25.

McIntosh, P (1989) 'White Privilege: Unpacking the Invisible Knapsack', *Peace and Freedom Magazine*, July/August, pp. 10–12.

Moreton-Robinson, A (2013) 'Towards an Australian Indigenous Women's Standpoint Theory: A Methodological Tool', *Australian Feminist Studies*, vol. 28, no. 78, pp. 331–347.

Mujcic, R and Frijters, P (2013) 'Still not Allowed on the Bus: It Matters if You're Black or White!', *IZA Discussion Paper No. 7300*.

Nakata, M (2007) 'The Cultural Interface', *The Australian Journal of Indigenous Education*, vol. 36, no. S1, pp. 7-14.

Nayak A (2003) *Race, Place and Globalization: Youth Cultures in a Changing World*. Berg.

Pager, D (2003) 'The Mark of a Criminal Record', *American Journal of Sociology*, vol. 108, no. 5, pp. 937-975.

Perea, JF (1997) 'The Black/White Binary Paradigm of Race: The "Normal Science" of American Racial Thought', *California Law Review*, vol. 85, no. 5, pp. 1213-1258.

Sumner, WG (1906) *Folkways: A Study of the Sociological Importance of Usages, Manners, Customs, Mores, and Morals*. Ginn and Company.

Tallbear, K (2014) 'The Emergence, Politics, and Marketplace of Native American DNA', in Kleinman, DL and Moore, K (eds) *Routledge Handbook of Science, Technology, and Society*. Routledge, pp. 21-37.

Vertovec, S (2007) 'Super-Diversity and Its Implications', *Ethnic and Racial Studies,* vol. 30, no. 6, pp. 1024-1054.

Wailoo, K, Nelson, A, and Lee, C (eds) (2012) *Genetics and the Unsettled Past: The Collision of DNA, Race, and History*. Rutgers University Press.

Walter, MM (2009) 'An Economy of Poverty? Power and the Domain of Aboriginality', *International Journal of Critical Indigenous Studies*, vol. 2, no. 1, pp. 2-14.

Wilson, WJ (2012) *The Declining Significance of Race: Blacks and Changing American Institutions* (3rd edn). University of Chicago Press.

10

CHANGING THE WORLD

As we were putting the finishing touches on this final chapter in 2020, it felt as if the whole world suddenly came to a stop as a new pandemic caused by the COVID-19 virus spread around the world. This chapter was finished during a period of lockdown while 'working from home', which quickly became such a well-used term that it garnered its own acronym (WFH). Hopefully when you are reading this, we have come out the other side of the pandemic. As we are writing it, we do not know what the future holds. Right now, the crisis is changing how we live. Family relationships and social life have been changed as we are isolating at home. Will this just be a pause before things go back to the way they were before or usher in an era of significant change? What we know already is that the contours of inequality that we have spent the last three chapters outlining – class, gender and race – are resulting in profound differences in the effects of the pandemic, who bears the brunt of the risks, and how things like 'social distancing', economic recession, and labour market and educational system transformations are experienced.

Crises are more than natural or physical phenomena and demand that we use our sociological imaginations. More than just a challenge for medicine or science, we will also as a society be making big decisions about how to live together and the type of world we want to have. This chapter will introduce the sociology of political power – who gets to make these decisions – and the way social movements have changed our world. We will finish by thinking about how sociology can be part of this process. As Mary Holmes has argued, while it is important for sociology to be critical of the myriad social problems in the world, it is also important for the discipline to maintain an optimism to contribute to responding to those problems and to create the knowledges and capacities to address them.

Political Power

We first introduced you to the concept of power in earlier chapters to understand the link between self and society. In this section we will focus on **political power** – the formal capacity to create laws and shape the behaviour of others. Obviously, some individuals and groups have more political power than others. We saw that in early sociology this type of power was often understood as founded on class relations. The government rules on behalf of those who own things. Many critical theories of class conflict continue in this vein and view the political and media fields as working on the behalf of the already powerful.

Marx believed that this would change as the workings of capitalism pushed the working class towards revolution. As we saw in Chapter 6, critical theorists spent the 20th century trying to tease out how cultural processes might explain why this did not occur, at least not in the context of advanced capitalist societies. While critical class perspectives have expanded to recognise how power is contested, those working in this tradition continue to locate power with capital. Yet, some compromises by the owners of capital highlight that multiple groups with competing aims may hold at least some form of power.

Michael Mann, a British-born sociologist who worked for much of his career in California, argues there are different sources of power, corresponding to the control over resources in four different social institutions. For Mann, **economic power,** which corresponds to the type of power that is the focus of traditional Marxists, is only one type of power. **Political power** corresponds to government, which interacts with economics, but neither is necessarily reducible to the other. Mann also argues that **military power**, the socially organised control over the use of violence, and **ideological power** are also relatively autonomous but overlapping networks of power. Ideological power designates the workings of the media and cultural industries, the power based on the human need to attribute meaning to events.

We can also see power in **pluralist** terms, a concept most closely associated with the American political scientist Robert Dahl. Pluralists argue that too many social scientists assume that one or at most a few groups are in power, often identifying beforehand who this is (for example, the capitalist class), and then conduct studies to see how this group wields power. Pluralists instead see many groups, representing many interests (including those seemingly less powerful) interacting and contesting political space and that it is sometimes difficult to predict what the outcome of this contest will be. Many actors are trying and, at least to some degree, succeeding in influencing the political process. For pluralists, it is unlikely that the interests of one small group will always dominate.

But are the people who become leaders of these different groups that contest power really representative of a plurality of positions? In 1911, Robert Michels outlined what he called the **iron law of oligarchy**, where all complex organisations always end up representing the interests of the very elite who take up positions in them, making representative democracy an unlikely source of equality or justice. Similarly, C. Wright Mills saw the leaders of different institutions – including the military, education, government and business – forming a **power elite**.

Seemingly representing different interests, members of the power elite go to the same parties, holiday destinations, clubs and universities, and send their children to the same schools. Those children are then sent on the same trajectory into powerful positions in society, making membership of the power elite informally, if not formally, an inherited position. Mills showed that those in the upper echelons of these important institutions in the USA often came from families that had been influential in US public life for many generations. For Mills, ordinary members of a society have very little influence relative to the power elite. This is similar to Bourdieu's analysis of the importance of cultural and social capital to the maintenance of elite networks and symbolic power.

In earlier chapters we introduced the ideas of Foucault, Butler and others, who see power as something that is embedded in particular ways of understanding the world, such as expert

discourses and performative norms. In other words, power is the practices and actions that positively, negatively or ambivalently affects people's lives, rather than something that groups or individuals own. As we have discussed, Foucault traced power that underpinned different social forms, particularly the emergence of modernity in the shift from sovereign to **disciplinary power**. In the late 1800s, the rise of the 'human sciences' meant more intense power and surveillance of people through defining, classifying, training and treating people. For instance, 'madness' was understood for the first time as an illness. Foucault called this disciplinary power. Interestingly, given this moment of public health emergency, he saw this type of power as largely concerned with knowledge about the health of populations. In his later work he used the term **biopower** to describe the contemporary world, as it was focused on the use of information and expertise to control subjects through intense surveillance of the general population in the name of monitoring and controlling hygiene, fertility and human life processes in general. For Foucault, the way political power is wielded is through what he called **governmentality**. This means that it is individuals who regulate themselves and those around them by following the expert advice to be good healthy citizens while living in a panopticon (discussed in Chapter 5).

These perspectives on power have tended to focus on what happens within specific nation-states, but importantly, political power between nation-states is equally important in our globalised world. Achille Mbembe, a social theorist born in Cameroon and now based in South Africa, develops the concept of biopower, adding a global and post-colonial lens to create the concept of **necropolitics**. Using examples from the suicide bomber to slavery to apartheid in South Africa, he theorises that power in the post-colonial world is predicated on who gets to live and die. The notion of national sovereignty – where nation-states control what happens within their own borders – was ignored in the colonial context and remains redundant in the post-colonial context as the right to kill people in other sovereign territory is claimed by some countries and groups, even though it is mostly illegal. Rather than a state of exception such as war, this can be normal everyday life for some people, for instance, where US drone strikes are flown under the banner of killing terrorists but there is considerable 'collateral damage' of innocent civilian deaths. The USA can seem to do this with impunity, despite United Nations' laws.

Mbembe says that this constant exposure to death can leave people in a kind of zombie existence of precarity, as if they are stuck between life and death. This way of living, he says, is unimaginable for most people in in the Global North, who only view such deaths as events through the media. The Greek-born and England-based media scholar Lilie Chouliaraki calls this the **ironic spectator** who is separated from the reality of the lives of the precarious. Such spectators often feel some empathy and anger about these injustices to the extent that they may express it through Facebook posts or wearing a wristband, before getting on with their own lives. This, according to Chouliaraki, has little to no influence on making actual change.

Mexican transfeminist theorist Sayak Valencia has further built on the idea of necropolitics to argue that violence itself is key to understanding what can be called **gore capitalism**. This is the undisguised price paid by those outside the Global North for being part of the global capitalist system. Valencia argues that the images of tortured, mutilated, or dead bodies of, for instance, members of Mexican drug cartels are consumed as little more than a spectacle in the Global North, where there are billion-dollar markets for drugs like cocaine. The term 'black market', for instance, not only is colloquial for illegalities, but Valencia suggests holds additional associations with Black and Brown people that those in the North depend on being exploited if their own relative material privilege is to be maintained.

Throughout this book we have introduced you to ways to think about the social web of connections at the foundations of our life, from global trade to our everyday interactions. Pandemics such as COVID-19 throw into stark relief the social divisions and inequalities that shape our lives globally and locally. While the virus has higher death rates for older people, it is not just age that shapes these outcomes. There are also gender, race and class dimensions to who gets to live and die, as Mbembe's necropolitics perspective highlights.

The way social life determines health is one of the most empirically robust findings in sociology. The British social epidemiologists Kate Pickett and Richard Wilkinson have shown how the unequal health patterns in a population are greatly intensified by inequalities. These inequalities matter whether comparing between different countries or comparing different regions within specific countries. They show how a culture of meritocracy – the idea that individuals get what they deserve – makes health inequalities worse. People blame themselves for the effects of social structure. Seemingly mundane everyday decisions about funding or policies therefore are intensely political: they help decide who lives and who dies.

It is clear that many suffer from the effects of power, even in questions of life and death, who do not in meaningful terms have access to mechanisms that can affect that power. Much of the contents of this book has emphasised how structures and institutions reflect the interests of certain groups, reproduce power relations, and engender inequalities. Yet throughout history, individuals and groups have banded together to argue for and fight for, and achieve, social change. So, while sociologists have theorised the ways things stay the same, and the role of unintended change, there are also many sociological concepts to help understand how social movements form around shared needs and purposes to then act on the world in the hope of changing it.

Resistance, Revolts and Revolutions

American sociologist and activist Frances Fox Piven discusses the power that ordinary people can wield, but also that this power is different from the economic, political, military and ideological power that is available to the elite. She highlights that the poor for example do not have access to the resources to shape the political process in regular ways. Instead, they must use **disruptive power**, tactics such as strikes, occupying space, not buying certain products, or refusing the demands of authority figures. In other words, power for those outside the power elite can come from causing trouble for the powerful, with all the risks of oppression and violence that entails, and that often means breaking the law.

For some sociologists, **resistance** to dominant norms can be performed through mundane everyday acts. For instance, for French theorist Michel de Certeau and UK sociologist Paul Willis, everyday consumption practices aren't just the actions of unthinking consumers or **'cultural dupes'** but can be creative. Creative consumption is a way of asserting freedom or challenging the systems of power and a way of expressing oneself, even resisting capitalist ideology, as per the discussion of subcultures in Chapter 6. This micro political action may be putting your favourite band's badge on your school uniform or turning a reality TV image into a satirical or critical meme. For De Certeau, there are spaces between the person, the product and how products are used that open possibilities for creativity, appropriation, adaptation, and rebellion. This rebellion is not revolutionary, it is about '**making do**'.

Sometimes people without access to the types of political power mentioned earlier in this chapter do come together to drive change much larger than making do, sometimes even leading to a **revolution** that profoundly changes the power structure of a society. Despite Marx's sophisticated theorising about the role of capitalism in social change, in practice this revolutionary class has tended not to be the working class.

Taking a global lens and focusing on colonialism, Frantz Fanon (introduced in the previous chapter for his concept of white masks), argued that peasants play a central role in revolution. He highlighted the role of race and colonial domination in revolution. While Marx saw race and ethnic divisions as having the potential to mystify the cohesion of the working class, Fanon turned this argument around. He argued that the existence of a working class could stifle revolutionary potential in much of the world under colonial domination. He showed how the working-class in colonised countries were partly aligned to the ruling class, as they were given some relative opportunities in the structure of colonial societies. It was the peasant who had nothing to lose and most to gain through violent revolution.

Similarly, looking at revolutions in England, France, China and Russia, the American sociologist and social historian Barrington-Moore Jr argues that it was the relationship between the emerging bourgeoisie class and peasants that shaped these countries trajectory towards either democracy or totalitarianism. Theda Skocpol, a political sociologist also based in the United States who was a student of Moore, similarly argues that recent revolutions are often driven by the interaction of different groups besides the working class. She adds that the role of the state and other social institutions besides the economy are crucial in understanding when a **revolt** – as an uprising by a lesser power or group – turns into a revolution. A revolution appears to require a weak state, often in crisis due to natural disaster, famine or war. When a revolutionary movement is successful, it also must manage the same constraints, even needing to rebuild the state, in a way that shapes the long-term future of the new system.

Social Movements

Groups of people, even the seemingly powerless at the time, have acted to change the world by forming **social movements**. Sociologists include a great diversity of groups under this label, from a group of people embracing a new resistant or deviant subculture, to a newly organised **political party**. They are (at least partly) organised social groups that aim to change something about society.

How does such a group emerge? For Herbert Blumer a social movement goes through four stages. He used the terms 'ferment', 'popular excitement', 'formalisation' and 'institutionalisation', but scholars following his work have renamed the stages as **emergence**, **coalescence**, **bureaucratisation** and **decline**. A movement **emerges** in response to persecutions and discrimination. Often this persecution continues for some time before a 'spark' sets off a new movement. One of the most famous examples is Rosa Parks, a civil rights activist in the Southern state of Alabama in the USA. As a young woman in the 1940s and 50s, Rosa lived in the segregated city of Montgomery. There were separate restaurants, toilets and other facilities for Black and white residents. Even public transport was segregated. Although Black and white Americans could catch the same buses, the seats at the front were reserved for whites. Black people often had to stand, even if there were empty seats at the front of the bus. In 1955 Rosa decided to challenge this segregation, getting on the bus and taking one of the 'reserved' seats at the front. She was arrested and fined. She refused to pay the fine and appealed to a higher court. Incidents like this can lubricate social change because people have something specific around which to organise.

Next a movement **coalesces** and becomes public. A number of civil rights organisations came forward to support Rosa Parks and an organisation, the Montgomery Improvement Association, was formed to support her challenge to segregation. This is the stage where the group publicly names its objectives and takes a collective form. These movements then **bureaucratise**, developing formal organisational structures and roles such as president and secretary. The first president of this new association in Montgomery, Martin Luther King Junior, would go on to lead a nation-wide civil rights movement. Dr King was trained in sociology and drew on his training in his activism.

Finally, a social movement then **declines**. This sounds rather pessimistic, but this includes all the ways a social movement may come to an end, including successfully meeting all their goals. The movement may also fail, through repression by government or other groups, or through co-option, where important figures are drawn into associating more closely with the group that was previously the target of the movement's protests – for example, if the government convinces activists to take public service positions to 'change things from the inside'. Sometimes a movement fades if new members are not recruited to the cause and previously passionate members become exhausted. The civil rights movement of the 1950s and 1960s (like the women's and queer rights movements) had many successes, but the struggle goes on with recent examples of social movements like 'Black Lives Matter' taking up the cause.

Social movements vary widely in their aims. David Aberle built a typology of social movements based on two dimensions: how much they want to change and how many people they want to change. Some movements call for modest change and are local in their scope, for example hoping to change a planning law to allow more public housing in their neighbourhood. Others may take a call for a relatively small change, for example to boycott a particular producer for underpaying their employees, all the way to a national or even global level. Others may try to totally reshape the way people live for a select group, such as a religious cult. Finally, some social movements push for radical change on a large and even global scale. The world communist movement or some environmental groups are examples of this type of movement.

Why social movements succeed or fail is still hotly debated by sociologists. A classic study of the success of social movements by William Gamson argued that highly organised and bureaucratic movements are more likely to succeed, but this also increases the chance of co-option. But others including Frances Fox Piven and Manuel Castells have argued that more flexible networks may be more successful, particularly in contemporary conditions. As we saw above, Skocpol points out that to understand why a group succeeds or fails requires attending equally to the social conditions and the strength of the state at the time. Importantly, social movements are not always progressive. Some formulate to stop or reverse change.

New Social Movements

Blumer and Aberle developed their theories of the formation and decline of social movements in the 1960s. In other chapters we have seen that many sociologists argue that the end of the 20th century saw a significant change in the way our societies are shaped. Many contemporary sociologists have similarly claimed that there are **new social movements** arising that correspond to the changing challenges of politics and ways that power works. While there are famous exceptions, such as the suffragettes and abolitionists, who fought for the right to vote for women and the end of slavery, social movements in modernity have been understood as largely focused on economic issues and shaped by class differences. For Anthony Giddens (a British sociologist) and Jürgen Habermas (a German sociologist and philosopher), while the labour movements, civil rights movements and women's movements of the past may indeed have been more pluralist in their aims and more fragmented than the distinction between old and new movements suggest, there has been a radical shift from **emancipatory movements**, focused on freeing groups from oppression and exploitation, to **lifestyle movements**, focused on recognition of different identities and access to opportunities for self-realisation. These scholars argue that struggles for new types of identities and lifestyles to gain recognition are becoming as or even more important than struggles for material equality.

For the Italian sociologist Alberto Melucci and the French sociologist Alain Touraine these new social movements have an expanded range of foci, increasingly the rights of individuals and groups. New social movements are an agglomeration of people sharing a broad agenda but with a variety of specific causes. Melucci gave examples such as the environmental movements and the third wave of the feminist movement, which worked as broad coalitions that came together and joined with other alliances around particular issues.

The aims of new social movements like this can be plural, ambivalent, and sometimes even contradictory, but that does not make them pointless, as they often help create awareness of an inequality and are experimenting with new ways of living and acting collectively. At the more radical end of these new social movements, instead of setting out a key plan for change, the hope is to experiment, aiming to create something new, to build new ways of living that are less consumerist and non-hierarchical, even if they do not have a clear sense yet of what this new form might be. For example, such experiments took place in the Occupy movements that emerged after the global financial crisis of the late 2000s.

Social Movements and Identity

Manuel Castells has argued that in what he called the information age, social movements would increasingly form around identities and be organised online. Castells saw that the world will be organised around three forces. Two of the forces are complementary: a 'technological revolution' and the 'global restructuring of capitalism', that revolutionise the way that we live. A contradictory force is the 'search for identity', as individuals are left to deal with rapid social change. He outlined three forms of identity that social movements would coalesce around. Firstly, there are **legitimising identities** that are promoted by states, governments and business. These reflect powerful social norms to work and consume. Secondly, there will be **resistance identities**, formed by people who feel that they are losing out from social changes. Castells' examples included Mexico's Zapatistas and Japan's Aum Shinrikyo, but more recent examples could be the Alt-Right, the Tea Party, One Nation (an Australian right-wing nationalist political party) and Brexit supporters. These groups want to return to the past, often in reactionary ways, as they feel social change has happened too quickly and that their own rights are being threatened. Thirdly, there are **project identities** that want to transform the way we live in progressive ways, reinventing dominant systems towards social justice and equality. These movements include feminism and environmental groups.

Public concern with environmental issues – such as climate change, soil degradation, peak oil, air and water pollution and waste, among many others – now seems a normal part of contemporary everyday politics. But this has not always been the case and is a result of groups working together to raise awareness of the damage being done to the environment by global capitalist production and its unsustainability.

Yet within environmental movements, just as within sociology, there is not necessarily agreement on what matters, what needs to be done or on what perspective to take on the relationship between humans and the environment. These differences have tended to be understood as linked to two different ways of understanding our relationship to the natural world (although as we show below, this might be too simple). A **social constructivist approach** questions how and why some environmental issues are seen as more significant than others, and why some issues are ignored or mispresented. This is reliant on the idea that nature cannot speak for itself and that the problems we emphasise may not be a direct reflection of reality or 'truth' but are subjective. The **realist approach** considers that environmental issues can be treated objectively, that they are real regardless of the politics and perceptions of them. This perspective believes we need to address concerns at face value based on the science and put measures in place to address them. This is a good example of the complexity of social movements. While they may be about the same problem or issue, such as mitigating climate change, there is often disagreement as to what is the best way to find a solution. These disagreements can happen in the academic ways of thinking about the problem in sociology and in the day-to-day organisation of social movements in terms of the different ways they are oriented towards the problem they are trying to fix. This can lead to infighting, ambivalence and lack of action that sees the status quo maintained.

Whose Side Are We On? Sociology and the Social Problems of the Contemporary World

Above we started to think about social movements and the environment. Big social questions mix the natural and social. Sociologists from Marx onward have never denied that material reality shapes our lives. However, some sociologists have bracketed out the natural to focus on culture and the social systems humans create. As we saw in Chapter 4, sociologists have persuasively argued that the main challenges facing us, including pandemics and climate change, mix the social and natural. For Ulrich Beck, for example, we live in **risk societies**, where the risks are largely due to the successes of modern human societies that result from scientific and technological progress. More of us can consume and travel (at least before the pandemic) in a way unimaginable even two generations ago, but in doing so we are pushing our environment in a way that might not just enable new viruses to emerge and spread easier than in the past but could even lead to the collapse of our climate system.

Some sociologists argue for a **new materialism** in sociology, different from the longstanding 'materialism' of sociologists who have drawn on Marx's focus on the way a society produces. Instead, this approach argues that a focus on subjectivities, identities and the social construction of reality has obscured the way our material existence is experienced. We have bodies and we interact with the non-social environment in everything we do. From this perspective sociology has also been too parochial, focused on humans and their rights and values while overlooking the damage humans have done to other animals and the natural world. Some sociologists taking this perspective want to highlight that humans do not just do things to non-humans. Non-humans act on humans. These scholars focus on the effects of relations between the human and non-human. Famously, French sociologists Bruno Latour and Michel Callon, and British sociologist John Law, have argued non-humans have agency, and we should take their agency just as seriously as human agency in our sociological accounts.

Understanding what agency means in sociology is difficult enough in the case of humans (see Chapter 5) and there is heated debate about what it would mean to give agency to things like tools, underground plumbing networks, great barrier reefs, or novel corona viruses. In one sense the claim is clear and sensible: for instance, IT infrastructure mediates human communication with algorithms increasingly acting using artificial intelligence. Buildings and traffic lights make city life possible, and our scientific instruments are what allow us to understand and intervene at a grand scale in the environment. Many sociologists maintain, however, that human agency has different properties from the way that non-human entities influence social life. To ignore this goes against the claim of new materialism to treat non-humans seriously, because it seems to be a type of anthropomorphism – forcing ideas of human intention and traits onto non-humans with their own, different properties.

It is important to add that these scholars who claim agency for non-humans also highlight that nothing can act on its own, but only has effects through being connected in a web of other things. There are not really actors or society in this approach but an infinite number of networks or assemblages of humans and non-humans that have effects in the world. Hence, arguably the most influential of these approaches is known as **actor-network theory**. These approaches attempt to break down the distinction between realism and social constructivism we introduced above. Everything is constructed but not only of social stuff.

Whether or not we treat the non-human as actors in our sociology, it is clear that sociology needs to think about diseases, pandemics and the climate if it is to help us understand how politics works and to possibly change the social world. Latour points out that we think of pre-modern life as much more closely connected to the natural environment but today we interact with the environment in a way impossible in the past, on a planetary scale. In a sense, the way humans have been able to mix the natural and social is the foundation for understanding contemporary society.

Similarly, we can create public health initiatives and medical interventions that have reshaped our notions of a natural lifespan, with advances expanding average life expectancy across the globe. It has more than doubled over the past century to around 70. There is great disparity across nations (up to 30 years) but the chance of living to old age has gone up at an amazing rate. The coronavirus pandemic hits people over 80 particularly hard, but this is the first time in human history that there has been a large population in their 70s and 80 to be impacted by a pandemic.

In some ways, we see evidence of progress around us. Some sociologists see the role of sociology to overcome a tendency in many societies towards an optimism bias that helps mask inequality and individualises responsibility. From this perspective, sociology's task is to critique the idea that the world is full of opportunities if you just lean in and do the work. There are approaches to sociology that have had a tendency towards being too optimistic or pessimistic. In the 1970s, American sociologist Alvin Gouldner challenged the approach to understanding social system functions built by Talcott Parsons and others – arguably the most influential sociological approach at the time – for being glowingly and naively optimistic about the role of social systems and in particular about American society. Gouldner probably oversimplified Parsons's approach in his critique (this is a common failing of many critiques). However, there is a tendency in Parsons and other such approaches to think that if a social institution exists, it must have a useful function.

Gouldner argued persuasively that sociology is intrinsically part of the societies in which it is created and cannot be objective in the way that the natural sciences perceive themselves to be objective. This does not mean being simply partisan. Sociology needs to be reflexive, constantly self-critical, looking at how social factors shape sociology as an approach and how sociology plays a role in society and how decisions are made about the future. Hence, Gouldner argued that sociology should be reflexively partisan, on the side of those pushing to change the world for the better. Other sociologists have made similar arguments, that sociology should be on the side of the oppressed, of social movements, and those advocating for emancipatory social change. Pierre Bourdieu, who we have discussed in several chapters, used the metaphor of sociology as a martial art that should only be used for self-defence of those with less power.

More recently the American-based British sociologist Michael Burawoy has argued that sociology is partisan in the way that all disciplines are. He argues that economics is concerned with expanding markets; political science is concerned with the state and stability; sociology therefore is concerned with the defence of social concerns and addressing inequality, from the perspective of **civil society**. Civil society includes non-government organisations, community groups, and social movements – in fact all organisations that are not-for-profit and not the state (hence it is also sometimes called the third sector).

Burawoy thinks sociology's partisan role is essential in a world facing ecological crises, huge material inequality, the rise of terrorism and fascism, and rapid social changes that make people feel insecure. He calls for a focus on **public sociology** – public facing sociology, working with social movements and civil society to defend humanity from these kinds of threats. This does not mean that sociologists need to stop their academically focused empirical work, as this is a foundation for good public sociology. But sociologists need to be cognisant of who the knowledge they produce is for and write in different ways that will be effective for reaching different audiences.

However, such partisan, public sociology might have its own limits if it becomes too focused on reducing everything to social construction, or ideology that creates 'dupes'. This has been a tendency in some types of critical sociology, including some work in the cultural-focused Marxist inspired tradition called **critical theory** that we have discussed in other chapters. Bruno Latour, related to his argument about treating non-humans seriously in our sociological accounts, argues that the type of critique underpinning critical theory – showing how what seem like facts are in fact social constructions controlled by the powerful – may verge on being dangerous. He sees some manifestations of this type of 'debunking' critical attitude within sociology as having a homology with conspiracy theories along the lines of the CIA were responsible for the attacks in New York and Washington on September 11, 2001, or that climate change is a hoax to destroy capitalism or get research funding, or today we might add that COVID-19 was created in a laboratory as a weapon of war or to enforce socialism.

In Chapter 1 we talked about how a good sociological imagination gives us an alternative explanation to conspiracy theories, allowing us to see that complex social facts can emerge without a small group of people actively controlling everything (remember the lizard people). We see the best sociology as using a mix of conceptual tools and lots of empirical work, including taking people's own experience of social life seriously, to look at the complex facts of social life, the interplay of social patterns and **social action**, and the way things change over time and how continuity is achieved.

With Bourdieu, Burawoy and others, we also believe sociology should be on the side of civil society, of social movements, and those trying to build a better world. Some famous leaders of social movements have used their sociology to change the world. Martin Luther King Junior, Jane Addams, Emily Blach and Alva Myrdal were all trained in sociology before winning the Nobel Peace Prize. However, this does not mean that everyone doing sociology, or sociology as a whole, will simply agree with exactly what participants within social movements believe and do (as we pointed out above, movements have their own internal politics and divisions and some have aims that we might find nefarious). Part of the role of sociology is to show how things might be harder to change than we realise, to show how change is linked to unintended consequences and how attempts to change the world can fail. Sociologists such as Les Back and Ken Plummer have argued that another part of our role is to sometimes be hopeful, highlighting what is good about our lives and that the world does continue to change. A better future is possible. Indeed, there are things to be hopeful about. As noted above, the sociologist Mary Holmes proposes a sociology for optimists, attuned to deep inequalities but also that not everything is getting worse. Holmes points out that sociologists too often overlook what makes life pleasurable and where humans find happiness. In her writing she shows numerous examples of people changing things for the better.

It is unlikely we would all ever agree on the right criteria for making an overall judgement on whether life is getting better or worse. For many sociologists, this is probably not the right question to ask, as the risks we face are now of a different kind that suggest an ambivalent attitude towards progress. We have an unparalleled capacity to shape the social and natural world. Yet, the capacity of the environment to surprise and potentially overwhelm us has not diminished, and the way humans have shaped our environment may be making this even more likely. Our public health systems have never been stronger, on average, yet we live in a way that allows new pathogens to emerge and travel around the world – in a matter of a months – that is also unparalleled in human history. Sociologists who call our current social world **risk societies** point out that we are living with the unintended consequences of modernity's success.

Will You Change the World?

As Holmes proposes, an approach to sociology that remains critical but is also optimistic is probably a necessary tool kit for sociologists if they are to be true to the human capacity to bring about social change. She suggests that the sociology of generations is an example of such an approach. The sociology of generations emerged as sociologists tried to think through the role of age, intergenerational relationships and social structures in social change. As both of us (Dan and Steve) work in the sociology of youth and young adulthood, we are going to finish the book by saying a little about young people and social change.

Whether you are young or not, there is a high chance you have heard young people described as apathetic. You might have even been called this yourself. In some countries the newspapers, politicians and many older people portray young people as disengaged from politics or use different groups of young people to scapegoat and blame for social problems that young people have very little control over. Sociologists who have studied young people give a more nuanced view. Some young people are disengaged from formal politics – such as voting in an election – and cynical about politicians and the way they wield power. This is the case across age cohorts – plenty of older people are also cynical about this. However, as we have seen in this chapter, power is much more than this and politics is much wider than the processes of formal government.

Have you marched in a protest or signed a petition? Have you engaged in debate about politics on Facebook or decided not to buy a product because of the behaviour of the company that produced it? Have you posted online about Me Too or Black Lives Matter? What about the young people in North Africa and West Asia who led what is called the Arab Spring and influenced young people from Spain to the USA to start their own occupations of public space, creating movements like Podemos and Occupy Wall Street. Even more recently, Greta Thunberg and other young people have led a renewed push to address the climate emergency. This does not mean that all young people are equally political or that they are all left wing. From the perspective of a sociology of generations, it means that there are new political issues and stakes that young people are shaping and engaging with. Thinking about youth and social change in these terms draws on foundational work undertaken by sociologists after the First World War, particularly the Hungarian-German sociologist Karl Mannheim.

Writing in the wake of the First World War, Mannheim argued that **generations**, in the sociological sense he gave them, did not unfold at regular intervals automatically as a people grew up and had children of their own. Instead following specific events, such as the aftermath of a world war, the ways of life pursued by the previous generation became impossible or unacceptable, particularly for the people most affected by the change (which is often the young, such as those most caught up in the fighting during a war). For Mannheim, such moments set the conditions for a new generational structure, that young people are both forced to navigate and are in some ways part of creating. Unlike many stereotypes of the Millennials or Generations X, Y and Z, Mannheim did not argue that all members of a generation think alike. A major event such as a war or a pandemic could create conditions for certain feelings, attitudes and tendencies to become more common and this could differ between age brackets, as the effects will be different based on people's age when the event took place. However, at the same time, Mannheim proposed there will often be deep oppositions *between* young people sharing a generational context.

A generation is defined by changing stakes, possibly climate or global health, over which people will disagree and take different positions. Recently, there are examples such as Me Too, Occupy, Students for Climate Change. We imagine there may be a strengthened movement for global health justice in the wake of the COVID-19 pandemic. Such movements are often led by the young. But other young people are part of the alt-right and a reactionary movement against inclusive youth cultures online and on campuses. The American sociologist Sarah Banet-Weiser has charted the role of young people in the rise of popular misogyny with the emergence of the Alt-Right, Incels and Men's Rights movements, the constant threats and abuse towards women online and the continuation of shocking statistics of men's violence against women in terms of domestic violence, sexual assault and murder (think also of the different approaches to gender among different young people outlined by Risman, which we covered in Chapter 8).

Mannheim called the different groups within a generation, **generational units**. A generational unit is defined in relation to changes from the generation before and also by its differences with others within the same generation, similar to the concept of subcultures we introduced in Chapter 6. Mannheim understood these differences as emerging through social factors. A generational location was only one of the social locations that shaped the concrete experience of a group of people; class and ethnicity, for example, are other such social locations mentioned in Mannheim's work. Now we would add gender, sexuality, geographical location, disability and other factors. Few contemporary sociologists would see generations in as concrete terms as Mannheim did; instead, today scholars using this framework see generational factors at play in people's lives alongside class, gender, race, disability and sexuality. In other words, generations can be part of an intersectional account.

We can also think about generations when we are being reflexive about sociology. In Chapter 3 we discussed the global political economy of social science. There may be generational change underway in sociology itself. Several of the sociologists we have spoken about in this book, including Ulrich Beck, Zygmunt Bauman and John Urry, have died over the past few years. They were among the most famous sociologists of their generation. These scholars have certain things in common – they are all from one part of the world and they are all men. As the sociologists from outside of Europe and North America, and feminist, race and post-colonial scholars we have introduced in this book have consistently pointed out, our present is shaped by our global history of inequality and colonisation. Patel, Bhambra, Connell and others we introduced you to in Chapter 3 and throughout this book push sociology to maintain a global sensibility and to draw from thinking across the globe. We have tried to introduce you to some of this sensibility in this book but there is still lots of work to do. This book still has a lot of white men in it, and it presents a view on sociology from our perspective – that of two white Australian men. The next generation of global scholars will shape sociology in a new way and hopefully be as influential as Beck, Bourdieu and Butler.

As we noted above, it can be difficult to agree on what progress means. This is also true within sociology and the social sciences. Some cynics suggest that social sciences never get any better. However, the sociologist Andrew Abbott argues this is only an appearance because how the social sciences progress is different from common understandings of how science improves over time. He argues that new schools of thought are more likely to be a reinvention of important concepts to fit the changing times and different conditions in different places as they are to be efforts to build better universal theories of stable phenomena. This is one of the reasons we have introduced you to key ideas from classical and contemporary sociology.

This conceptualisation of change and progress within social science has echoes of Mannheim's sociological model of generations. Mannheim was concerned with the way that a generation makes 'fresh contact' with a knowledge tradition, rejecting parts and reworking others. The next generation of sociologists – and we hope that this will include some of you who are reading this – will struggle with key sociological questions bestowed by our history and the history of sociology. But future sociologists will develop new approaches for the times and hopefully draw on a greater array of influences. Maybe you will be part of doing this.

Conclusion

Sociologists count a much wider sphere of human action as political action than the formal processes of government. But do these other ways of trying to wield power make a difference? Some sociologists continue to argue for a hierarchical understanding of power while others propose that nobody really has power, that power is found in practices or flows through networks. Importantly, we can see how forms of power constrain, marginalise and discriminate against particular people and groups, but also that individuals and groups can organise to resist and to remake the world.

Sociology is a discipline of multiple approaches, with some disagreements even about fundamental terms. Just like other conceptual couplings that have been used in sociology, like subject and object, structure and agency, continuity and change, the division between nature and society is not straightforward and needs to be critically challenged and rethought for contemporary times. This is important politically for facing huge human-induced problems such as climate change. However, there are meaningful distinctions that can be made. In our view, some of the most insightful sociology holds a tension between such key concepts. They are often not opposed, are almost always intertwined and often **co-constituted**, but they are not reducible one to the other or to some third factor.

The divisions and inequalities that shaped the past continue to shape the present. Continuity and change are best understood as a series of tensions. While there is much that looks like continuity, particularly in who wins or loses in society, this inequality does not unfold naturally or like clockwork. Social life is continually made and remade. In such a context, to keep things the same often means that people act differently, just as we will also have to act differently if we are to shape a better world. We live in an age where people are experimenting with new ways to influence how they are governed. We also live in a moment where a new generation faces the challenges of climate change, continuing inequalities, and global pandemics. Sociology will be essential in helping us understand our changing world and meet these challenges.

———————— **Key references for this chapter** ————————

Abbott, A (2001) *Chaos of Disciplines*. University of Chicago Press.

Aberle, DF (1966) *The Peyote Religion among the Navaho*. Aldine.

Back, L (2016) *Academic Diary: Or Why Higher Education Still Matters*. Goldsmiths Press.

Banet-Weiser, S (2018) *Empowered: Popular Feminism and Popular Misogyny*. Duke University Press.

Beck, U (1992) *Risk Society: Towards a New Modernity*. Sage.

Blumer, H (1969) 'Collective Behaviour', in Lee, AM (ed.) *Principles of Sociology*, 3rd edn. Barnes and Noble Books, pp. 165–221.

Burawoy, M (2005) 'For Public Sociology', *American Sociological Review*, vol. 70, no. 1, pp. 4–28.

Callon, M (1986) 'Some Elements of a Sociology of Translation: Domestication of the Scallops and the Fishermen of St Brieuc Bay', in Law, J (ed.) *Power, Action, and Belief: A New Sociology of Knowledge?* Routledge, pp. 196–223.

Castells, M (1997) *The Power of Identity*. Blackwell.

Castells, M (2015) *Networks of Outrage and Hope: Social Movements in the Internet Age*, 2nd edn. Polity Press.

Chouliaraki, L (2012) *The Ironic Spectator: Solidarity in the Age of Post-Humanitarianism*. Polity Press.

Dahl, RA (1961) *Who Governs?: Democracy and Power in an American City*. Yale University Press.

De Certeau, M (1984) *The Practice of Everyday Life*, trans. S Rendall. University of California Press.

Fanon, F (1965) *The Wretched of the Earth*. Grove Press.

Foucault, M (1998) *The History of Sexuality*, 3 vols., trans. R Hurley. Penguin Books.

Gamson, WA (1975) *The Strategy of Social Protest*. The Dorsey Press.

Giddens, A (1991) *Modernity and Self-identity*. Stanford University Press.

Gouldner, AW (1970) *The Coming Crisis of Western Sociology*. Basic Books.

Habermas, J (1981) 'New Social Movements', *Telos*, vol. 1981, no. 49, pp. 33–37.

Holmes, M (2016) *Sociology for Optimists*. Sage.

Latour, B (2004) 'Why Has Critique Run out of Steam? From Matters of Fact to Matters of Concern', *Critical Inquiry*, vol. 30, no. 2, pp. 225–248.

Latour, B (2005) *Reassembling the Social: An Introduction to Actor Network Theory*. Oxford University Press.

Law, J (2009) 'Actor Network Theory and Material Semiotics', in Turner, BS (ed.) *The New Blackwell Companion to Social Rheory*. Blackwell, pp. 141–158.

Mann, M (1986) *The Sources of Social Power*, vol. 1. Cambridge University Press.

Mannheim, K (1952) 'The Problem of Generations', in Kecskemeti, P (ed.) *Karl Mannheim: Essays on the Sociology of Knowledge*. Routledge & Kegan Paul, pp. 276–320.

Mbembe, A (2016) *Necropolitics*. Duke University Press.

Melucci, A (1980) 'The New Social Movements: A Theoretical Approach', *Social Science Information*, vol. 19, no. 2, pp. 199–226.

Michels, R (1915) *Political Parties: A Sociological Study of the Oligarchical Tendencies of Modern Democracy*. Hearst's International Library Co.

Mills, CW (1956) *The Power-Elite*. Oxford University Press.

Moore, B Jr. (1966) *Social Origins of Dictatorship and Democracy: Lord and Peasant in the Making of the Modern World*. Beacon Press.

Piven, FF (2006) *Challenging Authority: How Ordinary People Change America*. Rowman and Littlefield.

Skocpol, T (1979) *States and Social Revolutions: A Comparative Analysis of France, Russia and China*. Cambridge University Press.

Tilly, C (1978) *From Mobilization to Revolution*. Addison-Wesley.

Touraine, A (1992) 'Beyond Social Movements', *Theory, Culture & Society*, vol. 9, no. 1, pp.125–145.

Valencia, S (2018) *Gore Capitalism*, trans. J Pluecker. Semiotext(e).

Wilkinson, R and Pickett, K (2010) *The Spirit Level: Why Equality Is Better for Everyone*. Penguin.

GLOSSARY

Academic Dependency: The dependence of scholars and intellectuals from the Majority World on the institutions and ideas of Minority World social science.

Actor-Network Theory: A theoretical perspective which holds that reality is made up of networks of interrelated, interacting elements, including non-human elements such as objects and ideas. Actor-network theorists seek to trace the associations between these various elements.

Agency: The capacity to act in chosen or creative manner, to shape individual and social patterns.

Alienation: In Marxism, the process by which workers are separated or estranged from the products of their labour. Marx holds that in the capitalist system of production workers lose control over their labour and its products; as a result, their labour becomes something foreign to them.

Ambivalence: A feeling of contrasting or opposing commitments towards a particular entity or event.

Anomie: In Durkheim, a social state characterised by dramatic shifts in individual status, typically as the result of rapid, unregulated economic change. Feelings of anomie are associated with frustration, uncertainty, and unhappiness, and may cause *anomic suicide*.

Augmented Reality: A term proposed by Jurgenson to describe the merging of material reality and digital technologies.

Augmented Selves: A term proposed by Jurgenson to describe self-identities which combine physical and digital aspects, or which are developed through both online and offline interaction.

Base: In Marxism, the economic foundation of a society, including the relations and materials of production.

Big Data: A large amount of data, particularly as now being generated through new digital commerce and social media channels.

Biological Racism: The belief that certain racial or ethnic groups are superior to others based on intrinsic factors of biology.

Biopower: In Foucault, a term used to describe the way that modern nation-states regulate the bodily behaviours and life processes of their citizens. Biopower involves the control of population through practices of public health, risk regulation, shaping of reproduction, and so on.

Birmingham School: A group of scholars who developed an approach to the sociological study of cultures and subcultures, associated with the members of the Centre for Contemporary Cultural Studies at the University of Birmingham in England.

Black Feminism: An approach to feminism which focuses on the experiences of Black women and the intersection of racial and gender inequality.

Black Feminist Thought: A body of knowledge based around the assumptions and ideas of Black feminism.

Black/White Paradigm: A way of studying race which only examines relationships between white and Black people, rather than also considering non-black people of colour.

Blasé Attitude: In Simmel, a detached attitude towards events and other people required to navigate life in a city – also a flattening and homogenisation of spontaneity, unpredictability and ironically also of the individuality that city life appears to afford.

Bonding Social Capital: Relational resources tied to networks of individuals who are similar in some important way. Bonding social capital typically unites people *within* some specific group.

Border Thinking: A mode of thought which draws on the perspectives, knowledges, and forms of expression marginalised by colonial domination that focuses on experiences, lives and structures at the intersections of different borders.

Bourgeoisie: In Marxism, the class which owns and controls the means of production within the capitalist system.

Bricolage: A term used to describe the creation of new cultural forms via the combination, reworking, or alteration of existing cultural forms.

Bridging Social Capital: Relational resources tied to networks of individuals who are dissimilar in some important way. Bridging social capital typically relates people within a group to those *outside* of this group.

Bureaucracy: In Weber, a form of administrative organisation, characterised by hierarchy, chain of command, division of labour, formal procedures, and impersonal interaction.

Bureaucratisation: The third stage of a social movement, in which the social movement becomes an established organisation, often with a formal hierarchy and a paid staff.

Canon: A collection of classic works considered to be especially important and influential.

Capitalism: An economic system in which the means of production are held privately and operated for profit. Common features of capitalist systems include private property, wage labour, competitive markets, and voluntary exchange.

Captive Mind: A mode of thought in which the perspective of an external source is adopted in an uncritical and imitative manner. In Alatas's description, the external source is Western social science and humanities.

Charismatic Leadership: In Weber, a form of leadership is which authority depends on the charisma of the leader as experienced by the followers of that leader. Charismatic leaders are typically thought to possess exceptional abilities or qualities, setting them apart from other individuals.

Cisgender: An individual whose personal identity and gender corresponds with their assigned birth sex.

Civil Religion: In Bellah, a name given to an institutionalised collection of beliefs which has a quasi-religious or sacred character.

Civil Society: A term given to the sector of society which lies outside of the state or the market.

Civilisations: Distinct cultural groupings sharing foundational values, typically spanning a number of politically independent societies (e.g. 'Western civilization').

Civilising Process: In Elias, a term given to the long-term historical process by which manners and behaviour became increasingly refined in European societies.

Class: Categorisations of individuals based on economic status. Members of a class have been conceptualised as being similar in wealth, occupational type, lifestyles and disposition.

Class Ceiling: A term used to describe the collection of barriers which impede upward class mobility.

Class Consciousness: In Marxism, one's awareness of one's class, its interests, and its relationship to the means of production.

Closet: In Sedgwick, (coming out of the) closet is a broader metaphor of the workings of power in shaping sexuality in Global Northern societies, the assumptions made about people and the limitations of a heterosexual/homosexual binary.

Coalescence: The second stage of a social movement, in which people begin to organise around the issue identified.

Co-constituted: The view that two processes or outcomes are co-creating or reinforcing of each other – in the context of structure and agency in sociology, not separate or opposed forces, but as structures enabling agency and agency recreating structures.

Collective Effervescence: In Durkheim, the name given to a feeling of excitement and group unity aroused by participation in communal gatherings and rituals.

Colonisation: The process by which a nation establishes control over another territory or people, typically to provide economic benefits for the coloniser.

Colour-Line: In Du Bois, a term used to describe racial segregation, or social and legal barriers which separate people based on perceived race.

Conflict: In the context of sociology, an approach or theory that analyses social phenomena by examining their role in the creation or maintenance of group power.

Conspicuous Consumption: A term developed by Veblen, referring to the spending of money on goods or services which are primarily designed to signal an individual's status, taste, and economic power.

Consumption: The utilisation of goods or services.

Contingent Inclusion: A term used to describe the way that racial minorities can become included in communities on the basis of other characteristics.

Convivial Culture: In Gilroy, the lively, friendly interaction between different racial groups in a society.

Counterculture: A set of cultural patterns which are opposed to the dominant cultural patterns of a society.

Crip Theory: An approach playing on the term 'cripple' that has been reclaimed by the disability rights movement. Crip theory resists able-bodied heteronormativity as a taken-for-granted ideal.

Critical Theory: A style of social theory which is explicitly concerned with discovering and critiquing social injustices.

Cultural Appropriation: The adoption of elements in one culture, typically a minority culture, by another culture, typically a dominant culture. Cultural appropriation is typically seen as negative when cultural elements are misused or divorced from their original meaning.

Cultural Capital: In Bourdieu, non-economic resources that allow people to advance their position in a field. Such resources include dispositions, tastes, behaviours, credentials, skills, and so on.

Cultural Dupes: A term used to characterise and criticise theories which are seen as treating the individual as a blind follower or consumer of cultural trends or products. Such theories are thought to see individuals as cultural dupes lacking agency.

Cultural Identity: One's sense of belonging to a particular cultural group.

Cultural Imperialism: The process by which the culture, values, and norms of one society are imposed on another. Typically used in reference to the global dominance of Western culture and ideals.

Cultural Interface: A model, proposed by Nakata, in which cross-cultural interaction is described as a 'layered and very complex entanglement of concepts, theories and sets of meanings of a knowledge system'. Used to relate to Indigenous people's complex lives and social connections across cultural formations.

Cultural Racism: A belief that the culture of one 'race' or ethnic group is superior to, or alternatively under threat from, another. Cultural racism typically involves the belief that certain ethnic cultures are fundamentally incompatible; it is in this sense opposed to multiculturalism.

Cultural Sociology: A form of sociology which is specifically focused on interpreting the meanings, significance and effects of cultural forms and patterns.

Culture: A set of practices and norms widely shared by members of a group. Culture includes the traditions, symbols, language, gestures, norms, values and rituals that give meaning to our lives and that we use to understand our world.

Culture Industry: A term used by Adorno and Horkheimer to describe how popular culture in capitalist societies is produced in an industrial, standardised manner. For Adorno and Horkheimer, the products of the culture industry promote docility and passivity in citizens.

Cyborg: In Haraway, an entity which fuses elements of humans and machines.

Data: A collection of observations about the social world, gained through *methods*. With data, we can develop or test *theories*.

Decline: The final stage of a social movement, which occurs when change is successfully brought about or resisted or when the movement fails due to repression, co-optation, or a lack of support.

Dependency Theory: A theoretical perspective that arose in opposition to modernisation theory. Dependency theory argued that social development is linked to unequal power relationships between a 'periphery' made up of poorer countries and a 'core' of wealthier countries, where the wealthier core developed at the expense of the periphery.

Determinism: The belief that individual action is determined by forces outside of our control.

Deviance: Behaviour that does not conform to social norms.

Diaspora: A community of people who live outside of their shared country or region of ancestral origin.

Disciplinary Power: In Foucault, a kind of power, characteristic of modern societies, in which social control is maintained by means of surveillance, socialisation, and the instilling of routines and disciplines on the body.

Discourse: In Foucault, sets of widely accepted norms or ways of thinking about particular topics which are taken for granted in a particular time period or locale.

Discrimination: The unfair treatment of an individual or group based on their particular characteristics.

Disenchantment: In Weber, the name given to a kind of change by which individuals develop a more rational, scientific understanding of the world. Disenchantment is associated with the devaluation of religious ideas and practices.

Disgusted Subject: In Lawler, a gendered and classed form of self-definition through condescension and even 'disgust' towards those who cannot maintain middle-class feminised ways of acting.

Disruptive Power: In Piven, a form of political influence based on disruptive actions, such as strikes, boycotts, and sit-ins.

Distinctions: In Bourdieu, the means by which groups differentiate themselves from others, typically to establish their own superiority.

Division of Labour: The separation of tasks in a productive system. Generally divided into two forms: the division of labour in *manufacture*, referring to specialisation within organisations or manufactories, and the division of labour in *society*, referring to an increase in occupational distinctions.

Docile Bodies: In Foucault, individuals who have internalised disciplinary power, or who have been trained to behave in ways that preserve and maintain the present social order.

Double Consciousness: A feeling of internal conflict and estrangement arising from oppression. Double consciousness occurs when one's identity is bifurcated into distinct sets of thoughts, strivings, and ideals, which the individual struggles to reconcile. Coined by Du Bois in reference to the experience of African Americans.

Dramaturgical: A sociological perspective, developed by Goffman, which likens social behaviour to a dramatic performance.

Economic Power: In Mann, power derived from control of the production, distribution, exchange, and consumption of resources.

Elective Affinity: A relationship between cultural or social elements, in which each reinforces, supports, or affirms the other.

Emancipatory Movement: A type of social movement concerned with freeing groups from oppression, discrimination, and exploitation.

Embodiment: A term used to describe how social influences manifest in the bodily dispositions and behaviours of individuals.

Emergence: The first stage of a social movement, in which the movement begins to form around a particular issue or source of inspiration. Movements in this stage have little organisation; instead, feelings of discontent begin to crystalise.

Emotional Labour: Labour which involves the management of feelings or emotions, of both the customer and by the worker.

Emphasised Femininity: A set of idealised norms about female behaviour, which encourage women to behave in ways that conform to the needs and desires of men. Emphasised femininity encourages traits such as submissiveness and attractiveness.

Encoding and Decoding: A model of communication developed by Stuart Hall. Encoding refers to the production of a message, in which a sender attempts to convey information via symbols, gestures, and other such means. Decoding refers to the recipient's attempt to reconstruct the meaning of the message, or to interpret what the sender was attempting to convey with the chosen means.

Epistemology: The theory and study of knowledge, including what can be known and how.

Equality of Opportunity: Used to describe a situation in which individuals can compete on the same terms, or on a 'level playing field'.

Essentialism: The view that members of particular groups possess intrinsic and 'essential' traits which make them members of that group.

Ethnicity: A set of shared values, cultural practices, and ideas which are used to distinguish one group of people from another, often tied to ancestry. Aspects of ethnicity include rituals, religious beliefs, languages, social norms, and so on.

Ethnocentrism: The act of judging other cultures based on the standards, values, and ideas common to one's own culture. Ethnocentrism occurs when one evaluates the world from the perspective of their own culture and ignores the different perspectives of other groups.

Eugenics: A philosophy and social movement which holds that human populations or societies can be improved by encouraging certain groups to breed while discouraging others. Eugenicist ideas have often been implemented by force.

Eurocentrism: A form of ethnocentrism, in which the perspective being prioritised is that of European culture or society.

Expressive Role: In Parsons, a specialised role in groups, primarily concerned with the provision of emotional support for group members. In family groups, the expressive role is oriented towards the emotional needs of family members and involves such behaviours as caring for the young.

Extraversion: In Hountondji intellectual work is extraverted when oriented to the ideas and problems of other societies or cultures, particularly the way that colonised societies and settler colonial societies are oriented intellectually to the Global North.

False and True Needs: A distinction introduced by Marcuse. False needs are needs which are manufactured by institutions such as the media or the advertising industry. True needs are the intrinsic needs of individuals. Marcuse argued that advanced industrial societies fulfilled false needs at the expense of true needs.

Fatalism: In Durkheim, a social state characterised by excessively strong norms, or 'over-regulation' in which freedom of behaviour is heavily constrained. Feelings of fatalism are associated with a sense of oppression and hopelessness and may cause *fatalistic suicide*.

Femininity: A set of attributes or behaviours that have been characteristically associated with women.

Feminist Theories: Theories that analyse social phenomena by examining their role in the creation or maintenance of male dominance.

Feudalism: An economic and social system in which those who owned land (known as lords) controlled the peasants farming that land and had rights to a part of their produce, labour or to charge a rent.

Field: In Bourdieu, a system of social positions organised around particular stakes. Individuals occupy these positions and 'compete' over the stakes of the field, following the particular rules and norms of the field to advance their position. For example, individuals in the 'art' field compete for status, prestige, and recognition.

First-Wave Feminism: A social movement, occurring in the late 19th and early 20th centuries, which sought legal equality between men and women, especially in regard to voting and property rights.

Fordism: An approach to manufacturing, originally developed by Henry Ford to improve productive efficiency in the automotive industry. Principles of Fordism include greater standardisation via the use of machines, the employment of assembly line methods in manufacture, and the payment of sufficient wages to facilitate consumption.

Fourth-Wave Feminism: A social movement, beginning from around the early 2010s, focusing on women's empowerment and particularly linked with the use of digital tools and platforms. Fourth-wave feminism is thought to be especially concerned with issues such as body shaming and rape culture.

Frontstage and Backstage: A distinction introduced by Goffman to describe two different contexts of action. People engage in 'frontstage' behaviour when they know or anticipate that other people are watching them, while they engage in 'backstage' behaviour when their actions are comparatively less visible.

Functional Necessity: A social phenomenon considered to be necessary for society to exist or function properly.

Functional: In the context of sociology, a functional or functionalist approach analyses social phenomena by examining their role in the creation or maintenance of social order and functioning of society.

Gemeinschaft/Gesellschaft: Typically translated as *community* and *society*. *Gemeinschaft* refers to social ties based on personal interaction, such as those of family and friendship. *Gesellschaft* refers to social ties based on impersonal interaction, such as those of commerce.

Gender: A classification by which certain traits or behaviours are socially defined as masculine or feminine and attached to men or women. Has typically been distinguished from *sex*, a classification by which individuals have been defined as male or female (or more rarely intersex) on the basis of genetic and physiological characteristics.

Gender Order: A system of ideas and practices that define gender identities or roles in particular societies and determine their relationship to one another.

Gender-based Violence: Forms of violence which are motivated by or otherwise connected to gender norms.

Genderqueer: An individual who does not identify with or behave in accordance with traditional gender categories.

Generalised Other: In Mead, our sense of the general expectations which other people in a community or social group hold about appropriate beliefs and behaviours.

Generation: Interaction of changing social conditions, the life course and people's actions that create new experiences for youth cohorts that shape the unfolding of their adult lives. Generational change is created both by how young people navigate and how they create social change when older patterns of action and thought seem difficult, inappropriate or impossible in the changing context.

Generational Units: In Mannheim, subgroups within generations that form different responses to the particular historical situation based on differences other than age.

Genocide: An organised, systematised and coordinated effort to persecute and annihilate any human group or collectivity by another group with power (usually a state).

Gig Economy: An economic model in which short-term, temporary, or freelance work is commonplace.

Ghetto: In Elijah Anderson's analysis, the (iconic) ghetto is a widely held, sometimes tacit, stereotype of the neighbourhoods where African Americans live or grew up, embedded in popular culture.

Global Cities: In Sassen, the key places of globalisation. These are large urban centres like New York, London, Singapore or Beijing that are key nodes in regional and global networks, becoming even more important in late modernity. People and multinational companies will be increasingly drawn to them.

Global North: The use of a geographic reference, linked to the Northern hemisphere, to capture the political, economic and social status advantages and power of countries that were previously called 'Developed', which are mostly in this hemisphere. Similar to the Minority World.

Global South: Related to Global North, used to characterise the the political, economic and social status of countries that were previously called 'Third World' or 'Developing', countries primarily in the Southern hemisphere. Similar to the Majority World.

Globalisation: An ongoing process of social change by which regions and nations become increasingly interconnected with one another, especially in regard to economic, political or cultural phenomena.

Glocalisation: The idea that globalisation can increase or interact with the importance of local and regional level factors, rather than simply erasing them.

Gore Capitalism: A term used by Valencia to describe the idea that violence has become a commodity in the contemporary economy.

Governmentality: In Foucault, techniques of governing (broadly not just by 'the government') using practices aimed at shaping the conduct, beliefs and identities of people.

Great Transformation: A term coined by Polanyi to describe the social and political changes associated with the rise of modern market societies.

Habitus: In Bourdieu, a set of dispositions, tendencies, and preferences, through which we understand and participate in the world.

Hegemonic Masculinity: A set of idealised norms about male behaviour, which legitimise the subordination of women and of non-hegemonic men. Hegemonic masculinity encourages traits such as competitiveness, dominance, independence, muscularity, homophobia, and the devaluation of women and femininity.

Hegemony: In Marxism, a form of cultural domination in which the worldview of a ruling class becomes widely accepted as normal or correct, legitimising their power and justifying the status quo. For Gramsci, hegemony involves a mix of consent, coercion and even some comprise.

Heteronormativity: Heterosexuality as the social norm, preferred or assumed default category of sexual orientation and the social privileges attached to having this orientation.

Heterosexual Matrix: In Butler, a rigid set of linked categorisations in society that link sex, gender, and sexuality in a way that makes normative combinations seem natural.

Hidden Curriculum: Rules and lessons that are taught at schools outside of explicit curriculum and school policies, including 'cultural' expectations around gender, class or race.

Hipster Racism: Performing behaviours typically seen as racist in an ironic, self-aware, or satirical manner.

Holocaust: The systematic genocide of European Jews by Nazi Germany during the Second World War.

Homogeneity: A word used to describe a collection of elements which are each identical to one another.

Hybridity: In post-colonial studies, the creation of new transcultural forms and identities within the zone of cultural contact produced by colonisation and migration.

I and Me: A distinction introduced by Mead. The 'me' is made up of those aspects of the self that have been influenced more directly by or learned through interaction with others, while the 'I' consists of the individual's responses to the 'me', or the individual's response to the attitudes of others.

Identity: The qualities and attributes that people use to establish a person's individuality.

Identity Politics: A form of political action in which political alliances are formed around certain identity categories and their intersections, for example the categories of gender or race.

Ideological Power: In Mann, power derived from the human need to find meaning. Ideological power involves control over meaning, ritual, symbolism, and values.

Ideology: Beliefs, attitudes and cultural patterns justifying existing social institutions and hierarchies. Linked to power and the maintenance of inequalities.

Illusio: In Bourdieu, a commitment to participating in a particular field and the belief that the stakes of the field are worth competing over.

Imagined Community: In Anderson, the idea that nations are socially constructed entities, facilitated by a national media, based on individuals each believing that they are part of the national group.

Impression Management: In Goffman, a process by which we attempt to influence the perceptions that other people have of us, typically in order to achieve certain ends.

Indigenous Standpoint: The perspective on social phenomena afforded by experience as an Indigenous person and prioritising Indigenous ways of knowing and acting.

Individualisation: A name given to a general social trend, evident in many contemporary societies, which affords people greater options, and apparently more choices in regard to the way they live their lives but also new responsibilities to personally manage structural contradictions.

Industrial Revolution: A series of changes in production and manufacturing, occurring from the mid-18th century onwards. Key features of the industrial revolution include a greater use of machines, the organisation of labour in factories, and the use of new materials.

Information Age: A term used to describe the present historical age, especially in *post-industrial economies*. The information age is said to be marked by the growing importance of knowledge and information technology within the economy.

Instrumental Role: In Parsons, a specialised role in groups, primarily concerned with the completion of group tasks and the procurement of resources to do so. In family groups, the instrumental role is oriented towards the basic needs of the family and involves such things as the provision of financial support.

Internalised Racism: The acceptance, among racially marginalised groups, of ideas and stereotypes which portray them as inferior.

Intersectionality: The way that different social categorisations (such as race, gender, and class) intersect and overlap, forming new and complex forms of inequality.

Invisible Knapsack: A metaphor for privilege, developed by Peggy McIntosh, which posits that privilege is similar to an invisible collection of unearned assets that people can use to obtain success. Individuals who possess those assets are typically unaware that members of other groups (marginalised racial groups, for example) do not possess them, hence they are 'invisible' to them.

Iron Cage of Rationality: A situation in which people are increasingly compelled to act in accordance with dictates of efficiency, calculation, and rationality.

Iron Law of Oligarchy: The idea that an elite group of people will eventually take control within any democratic organisation.

Ironic Spectator: A term used by Chouliaraki to describe the detached, uninvested way that people may respond to human suffering in the current media environment. Ironic spectatorship involves outward gestures of solidarity and compassion that are more about benefiting one's own identity than genuinely helping others.

Islamophobia: Discrimination or prejudice against members of the Islamic faith.

Kaupapa Māori Theory: Theory based around the perspectives, aspirations, and values of the Māori community.

Kinsey Scale: A rating scale, used to measure sexuality on a gradation between homosexuality and heterosexuality.

Labelling Theory: A theory which proposes that identity and behaviour are influenced by how individuals are labelled, or by how certain terms are used to describe or categorise individuals.

Legitimising Identities: In Castells, forms of collective identity that are promoted by the dominant institutions of society in order to protect and reproduce the current social hierarchy.

Lifestyle Movement: A type of social movement concerned with achieving recognition or acceptance of new kinds of identity. In contrast to emancipatory movements, lifestyle movements are typically concerned with self-actualisation.

Liquid Modernity: In Bauman, a new type of modernity, associated with the contemporary era. Liquid modernity describes a condition of constant change, instability, and mobility, affecting all areas of human life.

Looking-Glass Self: In Cooley, our understanding of how other people perceive us, or our sense of how we appear to other people.

Majority World: The countries of the world outside the 'West', primarily in the Southern hemisphere, where most of the population resides. Developed as an alternative to terminology of 'Third World'.

Making Do: A term used by De Certeau to describe the tactics by which everyday people adapt to the strategies of control used by the powerful, often in innovative and resisting ways.

Manufactured Consensus: In Marcuse, the idea that commonly shared norms, ideas, and values are not the result of genuine agreement or free debate, but instead arise through efforts to manipulate and control the population.

Market Economy: An economic system in which decisions about the exchange of goods and services are ostensibly made by private individuals and businesses, rather than a central authority. Economic decisions in market economies are typically made in accordance with the logic of supply and demand.

Market Situation: In Weber, the various possibilities that exist for engaging in exchange. A shared market situation is like a type of shared class position.

Masculinity: A set of attributes or behaviours characteristically associated with men.

Material: In Marx, this includes all that is independent from thought and ideas but is most often used in references to economy and production.

McDonaldisation: In Ritzer, a process by which society adopts the characteristics or principles of a fast-food restaurant chain, namely, standardisation, homogenisation, and scientific management.

Mechanical Solidarity: In Durkheim, the integration of a group through similarity by way of shared values, norms, ideas, and behaviours.

Meritocratic: A system in which power or privilege is afforded to individuals on the basis of merit.

Mestiza Consciousness: In Anzaldúa, a term describing the unique experience of women with mixed ancestry, in particular Chicana women based on lived experience in hybrid cultural spaces, providing a basis for new understandings and resistance.

Methodological Cosmopolitanism: An approach to social science that sees social phenomena as taking place in an increasingly globalised context. Methodological cosmopolitanism involves attention to processes that transcend national borders.

Methodological Nationalism: An approach to social science that sees the nation-state as the primary object of analysis, or which largely focuses on processes within a single nation-state.

Methods: The procedures by which sociologists aim to gather reliable and accurate *data* about the social world.

Micro-aggressions: Small, commonplace behaviours or environmental features that communicate prejudicial attitudes towards members of marginalised groups.

Military Power: In Mann, power derived from the control of the social organisation of lethal violence, including the social organisation of military force.

Minority World: The wealthy countries of the 'West', which include a minority of the world's population but are responsible for a majority of consumption and have substantial influence over global politics. Used as as an alternative to terminology of 'First World' or 'Developed World'.

Misogyny: A strong contempt for women or femininity.

Mobilities: A research paradigm in contemporary sociology, focused on the study of movement. Mobilities scholars such as Urry study the movement of people, ideas, cultures, and things, and are often interested in topics such as transportation, migration, and tourism.

Modernisation Theory: A theoretical perspective that sought to describe and explain patterns of social development. Modernisation theories generally focused on the relationship between internal factors within societies (such as the relationship between economic development and democratic institutions) and argued that poor countries should emulate the structural patterns of wealthy countries.

Moral Panic: An instance of widespread panic or alarm in response to behaviours that are seen to threaten moral standards.

Multicultural Drift: The gradual drift towards acceptance of multicultural societies, created by everyday interactions and experiences.

Nation: A group of people who see themselves as a single, cohesive unit, based on various cultural, ancestral, or historical criteria. Members of a nation are typically similar in regard to their language, religious beliefs, cultural practices, and ethnic identities.

Nation-State: A *state* in which the majority of citizens belong to the same *nation*.

Nature/Nurture Debate: A debate about whether our behaviour is primarily determined by biological factors (nature) or by the influence of our social environment (nurture). Many approaches today focus on how these factors interact.

Necropolitics: A term used by Mbembe to describe the power to dictate who will live and who will die.

Network Capital: In Urry, an individual resource needed for success in the network society. Network capital involves technical and social skills, access to documents, technologies, and transportation, and ties with other individuals.

Network Society: In Castells, network-based social structure that increasing characterises the contemporary world, which builds upon new information and communication technologies and the connections they enable. Power is tied to the capacity to reallocate action and pathways across network nodes.

Networked Selves: A term used to describe the effects of social networking and digital technologies on one's sense of self.

New Materialism: A theoretical perspective which argues that scholars should consider how material objects and other non-human elements as well as embodiment shape social life.

New Racism: A form of racism based on a belief in the superiority or value of (or even need for protection of) the *culture* of a particular race or ethnic group, rather than primarily superiority in *biological* traits.

New Social Movements: A term used to describe the kinds of social movements that have emerged in Western societies from the mid-1960s onwards. New social movements are thought to be different from conventional social movements in the issues they pursue and how they do so.

Non-human Agency: The idea that non-human entities have agency, or a capacity to influence events and phenomena.

Northern Theory: Social science theories produced from the perspective of the Global North.

Occupation: A person's principal job or profession, the activity by which they earn their means of subsistence.

Ontology: Theory and study of what exists, of the types of beings in the world, how they emerge, change and are related to each other.

Ordinary Cosmopolitanism: Forms of cosmopolitan behaviour or ideas evident in everyday practice.

Organic Solidarity: In Durkheim, the integration of a group by way of mutual interdependence.

Orientalism: A particular perspective on Eastern culture, cultivated by Western academics, artists, and intellectuals. Orientalism involves depictions which paint Eastern culture as exotic, alien, irrational, or otherwise backwards in comparison to the West.

Other: An oppositional group against which self-image is constructed. The characteristics of the self are defined in opposition to the characteristics of the other.

Outsiders: Individuals who are thought to violate the established norms of a social group.

Panopticon: In Foucault and others, used as a metaphor for modern types of surveillance and self-formation. It is a type of prison designed by philosopher Jeremy Bentham and his brother in the 19th Century, in which cells are built around a central but not clearly visible (for the inmates) guard tower, such that prisoners come to assume they are being watched continuously, even if they are not.

Paranoid Nationalism: A concept developed by Hage, compared to an earlier form of 'defensive nationalism' that saw the threat to the nation as external. Paranoid nationalism is built on the newly vulnerable members of the working and middle class projecting this vulnerability on to anything deemed culturally alien, particularly within the nation's borders.

Party: In Weber, a group oriented to the acquisition of power. Parties are always directed towards the accomplishment of a particular goal.

Passing: When a member of one group is able to be seen by others as a member of a different group, particularly a light-skinned Black person may 'pass' as white.

Patriarchy: A form of social organisation in which power is primarily monopolised or held by men, to the exclusion of women.

Performativity: In Butler, the process by which gender identities are created and reinforced though behaviours, gestures, and elocutions.

Petty Bourgeoisie: In Marxism, a sub-class of the bourgeoisie made up of small-scale merchants and business people and professionals.

Platform Capitalism: A style of capitalism characterised by the widespread use of digital platforms.

Pluralism: A political theory which argues that power resources are distributed throughout society and are used by various groups to compete for influence.

Polarisation Effect: An aspect of moral panics, in which a split is created between two groups, typically the 'deviant' group and the 'correct' group.

Political Party: An organised group of people, sharing similar political positions, who field candidates for elections and attempt to gain access to institutional political power.

Political Power: In Mann, power held by a centralised, institutionalised, regulative body, in control of an associated territory.

Political Revolution: A substantial change in political governance based on a revolt against the existing order that is often violent, including the American and French revolutions of the late 18th century that are seen as constitutive of modernity.

Popular Culture: Forms of culture which are common or prevalent in a particular social group. Often defined in opposition to high or elite culture.

Post-colonial Feminism: Approaches to feminism which focus on the experiences of non-white, non-Western women.

Post-colonial Melancholy: A feeling of sadness, regret, and longing associated with a growing recognition of the negative aspects of colonisation but inability to acknowledge the violence it involved. Typically associated with elements of nostalgia for the time of empire, especially in Britain.

Post-colonial Studies: Academic approach that studies the ongoing social, cultural, and economic effects of colonialism and imperialism.

Post-colonial Theories: Theories that analyse social phenomena by examining their role in the creation or maintenance of Western/European dominance and study the current effects and historical legacy of colonisation.

Post-feminism: The view that feminism is no longer relevant or necessary as a political movement, and that gender equality has been achieved.

Post-Fordism: The dominant system of production in most contemporary industrialised economies, associated with a decline in mass production. Post-Fordism is typically thought to involve the rise of service professions, an emphasis on information and communication technologies, and a shift to small-batch production.

Post-industrial Economy: An economy in which the provision of services and information has higher relative importance than the provision of manufactured goods.

Post Modernity: A term used to describe cultural patterns or social structures which seem to depart from, or to otherwise break with, those characteristic of 'modern' societies.

Post-structuralism: A school of thought, emerging in 1960s France, which developed in reaction to the structuralist movement which preceded it.

Power: The ability of an entity, person, process or social formation to control, direct, or otherwise influence social processes, actions and outcomes.

Power Elite: In Mills, a term used to describe the leaders of military, corporate, and political groups, each of which are thought to share similar political interests and social networks.

Practices: In Bourdieu and others, a term used to describe the performance or carrying out of an action that provides a foundation for broader social patterns and selves.

Precariat: A social class comprised of people in precarious forms of employment.

Prejudice: The pre-emptive judging of a group or individual based on assumed characteristics.

Privilege: The idea that certain individuals or groups have advantages in society based on various characteristics, such as race, gender, sexuality, and so on.

Production: The provision of goods or services.

Project Identities: In Castells, forms of collective identity that allow people to redefine their social positions and to seek a transformation of the overall social structure.

Proletariat: In Marxism, the class which does not own and control the means of production within the capitalist system. To subsist, members of the proletariat must sell their labour power to the bourgeoisie for a wage.

Protestant Ethic: A belief in hard work, thrift, and personal discipline, seen as common to the values of the Protestant faith. For Weber, this was a cultural spark that had an elective affinity with capitalism and allowed it to grow in influence.

Pseudo-individualisation: In Adorno, the idea that elements of mass culture, such as products or popular songs, appear to be unique and different when they are in fact highly standardised. For Adorno, this creates an illusion of choice.

Public Sociology: A style of sociology which is explicitly concerned with engaging non-academic audiences and with addressing social problems.

Qualitative Methods: Researching social life from the perspective that not everything can be counted, and that understanding people's experiences and perspectives is a key aim of sociological research. Includes participant observation, ethnography, interviews and focus groups as major methods.

Quantified Self: A term proposed by Lupton to describe self-identities which are increasingly expressed or understood through numbers and measures.

Quantitative Methods: Methods that aim to quantify elements of social life, often to compare groups. These approaches, which include survey research and statistical analysis of the results, often aim to identify general patterns in society or within a group.

Queer Theory: A theoretical movement, emerging primarily in the 1990s, which is focused on the social construction of gender and sexual identities and how dominant forms of these constructions can be transgressed.

Race: A categorisation and taxonomy using apparent physical and genetic differences to claim biologically distinguishable groups within the human species.

Racialisation: The process by which an individual becomes categorised as part of a racial group.

Raciology: In Gilroy, the continued use of racial thinking, especially attempts to reassert essential or biological differences between human races. Often termed 'scientific racism'.

Racism: Prejudice or discrimination based on perceived race.

Rationality: In Weber, rationality (or rational action) is a type of orientation or social action, guided by conscious ideas, decisions and calculations of means towards ends. Can be opposed to *traditional* action, action guided by habit, or *affective* action, action guided by emotion.

Realist Approach: An approach to the study of social problems which argues that social problems are objective challenges which exist regardless of whether they are recognised as such.

Realm of Freedom: In Marx, a situation in which people are free to act as they please, unconstrained by material necessities.

Realm of Necessity: A situation in which individuals are constrained by the necessity of working to meet their material needs.

Redlining: The systematic denial of service (such as a loan or insurance) to particular groups, ostensibly on the basis of neighbourhood but practically and in its impact on the basis of perceived race.

Reflexive/Reflexivity: The capacity of an person to reflect on their behaviour, and to recognise the structural factors which shape, constrain, or otherwise inform it. Reflexivity is linked with the *sociological imagination*. Reflexivity is also sometimes used for the capacity of a group, or an academic discipline (such as sociology), to reflect on its own assumptions or apply its methods to itself.

Religion: Organised cultural practices and worldviews linking us to the supernatural.

Reserve Army of Labour: In Marxism, the unemployed population, whose presence is thought to depress working conditions and wages.

Resistance: A challenge to or refusal to accept or comply with the power of another.

Resistance Identities: In Castells, forms of collective identity that emerge when people feel disenfranchised or marginalised by social changes. Resistance identities entrench individuals against social change.

Revolt: An uprising in which subordinate groups challenge an established authority.

Revolting Subjects: In Tyler, subjectivities positioned by those with cultural power as disgusting or 'revolting', a type of symbolic violence. The label can also be used by those to which it is applied to resist or 'revolt' against this violence.

Revolution: A forcible overthrow of an existing government or social organisation. In Marxism, revolution specifically refers to the overthrow of a ruling class.

Risk Society/Societies: Societies that are increasingly dominated by a concern over risk and a desire to regulate and control risk, central of which are risks ironically caused by science and technology and a culture that believed risks can be fundamentally mitigated.

Roles: Commonly held expectations about how people should or will behave in certain social positions. Individuals are thought to 'play' roles when they conform their behaviour to these expectations.

Scapegoating: A process by which a particular group is blamed for outcomes that they are not responsible for.

Scientific Revolution: A series of changes in scientific inquiry, beginning from the mid-16th century. Key features of the scientific revolution include the emergence of science as a distinct discipline, the separation of science from religion, and the development of the scientific method.

Second Shift: Labour performed by women at home in addition to paid work performed in formal employment.

Second-Wave Feminism: A social movement, occurring from the 1960s to the 1980s, focusing on gender equality and discrimination against women. Second-wave feminism was especially concerned with inequalities in the workplace and the family.

Sect: A sub-group (typically religious) which has branched off or broken away from a main group.

Secular: Not religious (or not overtly religious). Secularisation is process of social change towards non-religious social institutions and values and away from overtly religious ones.

Self: A person's understanding and perception of their individuality, shaped by social processes.

Self-fulfilling Prophecy: The idea that a belief or expectation about a certain outcome can help to bring about that outcome.

Semiotics: An approach concerned with the study of signs and symbols, especially with their meaning.

Settler Colonial: A distinct type of colonial situation in which the existing inhabitants of a colonised territory are largely replaced by a new society of settlers.

Sex: A classification by which people are defined as male or female (or intersex) on the basis of genetics and/or physiological characteristics. Increasingly seen as more complex.

Sex Category: In West and Zimmerman, the biological sex that people are assumed to be, related to but distinguishable from both from the sexual characteristics by which they are assigned a sex when born and from the way they identify as a gender.

Sexism: Discrimination or prejudice against one sex, typically women, on the basis of their perceived inferiority.

Sexuality: An individual's sexual identity, including their sexual preferences, desires, tastes, and so on.

Significant Others: In Mead, people who are especially important to the development of our particular sense of self.

Social Action: An action that takes into account or is influenced by the actions of others.

Social Capital: In Bourdieu, resources which arise from social networks and relationships.

Social Constructivist Approach: An approach to the study of social life which focuses on how social processes and problems are 'constructed' by society, or how problems come to be recognised and thought of as problems.

Social Contract: A theory of society and political authority as founded on the consent of those governed or subordinated to the rules and laws of that society.

Social Control: The means by which societies enforce social norms and reduce expressions of deviance.

Social Dynamics: Analyses concerned with patterns and processes of social change. Contrasted with *social statics*.

Social Facts: In Durkheim, aspects of social structure, such as values or norms, which exercise control over individual behaviour, typically by influencing or eliciting certain actions.

Social Identity: The expectations and opinions others hold towards us based on the groups we belong to or the characteristics we are ascribed. Has a complex interactive relationship with a person's self-identity.

Social Movement: A group of people organised (often loosely) to achieve some social aim – typically to create or prevent social change.

Social Order: A situation of social stability, in which the norms or structures of a society are generally supported and maintained by its members.

Social Statics: Analyes concerned with the present structure of societies, or with understanding the stability of current social orders. Contrasted with social *dynamics*.

Socialisation: The process by which the individual learns the norms, values, and practices which are common to a particular social group.

Socio-economic Stratification: An aspect of social organisation, describing the degree to which people are organised into distinct categories or classes based on economic factors (such as wealth or occupation).

Sociological Imagination: From Mills, an ability to see relationships or draw links between personal experience and the wider social context and how it is changing over time.

Southern Theory: Social science theories produced from the perspective of the Global South. Connell argues that sociology has been dominated by Northern perspectives.

Sovereign Power: In Foucault, a kind of power, characteristic of medieval and feudal societies, in which a political leader attempts to maintain social control via public displays of force and authority.

Standpoint Theory: The position that marginalised groups have a unique, valuable perspective on social phenomena, particularly marginalisation and oppression. Standpoint theorists argue that groups have significantly different experiences and perspectives of the world, and that the exclusion of certain groups creates biased knowledge.

State: A political community with clearly defined borders and a single governing system, which has the power to police, defend and create laws over that territory.

Status: In Weber, social ranks determined by positive or negative estimations of honour.

Stereotypes: A generalised belief about a group of people, indiscriminately applied to all members of that group.

Stigma: An attribute or behaviour which is socially undesirable, or which causes one to be socially rejected.

Strain Theory: A criminological theory, developed by Robert Merton, which suggests that crime occurs when individuals use illegitimate means to obtain socially valued goals or ends.

Strength of Weak Ties: A term, coined by Granovetter, to refer to the importance of social networks between acquaintances.

Structure: Social factors, recurring patterns, and institutional forms that constrain and enable our actions (or agency).

Subaltern: The subjected or oppressed groups in societies; those subordinate to dominant or elite groups.

Subaltern Studies Group: A group of South Asian scholars, formed at the University of Sussex in 1970–80. The group is focused on the study of post-colonial societies, and on the representation of 'subaltern' groups: those who are subordinated on the basis of class, caste, gender, race, language and/or culture.

Subculture: A cultural group which exists within a larger culture and which adopts values, ideas, and cultural practices that are alternative to those of the larger culture.

Suffrage: The right to vote. Members of women's organisations, formed around the turn of the 20th century in many countries, campaigned for this right from women, some using militant action. These groups are central to First-wave feminism.

Super Diverse World: The idea that cultural diversity is increasing in societies, both in the number of ethnic groups within societies but also in the form of diversity in ethnic groups themselves.

Superstructure: In Marxism, the general ideals, norms, and values of a society. Marxist thought typically holds that the superstructure is largely determined by the *base*.

Surplus Value: In Marxism, the difference between the amount of money that a product is sold for and the amount of money the product costs to make. Surplus value is thought to be 'created' by the worker and 'appropriated', or taken, by the capitalist.

Survival Circuits: Dynamic networks of people and money which help support the economies of Majority World countries. Survival circuits often involve women, who, as low-wage migrant workers, send remittances back to their home countries.

Symbolic Interaction: The use of symbols to exchange meaning with other people (communication), seen by some sociologists as the foundation out of which society is constructed.

Symbolic Interactionism: A sociological theory that focuses on the creation of meaning through interpersonal communication as the foundation for social identity and social patterns.

Symbolic Violence: In Bourdieu, the process through which dominated groups are excluded from social spaces and come to accept their lower social position as natural, legitimate, or deserved.

Theories: General ideas, hypotheses, or assumptions about the social world. Theories offer potential answers to questions we have about social phenomena.

Third Space: In Bhabha, abstract social spaces 'between' recognised groups or identities (i.e. between distinct cultures), where new practices, ideas, and identities can emerge.

Third-Wave Feminism: A social movement, beginning in the 1990s as a reaction against second-wave feminism. Third-wave feminism criticised second-wave feminism for neglecting to address the relationship between gender inequality and other forms of inequality, such as inequalities in race and class.

Third World Feminisms: Approaches to feminism which focus on the experience of women in the 'Third World' or Majority World.

Transnational Capitalist Class: A global social class, which is thought to control supranational corporations, organisations, and other such institutions.

Values: Ideas or judgements about the kind of society in which people want to live, or about what constitutes a good society, which can guide action.

Vocation: Employment or occupation that someone is emotionally or morally drawn towards or to which they are particularly dedicated, qualified or well suited.

Voluntarism: The belief that individuals have free will or can freely choose their actions and behaviours. Voluntarism is opposed to *determinism*.

Voluntaristic Theories: Theories that emphasise *voluntarism*.

Waves of Globalisation: The idea that globalisation has progressed through several distinct periods of activity, rather than being a new or one continuous process.

Wealth: Income from investments, ownership of productive assets, salaries, bonuses, shares and property.

White Fragility: A reticence, possessed by white individuals, to talk about race and the structural benefits conveyed by whiteness. White fragility often involves defensive reactions and a dismissal of the existence of racism.

White Mask: From Fanon, when members of non-white racial groups adopt or imitate the behaviour of white groups, internalising the idea that these groups are superior.

Whiteness: The concept of whiteness (as a norm) is used by sociologists to highlight how a white identity is the 'default' identity around which societies are organised. Whiteness as norm involves the marginalisation of other racial identities, and the treatment of white culture and norms as the standard to which other groups should aspire.

Whiteness Studies: An interdisciplinary field focusing on the cultural, historical, and sociological aspects of whiteness, particularly on the ideology of white supremacy.

World Systems Theory: A theoretical perspective that sought to examine patterns of inequality in the global economy. World systems theory divided the world into core, semi-periphery, and periphery countries, and argued that the core countries exploited and dominated the others for their own gain.

INDEX

CPSIA information can be obtained
at www.ICGtesting.com
Printed in the USA
LVHW060022260523
748075LV00008B/63